DATE DUE

Crime Victim Rights and Remedies

Second Edition

Peggy M. Tobolowsky
Mario T. Gaboury
Arrick L. Jackson
Ashley G. Blackburn

CAROLINA ACADEMIC PRESS
Durham, North Carolina

Library of Congress Cataloging-in-Publication Data

Crime victim rights and remedies / Peggy M. Tobolowsky ... [et al.]. -- 2nd ed.
     p. cm.
   Rev. ed. of: Crime victim rights and remedies / Peggy M. Tobolowsky. c2001.
   Includes bibliographical references and index.
   ISBN 978-1-59460-578-9 (alk. paper)
   1. Victims of crimes--Legal status, laws, etc.--United States. I. Tobolowsky, Peggy M., 1952- II. Tobolowsky, Peggy M., 1952- Crime victim rights and remedies. III. Title.

KF9763.T63 2010
344.7303'288--dc22

                                        2009039191

CAROLINA ACADEMIC PRESS
700 Kent Street
Durham, North Carolina 27701
Telephone (919) 489-7486
Fax (919) 493-5668
www.cap-press.com

Printed in the United States of America

*Dedicated to our families
and to our colleagues at
the University of North Texas
and the University of New Haven.*

Contents

Preface   xiii

Chapter 1 · The Return of Crime Victim Rights and Remedies   3
   Introduction   3
   The Crime Victim in Ancient and Pre-Modern Times   4
   The Initial Role of the Crime Victim in the United States   5
   The Renewal of Interest in Crime Victims   6
   The Emergence of the Victims' Movement   8
   The President's Task Force on Victims of Crime   10
   Crime Victim Rights and Remedies: Then and Now   11

Chapter 2 · Crime Victim Rights of Participation in the Criminal
               Justice Process: An Introduction   15
   The Definition of a "Victim"   16
   The Definition of a "Crime"   19
   Conclusion   21

Chapter 3 · The Right to Notice of Proceedings and Outcomes in
               the Criminal Justice Process   23
   Notice of the Existence of Victim Rights   23
      Constitutional and Legislative Action   23
      Judicial Interpretation   25
      Implementation and Analysis of the Right   26
   Notice of Important Proceedings and Outcomes in the Criminal
      Justice Process   28
      President's Task Force and *New Directions from the Field*
          Recommendations   28
      Constitutional and Legislative Response   29
      Judicial Interpretation   34
         State Cases   34
         Federal Cases   40

Implementation and Analysis of the Right   43
Conclusion   46

Chapter 4 • The Right to Be Present at Criminal Justice Proceedings   49
Introduction   49
President's Task Force and *New Directions from the Field*
  Recommendations   50
Constitutional and Legislative Response   52
Judicial Interpretation   56
  State Cases   56
  Federal Cases   59
Implementation and Analysis of the Right   62
Conclusion   64

**Chapter 5 • The Right to Be Heard Regarding Charging Decisions
          and Pleas**   65
The Right to Be Heard Regarding the Initiation or Dismissal
  of a Charge   66
  President's Task Force and *New Directions from the Field*
    Recommendations   66
  Constitutional and Legislative Response   67
  Judicial Interpretation   69
    Overview   69
    State and Federal Cases   70
  Implementation and Analysis of the Right   74
  Conclusion   76
The Right to Be Heard Regarding Plea Negotiations and Agreements 76
  President's Task Force and *New Directions from the Field*
    Recommendations   77
  Constitutional and Legislative Response   77
  Judicial Interpretation   80
    State Cases   80
    Federal Cases   82
  Implementation and Analysis of the Right   84
  Conclusion   89

Chapter 6 • The Right to Be Heard Regarding Sentencing and Parole   91
The Right to Be Heard Regarding Sentencing   91
  President's Task Force and *New Directions from the Field*
    Recommendations   91

Constitutional and Legislative Response 93
Judicial Interpretation 95
   Capital Cases 96
   Noncapital State Cases 100
   Noncapital Federal Cases 104
Implementation and Analysis of the Right 108
   Utilization of the Right 108
   Impact on Criminal Justice System Administration and
     Efficiency 111
   Impact on Sentencing Outcome 112
   Impact on Victim Satisfaction 117
Conclusion 118
The Right to Be Heard Regarding Parole 119
   President's Task Force and *New Directions from the Field*
     Recommendations 119
Constitutional and Legislative Response 120
Judicial Interpretation 123
Implementation and Analysis of the Right 124
Conclusion 129

Chapter 7 · Remedies for Victim Rights Violations 131
Constitutional and Legislative Action 132
   Federal Provisions 132
   State Provisions 134
Judicial Interpretation 138
   State Cases 138
   Federal Cases 143
Implementation and Analysis 145
Conclusion 149

Chapter 8 · Restitution 151
Introduction 151
President's Task Force and *New Directions from the Field*
   Recommendations 153
Constitutional and Legislative Response 155
Judicial Interpretation 160
   Federal Cases 160
   State Cases 163
Implementation and Analysis of the Remedy 165
   Recovery of Victim Economic Loss 167

Recovery of Victim Psychological Loss and Victim Satisfaction   174
Reduced System Intrusiveness and Offender Recidivism   176
Reduced System Costs and Enhanced System Credibility   179
Conclusion   181

Chapter 9 · Crime Victim Compensation   183
Introduction   183
President's Task Force and *New Directions from the Field*
Recommendations   184
Constitutional and Legislative Response   186
Judicial Interpretation   190
Implementation and Analysis of the Remedy   192
Utilization of the Remedy   193
Low Visibility of the Remedy   197
Limited Program Staff and Funding   199
Victim Cooperation and Satisfaction   201
Conclusion   204

Chapter 10 · Civil Litigation   205
Introduction   205
Constitutional and Legislative Action   207
Judicial Interpretation   209
Intentional Tort and Related Direct Actions   209
Third Party Actions   213
Special Relationships Creating Duties of Reasonable Care   214
Duty to Control or to Warn of the Conduct of Others   220
Implementation and Analysis of the Remedy   223
Conclusion   225

Chapter 11 · The Future of Crime Victim Rights and Remedies   227
Introduction   227
Visions of the Future   228
Conclusion   234

Appendix 1 · President's Task Force on Victims of Crime Action
Recommendations   235
Proposed Executive and Legislative Action at the Federal and
State Levels   235
Recommendations for Federal and State Action   235
Proposed Federal Action   237

Proposed Action for Criminal Justice System Agencies   238
    Recommendations for Police   238
    Recommendations for Prosecutors   238
    Recommendations for the Judiciary   239
    Recommendations for Parole Boards   240
Recommendations for Other Organizations   240
    Recommendations for Hospitals   240
    Recommendations for the Ministry   241
    Recommendations for the Bar   241
    Recommendations for Schools   241
    Recommendations for the Mental Health Community   242
    Recommendations for the Private Sector   242
A Proposed Amendment to the Constitution   242

Appendix 2 · Proposed Federal Victim Rights Constitutional
            Amendment   245

Appendix 3 · State Victim Rights Constitutional Provisions   247
Alabama   247
Alaska   247
Arizona   248
California   249
Colorado   254
Connecticut   255
Florida   255
Idaho   256
Illinois   257
Indiana   257
Kansas   258
Louisiana   258
Maryland   259
Michigan   259
Mississippi   260
Missouri   260
Montana   261
Nebraska   262
Nevada   262
New Jersey   263
New Mexico   263
North Carolina   264

Ohio   265
Oklahoma   266
Oregon   266
Rhode Island   270
South Carolina   271
Tennessee   272
Texas   273
Utah   274
Virginia   274
Washington   275
Wisconsin   276

Notes   277

Table of Cases   339

Index   347

Preface

In 1982, President Ronald Reagan convened a Task Force on Victims of Crime. The recommendations made by this national Task Force have served as a guide for the development of crime victim rights and remedies in this country. In 2001, the initial edition of this text was published. It brought together a multifaceted set of materials reflecting the evolution of crime victim rights and remedies in the approximately twenty years since the Task Force's recommendations were published. The initial text described the applicable constitutional and statutory provisions addressing crime victim rights and remedies, as well as leading judicial opinions that interpreted them. In addition to presenting the current state of the law in this area, the text described the status of implementation of these rights and remedies, relevant empirical research, and a sampling of the pertinent policy analysis. This comprehensive portrait of the past and then current status of crime victim rights and remedies in this country was designed to inform the continued evolution of law and practice in this area.

In the years since the publishing of the initial edition of this text, the constitutional and statutory law in this area and judicial interpretation of it have continued to evolve, as well as the empirical research analyzing its development and implementation. Of particular note is the enactment of the federal Crime Victims' Rights Act of 2004, reflecting a significant expansion of federal statutory victim rights, and the federal court decisions that have begun to interpret it. Thus, this new edition of the text extends and expands the comprehensive description of crime victim rights and remedies provided in the initial edition. Now, almost thirty years since the President's Task Force issued its recommendations, progress in their implementation can once again be measured.

It is hoped that this new edition of the text will further facilitate the study of victim rights and remedies, and will serve as a general resource for those interested in victim rights and remedies in this country.

Crime Victim Rights
and Remedies

Chapter 1

The Return of Crime Victim Rights and Remedies

Introduction

Every year in the United States, millions of men, women, and children are victims of crime. In its 2008 National Crime Victimization Survey, based on a representative sample of Americans aged twelve and older, the United States Department of Justice Bureau of Justice Statistics estimated that this population experienced 21,312,400 violent and property crime victimizations in the categories of crime measured by the survey. Of these victimizations, 4,856,510 were for the measured violent offenses of sexual and non-sexual assault and robbery. The remaining 16,455,890 victimizations were in the property and non-violent offense categories of household burglary and personal, household, and motor vehicle theft.[1] In the 2008 Uniform Crime Reports, based on crimes reported to the police, the Federal Bureau of Investigation estimated that there were 11,149,927 offenses in the crime categories measured. This total included 1,382,012 murders, forcible rapes, robberies, and aggravated assaults and 9,767,915 burglaries, larceny-thefts, and motor vehicle thefts.[2] Even using the more conservative crime estimates contained in the Uniform Crime Reports, it is clear that crime affects substantial portions of the American population each year.

Researchers have attempted to measure the impact of crime on victims in a variety of ways.[3] One estimate of the $1,705,000,000,000 annual aggregate burden of crime on society included over $600,000,000,000 in property-related losses, almost $575,000,000,000 based on the value of crime-related fatalities and injuries, and over $90,000,000,000 in lost opportunity costs due to victim crime prevention efforts and lost workdays due to crime.[4] With regard to violent crime, treatment of victims is estimated to account for 14% of injury-related medical spending and as much as 20% of mental health care expenditures. The impact of violent crime is believed to result in wage losses equal to 1% of American earnings. The pain, suffering, and lifestyle changes resulting from

personal crime generally are estimated to reduce the quality of life of victimized families by almost 2%.[5]

Despite the significant number of individuals annually victimized by crime
and the personal and financial toll such victimization can have on them and
their families, crime victims have had relatively few rights and remedies in the
criminal justice process for much of this country's history. Since at least the middle of the nineteenth century, the primary goal of the American criminal justice system has been to identify, prosecute, and punish offenders rather than
to address the needs of crime victims. This offender-centered process is in direct contrast to the earliest criminal prosecutions in this country and elsewhere
which were victim-centered in process and outcome.[6] In the last thirty years,
however, there has been a dramatic increase in the rights and remedies available to crime victims. In this chapter, the evolution of events that led to the "return" of crime victim rights and remedies is traced.

The Crime Victim in Ancient
and Pre-Modern Times

In order to understand the evolution of the crime victim's role in the American criminal justice process, it is important to examine the historical antecedents to the development of the American criminal justice system. These
antecedents extend back to ancient times. In primitive societies, wrongs done
to a person or his property were subject to remedial action by a victim and his
family against an offender and his family. Norms of permissible retaliation and
recompense arose among tribal and family-based cultures for what are now
regarded as criminal offenses against individual victims.[7]

The early centrality of the victim in these primitive "criminal" proceedings
is evidenced by provisions of the Torah, the Code of Hammurabi, and other
ancient codes, that require offenders' repayment in kind or extent to those suffering criminal victimization in addition to or instead of prescribed retributive
sanctions.[8] For example, the proportionate sanction, or *lex talionis*, provisions
of the Torah that prescribe "life for life, eye for eye, tooth for tooth, hand for
hand, foot for foot, burn for burn, wound for wound, stripe for stripe"[9] co-
exist with provisions that allow an offender whose victim recovers from injuries sustained in a quarrel to "pay for the loss of his time [during his recovery],
and [to] have him thoroughly healed."[10] Through a prescribed measure of
physical retribution or a proportionate financial settlement, the goals of these
early legal systems were to make the victim whole and to minimize private re-
venge.[11]

This victim-centered system of redress continued in early Western law until approximately the eleventh century.[12] After this time, however, monarchs and their governments became increasingly involved in addressing harm inflicted by their subjects on each other. Historians attribute this shift in approach to various factors including the expansion of central authority and kingship, the growth and influence of the Church, the evolution of a structured court system, and evolving concepts of punishment.[13]

As the role of centralized authorities in these proceedings expanded, a transformation in notions of private, or civil, as opposed to public, or criminal, wrongs occurred. In early legal systems, only a few acts, including witchcraft, bestiality, and incest, were regarded as "criminal" offenses, i.e., wrongs against the community or public as a whole. Most acts against individuals, including homicide, assault, rape, and theft, were treated as private or civil wrongs for which there were recognized restitutive or retaliatory remedies for the victims. In this process of evolution, however, most individual acts committed against a person or his property became criminal offenses against the "king's peace" or the crown rather than private matters to be resolved by the affected parties. As such, they were increasingly subject to prosecution in the professional court system created, in part, to deal with these offenses.[14] Moreover, fines paid by the offender to the government and capital, corporal, and other forms of offender punishment increasingly accompanied and often replaced the previous requirements of offender restitution to the victim.[15] The crime victim's role was thus substantially reduced in the criminal proceedings that evolved over time generally to involve the government and the offender—not the victim—as parties.[16] The pursuit of restitution was largely transferred to private litigation initiated by the victim against the offender in the separate "civil" justice system.[17]

The Initial Role of the Crime Victim in the United States

In this country, a similar evolution from a private to a public prosecution system took place. In colonial America, law enforcement and the administration of justice were primarily conducted by individual victims with the assistance of public officials who charged fees for their services.[18] The victim was responsible for arresting his offender—either himself or with the aid of the local watchman, justice of the peace, or constable for whose assistance the victim paid. The victim was also responsible, at his own expense, for investigating the crime, filing the formal charges, and prosecuting the offender. In return for a successful prosecution, the victim could receive damages or keep or sell an indigent offender's services for a period corresponding to the amount of damages owed.[19]

By the time of the American Revolution, however, significant changes had begun to occur in the administration of justice.[20] Philosophically, these changes were motivated by Enlightenment notions that criminal prosecutions should serve societal interests of deterrence and retribution rather than individual victim interests in private redress.[21] Practically, the changes were influenced by the increasing urbanization and diversification of American life that rendered the previous private prosecution system ineffective and sometimes corrupt.[22] Consequently, professional government-operated police forces began to replace the previous system of volunteer or privately paid law enforcement officers, informers, and bounty hunters. Imprisonment and fines replaced capital and corporal punishments as the primary criminal sanctions. Restitutive damages to the victim were no longer actively pursued through the criminal justice process. Finally, a public prosecution system evolved in which a public prosecutor—not the victim—initiated and conducted the criminal prosecution on behalf of the government. By the middle of the nineteenth century, these changes had substantially transformed the American criminal justice system from a private to a public system. In this public prosecution system, the crime victim had become merely a witness in the government's prosecution and was generally relegated to the civil justice system for the recovery of restitution.[23]

The Renewal of Interest in Crime Victims

Other than occasional calls by penal reformers for greater use of victim restitution as a criminal sanction and its authorization by some American jurisdictions as a condition of the developing probation sanction or otherwise,[24] the crime victim remained effectively marginalized in the American criminal justice process until the convergence of several factors in the middle of the twentieth century. Just as Enlightenment philosophical and theoretical thought had shifted the focus of the criminal justice process from the victim to society in the eighteenth century,[25] a new theoretical approach that focused on the crime victim and became known as *victimology* emerged in the middle of the twentieth century. Most trace the modern study of victimology to the seminal works of Hans von Hentig and Beniamin Mendelsohn in the 1940s and 1950s. Both explored relationships between victims and offenders. They developed victim typologies that identified victim characteristics that might increase a person's risk of victimization, such as age or mental impairments that could make a person more vulnerable to crime, as well as characteristics that could contribute to or precipitate a crime, such as provocative behavior by the victim.[26]

Subsequent theorists expanded the study of victimology to encompass other aspects of crime victims and victimization generally and researchers collected empirical data regarding the evolving theories of victimization.[27] In addition to exploring theoretical and empirical bases for the study of victimology, researchers began to explore the psychological impact of victimization on victims, as well as the impact of their significant exclusion from the criminal justice process.[28] Researchers also began to identify proposed changes in the criminal justice system that they felt would be more responsive to victim needs and desires. Although there were no unanimous conclusions as to the most appropriate responses of the criminal justice system to crime victim needs, the restoration of restitutive remedies and greater victim participation and input in the criminal justice process were often included among proposed system changes.[29]

Theory was translated into action in this country in the 1960s as a result of a variety of factors. Following significant sustained increases in reported crime, there was a renewed American interest in and concern about crime. Crime and "law and order" issues were prominent features of public and political debate. Concerns about crime reached such a level that President Lyndon Johnson established The President's Commission on Law Enforcement and Administration of Justice to examine crime and the criminal justice system and to identify possible solutions to this growing problem. As part of its effort to understand the nature and extent of the crime problem, the Commission authorized a pilot national victimization survey that estimated a substantially higher rate of crime than reflected in the Uniform Crime Reports. This survey further increased awareness of the extent of crime victimization in this country. In addition, several aspects of the Commission's final report, in 1967, focused on crime victim-related issues. These included proposals to address crime victims' losses and needs for services, as well as suggestions to increase victim involvement in the criminal justice system.[30]

Among the Commission's proposals to address victims' losses from crime was a remedy in addition to the still largely dormant sanction of restitution. In this suggested supplemental system of victim compensation, the government would provide payment to the crime victim for unrecovered losses. The Commission's proposal followed the model of crime victim compensation introduced by reformer Margery Fry and initially enacted in New Zealand in 1963 and England in 1964, followed by initial legislation in the United States in California in 1965. New York, Hawaii, and Massachusetts soon followed California's example in establishing victim compensation programs. These victim compensation programs were among the first tangible responses to the renewed concern about crime victims during this period.[31]

Another outgrowth of the concern about crime in the 1960s was the establishment of the Law Enforcement Assistance Administration ("LEAA"). The mission of this federal government entity was to fund projects and proposals that could assist in the prevention and reduction of crime or address its effects. Among the projects funded through LEAA were victim and witness assistance programs in local prosecutors' offices and law enforcement agencies. In addition to these government-based programs, local projects began to be established to provide counseling and other assistance to victims of crime generally or of specific crimes, such as sexual assault.[32]

The Emergence of the Victims' Movement

By the early 1970s, interest in crime victims had increased to the degree that individual victims and victim service and support providers and advocates had begun to "network" at the local level. In 1973, the first national conference on victim assistance was held in the United States. An outgrowth of this conference was the establishment of the first national victim-related organization in 1975. This National Organization for Victim Assistance began to sponsor annual national conferences that addressed various victim issues as well as training programs for victim service providers. The remainder of the decade witnessed the creation of a number of other national victim-related organizations, including the National Coalition against Domestic Violence and the Victims Assistance Legal Organization, that were joined soon thereafter by Mothers Against Drunk Driving and the National Center for Victims of Crime (formerly the National Victim Center).[33]

Thus, by the end of the 1970s, it is fair to say that a *victims' movement* had developed in this country. Although this movement was influenced by the predecessor civil rights, anti-war, and other grassroots movements, it emerged more directly from the evolving women's movement. Many of the early leaders in the victims' movement were concerned about the criminal justice system treatment of the mostly female victims of sexual assault and domestic violence. They attributed what they viewed as inadequate system response to these crimes as symptomatic of women's lack of status and power. However, although many of the initial areas of interest of the victims' movement coincided with those of the women's movement, the focus of the victims' movement soon extended beyond these issues.[34]

Prompted by advocacy from those informally and formally aligned with the victims' movement, and with general support from the public at large, significant victim-centered achievements were accomplished during the 1970s. A majority of states initiated victim compensation programs and the National Association of Victim Compensation Boards was established to promote the creation of a national network of such programs. Victim assistance programs were established in many states and several states had networks of these programs.[35] The victimization survey piloted in conjunction with the President's Commission was refined and expanded and the United States Department of Justice Bureau of Justice Statistics began to administer it annually as the National Crime Victimization Survey (formerly the National Crime Survey).[36]

These victim-related accomplishments, however, were not always easily achieved. As one of the leaders of the victims' movement summarized,

> [t]he 1970s were marked by rapid progress in improving responses to victims, but they were also marked by turbulence, caused in part by the waxing and waning of federal financial support [due to the abolition of the LEAA at the end of the 1970s]. As national priorities shifted, stable funding became elusive, and programs often entered into internecine warfare over limited resources. Controversy also arose between programs that were driven by grassroots energy and those that were based in traditional criminal justice institutions. Many felt that there was an inherent conflict between the goals of prosecutors or law enforcement officers and the interests of victims. Some sought legal changes in the system, whereas others felt that change should take place through the formulation and revision of policies and procedures.[37]

In addition to the conflicts within the victims' movement, the evolving movement developed critics as well. Some philosophically disagreed with the movement's advocacy for institutionalized victim services out of a concern that the establishment of professional victim service providers would create dependency, distance victims from their own social networks, result in dissatisfaction and frustration from unmet expectations, create victim stereotypes, and delay the natural healing process from victimization.[38] As the victims' movement became more concerned with effecting changes in the criminal justice system to provide victims greater access and participation, some critics were concerned that victim activists intentionally or inadvertently were creating a "contest" of rights between victims and offenders or providing inappropriate responses to real victim needs.[39] Moreover, system changes sometimes espoused by those in or associated with the victims' movement (e.g., denial of bail, abolition of the exclusionary rule, mandatory sentencing, and elimination of parole) were criticized as a co-option of victim concerns by those with a "crime control" approach to criminal justice.[40]

The President's Task Force on Victims of Crime

Despite its internal conflicts and external critics, the victims' movement had begun to move well beyond its grassroots origins by the beginning of the 1980s.[41] The crime victims' movement and the victim rights it espoused were given a major endorsement when President Ronald Reagan proclaimed the first National Crime Victims' Rights Week in 1981.[42] This largely symbolic act was followed by a more substantive one, however, when President Reagan established the President's Task Force on Victims of Crime in 1982. The nine-member Task Force reviewed existing literature on criminal victimization and held hearings around the country to obtain input from professionals responsible for serving crime victims and from victims of crime themselves.[43]

In December 1982, the Task Force issued a *Final Report* that included over sixty action recommendations addressed to 1) the federal and state executive, legislative, and judicial branches; 2) criminal justice system agencies, including the police, prosecutors, and parole authorities; and 3) other professionals involved in crime victim service delivery, such as health care personnel, clergy, lawyers, educators, mental health care providers, and relevant private sector personnel. In these wide-ranging recommendations, the Task Force encouraged expansion of victim services and suggested practices to make the criminal justice process and related victim service delivery system more "victim friendly." The Task Force supported the expansion of state victim compensation programs through supplemental federal funding. It also recommended federal and state legislation requiring the imposition of restitution in all cases in which a victim had experienced financial loss, in the absence of compelling reasons to the contrary. The Task Force also proposed various changes in criminal justice process and procedure, such as the abolition of the exclusionary rule, establishment of preventive detention of suspects prior to trial, restrictions on judicial sentencing discretion, and abolition of parole, that it felt were required to better serve crime victims interests.[44]

In its *Final Report*, the Task Force also encouraged greater victim access to and participation in the criminal justice process. In this connection, the Task Force proposed that the Sixth Amendment to the United States Constitution be amended to add: "Likewise, the victim, in every criminal prosecution shall have the right to be present and to be heard at all critical stages of judicial proceedings."[45] The Task Force included specific recommendations to police and prosecutors to inform victims of the status of investigations and prosecutions. Applicable action recommendations were made to legislators, judges, prosecutors, and parole authorities that were designed to increase crime victim input regarding bail, pleas, sentencing, restitution, and parole decision making and to encourage victim presence at trial and parole proceedings.[46]

sentence, or both. A victim right to restitution is also included in several of the state constitutions. Various victim services are authorized and funded at the federal, state, and local level. The federal government and the majority of the states have constitutional or legislative provisions, or both, that require victim notification of important events and actions in the criminal justice process and allow, to varying degrees, crime victim presence and hearing at critical stages of the criminal justice process. In addition to these constitutional and legislative efforts, federal and state courts have construed and interpreted these newly authorized victim rights and remedies. Finally, researchers have attempted to assess the merits and effectiveness of these rights and remedies, when implemented.[54]

Although substantial progress has been made regarding crime victim rights and remedies since the issuance of the Task Force *Final Report*, the work envisioned by the Task Force is far from completed. Over ten years ago, the federal Department of Justice Office for Victims of Crime supported a project to assess the progress in the implementation of the Task Force recommendations. This collaborative effort by experts and practitioners in the crime victim field, as well as crime victims themselves, entitled, *New Directions from the Field: Victims' Rights and Services for the 21st Century*, noted areas of progress in the implementation of crime victim rights, ratified the continuing need for expanded implementation of many of the Task Force original recommendations, and issued scores of additional recommendations to participants within and outside of the criminal justice system that interact with crime victims.[55] Now, almost thirty years since the issuance of the Task Force *Final Report*, this book again assesses the progress that has been made on the implementation of the Task Force recommendations. The remainder of this book examines the constitutional, legislative, judicial, and research actions that have established, interpreted, and analyzed the primary crime victim rights and remedies since the "return" of such in the years following the Task Force *Final Report*.[56]

Chapter 2

Crime Victim Rights of Participation in the Criminal Justice Process: An Introduction

As noted in the previous chapter, at the time of the President's Task Force *Final Report*, crime victims had very limited formal rights of participation in the criminal justice process. As an introduction to its action recommendations, the Task Force presented a composite portrait of a crime victim's experience in which the victim of a violent crime was not notified of the defendant's pretrial release from custody, not given the opportunity to adequately consult with the prosecutor prior to required court appearances, not informed about the progress of the prosecution, not permitted to remain in the courtroom following the completion of trial testimony, not allowed to address the judge or directly provide input regarding the defendant's sentence, not allowed to attend parole release hearings, and not notified of the offender's parole release. Several of the Task Force action recommendations were designed to address these issues of limited victim access and participation in the criminal justice process.[1]

Since the issuance of the Task Force *Final Report*, the federal government and all of the states have enacted legislation that provides at least some victim rights of participation in the criminal justice process. The most frequently addressed rights of participation are the rights to be notified of key proceedings and outcomes, to consult with the prosecutor about important decisions in the prosecution, and to be present and heard at significant court or correctional proceedings.[2] In addition to this legislation, most of the over thirty states that have ratified "victim rights" constitutional amendments have included victim rights of participation to some degree.[3] The last federal victim rights constitutional amendment proposal introduced in Congress prior to the enactment of the federal statutory Crime Victims' Rights Act also included various victim rights of participation.[4]

These legislative and constitutional provisions and the court decisions interpreting them, however, vary widely. At the outset, although the federal government and all the states have either legislation or a constitutional provision, or both, regarding at least some of the victim rights of participation in the criminal justice process, not all of these provisions apply to all victims or to victims of all crimes.

The Definition of a "Victim"

The President's Task Force proposed extending some victim rights of participation not only to the direct crime victim, but also to the victim's family. For example, the proposed victim right to attend trial proceedings was also extended to a member of the victim's family. With regard to parole proceedings, the Task Force recommended that victims' families, as well as victims, be notified and be allowed to be present and heard.[5]

The federal government and the states typically extend their rights of participation to the direct crime victim. However, a victim's family member, or other designated representative, may usually exercise a direct victim's rights in instances in which a victim has been murdered, is incapacitated or incompetent, or is a minor. In this connection, the last federal victim rights constitutional amendment proposal introduced in Congress prior to the enactment of the federal statutory Crime Victims' Rights Act in 2004 gave standing to assert the rights provided to the "victim or the victim's lawful representative."[6] In addition to the crime victim and lawful representative, the federal Crime Victims' Rights Act extends standing to assert the crime victim's rights to the attorney for the Government and further defines the crime victims and representatives who are eligible for the prescribed rights:

> For the purposes of this chapter, the term "crime victim" means a person directly and proximately harmed as a result of the commission of a Federal offense or an offense in the District of Columbia. In the case of a crime victim who is under 18 years of age, incompetent, incapacitated, or deceased, the legal guardians of the crime victim or the representatives of the crime victim's estate, family members, or any other persons appointed as suitable by the court, may assume the crime victim's rights under this chapter, but in no event shall the defendant be named as such guardian or representative.[7]

In 2008, the Federal Rules of Criminal Procedure were amended to adopt the definition of crime victim contained in the Crime Victims' Rights Act.[8]

In their constitutional provisions, most states have given their legislatures the responsibility to define the victims covered by the provisions. They generally use such terminology as "crime victims, as defined by law"[9] or mention their legislatures by name, such as Connecticut's reference to a "victim, as the general assembly may define by law."[10] Several states also provide for the exercise of a victim's prescribed rights by the victim's "lawful representative."[11]

A few states do define the crime victims covered by their constitutional provisions. Perhaps the broadest and most detailed definition of victim status is contained in the recently amended California provision:

> As used in this section, a "victim" is a person who suffers direct or threatened physical, psychological, or financial harm as a result of the commission or attempted commission of a crime or delinquent act. The term "victim" also includes the person's spouse, parents, children, siblings, or guardian, and includes a lawful representative of a crime victim who is deceased, a minor, or physically or psychologically incapacitated. The term "victim" does not include a person in custody for an offense, the accused, or a person whom the court finds would not act in the best interests of a minor victim.[12]

In the absence of an individual victim, as defined in its amendment, Oregon considers its citizens generally, represented by the prosecutor, to be crime victims for purposes of its victim rights provisions.[13]

In their legislative victim rights provisions, some states use definitional language similar to the constitutional provisions described above.[14] Although a few states limit their coverage to direct crime victims only,[15] most states have extended their coverage to designated representatives of homicide victims, and a majority cover representatives of incapacitated, incompetent, or minor victims as well.[16] A few states extend certain participatory rights to family members of victims in circumstances not limited to their representative capacities.[17] Approximately ten states expressly exclude the defendant or any person in custody from their victim definitions.[18]

Although these definitional provisions would appear to be fairly straightforward, state appellate courts on occasion have been required to construe their terms in determining victim participatory rights. The Arizona Supreme Court held that an implementing statute and procedural rule that excluded police who had been victimized while on duty from exercising the state constitutional victim right to decline a pretrial defense interview were unconstitutional limitations of the definition of eligible crime victims provided in the constitutional provision.[19] The Arizona Supreme Court also held that the mother of children allegedly murdered by their father was still a victim under applicable law despite her potential, but, as yet uncharged, role in the offense.[20] An Arizona appellate court found that the driver of a car that was damaged, but who was not physically injured by a defendant in a driving while intoxicated prosecution was a victim for purposes of exercising victim rights in the prosecution.[21]

On the other hand, the South Carolina Supreme Court held that individuals who were identified as victims in charges involving the defendant that the prosecutor dismissed for unrelated reasons were not victims for purposes of exercising victim rights regarding a subsequent plea proceeding involving the defendant's resolution of other charges.[22] An Arizona appellate court found that individuals whose assertions of victimization by a defendant had not resulted in criminal charges against the defendant were not eligible for victim rights under applicable state law in the prosecution against the defendant on other charges.[23] The Arizona Supreme Court concluded that the cellmate victim of a defendant's assault was "in custody" and thus was excluded from the prescribed victim rights under state law.[24]

State appellate courts have also addressed the victim status of family members attempting to exercise victim participatory rights in a representative or independent capacity. For example, when permitted by law, appellate courts have generally upheld the exercise of victim rights by parents of minor child victims[25] and spouses of homicide victims.[26] In interpreting one of the more limited definitional provisions, however, the Indiana Supreme Court concluded that the applicable rights provision applied only to the direct crime victim and not to the homicide victim's mother.[27] An Arizona appellate court found that a person who committed suicide after a sexual assault was not murdered and thus her parents were not victims in the sexual assault prosecution for purposes of the state victim rights provisions.[28]

Federal courts have also begun to interpret the scope of the victim definition in the federal Crime Victims' Rights Act for purposes of the exercise of victim participatory rights and have reached sometimes differing conclusions. For example, although recognizing the conflicting legislative history and pre-existing case law, one federal trial judge adopted an "inclusive approach: absent an affirmative reason to think otherwise, I will presume that any person whom the government asserts was harmed by conduct attributed to a defendant, as well as any person who self-identifies as such, enjoys all of the procedural and substantive rights" of the statute. To implement his interpretation, the judge directed the prosecutor to identify all victims of the charged and uncharged crimes related to the defendant's alleged financial scheme. This judge also interpreted the statute's provisions defining a victim's lawful representative to permit a designated representative for competent as well as deceased, minor, incompetent, and incapacitated victims.[29] On the other hand, another federal trial judge, noting the same conflict in legislative history and pre-existing case law, concluded that victims of uncharged conduct would not be entitled to exercise participatory rights under the Act. Moreover, the judge found that a person who alleged that she had been physically and mentally abused by her former boyfriend whose conduct was influenced by the drugs that the defendant sold to him was not a person "directly and proximately harmed" by the defendant's drug crimes, as required for victim status under the Act.[30] Some federal courts have also noted that victim status and hence eligibility for victim rights under the Act may change as to specific rights at various points in the prosecution.[31]

Federal appellate courts have also begun to interpret the scope of victim status under the Act, as they review trial court rulings pursuant to the mandamus remedy provided in the Act for alleged violations of its provisions.[32] Contrary to the trial court, the Eleventh Circuit Court of Appeals held that home buyers whose mortgage loans were the subject of a conspiracy by a bank executive and a mortgage origination firm executive were "victims" of the bank executive's conspiracy to deprive the bank of honest services, even though only the bank was named in the criminal information as a victim. The appellate court found that the Act does not limit victim status to the individuals named in a criminal charging document, but includes all those who suffered direct and proximate harm from the offender's criminal conduct. Because the bank executive's conspiracy resulted in the charging of additional fees to the home buyers, they were directly and proximately harmed by the defendant's criminal conduct and qualified as victims under the Act.[33] On the other hand, the Tenth Circuit Court of Appeals denied mandamus relief and upheld a trial court determination that a homicide victim killed with a gun illegally transferred to a juvenile in violation of federal law was not a "victim" in the gun prosecution because the transfer of the gun and the subsequent homicide were "too factually and temporally attenuated" to establish the required direct and proximate harm.[34]

Thus, these definitional provisions concerning victim status are important determinants of eligibility for prescribed victim rights. These constitutional and legislative definitions, as interpreted by the courts, define who can exercise victim participatory rights.

The Definition of a "Crime"

Just as the federal and state jurisdictions have defined the victims to whom their rights provisions apply, they have also generally identified the crimes to which the rights apply. In this connection, most jurisdictions limit their victim participatory rights to certain crimes only.[35] Such a limitation in fact fol-

lows the model of the President's Task Force that restricted certain recommendations to victims of violent crime, such as the proposal for victim input
at sentencing.[36] The authors of the subsequent *New Directions from the Field*
study, however, recommended extending crime victim rights to victims of all
crimes, whether felony or misdemeanor and violent or non-violent.[37]

In the last federal victim rights constitutional amendment proposal introduced in Congress prior to the enactment of the federal statutory Crime Victims' Rights Act in 2004, the proposed rights were restricted to victims of
"violent crime."[38] The Crime Victims' Rights Act itself, however, does not restrict or limit the federal crimes to which it applies.[39]

In their victim rights constitutional provisions, most states entrust the definition of the crimes to be covered to their legislatures.[40] Of the nine states that
do not do so, Florida and Rhode Island provide no limitations on the victims
of crimes covered. California, New Jersey, and South Carolina extend their
provisions to those suffering physical, psychological, or financial (or property)
harm from crime. Oregon extends most of its rights to victims suffering financial, psychological, or physical harm from crime, but limits its plea consultation rights to violent felony victims. Washington limits its coverage to
victims of felony offenses, as does Utah unless its Legislature adds additional
crimes. New Mexico identifies specific serious offenses covered by the provisions.[41]

In their statutory provisions, most states place some limitations on the
crimes to which their victim rights apply. One frequently used limitation is
the restriction of these rights to victims of felony crimes of any kind or to
felonies and specifically identified misdemeanor offenses or offense categories.
For example, Idaho defines "criminal offense" for purposes of its victim rights
provision as "any charged felony or misdemeanor involving physical injury, or
the threat of physical injury, or a sexual offense."[42] Other states restrict their
rights provisions to victims of crimes involving physical or sexual violence or
injury. In this connection, in its victim rights provisions, Alabama defines
"criminal offense" as a "felony involving physical injury, the threat of physical
injury, or a sexual offense, or any offense involving spousal abuse or domestic violence."[43] Still other states limit their victim rights to victims of specifically enumerated offenses. The longest such list of offenses is provided by
Delaware that identifies over sixty specific offenses against persons, property,
children, incompetents, and public health, and relating to judicial proceedings, witnesses, and release of accused persons.[44]

Several states use a hybrid approach—restricting certain of the designated
rights to victims of specific types of crimes and authorizing other rights to
apply to broader categories of victims. For example, West Virginia apparently

places no restrictions on the crimes for which victims should receive notification of specified proceedings and outcomes, but limits victim consultation rights to victims of "serious" crimes, restricts notification of offender release rights to victims of specified offenses, and limits victim allocution rights at sentencing to victims of felony offenses.[45] Only a few states extend the authorized participatory rights to victims of virtually all crimes.[46] In addition to these restrictions based on the nature of the offense charged, most states provide some victim rights that are available only on victim request.[47] A few states limit their provision of victim rights to victims who "cooperate" with criminal justice authorities in the investigation and prosecution of the charged offense.[48] Although the state courts have infrequently interpreted these statutory definitions of eligible crimes, one state appellate court held that the legislature's more narrow definition of eligible crimes in its implementing statute was an unconstitutional limitation on the definition provided in the state constitutional victim rights amendment.[49]

Conclusion

The federal victim-related definitions for purposes of victim participatory rights are now fairly broad.[50] Although some of the restrictions resulting from the state definitions of the victims and crimes that are eligible for the prescribed rights are limited, others have the effect of significantly reducing the number of victims who qualify for the victim rights granted.[51] Therefore, these definitional and other limitations must be remembered as the specific participatory rights to victim notice, presence, and hearing in the criminal justice process are discussed in the following chapters.

Chapter 3

The Right to Notice of Proceedings and Outcomes in the Criminal Justice Process

Notice of the Existence of Victim Rights

In its *Final Report*, the President's Task Force directed action recommendations to the police, prosecutors, and correctional authorities to notify crime victims of various proceedings and outcomes in their cases.[1] As the authors of *New Directions from the Field* recognized, however, a preliminary notification area of concern is victim notification of the *existence* of these and other participatory rights. For crime victims to exercise their participatory rights, they must first be made aware that such rights exist. Obviously, the sooner that a victim is notified of the existence of these rights, the greater the opportunity the victim has to exercise them. Consequently, the *New Directions from the Field* authors recommended that law enforcement personnel initially advise crime victims of their rights, that the courts routinely advise victims of these rights, and that all justice system agencies and programs help ensure that victims receive meaningful information about their rights.[2] The federal system and most states require that victims be given notice of the existence of their participatory and other rights and expressly entrust the notification responsibility to the investigating law enforcement agency, the prosecutor, victim services personnel, or even the court. These notification provisions vary significantly.[3]

Constitutional and Legislative Action

The last federal victim rights constitutional amendment proposal introduced in Congress prior to the enactment of the federal statutory Crime Victims' Rights Act in 2004 did not contain a crime victim right to notice of the existence of the proposed rights.[4] The Act itself, however, requires that federal officers and employees "engaged in the detection, investigation, or prosecution of crime shall make their best efforts to see that crime victims are notified of, and accorded" the victim rights established in the Act. Although the Act also expressly requires the court to "ensure" that victims are afforded the prescribed substantive rights, this requirement does not expressly include ensuring that the Government has notified victims of the existence of the rights themselves. Fulfilling the express requirement to ensure that victims are afforded their rights, however, will likely often necessitate the court's ascertainment whether the Government has notified victims of the existence of prescribed rights.[5]

Ten states include the right to be notified of the available victim rights in their constitutional victim rights provisions and none of them designates any particular entity to make the notification.[6] In their statutory provisions, approximately twenty states require law enforcement personnel to make the rights availability notification. Most of the states require the notification to be given at the initial contact with the victim or within a specific or more general time period following the initial contact. For example, Georgia generally requires notification by law enforcement officers "upon initial contact" with the victim. Alabama requires notification "within 72 hours" after the initial victim contact. Ohio mandates notification "promptly" after the initial victim contact. Wyoming requires notification "without undue delay." California, however, specifies no general or specific time period for the rights notification by police officers.[7]

Approximately twenty states require prosecutors to notify victims of their rights. A few states identify a specific time period in which the rights notification must be made. Illustrating this approach are the New Mexico provision mandating notice of victim rights within seven working days after the filing of the formal charge and the Texas provision requiring notice within ten days after an indictment or information. Most states, however, prescribe either general or no time limits for the notice. For example, Delaware requires notification "promptly" after the commencement of prosecution. Minnesota mandates notification within a "reasonable time" after the offender is charged. Iowa designates no time period for the prosecutor's required notification to be made.[8]

Some states require notification by both the investigating law enforcement agency and prosecutor.[9] Approximately five states give the notification responsibility primarily to their victim assistance personnel.[10] A few states now also require judges to routinely announce crime victim rights at the commencement of proceedings.[11] A few states either do not expressly assign the responsibility to make this notification to any specific entity or do not expressly require that victims be notified of the existence of their rights.[12]

Judicial Interpretation

The potential significance of a victim's right to receive notice of the existence of her rights is illustrated by the appellate court's decision in *State ex rel. Hance v. Arizona Board of Pardons and Paroles*.[13] In this case, the offender was convicted of the victim's rape in 1974 and was sentenced to incarceration for twenty-five years to life. The parole board last notified the victim of an upcoming parole hearing, pursuant to then existing law, in 1984, when the notification letter was returned as undeliverable. After 1984, neither the parole board nor the local prosecutor had attempted to notify the victim of subsequent parole hearings. The offender was still in custody in 1990, when the Arizona victim rights constitutional amendment was ratified, and in 1992, when its implementing legislation became effective. These provisions require victim notification of the existence of applicable rights, such as the right to be informed of and to appear at post-conviction release proceedings and to be informed of all releases from custody. The implementing legislation also requires such notification only upon victim request.[14]

In 1993, a parole hearing was conducted, without notice to the victim, at which the offender's parole was denied, but his release to home arrest was approved. Information as to the offender's impending release reached the victim. She contacted the governor and the local prosecutor who unsuccessfully sought to have the parole board conduct a probable cause hearing to determine whether the release should be rescinded. The local prosecutor then initiated a "special action" proceeding on the victim's behalf in the appellate court shortly before the offender's scheduled release to home arrest. In this proceeding, the prosecutor sought to have the release order set aside and a re-examination hearing held, remedies available under Arizona law for violation of these notice provisions.[15]

The appellate court concluded that the victim was entitled to the above-described notification rights—including the right to notice of their existence—because the offender was still in custody when the provisions became effective.[16] The court rejected the board's assertion that it had no duty to notify this victim of the release proceedings because the victim had not requested such notice, as she was required to do under the statutory provisions.

> The state cannot now use the victim's failure to request notice as a defense against the victim's right to appear at the release proceeding because the state failed to first fulfill its constitutional obligation to inform her of that right. The constitutional mandate is clear: victims must be informed of their rights. Armed with this knowledge, victims may choose to exercise these rights. Conversely, an uninformed victim may not exercise her rights because she is unaware of them, or

unaware that the right to notice of a release hearing requires that she
first file a request for such a notice.

* * * * *

This victim was never informed of her constitutional right to request
notice of and to participate in post-conviction release proceedings. It
is this omission that violated her rights and rendered the release proceedings defective.[17]

As a result of this conclusion and the court's additional rejection of the parole
board's claim that it had made reasonable efforts to locate the victim, the appellate court set aside the offender's release order and ordered a re-examination hearing at which the victim could be present and heard.[18] Although this
decision represents a meaningful judicial effectuation of enacted victim notification rights, its significance is tempered by the fact that few states provide
such a remedy for notice violations, as discussed later in this chapter.

Implementation and Analysis of the Right

Nevertheless, as the *Hance* case illustrates, notification of the *existence* of a
victim's rights of participation in the criminal justice process is in many ways
the most important victim participatory right of all because it is the right on
which the exercise of all other rights depends. In recognition of its significance,
the federal system and most states provide this notification right to eligible
victims. The effectiveness of its actual implementation, however, determines
whether it is the linchpin of or the barrier to the exercise of the remaining participatory rights.

In a 2008 study of the implementation of the federal Crime Victims' Rights
Act of 2004, researchers surveyed a sample of federal crime victims whose cases
were initiated and completed during a twenty-three-month period beginning
at the outset of 2006. Of the approximately 250 victims who completed the
survey, victim awareness of each of the specific rights prescribed in the Act
ranged between approximately 48% and 78% of the respondents (plus additional respondents who indicated that they were not sure if they were aware of
each right). Only 23% of the respondents indicated their awareness of the
rights enforcement mechanisms in the Act and an additional 20% indicated
that they could not recall if they were aware of the mechanisms.[19]

In a 1998 survey of 4,000 respondents in nine northeastern states, researchers
posed questions about crime and the criminal justice system generally. To those
respondents who had been crime victims within the previous ten years, the
researchers asked specific questions about their experiences in the criminal

justice system. Surveyed victims of violent crimes resulting in arrest indicated that they were advised of their victim rights in 42% of cases. Victims of non-violent offenses stated that they received notification of their victim rights in only 30% of cases.[20] Although some of this disparity may be due to state laws requiring such notification only for victims of violent or specified offenses, less than 50% of *both* groups of victims indicated that they had received notice of the existence of their victim rights.

In a 1995 study seeking to determine the impact of constitutional and legislative provisions on crime victim rights, researchers identified two states that they characterized as "strong" and two states that they characterized as "weak," based on their provisions regarding the right to notification and other selected victim rights. The researchers then compiled responses from over 1,300 adult victims (or representatives) of primarily violent crimes from the four states regarding their experiences in the criminal justice process. The researchers also surveyed almost 200 criminal justice personnel and other officials. At least 70% of the applicable surveyed victims (i.e., based on the number of cases relevant to the inquiry) in the "strong" states indicated that they had been notified of their rights to discuss the case with a prosecutor, to make a victim impact statement regarding sentencing, to attend the parole hearing, and of the availability of victim services. Over 60% of the applicable victims in these states indicated that they were notified of the right to make an impact statement at the parole hearing and over 40% were informed of the right to be heard at the bond hearing. Less than 50% of the applicable victims in the "weak" states indicated that they had been advised of all of these rights, except the over 65% of such victims who had been told of their right to attend the parole hearing. Thus, especially in the "weak" states, but even in the "strong" states, significant portions of the surveyed victims stated that they had not received notification of available victim rights.[21] Added to these findings is a finding in a California study of victim allocution in which only 44% of 171 interviewed victims indicated an awareness of their right to appear at sentencing.[22]

The victims' recollections of their notification experiences in the four-state study contrasted somewhat with the criminal justice representatives' responses regarding their notification practices.[23] In addition, the nine-state survey called for victim recollections of events over a substantial period of time that could have impaired the accuracy of their recollections. Nevertheless, the victims' responses in all of these studies *at worst* indicate that substantial numbers of victims did not receive notice of the existence of their rights, and *at the least* may reflect that notification of the existence of the applicable rights was not accomplished *effectively* in significant numbers of cases. The absence of effective notification of rights would likely result in a reduction in victim exercise of these rights. Moreover, according to the researchers in the four-state study, victims who were notified of their rights were more satisfied with the criminal justice system than those who were not notified.[24]

Thus, it appears that despite the substantial constitutional and legislative efforts to provide victims notice of the existence of their rights, work remains to be done to ensure that this right is effectively implemented by those entrusted with this responsibility. As seen above, the effective implementation of this right not only is crucial in the exercise of other rights by crime victims, but it also impacts their perceptions of the criminal justice system itself.

Notice of Important Proceedings and Outcomes in the Criminal Justice Process

Just as a crime victim must be made aware of the existence of participatory rights in order to exercise them, the victim must be notified of the particular proceedings at which such rights may be exercised in order to use the rights. Even if a crime victim chooses not to actively participate in relevant proceedings, the victim can maintain involvement in the process if informed of important actions and outcomes in the prosecution and punishment of the offender. Prior to the issuance of the Task Force *Final Report*, only two states explicitly required that victims be notified of important developments in the proceedings.[25] In its *Final Report*, the President's Task Force proposed notification responsibilities for the police, prosecutors, and parole authorities.

President's Task Force and *New Directions from the Field* Recommendations

With regard to the police, the Task Force expressed the frustration of victims regarding the lack of information they received about the status of the police investigation of the crimes against them. Consequently, the Task Force recommended that police departments establish procedures to "ensure that victims of violent crime are periodically informed of the status and closing of investigations." More specifically, the Task Force proposed that these victims be informed of the arrest of a suspect or the closing of an investigation without an arrest. It also recommended that violent crime victims be given identifying and contact information regarding the case investigator to assist them in obtaining information about the status of the case.[26]

The Task Force felt that prosecutors are in the best position not only to be aware of all of the proceedings and outcomes in a case, but also to explain the legal significance of such to crime victims. Therefore, the Task Force recommended that prosecutors keep victims informed of the status of their cases from the initial charging decision to parole determinations. Although the Task Force recommendation was stated as to victims generally, its accompanying commentary addressed prosecutors' proposed notification responsibilities regarding victims of violent crime.[27]

The Task Force recommended the abolition of parole and hence parole boards. In the absence of immediate adoption of this recommendation, however, the Task Force proposed notification responsibilities for parole boards. The Task Force noted the lack of access to parole proceedings that many victims experienced. It also voiced victims' concerns regarding retaliation upon offenders' parole release. To address these concerns, the Task Force recommended that parole boards notify victims and their families in advance of parole hearings if their contact information has been provided. It also recommended that parole boards notify victims in advance of offenders' parole release so that victims can take whatever steps are necessary to prepare for such.[28]

Over fifteen years after the Task Force's *Final Report*, the authors of *New Directions from the Field* identified continuing gaps in victim notification processes, urged expanded use of technology to increase the effectiveness of victim notification, and recommended rights for all crime victims to notice of key public court proceedings (e.g., regarding bail, pleas, sentencing, and appeals), post-conviction release proceedings, significant changes in defendant status, and, on request, inmates' release, escape, or death. The *New Directions* authors made a number of specific recommendations to the police, prosecutors, and correctional authorities as to how they should fulfill these notification responsibilities, including expanded notification mechanisms to ensure actual notice to victims; requirements that certain notifications be made within a specified timeframe; and adoption of statewide, multilingual, toll-free correctional information systems regarding offender custody status.[29]

Constitutional and Legislative Response

The federal system and the vast majority of states currently require that crime victims be notified of significant proceedings and outcomes in the criminal justice process.[30] The last federal victim rights constitutional amendment proposal introduced in Congress prior to the enactment of the federal statutory Crime Victims' Rights Act in 2004 included the right of violent crime victims to "reasonable and timely notice of any public proceeding involving the crime and of any release or escape of the accused."[31] The Crime Victims' Rights Act provides a victim right to "reasonable, accurate, and timely notice of any public court proceeding, or any parole proceeding, involving the crime or of any release or escape of the accused."[32] The 2008 amendments to the Federal Rules of Criminal Procedure provide that the "government must use its best efforts to give the victim reasonable, accurate, and timely notice of any public court proceeding involving the crime."[33] A previously enacted victim services provision more specifically provides a variety of notifications that are required upon victim request:

> During the investigation and prosecution of a crime, a responsible official shall provide a victim the earliest possible notice of—
>
>> (A) the status of the investigation of the crime, to the extent it is appropriate to inform the victim and to the extent that it will not interfere with the investigation;
>> (B) the arrest of a suspected offender;
>> (C) the filing of charges against a suspected offender;
>> (D) the scheduling of each court proceeding that the witness is either required to attend or, under [the victim rights provision], is entitled to attend;
>> (E) the release or detention status of an offender or suspected offender;
>> (F) the acceptance of a plea of guilty or nolo contendere or the rendering of a verdict after trial; and
>> (G) the sentence imposed on an offender, including the date on which the offender will be eligible for parole.
>
> ****
>
> After trial, a responsible official shall provide a victim the earliest possible notice of—
>
>> (A) the scheduling of a parole hearing for the offender;
>> (B) the escape, work release, furlough, or any other form of release from custody of the offender; and
>> (C) the death of the offender, if the offender dies while in custody.[34]

Of the thirty-three states that currently have victim rights-related constitutional provisions, most include some type of notification provision. The most frequently provided notification right concerns notice of criminal justice proceedings, a right that is provided by twenty-nine of these states. It is most often stated in general terms, such as Connecticut's right to notification of "court proceedings," Mississippi's right to be "informed of ... public hearings," and

Colorado's right to be "informed [of] ... all critical stages of the criminal justice process," with these general terms subject to definition by the state legislature. In almost half of the states that provide this notification of proceedings right, the right is conditional in some way, such as Texas' provision of the right to notification of "court proceedings" only on a victim's request; Maryland's provision of the right to notice of a "criminal justice proceeding" "upon request and if practicable"; Indiana's provision of the right to be "informed of ... public hearings ... to the extent that exercising [this right] does not infringe upon the constitutional rights of the accused"; and South Carolina's provision of the right to be "informed of ... any criminal proceedings which are dispositive of the charges where the defendant has the right to be present."[35] Although some of these states' general notification provisions could be construed to include notice of appellate or parole proceedings, five states expressly include an unrestricted or conditional victim right to notification of parole proceedings in their constitutional amendments[36] and at least one state includes an express reference to the right to notice of appellate proceedings.[37] The most detailed constitutional notification of proceedings provision is that of Missouri, which includes "[u]pon request of the victim, the right to be informed of ... guilty pleas, bail hearings, sentencings, probation revocation hearings, and parole hearings, unless in the determination of the court the interests of justice require otherwise."[38]

In addition to provision of a right to notification of criminal justice proceedings, many states include a right to victim notification of certain outcomes in the proceedings in their constitutional amendments. Almost twenty states have a general or specific provision that includes an unrestricted or conditional victim right to notification of an offender's pretrial or parole release.[39] Twelve states have a general or specific provision that includes an unrestricted or conditional victim right to "information" about an offender's conviction or sentence.[40] Of the thirty-three states that currently have victim-related constitutional provisions, only Montana, New Jersey, and Rhode Island do not include any victim notification rights in their amendments.

In their statutory provisions, every state requires victim notification as to *something* and states continue to expand their notification requirements.[41] As to criminal justice proceedings themselves, notification is most frequently required regarding bail or pretrial release hearings, trial, sentencing, parole hearings, and cancelled or rescheduled proceedings. In their legislative provisions, some states explicitly require victim notification of some or all of these specific proceedings.[42] Other states more generally require victim notification regarding court or judicial proceedings, or hearings and proceedings in the case without a designation of the entity conducting such.[43] Although these undefined

provisions have typically not been judicially construed and thus are subject to
the interpretation of those officials entrusted with the notification responsibility, for purposes of this analysis, these general provisions are interpreted to
include at least the above-listed court proceedings and, when not so limited,
to include parole proceedings as well.

In terms of the statutory notification provisions regarding criminal justice
proceedings, over thirty-five states have specific or general notification provisions regarding bail or pretrial release hearings.[44] Moreover, over forty states
have specific or general provisions requiring victim notification of trial,[45] sentencing,[46] and parole[47] proceedings, and rescheduled or cancelled proceedings.[48] Approximately thirty states have victim notification requirements
regarding post-trial relief and appellate proceedings.[49]

A similar pattern is reflected in the legislative provisions regarding important actions or outcomes in the criminal justice process. More than thirty states
require victim notification of an offender's pretrial release[50] and final disposition or sentence.[51] Over forty states require victim notification regarding an
offender's plea bargain[52] and parole.[53] Many states also require victim notification of other outcomes in the criminal justice process, such as the dismissal
of a criminal charge, an offender's escape, pardon or commutation, or final discharge from sentence.[54] Almost twenty states require victim notification of a
suspect's arrest or the status of the investigation.[55]

Notification provisions as to these proceedings and outcomes appear to be
quite extensive, but many do have explicit or implicit limitations. For example, most states require notification of some or all of these proceedings and
outcomes only upon victim request.[56] Many states also give victims the responsibility to keep notifying authorities apprised of their current addresses.[57]
Some states make the rights contingent on victim cooperation with the prosecution.[58] Finally, as with most victim participatory rights, these provisions
are also subject to the definitional limitations of eligible victims and crimes
described in the previous chapter.

Moreover, although law enforcement, prosecution, or correctional authorities are usually given express responsibility for the applicable notification, the
procedures for notification often are not addressed at all in the provisions or
are addressed in widely varying levels of detail. Perhaps the most consistently
used procedural requirement is for the initial notification of the existence of
crime victim rights to be given in some type of written form.[59] Procedures for
subsequent notification of specific proceedings and outcomes range from general statements, such as California's allowance of notice "by any reasonable
means available" to very detailed procedures prescribed in Arizona.[60] Given
the often limited statutory guidance as to the procedures to carry out victim

notification, actual notice procedures may or may not provide effective victim notification. Further compounding the difficulties in achieving effective victim notification is the fact that many states statutorily limit their notification requirements to those that are "reasonable" or "practicable" under the circumstances.[61]

To address the challenges of effective victim notification, federal and statewide automated victim information and notification systems have been developed and expanded over the last fifteen years to provide case information or information regarding offender custody status or both through continuously available toll-free telephone numbers or through the Internet.[62] A majority of states now make some use of automated notification systems and states are increasingly adopting these notification systems in their notification provisions.[63] In the Crime Victims' Rights Act, Congress authorized $22,000,000 over a five-year period to enhance the federal automated notification system and an additional $25,000,000 to support the development and implementation of state and local notification systems.[64] As the authors of the *New Directions from the Field* study indicated, it is hoped that technology can increase the effectiveness of the victim notification requirements.[65]

Also potentially reducing the likelihood of effective victim notification is the absence of a remedy or sanction for any violation of notice requirements. As will be discussed in more detail in Chapter 7 of this text, although more jurisdictions are adopting some types of enforcement or compliance mechanisms, many states do not provide enforcement mechanisms or sanctions for victim rights violations of *any* kind. To the extent that jurisdictions specifically address notification rights violations, most provide no remedy or liability for the failure to provide victim notice.

At the federal level, the victim notification right is one of the statutory rights in the Crime Victims' Rights Act that federal courts are required to ensure and that is subject to an enforcement motion in the trial court and appellate mandamus action to enforce compliance, as will be described in more detail in Chapter 7. These enforcement mechanisms are referenced in the 2008 amendments to the Federal Rules of Criminal Procedure. However, following the lengthy list of notification responsibilities identified in the federal victim services statute outlined previously is the provision: "This section does not create a cause of action or defense in favor of any person arising out of the failure of a responsible person to provide [the above-described] information."[66]

With regard to the notifications required by its state statutory crime victims' bill of rights, Georgia expressly states that "[f]ailure to provide or timely provide any of the information or notifications required by this chapter shall not subject the person responsible for such notification or that person's employer

to any liability for damages." Specifically with regard to victim notification of
an offender's release, escape, or death, Georgia further expressly provides that
the custodial authority responsible for such notice "shall not be liable for a
failure to notify the victim."[67] With regard to victim notice of an offender's release from varying types of confinement, Maine also expressly provides that neither the applicable authorities' failure to perform nor compliance with the
notification requirements subjects them to liability in a civil action.[68]

A few states, however, do provide remedies for violations of victim notification provisions as to specific proceedings or more generally. If requested notice
has not been given to enable a victim to be present to make an impact statement at all "critical" stages of the prosecution, Louisiana judges "shall continue
the proceedings until proper notice is issued."[69] An Arizona procedural rule requires the court to inquire before applicable proceedings whether the victim has
been notified and, in the absence of the required notification, permits the court
to continue the proceeding or have the discretion to reconsider any ruling made.
The procedural rule is consistent with but also restricted by the statutory general rights violation provision that permits a re-examination hearing under certain circumstances subject to some statutory limitations as to convictions following
trial or plea and sentencings.[70] At least four states have remedies or sanctions
for the failure to provide victim notification of an offender's parole hearing or
parole release. Arizona, Oklahoma, and Tennessee provide the opportunity,
under specified circumstances, for a subsequent hearing to reconsider or re-
examine a parole or similar institutional release decision made as a result of a
hearing regarding which a victim did not receive requested notice, as described
previously in this chapter in the *Hance* case. In Hawaii, failure to provide requested notice of an offender's parole or final release can be the basis for a disciplinary action.[71]

Judicial Interpretation

State Cases

The presence or absence of remedial provisions concerning violations of
victim notification rights has often played an important role in the relatively
few cases in which state courts have addressed this right. In most instances,
reviewing courts have found either that there was no violation of an available
victim notification right in the circumstances presented or, upon finding a notification right violation, that the remedy sought was not available. Moreover,
in reaching their conclusions, state appellate courts have sometimes commented

on the limited nature of the crime victim rights being construed. Some courts, however, have granted victims some relief for notification rights violations.

The decision by the Kansas Supreme Court in *State v. Holt*[72] illustrates an instance in which a reviewing court found that the victim's right to notice had not been violated in the case. At a sentencing hearing following a plea agreement involving burglary charges, which the victim attended and at which she addressed the court, the trial judge sentenced the offender to a one-year term of incarceration plus restitution. The judge also stated that he would consider the offender's request for service of his sentence in the community at a future time. Subsequently, at a hearing that was called by the court *sua sponte* and of which the victim received no notice, the judge granted the offender parole release from his partially served sentence of incarceration. When the prosecutor objected to the hearing being conducted without notice to the victim and an opportunity to be present, the court stated that victim notification was required under the state victim rights provisions only for hearings required to be open to the public and that no such public hearing was required for the instant action of judicial parole release.[73]

In its appeal from the court's action, the state contended that the trial court erred in concluding that the victim had no right to notice of the parole proceedings. In determining this issue, the Kansas Supreme Court examined the state constitutional provision affording the victim right to be "informed of and to be present at public hearings, as defined by law" and the statutory provisions further defining the right. The court first noted that the Kansas victim rights statute established rights that were "merely directive or permissive" rather than mandatory and that they lacked enforcement provisions or sanctions for rights violations. Upon examination of the particular proceedings in this case, the Kansas Supreme Court upheld the trial court's conclusion that the hearing at which it granted parole to this offender was not a "public hearing" requiring notice to the victim. Although finding that the trial court was "legally correct" about the requirement to hold a public hearing in this case, the Kansas Supreme Court also recognized that it was within the court's discretion to do so and recommended "that trial judges carefully consider holding a public hearing and notifying crime victims in [such] cases where the court deems it advisable and when it can be accomplished without undue burden on the judicial system."[74] The Kansas legislature obviously found the state Supreme Court's concluding comments persuasive because the legislature subsequently expanded its definitions of "public" hearings and other proceedings regarding which a victim should receive notice to include hearings such as the one at issue in *Holt*.[75]

Using analysis somewhat similar to that employed in *Holt*, the California Supreme Court determined, in *Dix v. Superior Court ex rel. People*,[76] that rights provided under California statutory and constitutional provisions did not require victim notification of a trial court's action to "recall" a previously imposed sentence on an offender and to delay his subsequent resentencing. The California Supreme Court noted that the statutory right to notice and appearance at "sentencing proceedings" for specified purposes did not include continuance hearings regarding sentencing. Therefore, the victim's notice rights were not violated when his lawyer was refused the opportunity to object to resentencing continuances after the recall of the offender's sentence. Instead, at the time of the offender's ultimate resentencing, the victim would have a statutory right to receive notice, appear, and state his views. In addition, the state Supreme Court concluded that the existing constitutional and statutory victim rights provisions did not give the victim standing to challenge the recall action in the instant prohibition and mandamus action.[77] Of note, California's 2008 amended constitutional rights provision significantly expanded victims' rights to notice and includes a right to enforcement.[78]

Unlike the *Holt* and *Dix* courts that found no violations of the victims' notification rights or protected interests under the circumstances presented, other reviewing courts *have* found notification rights violations in the cases before them, but nevertheless have determined that the victims were not entitled to the relief or remedies requested. For example, in *People v. Pfeiffer*,[79] a Michigan appellate court held that the trial court erred in granting the prosecutor's motion for resentencing sought because of the prosecutor's failure to notify the victim regarding the original sentencing and resulting in the victim's inability to address the court. The appellate court held that the prosecutor's failure to notify the victim of the sentencing did not render the original sentence invalid under state law where the original sentencing proceeded without objection by the prosecutor and victim impact information was contained in the court's presentence report. The appellate court found that the state victim rights provisions did not "confer general remedial rights" on victims or establish an exception to state law that generally prohibited the modification of a valid sentence after imposition. The appellate court therefore set aside the second, increased sentence imposed and reinstated the defendant's original sentence.[80]

In *Hoile v. State*,[81] the Maryland Court of Appeals (the state's "supreme court") interpreted both a 2008 expansion of the state appellate rights provisions for crime victims as well as the merits of the claim regarding a violation of a victim's notification rights. Under the recently expanded appellate rights provisions, the court found that the victim, although not a party to the appeal, was permitted to participate in the offender's appeal "in the same manner as a party" regarding those issues involving the victim's rights only. On the merits of the issue affecting the victim's notification rights, however, the court held that the trial court erred in 1) granting the victim's motion to vacate a sentence imposed on the defendant at a reconsideration proceeding of which she had not been notified and 2) effectively reinstating an increased sentence. Despite the absence of notice to the victim, the sentence imposed at the reconsideration hearing was neither illegal nor irregular under state law in a manner that would allow its modification adversely to the defendant. Although the court acknowledged that its ruling would leave the victim without a remedy for the violation of her notification rights here, the court attributed that result to the legislature's choice not to provide such a post-sentencing remedy despite over twenty years of similar court interpretations of the scope of the state remedial provisions.[82]

> The Legislature has addressed some of the limitations on victims' rights, such as expanding a victim's right to apply to appeal, following *Lopez-Sanchez*. The Legislature, however, in the 23 years since *Lodowski* and 13 years since *Cianos*, has not given much substance to the illusory nature of the enforcement of victims' rights.... Although a victim now has more opportunity to participate in an appeal, there remains no effective tangible remedy for a victim to seek to "un-do" what already has been done in a criminal case. The Legislature has not amended the law to permit a victim, based on a violation of the victim's rights, to seek invalidation of an otherwise legal sentence. The victims' rights provisions in Maryland law still lack adult teeth. Thus, the victim is left largely with extra-judicial remedies.[83]

In *Bandoni v. State*,[84] the Rhode Island Supreme Court determined that neither a negligence cause of action nor a constitutional tort accrued when governmental officials failed to notify crime victims of their statutory and constitutional rights. The victims filed suit alleging common law negligence and constitutional tort actions against local and state entities and agents for the failure to notify them of the offender's plea agreement and sentencing. The victims asserted that they would have objected to the plea agreement and requested restitution had they been advised of the offender's court date. As damages for the defendants' failure to notify them of their rights, the victims essentially sought the amount of restitution they would have received following presentation of the impact statement they were not given the opportunity to present at the offender's sentencing.[85]

The Rhode Island Supreme Court concluded that no duty requiring that crime victims be notified of their rights existed at common law. Moreover, when the state legislature established the right to such notification in its victim rights provisions, it did not provide any statutory civil liability for the failure to inform victims of their rights, despite numerous opportunities to do so. The Rhode Island Supreme Court determined that "principles of judicial restraint prevent us from creating a cause of action [for damages in negligence] where a duty to apprise crime victims of their rights did not exist at common law and where our Legislature has neither by express terms nor by implication provided for civil liability."[86] The absence of a remedy for rights violations also proved fatal to the victims' constitutional tort claim. The court concluded that because the constitutional provision "expresses only general principles, and does not supply a sufficient rule of law by which even these general rights may be enjoyed, protected, or enforced, we must conclude that this provision is not self-executing."[87] Thus, although expressing the importance of the provision of established victim rights, the reviewing court declined to judicially create a cause of action based on a violation of the constitutional provisions.[88]

A few appellate courts have granted requested remedies for violations of notification provisions. For example, over the course of a year, the plaintiff in *Myers v. Daley*[89] received no response from the prosecutor to his original complaint of a violent victimization or his several requests for information as to the status of the investigation. The plaintiff finally filed the instant complaint against the prosecutor's office requesting that the court order the prosecutor to inform him of the status of the investigation of his complaint. Only after the filing of the lawsuit did the prosecutor's office inform the plaintiff that it had declined to initiate prosecution regarding his complaint. Although at that point both parties agreed to the dismissal of the suit, the plaintiff sought recovery of his court costs from the prosecutor's office. On appeal, the Illinois reviewing court determined that as the reported victim of a violent crime, the prosecutor had a legal duty to inform the plaintiff of the status of his case, upon his request, but that the prosecutor had failed to do so. As a result, the plaintiff would have been entitled to the relief he requested in the lawsuit and therefore the trial court properly awarded him the costs of his suit. The appellate court further noted, "[i]ndeed, the purpose of the Act would be frustrated if a victim were forced to file suit to learn the status of his case, and were also burdened by the costs of that suit."[90]

Requested relief for a notification rights violation was also granted by a California appellate court to the victim in *Melissa J. v. Superior Court ex rel. Williams*.[91] In this case, as part of the defendant's probation order, the trial court had imposed restitution to pay for the counseling of the defendant's molestation victim. Subsequently, without notice to the victim or an opportunity to object to the defendant's motion to terminate restitution, the court granted the motion. The victim sought a writ of mandate from the appellate court to direct the trial court to set aside the termination order issued in violation of the statutory requirement to notify the victim of all "sentencing proceedings." Although a prior appellate court had concluded that the California statutory provisions regarding victim notification of sentencing proceedings were "directory" rather than "mandatory" and thus could not form the basis for a victim's requested relief, the court in *Melissa J.* determined that the notice requirements had "greater force" in this case which involved the restitution rights of the victim. The reviewing court concluded that "[p]roper determination of restitution rights cannot take place without notice and an opportunity for the victim to be heard. Thus, as to restitution, the notice and right to appear requirements are mandatory. If the requirements are not satisfied, the victim may challenge a ruling regarding restitution" and "may assert his or her legitimate rights by the procedures available to parties" in the underlying criminal proceeding. The appellate court granted the victim's requested relief to direct the trial court to set aside its order terminating the previously ordered restitution.[92]

Further reflecting the types of potential relief available for victim notification rights violations and those that are unavailable is the Florida appellate court's ruling in *Ford v. State*[93] regarding the victim's attempt to declare a plea proceeding at which some restitution was ordered by the convicted defendants and charges against one defendant were dismissed void for insufficient notice to her. In her certiorari proceedings following the trial court's denial of her motion, the appellate court declined to vacate the pleas, noting that victims' constitutional rights must not interfere with those of the accused. However, the appellate court granted the victim's petition as to the restitution order and remanded the case for hearing with notice to the victims.[94] In *Alabama Board of Pardons and Paroles v. Brooks*,[95] the Alabama appellate court upheld the trial court's conclusion that a preliminary parole screening hearing conducted by parole authorities without notice to the victim sufficiently considered the possibility of parole to constitute a violation of the victim's right to notice concerning parole hearings. The appellate court further upheld the trial court's declaration that the parole granted at the subsequent parole hearing attended by the victim was void.[96] Finally, in *State v. Means*,[97] the New Jersey Supreme Court held that the prosecutor's failure to notify the victims prior to entering into a plea agreement, as required, was an insufficient basis *by itself* for the trial court to have set aside the plea agreement. Instead the trial court should have postponed the sentencing to allow victim notification of the plea agreement so that the court could make a more informed decision about whether to accept the agreement's terms. The appellate court ordered the reinstatement of the original plea agreement and remanded the case to the trial court for further proceedings.[98]

Thus, with only occasional exceptions, the state appellate courts that have interpreted victim notification provisions have generally *not* construed these provisions in a manner that would expand them beyond their clear constitutional or legislative terms. Instead, these courts have identified the limitations of the provisions when victims have sought to obtain more expansive judicial interpretations of their scope. Although often maintaining the importance of the victim notification rights at issue or expressing sympathy with victims whose notification rights have been violated, state appellate courts have been reluctant to use the tool of judicial interpretation to expand the reach of these rights.

Federal Cases

In addressing alleged violations of victim rights, under the Crime Victims' Rights Act, to "reasonable, accurate, and timely notice of any public court proceeding" concerning the crime or the accused's release or escape,[99] some federal courts have found no violation of the notification right under the circumstances presented. Other courts, while finding a violation, have been able to fashion an adequate remedy for it. In the few instances in which victims have thus far exercised the mandamus enforcement remedy for notification rights violations prescribed in the Act, their requested relief has been denied. Finally, in instances in which federal courts have addressed alleged federal civil rights violations based on violations of state victim rights provisions, they have not found a protectable federal interest based on the state rights granted.

In *In re W.R. Huff Asset Management*,[100] the Second Circuit Court of Appeals reviewed the notification procedures approved by a trial judge prior to his acceptance of a settlement agreement in a forfeiture action. The Government had proffered that there were tens of thousands of potential victims of the defendants' securities fraud in the case. The Government sought approval of an alternative notification plan regarding its proposed settlement agreement pursuant to the Act's provision allowing the court to devise "reasonable" procedures to provide victim rights that do not "unduly complicate or prolong the proceedings" in cases involving multiple victims. In this case, the Government used the Department of Justice website to post information about the proposed settlement. The Government also attempted to notify potential victims by informing various courts (and parties) handling related proceedings of the settlement proposal and by holding a press conference about it on national television and issuing a press release. At the hearing reviewing the Government's notification attempts, the trial court declined to adopt a proposal by one of the victim groups for additional notification efforts that would have delayed the proceedings for months, if not years. Having provided an opportunity for victims to file written objections to the proposed settlement agreement and to be heard at the hearing, the trial judge accepted the proposed settlement agreement at the conclusion of the hearing.[101] In a mandamus action, authorized under the Act for rights violations, the above group of victims sought to vacate the settlement agreement based on an alleged violation of the Act's notification right (and other grounds). In reviewing the claim, the appellate court adopted an abuse of discretion standard regarding the trial court's actions. The appellate court concluded that the trial court "did not abuse its discretion in determining that, given the time delays and the difficulty of identifying victims and calculating losses, the Government gave reasonable notice to crime victims in the extensive alternative notice procedures it employed." The appellate court further concluded that the trial court did not abuse its discretion in approving the settlement agreement and denied the mandamus petition.[102]

In *United States v. Turner*,[103] the trial judge found that the Government had failed to adequately notify victims of the initial appearance and detention hearing in a case and that he had not adequately inquired regarding the Government's notification efforts at the initial appearance. To remedy this deficiency, the judge instructed the Government to provide a written summary or transcript of the previous proceedings to victims in the case, as well as appropriate notification of the next scheduled proceeding regarding the defendant's release and their right to be heard, including revisiting the court's prior detention decision. The Government complied with the court's remedial order, although no victims chose to attend the subsequent detention hearing.[104] In *United States v. Ingrassia*,[105] the same trial judge found that the Government's use of the federal automated notification system provided inadequate notice of the preliminary plea proceeding at issue because the system provided inaccurate and incomplete information and only passively provided the over 200 victims with notice of this plea proceeding, at which no victim was present. The judge therefore ordered the Government to notify all victims by first-class mail (or other "reasonably equivalent" method) of the proposed plea, sentencing date, and the victims' right to be heard regarding the court's acceptance of the plea and the defendants' release conditions and sentencing. Because no final decision had been made as to whether the plea would be accepted by the court, the judge stated that this remedial action would be adequate to vindicate the victims' "legitimate interests" in the case.[106]

In the mandamus action in *In re Dean*,[107] the Fifth Circuit Court of Appeals reviewed the notification procedures regarding a plea agreement that the trial court had approved. Because of the large number of victims and the risk that media coverage would jeopardize the proposed plea agreement, the trial judge granted the Government's request to delay victim notification of the plea agreement until after it filed related criminal charges and the defendant signed the plea agreement. Following these events, the Government mailed three notices to victims informing them of the subsequent proceedings regarding the plea and their right to be heard. The trial court permitted all victims who wished to be heard regarding the acceptance of the plea to be heard; 134 victims also filed victim impact statements. After the trial judge denied the victims' request that he reject the plea agreement, the victims sought mandamus relief to require the trial court to reject the plea agreement.[108] The appellate court rejected the trial judge's rationale for the delayed notice of the plea agreement and found instead that the Government should have devised a "reasonable" way to inform the victims of the anticipated criminal charges and determine their views regarding the potential plea agreement. The appellate court further found, however, that the victims did receive notice of the plea agreement, albeit belated notice, and that they were allowed "substantial and meaningful" participation at the proceeding in which the defendant entered its plea. Rather than granting the requested mandamus relief to require the trial court to reject the plea agreement, the appellate court noted its confidence that the trial judge would be mindful of the violation of victim rights it had found and would fully consider the victims' objections to the plea agreement in making a final decision whether to accept the agreement. The appellate court therefore denied the mandamus relief.[109]

In addition to interpreting victim notification rights under the Crime Victims' Rights Act, federal courts have addressed whether alleged violations of state victim notification rights have created a federal civil rights violation. In *Dix v. County of Shasta*,[110] the Ninth Circuit Court of Appeals upheld the federal trial court's dismissal of the victim's complaint and found that the California victim rights provisions at issue—including the notice provisions— did not give the victim a liberty interest that was enforceable under the due process provisions. The appellate court also rejected the victim's claim that state governmental officials infringed his First and Sixth Amendment rights when they failed to notify him of the offender's sentencing proceedings. The appellate court expressed sympathy with the victim regarding the lack of notice he received. However, finding no federal cause of action, the reviewing court consigned the victim to remedies, if at all, in the California state courts or political process.[111]

Thus, federal courts have demonstrated increased efforts to ensure that victim notification rights are implemented under the Crime Victims' Rights Act. Those efforts, however, have not necessarily resulted in the relief requested by victims in instances in which notification rights have been violated. Similarly, victims have not yet found a federal remedy for violation of state victim notification rights provisions.

Implementation and Analysis of the Right

Reflecting the rapid expansion of the right to victim notification of certain events and outcomes in the criminal justice process, national surveys of prosecutors and correctional and parole authorities conducted in the mid-1990s reflected that approximately 80% of prosecutors' offices across the country were required to notify victims of felony case dispositions and at least 80% of correctional and parole authorities nationwide were notifying victims of changes in offender status.[112] Similarly, a survey of federal prosecutors, reported in 1990, reflected that over 80%–90% rated the quality of various aspects of prosecutors' notification efforts as "very well" or "well."[113] A 2004 evaluation of the North Carolina automated notification system regarding court events and offender custody status examined survey responses from twenty-nine sheriffs' offices and eighteen prosecutors' offices. Eighty percent of respondents felt that the automated system was very effective or effective for assisting the state's crime victims. They expressed general satisfaction with the technical aspects of the system and its positive impact on achieving their notification responsibilities and benefitting victims, but also noted the need to continue to increase public awareness about it and address technical problems as they arose.[114]

Surveys of victims regarding the effectiveness of victim notification have produced varying results. In its 2008 evaluation of the implementation of the Crime Victims' Rights Act, the General Accountability Office found that 78% of the 169 responding federal crime victims indicated that they were very or somewhat satisfied with the provision of their right to notice of public court proceedings (with an additional 15% expressing neutral or no opinion). The federal notification process includes an automated system.[115] In the 2004 North Carolina evaluation of its automated system regarding court events and offender custody status described above, victim survey respondents were subdivided into forty-one respondents from a court notification sample and forty-two respondents from an offender custody status sample. In both groups, 86% of respondents indicated general satisfaction with the accuracy of the provided information. Eighty percent of the court notification group and 85% of the offender custody group indicated that using the automated system provided them with a sense of safety and security.[116]

In the 1998 survey of the general public and crime victims in nine northeastern states, 83% of the approximately 4,000 individuals surveyed responded that it was important for crime victims to be informed of case progress and 56% responded that, based on what they knew or had heard, crime victims in their states were able to get information on case status and hearing dates. However, only 42% of the almost 500 respondents who had been victims of a crime in which a suspect had been arrested in the past ten years indicated that they felt that they had been kept informed about the progress of the police investigation. Of the victim respondents whose cases went to trial, 66% responded that they were informed in advance of the date and place of the trial and 43% were informed of all postponements or continuances of the trial dates. Of the victim respondents in whose cases the court held a sentencing hearing, 74% stated that they were informed about the sentencing hearing.[117]

In the four-state study involving over 1,300 crime victims in two "strong" and two "weak" victim rights states in 1995, researchers found that between approximately 90% and 97% of the surveyed victims rated as "very important" receiving information as to the arrest of a suspect, the defendant's pretrial release, and the date of the offender's earliest possible release from incarceration.[118] In terms of their reports of actual notifications made in their cases, crime victims in the two "strong" versus the two "weak" victim rights states reported the following notification of events and outcomes in their cases: suspect's arrest (93% vs. 86%), bond hearing (63% vs. 43%), defendant's pretrial release (38% vs. 26%), dismissal of charges (42% vs. 39%), plea negotiations (57% vs. 53%), trial (96% vs. 90%), sentencing hearing (92% vs. 73%), and parole hearings (70% vs. 35%).[119] Despite these varying degrees of notification (which sometimes contrasted with notification reports given by surveyed criminal justice personnel),[120] in their overall assessments of the efforts to inform them of their cases' progress, approximately 77% of the victims in the "strong" states and 60% of the victims in the "weak" states characterized such efforts as "adequate" or "more than adequate." Moreover, between approximately 70% and 80% of victims in "strong" and "weak" states said that they were "very" or "somewhat" satisfied with the police, prosecutors, and victim assistance staff—the personnel generally responsible for victim notification—as well as with the criminal justice system itself.[121]

Some of the findings of these surveys are consistent with surveys conducted at approximately the time of the President's Task Force, in which some researchers concluded that their crime victim respondents sought more information as to developments in their cases and that the provision of such information would increase their satisfaction with the dispositions in their cases and the criminal justice system generally. For example, in surveys of 389 victims of felony personal and property crimes in six sites around the country, researchers found that almost half of the victims indicated that they would have been more satisfied with the legal system if they had been better informed about the progress of their cases. Thirty percent of the surveyed victims also identified this as a means to improve relations between victims and the courts.[122] In personal interviews of 100 adult female rape victims in the metropolitan Washington, D.C. area, researchers determined that approximately half of the victims felt that they had been denied information about their cases. Among their suggestions for improving victim treatment at all stages of the prosecution, 21% suggested that victims be given more information on case developments. These researchers concluded that provision of such information was positively related to victim satisfaction with police and prosecution services.[123]

However, in a study of the results of an early victim assistance program in which victim liaisons notified victims of court dates, other researchers found no significant differences between the control and the experimental program groups in the percentage of victims who felt that they "had been treated well in court" or "had been kept informed of the status of their case." The researchers studied the effect of a Victim Involvement Project ("VIP") in a Brooklyn criminal court. A second Brooklyn court with similar types and dispositions of cases was used for control group purposes. Among other aspects of the study, almost 300 interviews were conducted with victims whose cases were concluded in these courts during a study period in the late 1970s. In terms of victims who felt that they had been treated well in court, the percentage for the VIP court victims was 44% compared to 37% for the control group. Interestingly, 27% of the VIP court group felt that they had been kept informed of the status of their cases versus 34% of the control group.[124]

Another study examined the effects of victims' knowledge of the disposition of their cases and of their court attendance on their perceptions of their defendants and on sentences imposed generally. This study involved approximately 200 victim interviews conducted after the initial charge had been filed and after the disposition in the case in Toronto suburbs during a study period in the late 1970s. The researchers found that knowledge of the case outcome increased the victims' assessment that sentences in general were "too easy." They further found that knowledge of case outcome only, i.e., without court attendance, produced the smallest reduction in demand for severity of sentencing of the combinations of court attendance and knowledge of disposition studied. Victims' knowledge of the case disposition did not have a significant impact on victims' perceptions of their offenders.[125]

Similarly, in a study to determine the effect of victim notification and various other forms of victim participation in the criminal justice process on victims' distress levels, researchers found that notification of court proceedings had no significant effect on victims' feelings of distress soon after their victimization or subsequently. This research was based, in part, on 125 completed surveys from victims whose felony cases were prosecuted in an Ohio county during a study period in the late 1980s. The victims were questioned as to various forms of their participation in the prosecution. Scales and other questions that measured victim distress levels after the crime and at the time of the survey were included.[126]

Several conclusions can be drawn from the above research regarding the implementation of the crime victim right to notice of significant criminal justice events and outcomes. At the outset, crime victims and the general public feel that such notification is important. With the tremendous increase in the statutory and constitutional requirements of victim notification, significant progress has been made in victim notification in certain areas. There remains a significant shortfall, however, in the number of victims who actually receive notice or at least believe that they have received notice of some events and outcomes. A portion of this shortfall can be accounted for by some degree of inaccuracy in the victims' recollections as to the notices they received and some can be explained by a certain degree of victim ineligibility for notification due to victims' failures to request notice or maintain current notification information, their victimization regarding crimes not eligible for notification, or other factors. Nevertheless, gaps between required and actual notification of important events and outcomes in the criminal justice process remain. One way to address these issues is the increased use of automated notification systems, adopted by the federal system and a growing number of states. As described in the North Carolina study above, its automated system was deemed generally effective by both criminal justice personnel and crime victims. Use of the system enhanced victims' sense of safety and security and reduced agency challenges in meeting mandated notification requirements. Based on the research that has been performed so far and contrary to early hypotheses, however, there does not seem to be a significant difference in victim perceptions of the criminal justice system and its participants or in victim distress as a result of the degree of notification victims have received.

Conclusion

The federal system and the states have obviously concluded that victim notification of important proceedings and outcomes in their cases can meaningfully enhance their experience in the criminal justice process. As a result, some degree of victim notification is required by constitutional or legislative provisions, or both, in the federal system and all states. As with most victim participatory rights, however, this notification right is generally limited to victims of certain crimes only and is frequently restricted to those victims who affirmatively request such notice. These limitations are compounded by the frequent use of vague language in the notification provisions, the absence of clearly articulated notification procedures, and the sometimes limited resources available to accomplish the notification requirements.[127] The incentive to perform notification requirements may also be reduced by the absence of victim remedies or sanctions for the violation of notification rights in most jurisdictions. As a result, gaps still remain between victim notification requirements and actual victim notice. Jurisdictions therefore should work toward the reduction of such gaps, through the adoption of automated systems or otherwise, not only to effectuate the victim notification rights themselves, but also because victim notification is a threshold right to the exercise of other substantive rights by victims interested in doing so.

Chapter 4

The Right to Be Present at Criminal Justice Proceedings

Introduction

Prior to the adoption of the public prosecutor system in this country during the nineteenth century, crime victims had broad rights to be present in court proceedings as private prosecutors or sponsors of prosecutions. After the adoption of the public prosecutor system, a crime victim—as any member of the general public—was still entitled to be present at most public court proceedings. This entitlement was often subject to restriction, however, in proceedings in which a victim was expected to testify as a witness. Moreover, some criminal justice proceedings were not generally open to the public or victims, such as parole hearings.[1]

These various traditions of inclusion and exclusion were based, in part, on the victim's varying roles in a criminal prosecution. As a member of the general public, a crime victim is the beneficiary of the constitutional principles that render most judicial proceedings open to the public. While the Sixth Amendment specifically guarantees the defendant the right to a public trial, the public's right to be present at judicial proceedings is derived from the First Amendment's guarantee of freedom of speech and of the press. This right has been held to apply to arraignments, pretrial release hearings, preliminary hearings, hearings on suppression motions, jury selection proceedings, trials, and sentencings.[2] It has been noted that the public nature of these proceedings "enhances the quality and safeguards the integrity of the factfinding process, with benefits to both the defendant and to society as a whole."[3]

Maintenance of the quality and integrity of the factfinding process, however, is the principal reason provided for the restriction of victim presence at judicial proceedings in which the victim also serves as a witness. The practice of excluding witnesses from the courtroom except during their testimony, upon the request of a party or the court, is often called the "rule on witnesses." This rule of exclusion is of ancient origin and was recognized at common law, with

49

its implementation left to judicial discretion. It was designed to help assure a fair trial for the accused by avoiding improper influences on witness testimony and preventing or exposing witness fabrication of testimony.[4]

Based on this common law precedent—or on the fair trial concepts incorporated in the due process protections of the Fifth and Fourteenth Amendments or on the view that the rule of witness exclusion might be necessary to provide the defendant with the right to *effective* confrontation of adverse witnesses guaranteed by the Sixth Amendment—the federal government and most states adopted this procedure of witness exclusion by evidentiary rule or otherwise. American jurisdictions either granted the parties an absolute right to exclude witnesses from the courtroom except during their testimony or allowed exclusion in the discretion of the court. The rule was interpreted to apply to the exclusion of witnesses not only during the taking of others' testimony, but also during opening statements and closing arguments in which testimony was described and after witnesses' initial testimony in the event of their recall for further testimony. Exceptions to the rule of exclusion were often provided, however, for parties or their representatives or for others whose presence could be demonstrated as essential in some way.[5]

Prior to the President's Task Force, victims' presence was not routinely considered "essential" and thus eligible for an exception from the exclusion rule. As a result, because victims were usually also witnesses in the criminal prosecution, and therefore subject to these rules of exclusion, they consequently had *fewer* rights to be present at certain judicial proceedings than the general public.[6] Moreover, there was also no widespread recognition of a general public or victim-specific right to be present at non-judicial proceedings, such as parole hearings. In this connection, fewer than ten states had "open" parole hearings prior to the Task Force recommendations.[7]

President's Task Force and *New Directions from the Field* Recommendations

In its *Final Report*, the President's Task Force addressed action recommendations to the judiciary and to parole authorities concerning crime victim presence. The Task Force also included a victim right of presence in its proposed modification of the Sixth Amendment to the federal constitution. Its proposed modification provided that the "victim, in every criminal prosecution, shall have the right to be present … at all critical stages of *judicial* proceedings."[8]

In its action recommendation to the judiciary, the Task Force recognized the competing interests involved in victim presence and exclusion from trial proceedings. The Task Force recognized that excluding witnesses from the court-room was one way that judges had maintained the integrity of the "truth-find-ing" process. Recognizing that the crime is often one of the most significant events in the lives of the victims and their families, however, "[t]hey, no less than the defendant, have a legitimate interest in the fair adjudication of the case, and should therefore, as an exception to the general rule providing for the exclu-sion of witnesses, be permitted to be present for the entire trial."[9] The Task Force also thought that this exception to the rule of exclusion should apply to a family member or other designated support person for the victim.[10] At-tempting to balance these competing interests supporting inclusion and ex-clusion, the Task Force ultimately recommended that judges "should allow the victim and a member of the victim's family to attend the trial, even if identi-fied as witnesses, *absent a compelling need to the contrary.*"[11]

Unlike its recommendation regarding victim presence at trial, The Task Force's recommendation concerning victim presence at parole hearings was not conditional. The Task Force recommended that parole boards allow crime victims, their families, or their representatives to attend parole hearings. It felt that victims' presence at parole hearings, and the accompanying recommended ability to make known the crime's impact upon them, would enhance the fair-ness of parole decision making. The Task Force challenged the supposition that only the offender was affected by a parole decision. It stated that victims had a "legitimate interest" not only in seeing their attackers appropriately pun-ished, but also in ensuring that they were not released prematurely to harm others. The Task Force also felt that crime victim presence at parole hearings would foster parole board accountability and reduce any abuses stemming from the fact that parole board decisions were often arrived at "behind closed doors."[12]

The authors of the *New Directions from the Field* study reiterated the im-portance of a victim right to attend court and parole proceedings. By the time of their study in 1998, a majority of states had made some or all of the fol-lowing adjustments to their laws: authorized a crime victim right to be pres-ent at at least some court proceedings, exempted crime victims to some degree from witness exclusion rules, and authorized their attendance at parole pro-ceedings. The authors recommended that federal and state laws should ensure that victims have the right to be present throughout "all public court pro-ceedings," including juvenile proceedings. To facilitate crime victim participa-tion in these proceedings, the *New Directions from the Field* authors recommended federal and state laws that would prohibit employers from tak-ing "adverse action" against victims who miss work to participate in criminal or juvenile justice proceedings. The study authors also recommended that judges facilitate the expanding rights of victims and their families to be present at court proceedings "unless the defendant proves that their presence would interfere with the defendant's right to a fair trial." Similarly, the study authors recommended that correctional authorities facilitate and expand victims' growing rights to attend parole proceedings.[13]

Constitutional and Legislative Response

As noted by the *New Directions from the Field* authors, since the President's Task Force, victim rights provisions regarding victim presence have largely focused on reaffirming victim rights of presence shared by the general public, reducing or eliminating the restrictions on victims' presence in proceedings in which they will testify as witnesses, and expanding victim entitlement to presence at certain non-public proceedings, such as parole hearings. Striking the proper balance between the defendant's right to a fair process and the victim's right to presence at important criminal justice proceedings is the task that has confronted the federal and state governments in the years since the President's Task Force.

The last federal victim rights constitutional amendment proposal introduced in Congress prior to the enactment of the statutory Crime Victims' Rights Act in 2004 included violent crime victims' right "not to be excluded from" any public proceeding involving the crime.[14] Between the issuance of the Task Force *Final Report* and the enactment of the Crime Victims' Rights Act, federal crime victims' right to be present evolved in several stages. In a victim rights provision enacted in 1990 (and repealed with the enactment of the Crime Victims' Rights Act), Congress required Executive Branch officials to use their "best efforts" to ensure that victims are provided the "right to be present at all public court proceedings related to the offense, unless the court determines that testimony by the victim would be materially affected if the victim heard other testimony at trial."[15]

Congress subsequently enacted two pieces of legislation facilitating victim presence, as a result of the proceedings arising out of the bombing of the federal building in Oklahoma City in 1995.[16] In this regard, Congress provided for closed circuit televising of criminal proceedings to victims and others with "compelling" interests in trials in which the venue of the trial is changed out of the state in which the case was filed and more than 350 miles from the location in which proceedings would have taken place, if these persons are unable to attend the proceedings due to the change of venue. The presiding judge in the trial retains the right to exclude an individual from the televised proceeding, however, if the court determines that the person's testimony would be "materially affected" by hearing other testimony at the trial.[17] In separate legislation, enacted in 1997, Congress prohibited a trial court from excluding a crime victim from the trial of an offense solely because the victim may make a statement or present information regarding an offender's sentence in a non-capital sentencing hearing or may testify as to the impact of the crime or other permissible factors at the sentencing hearing in a capital case.[18] In response to these separate statutes regarding victim presence, in 1998, Congress approved a modification of the federal evidentiary rule regarding exclusion of witnesses to exempt "a person authorized by statute to be present" from the exclusion rule.[19]

In the 2004 Crime Victims' Rights Act, Congress strengthened these provisions by including the victim right "not to be excluded from any such public court proceeding, unless the court, after receiving clear and convincing evidence, determines that testimony by the victim would be materially altered if the victim heard other testimony at that proceeding." Congress also provided that, before ordering exclusion, the court must make "every effort" to allow the victim's "fullest attendance possible," consider "reasonable alternatives" to the victim's exclusion from proceedings, and clearly state its reasons for exclusion on the record. In 2008, these provisions were substantially incorporated into the Federal Rules of Criminal Procedure.[20] Thus, although not absolute, the victim's right to be present in federal court proceedings has been significantly strengthened in the years since the Task Force *Final Report.*

All of the states have now explicitly recognized the victim's right to be present at court proceedings in some way. Most jurisdictions, however, condition the victim's presence at testimonial proceedings to some degree when the victim is also a testifying witness regarding the crime. In addition, a majority of states have recognized some victim rights to be present at parole hearings.[21]

Of the thirty-three states with victim rights constitutional amendments, thirty-one include a general or conditional victim right to be present at court proceedings or criminal justice proceedings.[22] Only Montana and Ohio do not include this victim right in their provisions.[23] Thirteen states authorize a crime victim to be present at court or judicial proceedings generally or at specifically identified court proceedings. Some of these states, however, allow limitations on the victim's court presence in cases in which the crime victim is going to testify at trial or otherwise.[24] For example, Illinois provides a victim right "to be present at the trial and all other court proceedings on the same basis as the accused, unless the victim is to testify and the court determines that the victim's testimony would be materially affected if the victim hears other testimony at the trial."[25]

Eighteen states authorize victim presence at "critical," "crucial," or "important" stages of the criminal justice process or criminal proceedings or generally at criminal justice or public proceedings in the case or the criminal justice process. Some of these states provide this right to the extent that it does not interfere with the constitutional rights of the accused.[26] Although in some instances these more general victim rights of presence could be construed to include parole or other post-conviction release hearings, California, Nebraska, and South Carolina expressly provide this victim right of presence in their constitutional provisions.[27]

In their statutory provisions, over ten states effectively authorize unrestricted victim presence at court proceedings either by providing victims the right to attend court proceedings generally[28] or all court proceedings that the defendant has the right to attend[29] or by creating an exception for victims to their rules of exclusion of witnesses.[30] Perhaps the most extensive victim rights of presence are provided by Alabama which not only authorizes victims to be present at court proceedings regarding the offense, to be exempt from rules of exclusion of witnesses, and to be exempt from exclusion except on the same grounds for which a defendant could be excluded from court proceedings, but also allows victims to be seated at counsel table with the prosecutor. These statutory provisions are, of course, subject to Alabama's constitutional right of victim presence "at all crucial stages of criminal proceedings, to the extent that [this right does] not interfere with the constitutional rights of the person accused of committing the crime."[31]

Approximately thirty states have modified their previous fairly automatic exclusions of victims at testimonial proceedings, but still condition a victim's right to be present at court proceedings to some degree. The most common condition is the provision of a victim's right to be present to the extent that the exercise of the right does not interfere with the defendant's constitutional rights.[32] Other jurisdictions have established a victim's right to be present subject to the court's determination that the victim's presence would not be prejudicial or contrary to the interests of justice or that the victim's testimony would not be materially affected or for other good cause the defendant may establish.[33] Still other jurisdictions preclude the victim's presence at testimonial proceedings until after the victim has testified.[34] In the most detailed of these provisions, California identifies specific criteria the court should consider in determining a motion to exclude a victim from criminal proceedings and provides the opportunity for a hearing with specific factual findings on the issue of exclusion, but makes these procedures subject to the court's authority to exclude victims who are subpoenaed as witnesses pursuant to state evidentiary statutes.[35]

The remaining states provide neither a general nor conditional statutory victim right to be present at court proceedings, but expressly refer to the victim's opportunity to be present only at sentencing proceedings.[36] On the other hand, in addition to the victim rights of presence at judicial proceedings described above, some states extend the victim's right of presence to members of the victim's family or support persons who are permitted to accompany a victim in court. Other states allow a designated representative of the victim to be present in instances in which a victim cannot or does not wish to personally exercise his right to be present.[37] Thus, although all of the states provide an express victim right of presence at court proceedings to some degree, *and* the express right of victim presence is often greater than prior to the President's Task Force, the extent of this right varies considerably.

Approximately forty states also allow crime victims to be present at parole hearings. The states that expressly address victim rights to be present at parole proceedings either provide the appearance right in connection with a right to orally address the parole authorities or provide the right to be present at parole proceedings generally.[38] Some states grant a victim right to be present at other post-conviction proceedings, such as pardon hearings.[39]

Those jurisdictions that have expressly addressed a victim's failure to exercise a granted right of presence at a proceeding have generally provided that such failure does not prevent the court from conducting the proceeding or provide a basis to set aside a conviction.[40] In a few states, however, the failure to provide a victim the right to be present at a post-conviction release proceeding or the failure to provide notice that would allow the victim to exercise such a right to be present can result in either a postponement of the proceeding or a reconsideration of any release decision reached at it.[41]

In addition to their rights to be present at various proceedings, victims in approximately forty states have employer-related rights that facilitate their rights to presence. These rights include the prohibition of an employer from firing or threatening to fire victims who miss work to attend criminal justice proceedings or employer intercession services to resolve problems arising from victims missing work to attend criminal justice proceedings, or both.[42] Although many states include these provisions within their general victim rights provisions making them subject to the general (and often limited) remedies for rights violations, some states have specific sanctions for violations of their employer prohibition provisions. For example, Michigan provides a criminal penalty for employer violations and Minnesota provides both criminal penalties and a civil action regarding such violations.[43]

Judicial Interpretation

State Cases

Other than the cases described in Chapter 3 regarding the failure to notify victims of proceedings and thus the denial of their rights to attend such proceedings, there have been few state cases that have directly addressed victims' assertions of or claims of denial of their right to be present at authorized proceedings. Although recognizing the importance of the right, courts have not always been able to grant the requested relief. Courts have more frequently addressed offender challenges to victims' presence at testimonial proceedings. Reviewing courts have typically upheld the degree of victim presence authorized by state law, including trial courts' discretionary rulings implementing such. Reviewing courts have not foreclosed the possibility that a defendant might demonstrate circumstances in which a victim's authorized presence could jeopardize the defendant's right to a fair trial. However, they have generally found no prejudice to a defendant's rights from a trial court's allowance of a victim's presence during trial or other testimonial proceedings before the victim's initial or subsequent testimony or after the testimony has been completed—as authorized by applicable law and under the circumstances presented.[44]

In *State v. Timmendequas*,[45] the New Jersey Supreme Court reviewed the trial court's decision to empanel a jury from another county rather than changing the venue of a murder trial due to extensive publicity. After approving a change of venue for the trial, the trial court adopted this alternative approach regarding venue following the Government's motion to reconsider in which it presented evidence of the emotional and financial hardship that a change of venue would pose for the deceased victim's family. On appeal, the defendant challenged the trial court's consideration of the impact of the venue change on the victim's family. The New Jersey Supreme Court stated that such consideration was proper pursuant to state constitutional and statutory victim rights provisions concerning the victims' right to be present at public judicial proceedings and to have inconveniences associated with their participation in the criminal justice process minimized to the extent possible, provisions that reflected the increased efforts in the state and nation to protect crime victims and enhance their participation in the criminal justice system. The appellate court found that the trial court was also required to consider the defendant's constitutional rights: "Taking the concerns of the victim's family into account does not constitute error, *provided* that the constitutional rights of the defendant are not denied or infringed on by that decision." The New Jersey Supreme Court upheld the trial court's determination that the alternative venue procedure did not infringe or diminish the defendant's constitutional rights here.[46]

In *State ex rel. Goldesberry v. Taylor*,[47] the requested relief was not available to the victim who was not able to exercise his right to be present at a plea and sentencing proceeding due to lack of notice. A Missouri appellate court rejected the prosecutor's initially successful efforts in the trial court to set aside the judgment and sentence due to the violation of the victim's right to be present and heard at the proceedings. In the defendant's appellate challenge to the trial court's action, the trial judge contended that the violation of the victim's right to be present constituted "manifest injustice" that authorized setting aside the plea and sentence under applicable provisions. Although the state constitutional right to be present was supported by implementing legislation stating that the "victim's rights are paramount to the defendant's rights," the constitutional victim rights provision also expressly did *not* authorize setting aside a guilt finding or plea based on the rights provision. Finding no other basis to support the trial court's action, the appellate court found that the trial court's jurisdiction in this case terminated with the initial entry of the plea and sentence and that its subsequent action to set them aside was void.[48]

Most appellate court rulings have addressed offenders' challenges to victims' presence at testimonial proceedings. In most instances, reviewing courts have upheld the state laws and rules governing victim inclusion and witness exclusion at proceedings, as well as trial courts' discretionary rulings implementing such. For example, in *Stephens v. State*,[49] the Arkansas Supreme Court rejected the offender's constitutional challenge to the state evidentiary rule allowing crime victims to be present during trial notwithstanding the state's witness exclusion provisions. Finding no express constitutional right to the exclusion of witnesses, the appellate court found that the defendant had failed to demonstrate how a crime victim's presence was "inherently unfair" or was unfair in this case in which the victim was the second witness and testified based on her own knowledge without influence from the previous testimony.[50] In *State v. Fulminante*,[51] the Arizona Supreme Court similarly concluded that the crime victim exception to the state witness exclusion rule did not violate due process generally and the defendant had failed to demonstrate actual prejudice from the presence of the deceased victim's mother (his ex-wife) in court prior to her testimony.[52]

In *State v. Beltran-Felix*,[53] a Utah appellate court rejected the defendant's due process challenge to the state's constitutional and statutory victim rights to presence at important criminal justice proceedings. The appellate court further found no unconstitutional application of the rights in this case in which the victim was present in court throughout the trial and testified as the final prosecution witness. The reviewing court found "no suggestion that the critical elements of the case" turned on the victim's testimony or that her testimony was significantly altered to conform with other witnesses and rejected the defendant's claim that the prosecutor had improperly referred to the victim's presence.[54]

Conversely, the Texas appellate court in *Jimenez v. State*,[55] concluded that the trial court had abused its discretion by failing to exclude the victim from the pretrial hearing on the defendant's motion to suppress identification. State law authorized the victim's presence, if approved by the court. In this case, however, the appellate court found that the critical and only contested issue was the reliability and admissibility of the victim's identification, the subject matter of the hearing. Given the risk that the victim's presence during other testimony and argument at the hearing tainted subsequent identification testimony, the trial court's abuse of discretion in allowing the victim's presence formed part of the reversible error regarding the identification testimony.[56]

In some cases, the determination of error from a victim's presence has been based on whether the presence was permitted by applicable law, in addition to the resulting prejudice from it. For example, in *Claiborne v. State*,[57] the Arkansas Supreme Court upheld the presence, at a hearing on the defendant's motion to suppress identification, of an identification witness from one burglarized residence during the identification testimony of her neighbor whose residence had also been burglarized. Despite the critical nature of the identification testimony in both cases and this witness' previous equivocal identification, the reviewing court determined that this victim was not a "witness" to her neighbor's burglary and thus was not subject to exclusion during his testimony and that she was otherwise entitled under state law to be present at the suppression hearing due to her own victim status.[58]

On the other hand, in *Solomon v. State*,[59] the Arkansas Supreme Court found that the trial court had *erroneously* ruled that a homicide victim's daughters were entitled to be present in the courtroom during trial although they were not included in the victim's exception to the state rule on exclusion of witnesses. The daughters testified after several prosecution witnesses and offered important testimony as to the intent of their father, the defendant. In this case, the defendant's intent was the critical issue in the case because the defendant claimed that he had accidentally, not intentionally, shot his wife. Given the substance and the nature of the daughters' testimony on this crucial contested issue and the possibility that their testimony could have been influenced by that of preceding witnesses, the Arkansas Supreme Court concluded that the defendant had demonstrated sufficient prejudice from the trial court's erroneous ruling to require reversal of the defendant's conviction and a remand of the case for retrial.[60]

Appellate court action regarding a trial court's permitting a victim not only to be present in court, but also to be seated at counsel table has also been based, in part, on whether such action was permitted by applicable law. In one case in which the trial court had erroneously allowed a victim not only to be present during trial (which was authorized by law), but also to sit at counsel table (which was not authorized by law), a reviewing court found a danger that the seating of the victim at counsel table could be perceived as the trial court's expression of opinion on her credibility as a witness and therefore presented sufficient prejudice to the defendant to reverse his conviction.[61] In another case, the appellate court concluded that state constitutional victim rights provisions did not "permit victims or their families to actively participate in the conduct of the trial by sitting at counsel table or being introduced to the jury" as the trial court had erroneously permitted regarding the homicide victim's son.[62] In some instances, the finding of error has been based on the victim's emotional or other conduct while seated at or near counsel table.[63] Alabama courts, however, have consistently rejected defendants' challenges to the state's law permitting victims, or their representatives, to sit at counsel table with the prosecutor.[64] An Indiana appellate court also upheld a trial court's ruling permitting the victim to sit at counsel table after his testimony and prior to his recall by the defense when the prosecutor selected him as the authorized person to sit at counsel table and "assist" the prosecutor during the trial.[65]

Thus, although state reviewing courts have not extended victims' rights of presence beyond their clear constitutional, statutory, or procedural limits, they have generally upheld such provisions granting victim rights to be present when challenged and have rejected offenders' challenges to trial courts' actions implementing the provisions. Reviewing courts have also not hesitated to reverse offenders' convictions, however, in those instances in which a victim's presence has been clearly shown to have jeopardized an offender's right to a fair trial or to reverse trial court actions that have exceeded those authorized.

Federal Cases

The Ninth Circuit Court of Appeals opinion in *United States v. McVeigh*[66] represents one of the few federal cases specifically addressing a victim's claim of the denial of a right to be present prior to the enactment of the Crime Victims' Rights Act in 2004. This case involved the trial of one of the defendants in the bombing of the federal building in Oklahoma City. Pursuant to the then existing federal witness exclusion rule, the trial judge entered a pretrial order prohibiting victims who would offer victim impact testimony at the sentencing proceeding from attending the trial proceedings. Both the Government and the excluded witnesses filed appeals from the trial court's order and requests for mandamus. The appellate court determined that the subject matter of the Government's appeal did not fall within the statutorily designated areas of permissible governmental appeals and was not appropriate for mandamus review.[67]

In dismissing the excluded witnesses' appeal and mandamus petition for lack of standing, the appellate court reviewed the proffered statutory and constitutional bases of their claims. The appellate court found that the existing federal victim rights provision that tasked Executive Branch officials to make their "best efforts" to ensure victims' right to be present at public court proceedings, that was subject to certain judicial exclusions regarding victims who were also witnesses, and that prohibited a cause of action based on its violation did not provide a "legally protected interest" required for standing. The appellate court also concluded that the general First Amendment-based public right of access to proceedings did not create a *personal* constitutional right to attend the proceedings that would establish the victims' standing here.[68] In direct response to and shortly after the appellate court's ruling dismissing the victims' suit, Congress enacted legislation, described previously in this chapter, that prohibited trial courts from excluding victims from trial proceedings solely because such victims may testify concerning sentencing-related matters during the sentencing hearing.[69]

In the Crime Victims' Rights Act of 2004, Congress attempted to address other deficiencies of the previous legislation identified in the *McVeigh* decision by strengthening the victim rights provisions, including those regarding victim presence, and providing remedies (and accompanying standing) for their violation.[70] Federal courts have begun to interpret both the strengthened victim presence right and the remedy prescribed for its violation.

For example, the trial judge in *United States v. Johnson*[71] granted the Government's motion for family members of the deceased victims who would testify during the trial and at sentencing to be present during the trial. The trial court found that all of the family members qualified as "victims" under the Act, that their testimony during trial would be as to "discrete factual events" not subject to "material alteration" from hearing other testimony (as required for their exclusion), and that the defendant acknowledged the application of the Act here and proffered no grounds for exclusion under it.[72]

In ruling on the Government's motion to allow the deceased victim's family access to certain information and proceedings in *United States v. L.M.*,[73] the trial court interpreted whether the federal victim right to be present at "public" court proceedings applied to juvenile proceedings. The court held that this victim right applied to juvenile proceedings only if they were open to the general public, a determination that federal courts make on a case-by-case basis regarding various juvenile proceedings. Although the court granted the Government's request to notify the deceased victim's family of scheduled juvenile proceedings and access to certain redacted case records, the court held that the upcoming transfer hearing to determine whether the juvenile would be tried as an adult involved the kind of sensitive background information concerning the juvenile that warranted that it be closed to the public. Hence, the victim's family would not be permitted to attend this transfer proceeding. The trial court reserved ruling on the public nature of any future proceedings.[74]

In *In re Mikhel*,[75] the Ninth Circuit Court of Appeals reviewed a mandamus petition filed by the Government pursuant to the Act after the trial judge denied its unopposed motion to permit the murder victim's family members to be present throughout the defendant's trial. Instead, the trial judge required that family members who were testifying during the guilt proceedings be excluded until after their testimony and required a similar procedure for the sentencing to "prevent collusive witness testimony and to ensure proper courtroom decorum." The appellate court noted that the Crime Victims' Rights Act established a statutory exception to the general federal witness exclusion rule and further established the factual findings that a trial court must make before requiring victim-witness exclusion from proceedings. While the pre-Act witness exclusion rule might have permitted the judge's summary ruling regarding the testifying victims, the Act requires more than a "mere *possibility*" that victim testimony might be altered. Instead, "a district court must find by clear and convincing evidence that it is *highly likely*, not merely *possible*, that the victim-witness will alter his or her testimony" and must consider reasonable alternatives before ordering victim exclusion. Rather than ordering the trial judge to permit the victim-witnesses to be present, however, the appellate court remanded the matter to the trial court to determine whether there was clear and convincing evidence that the victim-witnesses' testimony would be "materially altered" by their presence, as required by the Act, and to otherwise reconsider its exclusion ruling in light of the appellate court's opinion and the Act's requirements.[76]

In an additional interpretive review of the Crime Victims' Rights Act in *United States v. Turner*,[77] a federal trial judge noted the expansion of the Act's right to presence provisions as well as their limitations. As in the above case, the judge observed the impact that the Act had on the general federal witness exclusion rule. The judge also noted the limitations of the Act's right to be present:

> [T]he phrasing of this provision does have important implications for all proceedings in a criminal case: the right is phrased in the negative (*i.e.*, the crime victim has the right "not to be excluded") rather than as an affirmative right to attend. This is to guard against arguments

that the government has some affirmative duty to make it possible for indigent or incarcerated victims to be present in the courtroom. The negative phrasing also suggests that the fact that a properly notified victim cannot be present is not in itself a circumstance that requires a proceeding to be adjourned. Essentially, a judge conducting a public proceeding involving a crime may not close the courtroom door to a crime victim who seeks entry but has no obligation to ensure the victim actually arrives there.[78]

Future federal court decisions will, of course, continue to interpret the scope of this victim right under the Act and the remedies available to secure it.

In addition to ruling on victims' right to be present in court under the Act, federal courts also have continued to address offender appellate claims based on crime victim presence. In *United States v. Visinaiz*,[79] the Tenth Circuit Court of Appeals found that the trial court did not err in permitting the deceased victim's son to remain in the courtroom after his testimony. The appellate court found that the victim's son was properly determined to be a victim under pre-Act statutes and thus exempt from the federal witness exclusion rule, that there had been no request for a cautionary instruction to him to not discuss his testimony with others, and that there was no indication that he had done so.[80] In *United States v. Sampson*,[81] the First Circuit Court of Appeals found no abuse of discretion in the trial court's denial of the defendant's mistrial motion based on the reactions of the victims' families and others to evidence presented in his capital sentencing proceeding. The appellate court noted the victims' families right to attend the proceeding under pre-Act law and the efforts of the trial judge to reduce the risk of "unfair prejudice" from the gallery reactions to evidence, including instructing the jury to decide the case based only on the evidence, individually questioning jurors in response to defense concerns, and moving the victims' family in and even outside of the courtroom when especially disturbing evidence was presented to minimize juror exposure to their reactions.[82]

Implementation and Analysis of the Right

The extent to which crime victims actually take advantage of their rights of presence has not been widely documented. In its 2008 evaluation of the implementation of the Crime Victims' Rights Act, the General Accountability Office found that 45% of 174 responding victim-witness professionals reported at least some increase in victim attendance as a result of the Act and 27% reported a great or very great increase in attendance. However, almost 85% of the 167 responding crime victims *did not attend* any of the proceedings in their cases for which they received notice, most frequently citing the distant location of the court and lack of interest in attending.[83] These more recent results do not reflect increases in victim court attendance over earlier studies. In a local study in Ohio in the late 1980s, according to official records, approximately 20% of the studied victims were present in court during trial or sentencing. In a survey of a subgroup of these victims, 23% indicated that they were present for the offender's plea and 34% reported that they had attended the sentencing.[84] In a 1985 survey of probation staff and prosecutors in thirty-three states, it was estimated that 18%-26% of victims attended sentencing hearings.[85]

In the 1995 survey of crime victims in two "strong" and two "weak" victim rights states, however, over 70% of victims in "strong" *and* "weak" states who had been notified of the sentencing hearing, attended it. On the other hand, only approximately 14% of victims in the "strong" states and 18% of victims in the "weak" states who had been informed of the parole hearing chose to attend it. Surveyed criminal justice personnel reported that victims were excluded from trial in 30% of cases or less in "strong" states and 10% of cases or less in "weak" states, with such exclusion most frequently based on the fact that the crime victims might testify at trial. Researchers in this study hypothesized that being given the opportunity to participate in criminal justice proceedings would be a more important predictor of victim satisfaction than victims' actual participation because being given the opportunity to participate returns control to the victim and allows the victim to choose whether to participate or not.[86]

A few researchers have attempted to assess the effect or impact of victims' presence at criminal justice proceedings. One study, involving approximately 200 victim interviews conducted after initial charge and after disposition in cases in Toronto suburbs in the late 1970s, examined the effects of victims' court attendance on their perceptions of their offenders and on sentences imposed generally. Researchers found that court attendance appeared to improve victims' perceptions of sentencing outcomes generally, but had no impact on their perceptions of their offenders.[87] Other researchers, in a late 1980s study of 500 felony cases prosecuted in an Ohio county and 125 completed victim surveys, found that court attendance had a correlation with whether offenders received sentences of incarceration or probation and the length of the incarceration sentences imposed. However, court attendance had no significant impact on victims' satisfaction with the sentences imposed or with the criminal justice system generally.[88] These researchers also found that court attendance had a limited positive effect on victims' distress levels.[89]

Thus, the results of this limited empirical research regarding the implementation and the effects of the victim right to be present at criminal justice proceedings are somewhat inconclusive. Although the percentage of crime victims who actually attend criminal justice proceedings appears to vary in the few studies done, it is clear that significant numbers of victims are *not* attending such proceedings. This result could be due to remaining restrictions of the right to attend various proceedings or of victims eligible for such a right; the lack of adequate notification of the proceedings which forecloses the exercise of the right of attendance; the lesser value that victims place on attendance than previously believed; or the hypothesis previously stated that the opportunity to attend criminal justice proceedings is a more valued right than actual attendance. The limited research results regarding the effect of court attendance on victim perceptions and satisfaction also produced mixed results.

Conclusion

In the years since the President's Task Force, victim rights of presence at court and post-conviction proceedings have been significantly expanded. These rights, however, often remain conditional in instances in which the victim's role as a prosecution witness risks conflict with the defendant's right to a fair trial. Reviewing courts have generally upheld the balance between these interests which has been established through constitutional or legislative provisions and implemented by trial courts. Future movement in this area of victim rights will likely reflect the continuing efforts of legislatures and courts to strike the proper balance between the respective rights of victims and defendants.[90]

Chapter 5

The Right to Be Heard Regarding Charging Decisions and Pleas

Although obtaining victim rights to notification of important events and outcomes in the criminal justice process and to presence at criminal justice proceedings have been important goals of the victims' movement in the years since the President's Task Force on Victims of Crime, the ultimate goal, in terms of participatory rights, has been to achieve greater victim input into the central decisions affecting the prosecution.[1] Prior to the President's Task Force, there were few requirements that prosecutors, judges, or parole authorities obtain or listen to the views of victims regarding important decisions in their cases. In a few areas, such as the prosecutor's charging decisions, there has been some expansion of the right to be consulted by the prosecutor, but limited change in the victim's formal right to be heard by the court. In other areas, such as regarding plea negotiations, there has been a significant expansion of victims' formal right to be consulted by the prosecutor and some meaningful expansion of the right to be heard by the court. In areas such as sentencing and parole decisions, as discussed in Chapter 6, victims' rights to be heard have been widely recognized.

The various mechanisms for victims to provide input into these criminal justice decisions are collectively referred to as the "right to be heard." Jurisdictions may give victims a right to provide input orally, or in writing, or both. In addition, some jurisdictions provide various victim rights to be heard without attempting to define the means by which such a hearing can be achieved or the extent of the right granted. For purposes of the analysis in this text, the right to be heard includes a victim right to provide input orally or in writing or through any other means reasonably designed to transmit such input.

The Right to Be Heard Regarding the Initiation or Dismissal of a Charge

Through a victim's decision to report an alleged crime to the authorities or his choice to decline to make such a report, a crime victim has always had significant input into the decision to charge a suspect with a crime. Estimates in the 2008 National Crime Victimization Survey indicate that victims reported to the police approximately 47% of that year's violent crime victimizations and approximately 40% of the property crime victimizations.[2] Thus, by failing to report the crime to the authorities, victims in a majority of victimizations provide *negative* and usually decisive input regarding the initiation of criminal charges in their cases.

Once a crime has come to the attention of the authorities, however, the decisions to file formal charges against a suspect, as to what charges should be filed, and as to whether the filed charges should be dismissed have generally been entrusted to the prosecutor's discretion since the adoption of a public prosecution system in this country.[3] Of course, a prosecutor has always had discretion to and often does consult the victim about these charging decisions.[4] Prior to the President's Task Force, however, such consultation was rarely formally required and mechanisms for a victim to challenge the prosecutor's charging decisions were also rare.[5]

President's Task Force and *New Directions from the Field* Recommendations

Prior to the President's Task Force, only one state required victim input into key prosecutorial decisions.[6] In its action recommendations to prosecutors, the Task Force recommended that prosecutors "inform" victims about the status of their cases, beginning with the initial decision to charge or to decline prosecution. It also generally recommended that prosecutors consult with victims during the "various stages" of the prosecution, which could include charging decisions. Specifically with respect to the decision to dismiss a case, the Task Force recommended that a prosecutor should consult in advance with a victim of a violent crime and tell the victim the reasons for the prosecutor's decision to dismiss the case. The Task Force included case dismissals among the prosecutorial actions regarding which prosecutors should ensure that victims of violent crime are given an opportunity to make their views known and regarding which it recommended that prosecutors had an obligation to bring such victims' views to the attention of the court.[7] The Task Force also included

a crime victim right "to be heard at all critical stages of judicial proceedings" —
which arguably could include certain dismissal if not charging decisions—in
its proposed federal constitutional amendment.[8]

The authors of the New Directions from the Field study reiterated the importance of "meaningful" prosecutor consultation with victims prior to major
case decisions, including charge initiation, reduction, and dismissal. In their
view, such consultation not only is important to permit victim input into
charging decisions and information about the status of the prosecution, but also
helps prosecutors make informed decisions about their cases.[9] Although there
has been expansion of the prosecutor's general duty to confer with the victim,
there has been only modest expansion of a victim's formal and express right to
be heard regarding charging decisions in the years since the President's Task Force.[10]

Constitutional and Legislative Response

The last federal victim rights constitutional amendment proposal introduced in Congress prior to the enactment of the federal statutory Crime Victims' Rights Act in 2004 did not contain a victim right to consult with the
prosecutor or an express right to be heard regarding the decision to initiate or
dismiss a criminal charge.[11] The Act itself contains a victim's "reasonable" general right to confer with the case prosecutor, but also a provision that none of
the victim rights provided should be construed to "impair" prosecutorial discretion.[12] Similarly, the Attorney General Guidelines for Victim and Witness Assistance require prosecutor availability for consultation with victims about
"major" case decisions (including dismissals), but permit such consultation to
be limited to gathering information from victims and providing only public information and non-sensitive data.[13]

In their constitutional provisions, twelve states include a general right to confer or consult with the prosecutor, which could include consultation regarding charging decisions.[14] California specifically provides a right to "reasonably" confer with
the prosecutor regarding the charges filed. Arizona and South Carolina provide
a constitutional victim right to confer with the prosecutor "after the crime against
the victim has been charged … or before any disposition." Louisiana provides a
right to confer prior to final case disposition.[15] Eight states provide a constitutional right to be heard at important or critical stages of the criminal process or
proceedings or generally at criminal justice, public, or court proceedings[16]—
which again could arguably include dismissal if not charging decisions.

In their statutory provisions, approximately ten states have general provisions regarding a victim right to consult with the prosecutor or a requirement
that victims' views be ascertained during the criminal justice process or pro-

ceedings,[17] which could include charging decisions. A few states have express provisions authorizing or requiring prosecutor consultation with victims or otherwise allowing victim input prior to filing charges or making a decision to decline to file charges. For example, upon a victim's request in Arizona, the prosecutor must confer with the victim, including the "victim's views" about a decision not to proceed with a criminal prosecution. In New Jersey, victims have the right to submit a written statement about the crime's impact to the prosecutor which the prosecutor must consider before making a final decision about whether to file charges.[18] Approximately twenty states have provisions authorizing or requiring victim consultation with or input to the prosecutor regarding case dismissals. For example, Pennsylvania gives victims of certain crimes the right to submit "prior comment" to the prosecutor on the "potential dropping" of any charge. Louisiana requires that the prosecutor, on the request of victims of certain crimes, consults to "obtain their view" regarding dismissal of the case.[19]

In addition to often making the consultation right available only on victim request, several of these states include in their consultation provisions a further provision that the prescribed consultation does not include crime victim authority to "direct the prosecution" of the case[20] or a provision that the failure to conduct the prescribed consultation does not affect the validity of the prosecutorial action taken.[21] In their victim rights statutes, jurisdictions have not generally included a specific victim right to be heard in court regarding the prosecutor's charging decisions.[22]

In addition to or instead of the "right to be heard" provisions regarding charging decisions contained in state victim rights provisions, some states have maintained common law or pre-public prosecution traditions or have enacted specific laws that allow victims or other members of the public to challenge a prosecutor's decision to decline prosecution or that enable a victim to initiate and, in some instances, to prosecute criminal charges.[23] For example, Colorado allows any person to file an affidavit with a court alleging the commission of a crime and the "unjustified refusal" of the prosecutor to prosecute. The court, in turn, "may" require the prosecutor to appear and explain the refusal to prosecute. If the judge finds that the prosecutor's refusal to prosecute was "arbitrary or capricious and without reasonable excuse," the judge may order the prosecutor to file charges and prosecute the action or may appoint a special prosecutor to do so.[24] Wisconsin has statutory provisions that allow citizens to seek a judicial determination of whether a criminal complaint should be filed when a prosecutor has refused to file a complaint or otherwise.[25] Some states maintain common law or other traditions that allow citizens unrestricted or conditional access to grand juries to present evidence of criminal conduct for investigation and initiation of prosecution.[26] Finally, many states allow a crime victim to retain a private attorney to consult with the prosecutor about the case or assist the prosecutor in the case's prosecution. Some states even allow such private counsel to conduct the prosecution in minor cases with the permission of the prosecutor.[27] Thus, although entrusting charging decisions to the public prosecutor is clearly the norm in the contemporary American criminal justice system, states have often maintained certain traditions of the earlier victim-centered prosecution process that can extend the victim's right to be heard regarding charging decisions to some degree.

Judicial Interpretation

Overview

Jurisdictions' failure to significantly expand their victim rights provisions concerning the right to be heard regarding charging decisions is consistent with courts' traditional reluctance to review prosecutors' charging decisions. Courts most frequently decline such review on separation of powers grounds, refusing review of this executive branch function in circumstances in which the charging decision is not based on illegal or improper considerations.[28] Other courts have recognized that the factors that determine a prosecutor's charging decision, such as the strength of a prosecutor's case, the prosecution's deterrence value, or the government's enforcement priorities, are "ill-suited" to judicial review and that such review could undermine prosecutorial effectiveness.[29]

In some instances, courts have rejected challenges to the prosecutor's charging decision on standing grounds. For example, the United States Supreme Court rejected a woman's attempt to force a prosecutor to initiate criminal non-support charges against the father of her child in *Linda R.S. v. Richard D.*[30] due to her lack of standing. The woman had filed a class action suit to enjoin the application of the Texas criminal non-support statute, which had been judicially construed to apply only to married parents. The woman, the parent of a child born out of wedlock, sought to enjoin the local prosecutor from refusing to prosecute the father of her child for non-support. The Court noted that, "in American jurisprudence at least, a private citizen lacks a judicially cognizable interest in the prosecution or nonprosecution of another."[31] Although the woman had an interest in the support of her child, she had not demonstrated that her failure to obtain support payments resulted from the non-enforcement of the criminal statute as to the child's father or that her requested relief of prosecution would result in payment of support by the child's father. The Court therefore concluded that she lacked standing to pursue her action.[32]

Finally, other courts have rejected efforts to challenge a prosecutor's charging decision on the merits by simply finding no governmental duty to a citizen to initiate or maintain a prosecution and hence no cause of action in mandamus or otherwise to compel prosecution.[33] In light of courts' general reluctance to intervene in prosecutors' charging decisions, it is not surprising that state and federal reviewing courts have generally *not* found that the limited victim rights provisions in this area have significantly expanded the victim's role in charging decisions.

State and Federal Cases

State reviewing courts have generally not attempted to expand constitutional or legislative victim rights provisions in addressing prosecutor or offender challenges to victim assertions of their right to be heard regarding charging decisions. For example, in *State v. Layman*,[34] the Tennessee Supreme Court found that the trial court had erroneously permitted the deceased victim's family and its attorney to participate in the hearings regarding the prosecutor's attempt to dismiss a more serious homicide charge in favor of a reduced charge. The appellate court found that their participation in opposition to the prosecutor in the hearings exceeded the statutory victim right to confer with the prosecution and constituted an attempt to direct the prosecution. The court also found that their participation was not authorized under the statutory "right to be heard" provisions because the dismissal hearings at issue were not statutorily identified as proceedings at which victims have a right to be heard. Although the Tennessee Supreme Court found the trial court's permission of this type of participation harmless error under the circumstances, it concluded that the trial court had abused its discretion in rejecting the prosecutor's attempt to dismiss the higher charge.[35] In addressing governmental appeals of trial courts' dismissals of charges based on crime victim requests, other state appellate courts have upheld such dismissals only when specifically authorized by statutory provisions concerning victims.[36]

In *Gansz v. People*,[37] the Colorado Supreme Court specifically addressed whether any of the state constitutional or statutory victim rights provisions gave a crime victim standing or the right to challenge or appeal a prosecutor's discretionary dismissal of charges against the alleged perpetrator of the crime. In this case, the defendant had initially been charged with assault. After reviewing the case for trial, however, the prosecutor determined that the victim was not a credible witness and that the case could not be proven beyond a reasonable doubt. The trial court granted the prosecutor's motion to dismiss the case without a hearing. The trial court vacated the dismissal and ordered a hearing, however, after receiving a letter from the victim objecting to the dismissal. At the hearing, the trial court ruled that the victim lacked standing to challenge the dismissal and again granted the prosecutor's dismissal motion.[38]

In the victim's attempted appeal from the trial court's action, the Colorado Supreme Court noted that the prosecutor's statutory obligation to consult with a victim, where practicable, regarding decisions concerning case dismissal provided that noncompliance with the provision would not invalidate any decision or disposition made. The appellate court concluded that this consultation right did not provide the victim with a "right to be heard in the context of an appeal of the dismissal of criminal charges."[39] Moreover, although the state constitutional provision granted victims the right to be heard at all "critical stages of the criminal justice process" as defined by the state legislature, the legislature had limited this right to proceedings involving pretrial release, the acceptance of plea agreements, and sentencing. As a result, the Colorado Supreme Court concluded that the state victim rights provisions did not give the victim the right to challenge the prosecutor's dismissal motion in the trial court or standing to appeal the court's order granting it.[40]

Although the *Gansz* court rejected the victim's standing to appeal the case dismissal pursuant to the state's victim rights provisions, it acknowledged her standing to seek future relief under the general statutory provisions permitting citizen challenge of a prosecutor's "unjustified" failure to prosecute a case,[41] described previously in this chapter. It is pursuant to such general statutory provisions or common law traditions—rather than victim rights provisions— that crime victims have thus far obtained judicial recognition of even a limited opportunity to be heard regarding prosecutors' charging decisions. For example, in *Sandoval v. Farish*,[42] the Colorado Supreme Court considered a victim challenge to the prosecutor's failure to bring criminal charges under the Colorado provision described above. Even in acknowledging the availability of the remedy, however, the reviewing court recognized the limited review provided by the statute. The appellate court noted that the procedure does not permit a judge to "substitute his own judgment" for that of the prosecutor, but rather requires the challenging party to prove by clear and convincing evidence that the prosecutor's refusal to prosecute was arbitrary or capricious or without reasonable cause. After noting the wide range of permissible factors appropriate for prosecutorial consideration in the charging decision, the court upheld the prosecutor's action.[43] In a subsequent case in which a Colorado appellate court determined that this challenge process included "minimum procedural requirements" of discovery and a hearing, the reviewing court also noted that "[e]xperience teaches that in most cases in which this statute is invoked the diligence and judgment of prosecutors in the exercise of their discretion will be recognized and exonerated."[44]

Reviewing courts in other states have also examined the range and limits of citizen involvement in charging decisions. Wisconsin appellate courts have upheld statutory mechanisms for citizens to seek a judicial determination that criminal charges should be filed in the absence of prosecutorial action, but have recognized the limitations of the remedy. In *State v. Unnamed Defendant*,[45] the Wisconsin Supreme Court recognized the state's long-standing tradition and authorization of "John Doe" and related procedures which permit citizens to seek judicial investigation of a criminal complaint and subsequent initiation of a criminal charge upon a probable cause finding, in circumstances in which a prosecutor has not acted. Although the Justices debated the merits of the procedures from a public policy perspective, they concluded that these procedures did not violate constitutional separation of powers doctrines.[46] Wisconsin appellate courts, however, have also concluded that a judge cannot require a prosecutor to alter a previously filed charge pursuant to these provisions [47] and that a judge's refusal to initiate criminal charges following a person's request under these provisions is not subject to appellate review.[48]

In *Commonwealth v. Benz*,[49] the Pennsylvania Supreme Court reviewed the application of a Pennsylvania procedural rule that permitted a private individual to seek judicial approval of a complaint upon its disapproval by a prosecutor. It determined that a trial court's conclusion that the prosecutor had not abused his discretion in declining prosecution was subject to appellate review, at least when the declination of prosecution was premised on insufficiency of the evidence rather than prosecutorial discretion in matters of policy.[50] Pennsylvania appellate courts have noted, however, that the judicial independent review of a disapproved complaint "should not interfere with the exercise of prosecutorial discretion unless it is determined that there has been a 'gross abuse of discretion.'"[51]

The Kansas Supreme Court, in *State ex rel. Rome v. Fountain*,[52] reviewed that state's statutory provisions and judicial precedent in determining whether a complainant had standing to appeal from a dismissal of a prosecution sought jointly by the prosecutor and the defendants. Although the complainant had permissibly initiated the prosecution by filing a complaint with the proper judicial authority, as authorized under state law, the reviewing court could find no similar legal authorization for an appeal by the complainant from a subsequent dismissal of the complaint. Noting the state's long-standing tradition of public prosecution, the Kansas Supreme Court concluded that the complainant had no standing to appeal the dismissal of the complaint.[53]

Thus, although state reviewing courts have generally upheld statutory authorizations of citizen initiation or challenge of charging decisions, they have not typically expanded such authorizations beyond their express terms and have construed them in a manner mindful of the prosecutor's considerable discretion regarding charging decisions. Similarly, although state reviewing courts in most jurisdictions have generally upheld statutory or common law authorizations of a victim's retention of a private attorney to *assist* the public prosecutor in the conduct of the prosecution, they have generally required that such assistance be rendered under the direction or control or with the knowledge of the prosecutor. Absent a showing of misconduct by the private counsel or prejudice to the defendant, the permission of the assistance of private counsel has generally been entrusted to the discretion of the public prosecutor or the trial court.[54]

In determining whether the assistance of a private attorney has violated a defendant's due process protections, however, federal reviewing courts have been especially sensitive to any exercise of control by a "private prosecutor" over crucial prosecutorial decisions, such as the initiation of charges or the selection of the targets of a prosecution, that can determine the fairness of particular prosecutions.[55] This concern led the United States Supreme Court, in *Young v. United States ex rel. Vuitton et Fils S.A.*,[56] to exercise its supervisory authority to reverse the criminal contempt convictions of defendants whose contempt prosecution had been requested by the attorney for a litigant in a civil suit in which the court's injunction had been violated and who was also appointed by the trial court to serve as special prosecutor for the contempt proceedings. Among the Court's areas of concern were the appearance of impropriety, the potential for conflicts of interest, and private counsel control over charging decisions and other prosecutorial functions.[57]

In the only case thus far addressing the victim right to be heard regarding charging decisions pursuant to the Crime Victims' Rights Act, a federal trial judge in *United States v. Heaton*[58] determined that the victim's reasonable right to confer with the prosecutor applied to any critical stage or disposition of the case, including the Government's motion to dismiss the prosecution. Similarly, the victim's right to be treated with fairness under the Act also applied to the court's ruling on the dismissal motion and required consideration of the victim's views regarding the dismissal. Before ruling on the dismissal motion in this case (and future "victim-related" cases), the trial judge therefore required the prosecutor to inform the court that the victim had been consulted regarding the dismissal and to indicate the victim's views regarding the dismissal.[59]

In conclusion, reviewing courts have not generally construed crime victim "right to be heard" provisions in a manner that would significantly expand the victim's right to be heard regarding the initiation or dismissal of criminal charges beyond its express terms. Similarly, although typically upholding general statutory provisions permitting citizens to initiate or challenge prosecutors' charging decisions, reviewing courts have construed these provisions with deference to prosecutors' broad discretion regarding charging decisions. Finally, while generally upholding statutory provisions or common law traditions that permit the assistance of "private prosecutors" in the conduct of public prosecutions, reviewing courts have sought to ensure that public prosecutors retain control over and responsibility for the prosecution, especially regarding charging decisions.

Implementation and Analysis of the Right

Perhaps because of the limited nature of the right to be heard regarding charging decisions, empirical research concerning this right is also limited. In the four-state study involving over 1,300 crime victims from two "strong" and two "weak" victim rights states in 1995, researchers found that approximately 89% of the surveyed victims thought that it was "very important" for victims to have the right to discuss their cases with the prosecutor's office and approximately 91% thought that it was "very important" to have the right to be involved in decisions regarding "dropping" a case.[60] In a 1998 survey of approximately 4,000 members of the general public and crime victims in nine northeastern states, less than 50% in each state, and approximately 40% overall, indicated that crime victims are "usually" able to discuss their cases with prosecutors,[61] presumably including discussions regarding charging decisions. In its 2008 evaluation of the Crime Victims' Rights Act, the General Accountability Office found that 31% of the 229 responding federal victims were somewhat or very satisfied with their right to confer with the prosecutor (presumably including charging decision discussions), with another 53% expressing a neutral or no opinion regarding their satisfaction.[62]

These victim surveys can be compared with surveys of criminal justice personnel regarding their consultation with crime victims regarding case charging decisions. The accompanying 1995 survey of criminal justice personnel in the "strong" and "weak" victim rights states revealed that 73% of such personnel from "strong" states "always or usually" consulted with victims prior to case dismissals and that an additional 18% "sometimes" did so. This compared with 43% of the personnel from "weak" states who "always or usually" engaged in such consultation and the additional 38% who "sometimes" did so.[63] The percentages from the "strong" states are comparable to those in a survey of federal prosecutors, reported in 1990, in which 73% gave ratings of "very well" or "well" regarding the quality of prosecutors' consultation with victims concerning declination or dismissal of charges.[64]

Limited empirical research reflects the degree of change in the impact of victim input regarding charging decisions in the years since the President's Task Force. In a six-site national study conducted in the early 1980s using hypothetical scenarios with about 100 prosecutors and other criminal justice personnel, researchers found that evidence characteristics and the presence of physical injury to the victim predicted prosecutors' acceptance of cases for prosecution more often than other factors, such as victim input.[65] A study published in 2007, based on a survey of 102 responding local Texas prosecutors, revealed that 44% gave 50% or more weight to the victim's preference in the charging decision and 56% of the respondents gave victim preference 25% weight or less. Although 10% of the responding prosecutors indicated that victims have no influence in the charging decision, 86% responded that the influence that victims have in the charging decision is "about right." To the extent that prosecutors gave greater weight to victim input in charging decisions, these researchers suggested they were following a victim satisfaction model, conferring "de facto party status" on victims or serving as quasi-attorneys for the victims in these charging determinations.[66]

Given the limited nature of this research, commentators who have debated the merits of a potential expanded victim right to be heard regarding charging decisions have done so on policy grounds rather than research results. The policy grounds for maintaining victims' limited formal participatory role regarding charging decisions have been articulated in the judicial opinions described in this chapter. After weighing various costs and benefits to the interested criminal justice participants of victim participation in the charging decision, one scholar proposed granting the crime victim a right to express his views to the prosecutor on the charging decision orally or in writing before the charging decision is made. This participation right would be limited to a right of consultation only with no victim right to appeal or challenge the prosecutor's charging decision if contrary to the victim's views. This commentator would characterize the prosecutor's consultation duty as an ethical duty. In the event that a prosecutor failed to consult a victim regarding a charging decision, the victim could pursue disciplinary sanctions against the prosecutor, in order to deter the prosecutor's future violations of his consultation duty. This scholar believed that this potential remedy for violations would have fewer drawbacks than the recognition of a victim cause of action for prosecutorial abuse of discretion with required consultation as a remedy, but no right to challenge the prosecutor's final charging decision. In this commentator's view, the described consultation right—which would provide the victim a right to be heard, but not a right to determine the substance of the charging decision—would maximize the benefits and reduce the drawbacks of victim participation in the charging decision.[67]

After conducting his own analysis of the interests of the various parties in-volved in a criminal prosecution, another scholar noted the "more inviolate" nature of the initial charging decision than other subsequent prosecutorial de-cisions. He nevertheless also noted that nothing prevented a prosecutor from routinely inviting the victim and his counsel, if any, to a pre-charge confer-ence and soliciting the victim's views on what the charge should be. Moreover, as to hearings on charge dismissals, this scholar would authorize the victim to participate as a party and thus "force the prosecutor to justify to the court his decision not to proceed, or to proceed on assumptions about the facts and the law that differ from the victim's account."[68] Based on this same rationale, other commentators have also proposed providing victims the right to seek judicial, grand jury, or higher prosecutorial review of prosecutors' decisions not to ini-tiate charges.[69] Finally, some commentators have advocated a return to vari-ous forms of private prosecution in which victims could actually initiate prosecutions in certain types of cases when prosecutors failed to do so or join their private actions with the public prosecution.[70]

Conclusion

The multi-faceted decisions to initiate and dismiss criminal charges are closely associated with the discretion incorporated in the public prosecution system. In the years since the President's Task Force, there has been some ex-pansion of the victim's formal right to confer or consult with the prosecutor generally and, in some instances, specifically regarding these decisions. How-ever, there has been limited change in the victim's ability to challenge the pros-ecutor's charging decisions or otherwise be heard by the court regarding them.

The Right to Be Heard Regarding Plea Negotiations and Agreements

Unlike the more limited change regarding the crime victim's right to be heard concerning charging decisions, there has been a significant expansion of the victim's right to be heard by the prosecutor and a meaningful expan-sion of the right to be heard by the court regarding plea negotiations and agree-ments since the issuance of the President's Task Force recommendations.[71] Moreover, because it is generally estimated that at least 90% of criminal con-victions are obtained through negotiated pleas of guilt,[72] an expanded victim right to be heard regarding such plea negotiations and agreements is especially significant.

President's Task Force and *New Directions from the Field* Recommendations

As stated in the previous section, only one state required victim input into key prosecutorial decisions prior to the President's Task Force.[73] In the commentary to its action recommendations to prosecutors, the Task Force recommended that prosecutors consult with every victim of a violent crime regarding how the plea negotiation system operates, the negotiating posture that the prosecutor has taken in the case, and the rationale for this position. The Task Force recommended that prosecutors should always consider the victim's views before reaching a final decision on a plea agreement. In this connection, the Task Force noted that "[a]lthough lawyers and judges rely on plea bargaining as a tool of calendar management, victims legitimately view the resolution of and sentencing in a case as an evaluation of the harm done to them."[74] As a result, the Task Force formally recommended that prosecutors have an "obligation to bring to the attention of the court the views of victims of violent crimes on ... plea bargains. They should establish procedures to ensure that such victims are given the opportunity to make their views on these matters known."[75] In addition, the Task Force's proposal for a federal constitutional amendment providing a crime victim right "to be heard at all critical stages of judicial proceedings"[76] would certainly include such a right regarding plea proceedings.

The authors of the *New Directions from the Field* study reiterated that prosecutors should meaningfully consult with victims regarding plea agreements. They also recommended that judges should not accept plea agreements without first confirming that prosecutors have consulted the victim in the case. Prosecutors should convey the victim's views regarding the plea agreement to the court, whenever possible. Moreover, because most criminal cases are resolved by negotiated pleas, the study authors maintained that crime victims should have the right to be heard in court before a plea is accepted. Not only would this provide victim access to this critical stage of the prosecution, but it would also permit more informed decision making by the court regarding the acceptance of a proposed plea agreement.[77]

Constitutional and Legislative Response

Although a victim right to confer with the prosecutor is not included in the last federal victim rights constitutional amendment proposal introduced in Congress prior to the enactment of the federal statutory Crime Victims' Rights Act in 2004, this proposal did include a victim right "reasonably" to be heard at public plea proceedings.[78] The Act itself includes both a victim's "reasonable" right to confer with the prosecutor and a right to be "reasonably" heard in trial court public plea proceedings. The Act also permits a victim to move to re-open a plea if the victim has asserted and been denied the right to be heard before or during a plea proceeding, the victim has sought appellate mandamus review of the rights denial within ten days, and the defendant has not entered a plea to the highest offense charged.[79] The Act's victim right to be heard in court plea proceedings and authorized remedy for its denial are included in the 2008 amendments to the Federal Rules of Criminal Procedure.[80] Finally, the Attorney General Guidelines for Victim and Witness Assistance direct prosecutors to make "reasonable efforts" to notify victims of and consider victim views about proposed plea negotiations and identify a variety of factors to consider in determining the reasonableness of such efforts.[81]

In their constitutional provisions, twelve states include a general right to confer or consult with the prosecutor and four states include a specific right of consultation before any disposition, all of which could include consultation regarding plea negotiations and agreements. One state includes a specific right of consultation regarding plea negotiations for certain offenses.[82] Eight states provide a constitutional right to be heard at important or critical stages of the criminal process or proceedings or generally at criminal justice, public, or court proceedings—all of which should include plea agreements and proceedings.[83] In addition, seven states provide a specific constitutional right to be heard at proceedings regarding pleas, plea agreements, or case dispositions.[84]

In their statutory provisions, approximately forty states either specifically authorize or require prosecutor consultation with crime victims regarding plea negotiations or agreements, or provide a general crime victim right to confer or consult with the prosecutor (which could include consultation regarding plea agreements), or both.[85] A few additional states do not provide an express consultation right regarding plea agreements, but their requirement of victim notification of plea discussions or negotiations must be accomplished prior to the entry of the negotiated plea, which could consequently give rise to victim-prosecutor consultations.[86] Thus, most states have statutory provisions that directly require or indirectly promote prosecutors' consultation with crime victims regarding plea agreements.

With regard to the states that have an express statutory authorization or requirement of victim consultation regarding plea negotiations or agreements, some states require only that prosecutors consult or confer with victims regarding their plea negotiations, leaving the content of such consultation undefined.[87] Other states use language that requires prosecutors to affirmatively obtain victims' views or input regarding plea negotiations.[88] For example, Florida's provision requires prosecutors to consult with victims "in order to obtain the views of the victim or family about the disposition of any criminal ... case," including the victim's views about plea agreements.[89] Pennsylvania's statute gives victims the right to "submit prior comment" to the prosecutor's office on the potential reduction or dropping of any charge or changing of a plea.[90] New Jersey allows victims to submit a written impact statement to prosecutors that prosecutors must consider prior to accepting a negotiated plea agreement containing sentence recommendations, and also authorizes victims to receive an explanation of the terms of and reasons for the agreement.[91]

To ensure that the required consultations take place, several of these states require prosecutors to disclose to the court the substance or nature of their consultations or attempts to have such consultations prior to the court's acceptance of a plea agreement.[92] For example, South Dakota not only requires prosecutors to make a "reasonable effort" to provide crime victims an opportunity to comment on the terms of any proposed plea agreement, but also requires the prosecutor to disclose the victim's comments on the plea agreement to the court prior to the court's acceptance of any plea agreement.[93] In Ohio, if the court is informed of the prosecutor's failure to consult with the victim regarding a negotiated plea, the court must note the prosecutor's failure and the reasons for it on the record.[94] Prior to the court's acceptance of a plea agreement in Arizona, a prosecutor must advise the court that reasonable efforts were made to confer with the victim about the negotiated plea and of the victim's position regarding the negotiated plea, if known, as well as that reasonable efforts were made to notify the victim of the plea proceeding and the victim's right to be present and heard at it.[95]

Despite the significant number of states that have provisions regarding crime victim consultation concerning plea agreements, many states provide a right to such consultation only for victims of certain crimes or on victim request [96] or include limiting language regarding the consultation right, such as requiring only "reasonable efforts" to consult or consultation "where practicable."[97] In addition, several states include in their consultation provisions a further provision that a prosecutor's failure to confer with a victim regarding the plea agreement either does not affect the validity of the plea agreement or the resulting disposition or serve as a cause for delaying the plea proceedings.[98] Arizona also makes clear that its consultation right does not include victim authority to "direct the prosecution" of the case.[99]

In addition to the victim right to confer with the prosecutor regarding plea agreements, over twenty states provide specific statutory victim rights to be heard in court in connection with plea agreements[100] or general rights to be heard regarding important criminal justice proceedings, for which status plea proceedings should certainly qualify.[101] Many of these states do not define the content of this right to be heard. Some states, however, do describe a particular area of content for the right—most frequently the crime's impact on the victim. For example, New Hampshire provides a victim right to "appear and make a written or oral victim impact statement … prior to any plea bargain agreement."[102] The few states that have statutorily addressed the effect of a victim's failure to exercise a provided right to be heard at a plea proceeding have indicated that such failure does not prevent the court from conducting the proceeding or serve as a basis to set aside the disposition. Arizona, however, has adopted a victim remedy to re-open a plea if the victim has asserted and been denied the right to be heard before or during the plea proceeding and the defendant has not entered a plea to the highest offense charged.[103]

Thus, since the President's Task Force, there has been a substantial adoption by the states of the victim's formal right to be heard by the prosecutor through consultation concerning plea agreements. Moreover, there has been a meaningful expansion of the crime victim's constitutional and statutory right to be heard in court regarding plea agreements. These rights are often conditional, however, and the effectiveness of their implementation determines the actual significance of the expansion of these rights to be heard.

Judicial Interpretation

State Cases

Few state courts have addressed prescribed victim rights to be heard in the context of plea agreements. In *State v. Casey*,[104] the mother of a minor victim of sexual conduct advised the prosecutor before and during a hearing reducing the pending charge from a felony to a misdemeanor pursuant to a plea agreement that both wanted to be heard by the court regarding the plea. The prosecutor did not inform the judge of this desire and neither the victim nor his mother directly asked the judge to be heard at the hearing. The judge accepted the negotiated plea. With the assistance of counsel, the victim and his mother subsequently moved to set aside the plea. At the sentencing hearing, the judge heard testimony from the victim and his mother and argument from their attorney regarding the appropriateness of the plea, informally "re-opened" the plea to accept the testimony, and then reaffirmed the plea and denied the victim motions to set it aside.[105]

After reviewing the state constitutional and statutory victim rights provisions, the Utah Supreme Court concluded that the victim right to be heard at "important" criminal justice proceedings included the plea proceeding at issue. The appellate court further concluded that a victim request to be heard to the prosecutor adequately "triggered" this right and that the victim and his mother had made such a request. The prosecutor's failure to inform the court of the victim's request to be heard constituted a failure of his duties under the victim rights provisions and as an officer of the court. This failure resulted in a denial of the victim's right to be heard at the plea proceeding. Under Utah victim rights provisions, the victim was entitled to appellate review of the trial court's rulings regarding his right to be heard. However, the Utah Supreme Court determined that the judge's actions in permitting the victim and his mother to address the court at the sentencing proceeding and his "re-opening" the plea to accept such testimony before reaffirming the plea, remedied the rights violation that occurred at the plea hearing.[106]

In *People v. Stringham*,[107] the prosecutor and defendant agreed that the defendant would enter guilty pleas to voluntary manslaughter and kidnapping in exchange for dismissal of murder and related charges. One judge conditionally accepted the plea agreement, but subsequently recused himself prior to the sentencing hearing. At the sentencing hearing before the new judge, the victim's father criticized the plea bargain and the prosecutor and urged that the defendant be charged as a "murderer." After a subsequent hearing, this judge rejected the plea agreement, as permitted under California law. In his appeal from his trial conviction of second degree murder and related charges, the offender contended that his plea agreement had been erroneously rejected and sought to have the agreement specifically enforced. In support of his contentions, he challenged the victim's father's right to address the court regarding the appropriateness of the plea and the impact of the receipt of this information on the judge's ultimate decision to reject the plea agreement.[108]

The appellate court noted that the California victim rights provisions did not specifically provide a right to be heard at plea proceedings, but did provide a victim the right to attend sentencing proceedings and "reasonably express" his views regarding the crime and the defendant, which views were to be considered by the court. The appellate court construed these provisions to allow a victim or his next of kin, such as the victim's father in this case, to attack a plea bargain at a sentencing proceeding following the initial acceptance of the plea. The appellate court concluded not only that the victim's father had standing to make the statements to the court, but also that the actual statements made did not exceed the scope of the statutory provisions. Finally, the appellate court found that the victim's father's statements had not exerted "overbearing pressure" on the judge who had made an independent review of the case and whose stated grounds for rejecting the plea agreement did not even involve the contested statements.[109]

Similarly, a few other appellate courts have rejected a defendant's attempt to withdraw his negotiated plea in circumstances in which the prosecutor had agreed not to allocute as to some or all sentencing issues, but the victim, or a family member, had addressed the court on such sentencing issues. These courts determined that, in the absence of explicit victim agreement to be bound by the prosecutor's position on allocution or of collusion by the prosecutor to circumvent the plea agreement through the victim, the victim's exercise of his rights to be heard regarding the sentencing of the defendant did not violate the prosecutor's plea agreement or provide a sufficient basis for the defendant to withdraw his guilty plea.[110]

Although in these decisions appellate courts have ensured that victims' rights to be heard are not foreclosed by prosecutors' plea agreements, reviewing courts have also not expanded these rights to be heard beyond their express terms. For example, in *State v. McDonnell*,[111] the prosecutor had effectively offered to waive pursuit of the death penalty in exchange for the defendant's guilty plea to aggravated murder—subject to the victim's parents' agreement. Although the plea agreement was acceptable to the defendant, it was not acceptable to the victim's parents. Upon the prosecutor's subsequent election to proceed to trial and to seek the death penalty, the defendant sought to have the court enforce the previously proposed plea agreement. The trial court rejected this attempt to enforce the agreement and the defendant was sentenced to death upon his conviction at trial. On appeal, the offender contended that the prosecutor had based his decision not to proceed with the plea agreement on "improper considerations" and sought to enforce the agreement.[112]

The state conceded that, under Oregon statutes governing prosecutors' authority to enter into plea agreements, a prosecutor cannot let victims or their families play the decisive role in plea negotiations by deferring to their judgment as to whether a plea agreement is appropriate. The state thus conceded that the prosecutor's refusal of the plea agreement on this basis was error. Although consultation with crime victims is important in the plea negotiation process, the Oregon Supreme Court agreed that the prosecutor could not improperly delegate the decision to enter into plea negotiations to the victim's parents. In order to determine whether the initial agreement should be enforced, the Oregon Supreme Court remanded the case for an evidentiary hearing to determine whether the prosecutor would have entered into the plea agreement, if only proper criteria for the decision had been considered.[113]

Federal Cases

The few federal cases regarding victim rights to confer with the prosecution and to be heard by the court regarding pleas pursuant to the Crime Victims' Rights Act have reached fairly similar results to the state cases. In *In re Dean*,[114] the Fifth Circuit Court of Appeals considered a mandamus action filed by crime victims seeking to require the trial court to reject a plea agreement of which they had received no prior notice or opportunity to confer with the prosecutor. Prior to the actual entry of the plea in court pursuant to the agreement, some victims had presented their opposition to it and other victims (or their attorneys) attended and spoke at the plea proceeding in opposition to the agreement. Subsequent to the plea proceeding, the trial court judge denied the victims' requests to reject the plea agreement.[115] In the mandamus action, the Fifth Circuit Court of Appeals found that the Act envisions that "victims have a right to inform the plea negotiation process by conferring with prosecutors before a plea agreement is reached." This consultation does not infringe the Government's "independent prosecutorial discretion"; "instead, it is only a requirement that the government confer in some reasonable way with the victims before ultimately exercising its broad discretion."[116] The appellate court concluded that the prosecutor should have undertaken a "reasonable" effort to ascertain the victim's views regarding the proposed plea prior to entering into the agreement. However, because the trial court heard from the victims at the time of the plea hearing, the appellate court indicated its belief that the trial court would consider the victims' views in any final determination regarding the plea agreement or ultimate sentence and therefore declined to grant the requested mandamus relief.[117]

To avoid the factual situation described above and to make "meaningful" victims' rights under the Act to be heard regarding pleas and to be treated with fairness, one trial judge required the prosecutor to notify the victims of its proposed plea agreement and provide a statement explaining the Government's decision to enter into the proposed agreement. This advance disclosure would permit the victims who chose to exercise their right to be heard at the plea proceedings to do so most effectively.[118] In another case, the Second Circuit Court of Appeals found that the victims' exercise of the Act's right to be heard provisions was not an attempt by the Government to circumvent its obligations under a plea agreement by using "victim-surrogates" who sought a harsh punishment at the sentencing proceeding.[119]

On the other hand, in reviewing a crime victim complaint about an alleged violation of the right to confer with the prosecutor regarding a settlement agreement, the Second Circuit Court of Appeals determined that the Government had not denied any victim the opportunity to confer and stated that the Act does not require the Government to "seek approval from crime victims before negotiating or entering into a settlement agreement."[120] Similarly, with regard to the right to be heard concerning a plea, one trial court noted that this right does not give victims "veto power over any prosecutorial decision, strategy or tactic" regarding a plea. Moreover, even if a plea is re-opened as a result of a violation of the victim right to be heard, the Act "only entitles the victim to be reasonably heard as to why the Court should not accept the plea on the otherwise agreed terms."[121] Thus, while maintaining the importance of a victim's right to confer and to be heard in the context of plea agreements, state and federal courts have not extended this right to include a right to control the agreements themselves.

Implementation and Analysis of the Right

Both before and after the President's Task Force recommendations, researchers have attempted to assess the extent to which prosecutors and judges have elicited and considered victims' views regarding plea agreements in their cases. Such research has produced mixed results as to the use and effectiveness of such consultation and consideration. Of course, in the time period prior to the President's Task Force recommendations, prosecutors and judges generally were not formally required to consider victims' views regarding plea agreements. The absence of a formal victim right to be heard regarding plea agreements explains, in part, the significantly varying degrees to which prosecutors and judges in pre-Task Force studies indicated that they considered victims' views regarding plea agreements.[122]

For example, based on interviews of Nashville prosecutors conducted in the 1970s, one researcher concluded that victims played a "very significant" role in the plea bargaining process and that their views were considered by prosecutors in decisions to submit or accept plea offers.[123] In a Connecticut study conducted in the late 1970s, researchers found that the victim's attitude toward the case was one of prosecutors' most frequently cited aspects of their case evaluations and that it was of "pivotal" importance in assault and sexual assault cases.[124] In a six-site national survey conducted at the approximate time of the President's Task Force, 49% of the forty-three surveyed prosecutors said that they rarely heard from victims concerning their views regarding plea proposals. Forty-four percent reported that they gave victims' views regarding pleas little or no weight, with 28% saying that they gave victims' wishes "some or a lot" of weight and another 28% indicating that the weight given depended on the particular case. These researchers concluded that victims' wishes were usually "weighed heavily" in plea bargain decision making in cases of violent or nonstranger crimes. In a burglary case simulation conducted in connection with this research, only 41% of 134 prosecutors identified the "victim's attitude toward bargain" as an item considered necessary in deciding the appropriate plea offer. Percentages of fifty surveyed judges who said that they sought victims' opinions of plea agreements before accepting them ranged from 0 to over 90%.[125]

In the years since the President's Task Force, considerable variation remains in the degree to which victims are being heard and the degree to which they perceive they are being heard regarding plea agreements. In a five-state survey of over 350 victims in the late 1980s, approximately half of the victims indicated that they were not satisfied with their opportunity to provide input regarding guilty pleas.[126] In a survey of federal prosecutors, reported in 1990, 72% rated as "very well" or "well" the quality of their provision of consultation with victims on plea agreements and sentencing recommendations.[127] In a 1998 survey of approximately 4,000 members of the general public and crime victims in nine northeastern states, less than 50% of the general public and of victims in each state, and approximately 40% overall, indicated that crime victims are "usually" able to discuss their cases with prosecutors,[128] which presumably includes consultation regarding plea agreements.

Researchers in the 1995 study of over 1,300 crime victims and approximately 200 criminal justice personnel and other officials in two "strong" and two "weak" victim rights states examined various aspects of the implementation of the victim right to be heard concerning plea agreements in greater detail. At the outset, 87% of the crime victims overall rated as "very important" the right to "talk about" whether a plea to lesser charges by the defendant should be accepted.[129] Only 52% of the applicable crime victims (i.e., relevant to the inquiry) in the "strong" states and 56% in "weak" states, however, indicated that they had actually talked with the prosecutor about accepting a plea to a lesser charge. On a more general note, approximately 64% of "strong" state victims and 51% of "weak" state victims rated their ability to have input in their cases as "adequate" or "more than adequate." These percentages can be compared with the 69% of the criminal justice personnel in "strong" states and 56% in "weak" states who indicated that they "always or usually" consulted crime victims regarding plea bargains and the additional 19% of personnel in "strong" states and 44% in "weak" states who indicated that they "sometimes" had such consultations.[130]

Crime victims and criminal justice personnel differed significantly as to the impact of their consultation regarding plea agreements. Of the criminal justice personnel from "strong" states, 64% said that the victim consultation had "a lot" of impact and an additional 36% said that it had "some" impact. Of the "weak" state personnel, 39% indicated that the consultation had "a lot" of impact and another 42% said that it had "some" impact. On the other hand, 47% of applicable "strong" state victims and 9% of applicable "weak" state victims said that the consultation had "a lot" of impact and 21% of "strong" state victims and 38% of "weak" state victims said that it had "some" impact.[131] The degree to which these crime victims perceived that their consultation had an impact is perhaps also reflected in their ratings of the "fairness" of the verdict or plea bargain. Only approximately 53% of "strong" state victims and 42% of "weak" state victims rated the fairness of the verdict or plea bargain as "adequate" or "more than adequate." Case outcome was also one of the most frequently mentioned factors regarding victim satisfaction or dissatisfaction with the prosecutor—this factor mentioned much more frequently than prosecutor communication with the victim.[132] These survey findings reflect differing results regarding both the implementation and perceived effectiveness of crime victims' right or ability to have their views regarding plea agreements heard.

In the more recent study published in 2007, based on a survey of 102 responding local Texas prosecutors, 59% gave 50% or more weight to the victim's preference during plea negotiations and 41% of the respondents gave victim preference 25% weight or less. Although only 4% of the responding prosecutors indicated that victims have no influence in plea negotiations, 89% responded that the influence that victims have in plea negotiations is "about right." When asked, however, if they were more likely to defer to a victim's desire for a jury trial despite their own desire to enter a plea agreement, only 18% of the respondents agreed or strongly agreed and 54% disagreed or strongly disagreed (with the rest being "neutral").[133]

Although most of the research in this area has utilized survey methodology, a few researchers have taken other approaches to assess the effectiveness of a victim right to be heard regarding plea agreements. One of these efforts was a field experiment conducted in the late 1970s to evaluate the use of pretrial settlement conferences to which the judge, prosecutor, defense attorney, defendant, victim, and investigating police officer were invited. Over 1,000 felony cases assigned to test and control group judges were included in the Miami area study, with over 350 assigned to the experimental settlement conference group. Researchers attended the settlement conferences and conducted interviews with the judges, attorneys, defendants, victims, and police officers in the test and control group cases.[134]

The research results provide support for policy advocates on *all* sides of the issue of the effectiveness of a victim right to be heard regarding pleas. From a systems standpoint, the conferences seemingly shortened the length of time it took to close cases, but did not cause significant changes in the proportion of cases litigated or defendants convicted. The fact that all key decision makers were potentially present at the conferences actually seemed to increase case handling efficiency, perhaps by lowering information costs and needs. The sessions themselves averaged only ten minutes in length and resulted in final or tentative agreement regarding disposition in three-fourths of the cases. The time to disposition in the test courtrooms was reduced by approximately three weeks by the conference procedure.[135]

In terms of the dynamics of the conferences, they were dominated by the professionals with lay members mainly providing requested information. The judges, in particular, typically controlled the conference discussions. The sessions were attended by only one-third of the invited victims. Although some of the professionals suggested that victims' poor attendance reflected their lack of interest, notification problems in the research project were most frequently cited by victims as the reason for nonattendance. Only 25% of attending victims made more than five comments during the sessions. Contrary to the expectations of some participants, victims were usually supportive of the dispositions proposed by the judges and attorneys—rather than demanding the maximum punishment allowed. Perhaps because of the limited role victims played at the conferences, by the end of the project, some of the professionals questioned the significance of their participation. Victims and other lay participants, however, indicated modest gains in information and satisfaction with their treatment as compared to non-participants. In this connection, victims who attended the conferences were much more likely to indicate that they knew the dispositions in their cases, but they were not *significantly* more satisfied with the dispositions or processing of their cases than victims who did not attend the conferences.[136]

Subsequent field tests at three locations generally confirmed these research results. In these field tests, victims were allowed to participate in plea conferences presided over by judges. Approximately 50% of eligible victims participated in the conferences, with their participation accounting for approximately 10% of the speaking time at the conferences. The majority of the victim participants did not believe that their participation affected the outcome of the plea negotiations, but they were more satisfied with the pleas negotiated and plea bargaining generally than victims who did not participate.[137]

Confirming the original Florida study's findings regarding the consistency of the victim's view regarding the plea agreement with that of the professionals are the results of a Buffalo area study conducted in the mid-1970s in which researchers observed twenty-eight plea negotiation sessions in which victims were present. In the majority of these sessions, the prosecutors sought or acknowledged and, in the researchers' view, considered the victims' opinions regarding the plea agreements. In 86% of these sessions, the victim's view coincided with the disposition reached regarding the case. These researchers also found that there was no statistically significant variance between the disposition outcomes in cases in which victims attended plea negotiation sessions and those in which victims did not attend.[138]

Various aspects of these studies provide support for competing policy positions concerning increased crime victim input regarding plea agreements.

Those opposed to greater formal victim involvement question whether such increased input would provide substantial additional insight for the decision makers. They also raise concerns about the increased administrative burden resulting from expanded formal victim input. Most fundamentally, however, they cite issues of prosecutorial discretion and policy and the larger public interest, similar to those concerning charging decisions, which could be adversely impacted by an increased victim participatory role regarding plea negotiations and agreements.[139]

Other commentators have advocated the benefits of various mechanisms through which victims could provide expanded input regarding plea negotiations and agreements. One commentator determined that the victim's right of participation regarding plea agreements should include the right to be heard by the court regarding the proposed plea agreement, orally or in writing, rather than simply the right to consult with the prosecutor. Such direct communication with the ultimate decision maker regarding the plea enhances the victim's sense of participation in the plea process. Moreover, in cases in which the victim's views of the plea agreement differ from those of the prosecutor, direct victim communication with the court avoids conflict in the prosecutor's role and ensures that the victim's views will be communicated to the court. In this scholar's procedure, the crime victim's right of participation regarding plea agreements would be limited to a right to be heard by the court. The court would not be bound by the victim's views and the victim would have no right to appeal the judge's acceptance of the plea agreement over the victim's objection. If the trial judge denied the victim the opportunity to be heard regarding the plea agreement, this denial could be deemed a violation of the code of judicial conduct for which the victim could file a grievance against the trial judge with the appropriate commission. In this commentator's view, this procedure would avoid constitutional, administrative, and other difficulties that might arise from giving crime victims greater control over or the right to appeal from plea agreements.[140]

Another commentator would extend the victim's right to be heard by the court regarding plea agreements to a right to participate as a "party" in hearings regarding guilty pleas. The purpose of such a party status for the victim would be "not only to make the victim feel better but also to assure fuller consideration of issues of accuracy and legality where there is a risk that such issues will be submerged by the pressures of bureaucracy and politics and plea bargaining."[141] Although this scholar did not address the issue of whether this limited victim party status would include a victim right to appeal, another commentator would extend the victim's right to be heard by the court to include a right to seek discretionary appellate review of the offender's sentence, despite concerns about double jeopardy and due process constraints.[142]

A few commentators have proposed giving victims formal veto power over plea offers before they are negotiated with the defendant.[143] In one of the more detailed of such proposals, one commentator would require the prosecutor to notify the victim of a proposed plea offer and provide a fixed time period during which the victim could veto the offer if the victim found it excessively lenient or harsh. If the victim failed to respond within the prescribed time period, the prosecutor would be free to communicate the offer to the defense. This commentator concluded that the victim veto procedure would increase a victim's input in the outcome of the case, with resulting increased crime reporting and participation in and satisfaction with the criminal justice system. It would also provide "substantial symbolic importance, as it finally recognizes the reemergence of crime victims as prominent actors in the criminal justice system."[144]

Conclusion

No jurisdiction has formally adopted a crime victim veto as part of a victim right to be heard regarding plea negotiations and agreements. Moreover, many jurisdictions have not found the rationales of the above proposals persuasive enough to extend this express right to be heard beyond consultation with the prosecutor. Nevertheless, support for greater victim input in this area has resulted in a significant expansion of victims' rights to be heard by the prosecutor and the court concerning plea agreements in the years since the President's Task Force. The expansion of these hearing rights is particularly meaningful because it has given eligible victims input into a disposition decision regarding which victims previously had limited formal access. Moreover, this input pertains to a dispositional decision making process through which most criminal convictions are obtained. As a result, the impact of the effective implementation of this victim right to be heard can be substantial.

Chapter 6

The Right to Be Heard
Regarding Sentencing and Parole

A crime victim's right to be heard regarding sentencing has been one of the most widely adopted victim rights in the years since the President's Task Force on Victims of Crime. The federal system and every state provide eligible victims an opportunity to offer input to the court regarding sentencing either in writing or orally, or both. Through submission of a victim impact statement or oral statement or testimony, a victim can generally communicate to the sentencing judge the direct physical, psychological, and economic impact of the crime and, in some states, the victim's opinion as to the crime, the offender, or the desired sentence. Virtually every state now also provides some type of victim right to be heard regarding an offender's parole.[1]

The Right to Be Heard Regarding Sentencing

President's Task Force and *New Directions from the Field* Recommendations

Prior to the President's Task Force recommendations, eight states required a victim impact statement at sentencing and three states authorized victim allocution, i.e., an oral statement to the court, at sentencing.[2] Before the completion of the Task Force's work, Congress enacted the Victim and Witness Protection Act of 1982, which required the inclusion of victim impact information in the federal presentence reports that are prepared for the judge's use in sentencing.[3] In its *Final Report*, the Task Force noted the recent enactment of the federal law and also recommended state executive and legislative action to require victim impact statements at sentencing.[4]

In the commentary to its recommendations to prosecutors, the Task Force noted prosecutors' responsibility to ensure that victims of violent crime are informed about the presentence report process and that they have an opportunity to have their views reflected in these reports. Prosecutors should also ensure that victims have the opportunity to appear and be heard by the court at sentencing. In support of these recommendations, the Task Force noted that the victim's life, as well as the defendant's life, is profoundly affected by the sentence imposed. It felt that the court must hear from both sides to make an informed sentencing decision. The Task Force thus included sentencing among the stages of the prosecution regarding which it recommended that prosecutors had an obligation to bring the views of victims of violent crime to the attention of the court and regarding which prosecutors should establish procedures to ensure that these victims have the opportunity to make their views known.[5]

In its recommendations to the judiciary, the Task Force recommended that judges should "allow for, and give appropriate weight to, input at sentencing from victims of violent crime."[6] In addition, the Task Force's proposal for a federal constitutional amendment providing a crime victim right "to be heard at all critical stages of judicial proceedings"[7] would clearly include such a right regarding sentencing proceedings. The Task Force's commentary regarding its recommendation to judges is one of the most strongly stated commentaries in the *Final Report*. In recognition of the important role that sentencing plays in the criminal justice process, the Task Force recommended that violent crime victims be allowed both to provide information about the crime's impact and to speak at the sentencing proceeding. The Task Force stated that inclusion of the crime victim in the sentencing process is a crucial recognition of the impact of the crime on the victim, and is essential to ensure that the court has all the necessary information to reach a just and balanced sentence.[8]

> Victims, no less than defendants, are entitled to their day in court. Victims, no less than defendants, are entitled to have their views considered. A judge cannot evaluate the seriousness of a defendant's conduct without knowing how the crime has burdened the victim. A judge cannot reach an informed determination of the danger posed by a defendant without hearing from the person he has victimized.[9]

Jurisdictions responded to the Task Force's strong recommendations regarding victim input at sentencing. By the time of the *New Directions from the Field* study, its authors noted that all American jurisdictions had adopted some type of victim right to input regarding sentencing. However, not all states permitted victims to be heard orally at sentencing, in addition to providing input for the written victim impact statement presented to the court. In addition, some jurisdictions did not permit victim input regarding all crimes. To facilitate the provision of victim input at sentencing, the study authors recommended that jurisdictions allow the provision of such input via electronic means (e.g., videotape or audiotape) and that judges require prosecutors to describe on the record their efforts to seek victim input regarding sentencing. The study authors thus noted areas for continued progress even regarding the now well-recognized victim right to be heard concerning sentencing.[10]

Constitutional and Legislative Response

The last federal victim rights constitutional amendment proposal introduced in Congress prior to the enactment of the federal statutory Crime Victims' Rights Act in 2004 did not include a right to confer with the prosecutor regarding sentencing, but it did include a victim right "reasonably" to be heard at sentencing proceedings.[11] The Act itself expands previous federal legislation and includes both a victim's "reasonable" right to confer with the prosecutor and a right to be "reasonably" heard in trial court sentencing proceedings. The Act also permits a victim to move to re-open a sentence if the victim has asserted and been denied the right to be heard before or during the sentencing proceeding and the victim has sought appellate mandamus review of the rights denial within ten days.[12] The 2008 amendments to the Federal Rules of Criminal Procedure removed some constraints on victim impact information provided for the presentence report by deleting verification and "nonargumentative" style requirements. These amendments incorporated the expanded victim right to be heard at court sentencing proceedings established in the Act by deleting its previous restriction to victims of certain crimes only and providing under the section entitled, "Opportunity to Speak": "Before imposing sentence, the court must address any victim of the crime [as defined in the Act] who is present at sentencing and must permit the victim to be reasonably heard." Finally these 2008 amendments incorporated the Act's authorized remedy for re-opening a sentence in the case of a rights denial regarding the right to be heard.[13]

In their constitutional provisions, seventeen states include a general or specific victim right to confer or consult with the prosecutor, which should include consultation regarding sentencing.[14] Eight states provide victims a constitutional right to be heard at important or critical stages of the criminal process or proceedings or generally at criminal justice, public, or court proceedings — all of which should include sentencing proceedings.[15] In addition, twenty states provide victims a specific constitutional right to be heard at sentencing proceedings.[16] Thus, twenty-eight of the thirty-three states with victim rights constitutional amendments provide crime victims a general or specific constitutional right to be heard at sentencing proceedings.

In their statutory provisions, although most states have general or specific provisions authorizing or requiring prosecutor consultation with victims regarding pleas (which could include sentencing issues),[17] less than twenty states have general or specific provisions authorizing or requiring prosecutor consultation with victims regarding sentencing.[18] Although prosecutors in other jurisdictions are free to and often do discuss sentencing issues with crime victims, the express victim right to be heard regarding sentencing has primarily been adopted through provision of a victim's opportunity to be heard by the court rather than the prosecutor.

Every state has statutory provisions authorizing some type of crime victim right to be heard by the court regarding sentencing. Most states authorize a victim to provide input to the court regarding sentencing both orally and in writing.[19] Only a few states currently restrict victim input to the court to the victim submissions in the presentence report or other written submissions.[20] However, the *most frequently used* method for presentation of victim information is its submission in written form as part of the presentence investigation report prepared for the sentencing judge by probation office personnel.[21] Whether delivered orally or in writing, the prescribed content of the victim input regarding sentencing varies considerably. Some states expressly authorize victim input only as to the crime's direct physical, psychological, financial, and sometimes social impact.[22] Other states also allow input as to the victim's opinions or beliefs regarding the crime, the offender, or the desired sentence.[23] Still other states give only general guidance as to the content of the input or no guidance at all.[24] Regardless of the specific statutory authorizations, courts frequently receive additional input from victims regarding sentencing.[25] In addition to provisions identifying the content of victim input regarding sentencing, several states also expressly require the court to *consider* the victim input in determining the defendant's sentence.[26]

As the above description reflects, there is substantial variation among the states concerning the express scope of the crime victim right to be heard by the court regarding sentencing. For example, although Kentucky does not provide for an in-court address to the court, the content of the written victim impact statement, which must be considered by the court prior to sentencing for certain offenses, may contain, "but need not be limited to, a description of the nature and extent of any physical, psychological or financial harm suffered by the victim, the victim's need for restitution and ... the victim's recommendation for an appropriate sentence."[27] In Missouri, the victim is entitled to both a presentence report statement and an in-court oral or written victim statement, but the prescribed focus is limited to the "facts of the case and any personal injuries or financial loss incurred by the victim."[28] In Arizona, although the victim's presentence report statement for the prescribed offenses concerns the "economic, physical and psychological impact" of the crime, his in-court presentation can consist of "evidence, information and opinions that concern the criminal offense, the defendant, the sentence or the need for restitution."[29] In Minnesota, both the victim's input into the presentence report and her oral or written in-court statement for the prescribed crimes can include information regarding the crime's impact as well as the victim's views regarding any proposed disposition or sentence.[30]

As with previous participatory rights, many states limit either the right to have a victim impact statement as part of a presentence report or the right to be heard in court regarding sentencing, or both, to victims of designated crimes or crime categories only. Some states also make the right to be heard in court discretionary or available only on victim request.[31] Some states require the victim's in-court statement to be given under oath and subject to cross-examination.[32] Finally, some states that have specifically addressed violations of or failures to exercise this right have indicated that such violations or failures do not prevent the court from conducting the sentencing proceedings or serve as a basis to set aside the disposition, or both.[33] Arizona, however, provides a victim right to re-open a sentence for a victim who has asserted and been denied the right to be heard before or during the proceeding and Maryland provides a victim right to appeal regarding the denial of the right to be heard by the court at sentencing.[34] Thus, despite the provision of a victim's right to be heard regarding sentencing by the federal system and all of the states, the extent of and limitations on the right can vary considerably.

Judicial Interpretation

Perhaps reflecting the wide adoption and significance of this victim right to be heard, courts have been more actively engaged in its interpretation than that regarding other victim rights. Of course, the provision of an express victim right to be heard regarding sentencing in some ways simply formalizes a source of sentencing information to which courts previously have had informal access.[35] As the United States Supreme Court noted over sixty years ago, in rejecting a defendant's contention that a sentencing judge should be restricted to consideration of sentencing information received in open court, American sentencing judges have always had "wide discretion in the sources and types of evidence used to assist [them] in determining the kind and extent of punishment to be imposed within limits fixed by law."[36] Nevertheless, once victim input regarding sentencing began to be *required*, rather than permitted, it began to receive much more judicial scrutiny.

Capital Cases

Not surprisingly, the closest scrutiny of the appropriateness of victim input came in the context of sentencing proceedings in capital cases. In a trilogy of capital cases decided within a five-year period, the United States Supreme Court established and then rejected certain limitations on victim impact information in capital sentencing proceedings. In *Booth v. Maryland*,[37] a narrow Court majority concluded that information in a victim impact statement which described the victims' personal characteristics and the crime's emotional impact on the victims' family, as well as family members' opinions and characterizations of the offender and the crime, was "irrelevant to a capital sentencing decision, and that its admission creates a constitutionally unacceptable risk that the jury may impose the death penalty in an arbitrary and capricious manner."[38]

The information, concerning the brutal murder of an elderly couple in the course of a burglary, was included in the victim impact statement required under state law as part of the presentence report in felony cases. The information, which was very dramatic and descriptive, was obtained by probation staff from the victims' children and other family members. Defense counsel moved to suppress the statement, contending that its use in a capital case violated the Eighth Amendment. After the trial court denied this motion, the prosecutor nevertheless agreed to read the impact statement to the jury rather than call the family members as witnesses, in an attempt by defense counsel to limit the "inflammatory effect" of the information.[39]

The Court concluded that the introduction of this victim-related information in a capital sentencing proceeding violated the Eighth Amendment. It introduced information of which the defendant might not have been aware or that was irrelevant to his decision to kill and potentially diverted the jury's focus away from the key constitutional capital sentencing areas regarding the defendant's background and record and the circumstances of the crime. Thus, in the "unique circumstances" of a capital sentencing hearing in which the focus is on the defendant's moral blameworthiness, the Court determined that the victim's personal characteristics and the crime's impact on the victim's family were not "proper" sentencing considerations. Similarly, the Court concluded that the admission of family members' opinions and characterizations regarding the crime and the offender served only to "inflame the jury and divert it from deciding the case on the relevant evidence concerning the crime and the defendant" and was inconsistent with the "reasoned decisionmaking" required in capital cases.[40]

Two years later, in *South Carolina v. Gathers*,[41] the Court extended its ruling in *Booth* to bar prosecutors' comments regarding personal characteristics of the victim in a capital sentencing proceeding, in the absence of evidence that the defendant was aware of such characteristics or that they played a role in the defendant's decision to kill. During his closing argument at the sentencing in *Gathers*, the prosecutor read from a religious tract and noted a voter registration card, both of which the victim had in his possession when he was murdered and which had been admitted into evidence. The prosecutor commented on the victim's perceived religious characteristics as well as the implications of his good citizenship. The Court concluded that this information regarding the content of these items was not relevant to establish the circumstances of the crime or the defendant's personal characteristics in the absence of evidence establishing their relevance to the commission of the crime. This information thus fell under the exclusion of victim characteristic evidence established in *Booth*.[42]

The Court's holdings in *Booth* and *Gathers* barred the *mandatory* consideration of victim impact evidence in capital sentencing proceedings as well as the admission of this evidence in circumstances in which it was not relevant to an assessment of the defendant's "moral blameworthiness," the focal point of capital sentencing determinations. As to the victim impact evidence (but not the victim opinion evidence regarding the offender or sentence), however, the Court in *Booth* acknowledged that similar types of information might be admissible if they related directly to the circumstances of the crime or were relevant to rebut an argument raised by the defendant. In such circumstances, the trial judge could determine the relevance of the information to a "legitimate consideration" and weigh its probative versus prejudicial value. The Court also implied no opinion regarding the use of victim impact statements in noncapital cases and even noted that facts about the victim and his family may be relevant in a noncapital trial.[43]

Two years after *Gathers* and after a change in Court membership, the Court expanded its concept of evidence that could constitutionally be deemed relevant to the capital sentencing decision to include victim impact evidence. In *Payne v. Tennessee*,[44] the challenged evidence and information concerned testimony of the victims' mother and grandmother on the emotional impact that the murders of her daughter and granddaughter had had on her surviving grandson and the prosecutor's closing argument about this impact. The Court held that the Eighth Amendment does not create a *per se* bar prohibiting capital sentencing juries from considering or prosecutors from commenting on evidence as to a victim's personal characteristics and the emotional impact of the murder on the victim's family. The Court overruled *Booth* and *Gathers* to the extent that they reached contrary conclusions. Unlike the Court majorities that had decided these cases, the *Payne* majority concluded that evidence as to the extent of the harm caused by a defendant, in addition to or as part of the evidence as to his "blameworthiness," could be relevant to a capital sentencing decision, and that victim impact evidence could help establish the actual harm caused by a particular crime. Introduction of this victim impact evidence also permitted the victim to be treated as an individual at the capital sentencing, just as the defendant was. Although the *Payne* Court found that the Eighth Amendment did not bar states' authorization of victim impact evidence at capital sentencing proceedings and prosecutorial comment upon it, the Court noted that the Fourteenth Amendment Due Process Clause provided a "mechanism for relief" if such victim impact evidence is "so unduly prejudicial that it renders the trial fundamentally unfair."[45]

The *Payne* Court's holding overruling *Booth* and *Gathers* was limited to these cases' holdings that "evidence and argument relating to the victim and the impact of the victim's death on the victim's family are inadmissible at a capital sentencing hearing." Because no evidence was introduced in *Payne* regarding "family members' characterizations and opinions about the crime, the defendant, and the appropriate sentence," *Booth's* holding that the admission of such evidence violates the Eighth Amendment in capital sentencing hearings was left undisturbed by *Payne*.[46] By removing the Eighth Amendment bar to the admission of evidence about the victim and the crime's impact on the victim's family and related prosecutorial argument, however, the Court allowed the federal system and the states to determine the relevance of such information to the capital sentencing decision, subject to any overriding due process constraints.[47] The federal system and most of the capital punishment states that have addressed the issue have concluded that victim impact evidence is admissible in capital sentencing proceedings, as long as it is not unduly prejudicial or inflammatory. Reviewing courts have reached this conclusion by interpreting death penalty, sentencing, or victim rights provisions existing at the time of the *Payne* decision or provisions that have been added or amended following *Payne* to expressly authorize victim impact evidence in capital punishment sentencing proceedings.[48]

In their rulings regarding the admission of specific victim impact evidence, state reviewing courts have generally found either no error or no reversible error from the admission of such evidence. For example, the Arkansas Supreme Court found no error from the presentation of a silent videotape that included approximately 160 photographs covering the victim's entire life, was almost fourteen minutes long, and was narrated with some emotion by the victim's brother.[49] The Missouri Supreme Court found no plain error from the reading to the sentencing judge of prepared statements by thirteen victim impact witnesses, some of which included requests that "justice" be served through the sentence imposed, and the introduction of pictures, awards, and other evidence about the victim's life.[50] On the other hand, the Oklahoma Court of Criminal Appeals specifically identified victim impact statements including that the victim was "butchered like an animal" and that the defendant acted "like [a] blood thirsty animal," as contributing factors to its vacation of the defendant's death sentence and remand for resentencing.[51] The Indiana Supreme Court found the erroneous admission of victim impact evidence unrelated to statutory aggravating and mitigating factors was harmless because the judge determined the sentence and said she would not consider inadmissible portions of the evidence.[52] This appellate court also found that the erroneous admission of a victim's family's recommendation of the death penalty was harmless because the judge, rather than a jury, determined the sentence and stated that she would not consider inadmissible evidence.[53] When such sentencing recommendation impact information was presented to a capital sentencing jury, however, the Idaho Supreme Court found that it was reversible error.[54] Finally, although most capital punishment states have not adopted specific procedures for the admission of victim impact information at capital sentencing proceedings, the New Jersey Supreme Court and the Oklahoma Court of Criminal Appeals have prescribed the most extensive such procedures, including prior notice to the defendant, prior hearing regarding admissibility, and jury instructions regarding the consideration of the evidence.[55]

In applying the post-*Payne* federal death penalty provisions that permit introduction of victim impact evidence as a non-statutory aggravating factor in capital sentencing proceedings,[56] federal trial courts have permitted family members, co-workers, friends, and neighbors to offer evidence of victim characteristics and the crime's impact, but have generally excluded evidence regarding sentencing recommendations, characterizations of the defendant, and the impact of crimes other than those for which the defendant is being sentenced.[57] The trial courts have applied the statute's prior notice provisions and some have adopted additional procedures to reduce the risk of prejudice at the sentencing proceedings.[58]

As in the state court systems, federal reviewing courts have generally found no error or no reversible error in the admission of victim impact evidence in federal capital proceedings. For example, the Tenth Circuit Court of Appeals in the Oklahoma City bombing case found no constitutional error in challenged portions of the victim impact testimony from almost forty individuals, including family members of victims, survivors, and medical, rescue, and victim assistance workers. The appellate court found that specifically challenged areas of testimony and the "poignant and emotional" evidence taken as a whole fell within the permissible limits established in *Payne*. The reviewing court also noted the prosecutor's "self-restraint" in the presentation of the evidence and the trial court's efforts that "significantly minimized" the overall impact of the testimony.[59] Although finding error in the admission of specific victim impact evidence, other reviewing courts have generally found the error to be insufficient to require reversal or vacation of the death sentences imposed. For example, in a case construing the consideration of evidence of victim vulnerability and victim impact under the federal death penalty provisions, the United States Supreme Court found that any error in the "loose drafting of [these] nonstatutory aggravating factors" was harmless. In this connection, the Court particularly pointed to the prosecutor's argument to the jury which "cured" these "appropriate subjects for the capital sentencer's consideration" of "any infirmity as written."[60] The Fifth Circuit Court of Appeals also found the erroneous admission of written victim impact evidence that characterized the defendants harmless error.[61]

Thus, in the years following *Payne*, federal and state reviewing courts for the most part have upheld the admissibility of victim impact evidence in capital sentencing proceedings. They have also generally found no error, or no reversible error, in the particular pieces of victim impact evidence admitted. In addition to their standard review to ensure that the probative value of introduced victim impact evidence outweighs its prejudicial effect, some reviewing courts have established special procedural safeguards governing the introduction of this evidence in the "unique circumstances" of capital cases.[62]

Noncapital State Cases

Because even the *Booth* Court had not precluded the potential use of victim impact information in noncapital sentencing proceedings, the *Payne* Court's ruling as to the general admissibility of such information in capital sentencing did not alter any existing legal precedents in noncapital cases. State reviewing courts in noncapital cases have maintained their ongoing responsibility to ensure that the probative value of victim impact evidence exceeds its prejudicial effect, but they also have generally found no error, or at least no reversible error, from the admission of such evidence.[63] For example, an Illinois appellate court permitted victim impact information that included poetry.[64] An Idaho appellate court held that video and photographic images can constitute a proper exercise of a victim's right to be heard at sentencing and further found that the admission of a moving DVD of less than five minutes that was accompanied by music and included an image of the victim's children at her grave did not result in manifest injustice to the defendant.[65] A New York appellate court found that evidence of the psychological impact of a rape on the victim was a proper factor to be considered by the sentencing judge.[66]

State reviewing courts in noncapital cases have also generally found no reversible error from the admission of victim impact evidence on additional subjects than those expressly specified in statutory authorizations regarding this evidence. In such instances, reviewing courts have often concluded that these enactments prescribe the types of victim impact evidence that the court is *required* to receive, but do not limit the trial court's traditional ability to receive additional information relevant to sentencing.[67] For example, appellate courts have typically found no error, or alternatively no reversible error, from a victim's opinion regarding the offender or a sentence recommendation in instances in which these topics were not expressly authorized in victim impact statutes.[68] Some appellate courts have found no reversible error from the admission of impact information regarding uncharged or past victims.[69] Some appellate courts have upheld the admission of testimony or information from additional victims or witnesses than the number or type authorized by statute.[70] For example, although faulting the prosecutor's failure to provide sufficient advance notice to the defense about the receipt and submission to the judge of almost 200 letters from the public urging the imposition of the maximum sentence, a New Mexico appellate court found that the letters were admissible in the sentencing proceeding in addition to the impact evidence of family members and that the defense was not prejudiced by their admission, in part, because the judge did not rely on the letters in imposing the maximum sentence on the defendant.[71]

Reviewing courts have differed, however, as to whether this expanded victim impact evidence requires greater formalities, such as the requirements of victim testimony under oath or subject to cross-examination. For example, the Nevada Supreme Court established rules regarding when prior notice, testimony under oath, and cross-examination are required concerning oral victim impact testimony. All are required when impact testimony includes a defendant's prior "bad acts," as in the case under review. When impact testimony is more limited, the victim still must be placed under oath, but prior notice and cross-examination may not be required. The absence of the required formalities given and the nature of the impact testimony in conjunction with other errors regarding sentencing constituted reversible error in the case under review.[72] Also reflecting a concern about the absence of formalities regarding the receipt of victim impact information, the Maine Supreme Court found that a judge's consideration of information in a submitted letter regarding uncharged offenses violated the defendant's due process rights and required vacation of his sentence in the absence of any steps taken to ensure its factual reliability.[73]

Other appellate courts, however, have not required that victims be placed under oath or be subject to cross-examination when providing victim impact evidence.[74] These courts have also not found a violation of a defendant's due process or confrontation rights from the court's consideration of written impact information as long as the defendant is given notice of such and an opportunity to respond.[75] Some reviewing courts have even found no reversible error in the trial court's receipt of victim impact information outside of normal channels of victim impact statements or oral allocution at sentencing, such as through *ex parte* conversations or statements.[76] The norm, however, is to provide defense attorneys an opportunity to challenge the information in victim impact statements or testimony at sentencing, if not to cross-examine the victim himself regarding this information.[77] Thus, on review, the admission of victim impact evidence in state noncapital cases has generally been upheld, with some variation in terms of the procedural formalities accompanying its receipt.[78]

Despite this general judicial support for the admission of victim impact evidence, state reviewing courts have also placed limits on the extent of a victim's right to be heard regarding sentencing. In *People v. Pfeiffer*,[79] a Michigan appellate court concluded that the state victim rights provisions did not provide a basis for the trial court to reconsider and modify a validly imposed sentence that the offender had begun serving. At the initial sentencing hearing in this case, the prosecutor referred to and the trial court had before it victim impact information in the presentence report, but the victim was not present. The prosecutor at the sentencing made no objection to or request to delay the proceeding. After the mistaken failure to notify the victim of the hearing was detected, the prosecutor assigned to the case moved for a resentencing on the grounds that the victim's right to be heard at sentencing had been violated. At the resulting hearing, at which the victim's mother testified, the trial court resentenced the defendant to an increased term of incarceration. Although the appellate court acknowledged the victim's statutory right to offer oral allocution at sentencing, the court concluded that the victim rights statute provided no general remedial rights to victims for violations that would render the initial sentence invalid and subject to modification under state law. The Michigan appellate court therefore ordered the defendant's initial sentence reinstated.[80]

In *State v. Bruce*,[81] a case that did not rely on the state victim rights laws, however, an Ohio appellate court upheld a trial court's resentencing of a defendant in circumstances in which the trial court had initially imposed an "incorrect" sentence under state law at a sentencing proceeding that the victim mistakenly did not attend. At a resentencing hearing the next day, prior to the execution or formal entry of the sentence, the victim testified regarding her injuries from the offense and the trial court imposed a "correct," albeit more severe, sentence. The appellate court concluded that the trial court had the authority to correct the initial incorrect sentence and that the additional information from the victim justified the increased sentence of incarceration imposed in the resentencing proceeding.[82]

State appellate courts have also rejected the notion that victim rights to be heard regarding sentencing give victims standing as "aggrieved parties" in the prosecution with rights to petition for relief from or seek appellate review of courts' sentencing decisions. In *Schroering v. McKinney*,[83] the Kentucky Supreme Court concluded that the victim's widow, although having a "personal interest in the outcome," did not have standing to seek mandamus to have a trial court's order granting shock probation to the defendant set aside. The reviewing court concluded that there had been no violation of the state statute requiring the court to consider a victim impact statement before granting shock probation and that the trial court had otherwise not exceeded its authority in granting shock probation without a hearing.[84] In *Dix v. Superior Court ex rel. People*,[85] the California Supreme Court concluded that, even in light of California's constitutional and legislative victim rights provisions, the victim had no standing to seek mandamus or prohibition to overturn a trial court's order "recalling" its previously imposed sentencing order and continuing the matter for resentencing. Rather than the instant action the victim sought, he would be able to be notified of and express his views at the defendant's subsequent resentencing, as provided under California's victim rights provisions.[86]

Similarly, in *State v. Lamberton*,[87] the Arizona Supreme Court held that the state's constitutional and statutory victim rights provisions, which included rights to be heard at sentencing and post-conviction relief proceedings, did not give the victim the right to file an independent petition of review challenging the merits of a trial court's grant of the defendant's motion for post-conviction relief following an evidentiary hearing at which the victim testified. Even the state's provision of a victim right to seek an order or a "special action" to assert or challenge the denial of victim rights did "not give the Victim standing to argue before an appellate court that the trial court's ruling in a criminal proceeding was error or to bring the types of action against the defendant that the State can bring."[88] The Arizona Supreme Court also rejected the victim's assertion that the only meaningful way to maintain her constitutional right to be heard at sentencing was by filing her own petition for review. To the contrary, the victim's positions regarding such would be reflected in the trial court records reviewed in connection with the prosecutor's petition for review. In addition, the victim's views could be communicated to the prosecutor through the prescribed consultation and notification requirements regarding post-conviction and appellate proceedings.[89] Finally, in *Cooper v. District Court*,[90] an Alaska appellate court concluded that neither the victim nor the state Office of Victims' Rights (legislatively charged with advocacy on behalf of victims) had standing to seek appellate review of what they considered to be an error in the court's sentence following a sentencing proceeding in which the victim had exercised her right to be heard. The appellate court concluded that the victim's right to be heard regarding sentencing did not "guarantee crime victims a right to attack the sentencing decision if the judge fails to adhere to the crime victim's views regarding the proper sentence."[91]

Despite these limiting state court interpretations of the extent of a victim's right to be heard regarding sentencing in noncapital cases, this victim right remains quite extensive. Reviewing state courts have generally found no error, or no reversible error, in the admission of victim impact information and evidence and even victim opinions regarding the crime, the offender, and the appropriate sentence. Thus, the victim right to be heard regarding sentencing, as adopted by state constitutional and statutory law and interpreted judicially in the state systems, remains one of the most widely adopted victim rights since the President's Task Force on Victims of Crime.

Noncapital Federal Cases

Both before and after the enactment of the Crime Victims' Rights Act in 2004, federal courts have addressed the same type of admissibility issues concerning the introduction of victim impact evidence in noncapital cases as the state courts and have generally found no error or no reversible error due to the admission of such evidence.[92] The Act, however, expanded the right to be heard at sentencing to all victims directly and proximately harmed by federal crimes (rather than only victims of violent crime or sexual abuse)[93] and has also resulted in some interpretive decisions concerning its scope.[94]

One of the first major interpretive issues that some federal courts have addressed is whether the Act's right to be "reasonably heard" at public sentencing proceedings includes a victim right to orally address the sentencing court. After reviewing the language of the Act and the legislative history accompanying its enactment, one federal trial judge concluded that victims of non-violent as well as violent crimes have a right to be heard at sentencing under the Act; that this right includes a right to be heard orally by and to personally address the court; and that this right is mandatory rather than discretionary. This trial judge deemed this interpretation necessary to make victims "independent" participants in the sentencing proceedings, as contemplated by the Act.[95]

In *Kenna v. United States District Court*,[96] the Ninth Circuit Court of Appeals addressed this same issue in a mandamus proceeding arising out of a financial fraud case in which the two defendants had caused losses to scores of victims of almost $100,000,000. More than sixty victims submitted written impact statements. At the sentencing proceeding for the first of the defendants, several of the victims orally addressed the court regarding their losses. At the sentencing proceeding for the second defendant, three months later, the trial court denied any of the victims the right to speak, indicating that in light of the previous oral statements at the first sentencing and his re-review of the written statements, the judge did not believe that there was any additional information that the victims could provide that would have any additional impact. If there were any changed developments since the initial sentencing, the prosecutor could bring those to the judge's attention. One of the victims who had spoken at the initial sentencing filed a mandamus action pursuant to the Act, asserting that his right to be heard included a right to speak in open court and that the trial judge had denied that right. He sought a vacation of the second defendant's sentence and an order requiring that the trial judge permit victims to speak at a resentencing.[97]

In the mandamus proceeding, the victim and the trial judge offered competing interpretations of the right to be "reasonably heard" language in the Act: the absolute right to speak, if desired, subject to reasonable constraints on duration and content versus a right to make the victim's "position known by whatever means the court reasonably determines," including a limitation to written submissions or prior oral statements. The appellate court found both textual interpretations of the Act "plausible" and thus found that the right to be heard language in the Act was ambiguous. The appellate court therefore consulted the sparse legislative history of the Act and that of the contemporaneous proposed federal constitutional victim rights amendment. This legislative history "disclose[d] a clear congressional intent to give crime victims the right to speak" at the proceedings addressed by the Act. This interpretation put crime victims on the same footing as the prosecutor and defendant in their ability to address the sentencing court and made them "full participants" in the proceeding, as contemplated in the Act. Moreover, although the appellate court acknowledged the Act's authorization of "reasonable" procedures in cases with multiple victims such as this one, when cases involve multiple defendants at separate sentencing proceedings, victims have the right to "confront every defendant who has wronged them" rather than relying on submissions at previous proceedings involving other defendants.[98] The Ninth Circuit Court of Appeals granted the mandamus petition, but rather than vacating the sentence, remanded the case to the federal trial court to determine whether it would re-open the sentencing due to the victim rights violation, as authorized by the Act.[99]

The victim in *Kenna* initiated a subsequent mandamus action after the trial court rejected his argument that the Act gives crime victims a general right to obtain disclosure of the presentence report prepared for the court. In declining to disclose the entire presentence report concerning the second defendant in connection with the re-opening of his sentencing proceeding, the trial judge had offered to consider disclosing specific portions of the report, but found that the victim had failed to demonstrate sufficient grounds that outweighed the traditional confidentiality afforded the report to justify its entire disclosure. The victim refused any partial disclosure of the report and sought disclosure of the entire report in the mandamus action. The Ninth Circuit Court of Appeals held that the Act does not give victims a general right to obtain the presentence report and that the trial judge had not abused his discretion or committed legal error in his ruling on the victim's request in this case.[100] In *In re Brock*,[101] the Fourth Circuit Court of Appeals also denied mandamus relief to a victim who asserted that his ability to meaningfully exercise his right to be heard had been denied, in part, because the trial judge declined to provide his access to requested portions of the presentence report. The appellate court found no abuse of discretion in the trial court's ruling where the record disclosed that the victim was provided "ample" information regarding the sentencing issues, including the Government's sentencing memoranda, and did not need the presentence report to describe the crime's impact on him.[102] Other federal courts have declined requests to provide victims with other non-public information sought in connection with the right to be heard.[103]

The federal appellate courts have also begun to explore other interpretive issues regarding the scope of the victim right to be reasonably heard at sentencing under the Act. In the *Brock* case, the victim had submitted a written victim impact statement and a restitution affidavit and was permitted to provide additional impact information orally to the court at the sentencing hearing. The victim described the impact of the crime on him, expressed his dissatisfaction with the court's characterization of the crime's severity, and urged the court to consider all of the evidence in sentencing. The trial judge, however, declined to hear the victim's testimony and arguments regarding his sentencing calculations under the federal guidelines. In his mandamus action, the victim asserted that the trial judge's refusal to hear his information concerning the guidelines calculations violated his right to be heard. The Fourth Circuit Court of Appeals found that the trial judge had considered the victim's written and oral information regarding the crime and its impact and that the court's refusal to consider the victim's arguments regarding the guidelines calculations did not prevent him from being reasonably heard under the Act, especially when the trial judge indicated that his sentences would have been the same regardless of the guideline calculations.[104]

Federal appellate courts have also concluded that the Act does not provide crime victims a basis to utilize the Act's mandamus remedy to appeal a defendant's sentence or to exercise an independent right to appeal a sentence or a rights violation. In the *Brock* mandamus action, the victim contended that the trial judge's incorrect sentencing guidelines calculations had deprived him of his right to be heard. The Fourth Circuit Court of Appeals found that the Act "does not provide victims with a right to appeal a defendant's sentence by challenging the district court's calculation of the Guidelines range." The appellate court found that the victim was reasonably heard regardless whether the trial judge's guidelines calculations were correct.[105]

In *United States v. Hunter*,[106] the Tenth Circuit Court of Appeals dismissed an attempted independent appeal by a homicide victim's family members from a defendant's conviction and sentence and regarding an asserted rights denial by the trial court. In a previous mandamus action, the appellate court had denied relief to the family members who sought to be declared victims of a defendant who had sold a gun to the person who murdered their daughter eight months later. The trial court had ruled that the family members had not shown that the unlawful gun sale for which the defendant was being prosecuted was the proximate cause of their daughter's death. The defendant subsequently entered a plea agreement with the Government and was sentenced. Neither the Government nor the defendant appealed, but the family members filed a notice of appeal from the defendant's conviction and sentence and due to the trial court's denial of their victim status.[107]

The Tenth Circuit Court of Appeals held that a "crime victim does not have an express right under the [Crime Victims' Rights Act] to appeal the defendant's conviction and sentence based on alleged violations of the statute."[108] The appellate court concluded that its holding was consistent with the general principle that only parties to litigation can appeal an adverse judgment and with the specific provisions of the Act. The appellate court found that the Act prescribed the mandamus remedy as the sole express vehicle for victims to assert rights violations, and only authorized the Government to assert any victim rights denials as errors in the course of an appeal. The Act's prescribed remedy of re-opening a plea or sentence requires prior pursuit of mandamus (not appellate) relief regarding an asserted rights denial. The Act's provision that it should not be construed to "impair" prosecutorial discretion would be undermined by permitting sentences to be re-opened via victim appeals after victims have asserted their rights in the trial court and through mandamus.[109] Finally, the appellate court reviewed the precedent presented and found "no precedent nor any compelling justification for allowing a non-party, post-judgment appeal that would reopen a defendant's sentence and affect the defendant's rights." Holding that persons claiming to be victims under the Act may not appeal from an alleged denial of rights pursuant to the Act except through the mandamus remedy prescribed by the Act, the appellate court therefore dismissed the family members' appeal.[110]

Thus, as in the state court systems, the federal courts have generally found no error or no reversible error in the introduction of victim impact evidence in noncapital cases. As more federal courts interpret the Act's provisions regarding the victim right to be reasonably heard at sentencing, it is anticipated that the scope of these provisions will be further clarified.[111]

Implementation and Analysis of the Right

The victim right to be heard regarding sentencing has been adopted and implemented in the midst of a lively debate among legal commentators, policy advocates, and social scientists as to the merits of such a right. Opponents of the grant of a victim right to be heard regarding sentencing have argued that including the victim's input in sentencing would reduce the objectivity of the process; shift the focus away from legitimate sentencing factors and toward inappropriate considerations of victim retaliation and vengeance; result in inequitable, disparate, or harsher sentencing; erode the prosecutor's function and control over the prosecution; be administratively cumbersome and time consuming; or further traumatize victims either by creating unmet expectations as to the effect of their input or by forcing them to participate in the sentencing process against their wishes. Advocates of a victim right to be heard regarding sentencing, however, have contended that such victim input would promote more informed, accurate, and democratic sentencing decisions; recognize the victim's status as the injured party in the prosecution; assist the victim's healing and regaining of control following the victimization; increase victim satisfaction and cooperation with the criminal justice system; and promote the sentencing goals of rehabilitation by confronting the offender with the reality of the impact of his crime and of retribution by identifying the degree of harm done, and other sentencing goals.[112] As the victim's right to be heard at sentencing has been implemented in the years since the President's Task Force, the results have neither matched the highest expectations of its advocates nor realized the worst fears of its critics.

Utilization of the Right

At the outset, despite advocates' and analysts' portrayal of victims' *desire* for greater participation in the criminal justice process, and especially the sentencing process,[113] estimates of the extent to which victims have taken full advantage of their rights to be heard at sentencing have varied considerably. Studies done in the 1980s often reflected significant gaps between the formal provision of and the exercise of victim rights to be heard regarding sentencing. For example, based on a survey of probation staff and prosecutors in thirty-three states, one researcher concluded that victim impact statements were prepared, on average, in over three-fourths of felony cases. Only 18%–26% of victims, however, were present at sentencing; approximately 15% submitted authorized written statements independently of the victim impact statement included in the presentence report; and 9%–13% made oral allocution statements at sentencing.[114] In a survey of over 350 victims in five states, other researchers found that while almost 50% of victims reported having been consulted about the sentences in their cases, only 27% reported actually making a victim impact statement.[115] Researchers in a study of over 400 sexual assault victims in a metropolitan Ohio county found that sentence recommendations were made by approximately 60% of the victims in their victim impact statements.[116] Other researchers conducting a local study of 500 felony victims in Ohio found that 55% of the victims submitted a victim impact statement, 18% were present during trial or sentencing, and 6% exercised their oral allocution right at sentencing.[117] This final figure is comparable to a three-site California study involving approximately 170 victims which concluded that oral or written allocution at sentencing was exercised in less than 3% of the felony cases studied.[118]

More recent studies reflect some reduction in the gap between availability and exercise of the right to be heard regarding sentencing. In the four-state study involving over 1,300 crime victims in two "strong" and two "weak" victim rights states in 1995, victim interest in making an impact statement before sentencing remained high, with 82% of surveyed victims indicating that this right was "very important." In addition, 79% of responding victims said that it was "very important" to be involved in the decision about the sentence the defendant should receive. Of those victims who received notice of the sentencing, 73% of victims in "strong" states and 72% of victims in "weak" states said that they attended the sentencing hearing. In both "strong" and "weak" states, 93% of victims given the opportunity to make an impact statement indicated that they did so. In their impact statements, 79% of victims in "strong" states and 60% of victims in "weak" states gave their opinions about the sentence.[119]

These figures must be compared with those from the survey of approximately 150 criminal justice personnel in these states in which 88% of "strong" state personnel and 63% of "weak" state personnel indicated that they "always or usually" allowed victims to make an impact statement and an additional 7% of "strong" state personnel and 25% of "weak" state personnel said that they "sometimes" did so. Their estimated percentages of cases in which victims actually made an impact statement, however, were 39% in the "strong" states and 43% in the "weak" states. Additionally, 73% of "strong" state personnel and 80% of "weak" state personnel said that they "always," "usually," or "sometimes" consulted with victims regarding sentencing.[120]

However, the most recent studies regarding utilization of the right to be heard at sentencing do not consistently reflect significant victim utilization of the right. In its 2008 evaluation of the implementation of the Crime Victims' Rights Act, the General Accountability Office found that 40% of 174 responding victim-witness professionals reported at least some increase in victims submitting written statements or speaking at court proceedings, with an additional 37% indicating a great or very great increase in these activities. However, 92% of the 182 responding federal crime victims reported that they *did not speak* at the sentencing hearings in their cases.[121] Disappointing rates of victim participation are also reflected in the 22% return rate of victim impact statements from victims, reported by the Texas Crime Victim Clearinghouse in 2004.[122] In a study of 233 Texas victim impact statements submitted between 2003 and 2005, researchers found that these statements were most often submitted by or on behalf of female victims of violent crime who were under thirty years old.[123]

The contrasting figures in the more recent studies reflect that there are still gaps between the availability and exercise of the right to be heard. Proffered explanations for these gaps include victim unawareness of the rights regarding sentencing due to lack of notification, discouragement or the absence of active encouragement by criminal justice personnel of their exercise, and actual victim choice of nonparticipation.[124] Research supports several of these explanations.

As discussed more fully in Chapter 3, difficulties with and lack of notification of participatory rights have often been mentioned as impediments to their exercise.[125] Illustrating such difficulties in the sentencing area, in the 1998 survey of victims in nine northeastern states, only 53% of applicable victims indicated that they were given the opportunity for a victim impact statement.[126] In the 1980s California study of victim allocution, only 44% of 171 interviewed victims indicated an awareness of their right to appear at sentencing.[127] In its 2008 evaluation of the implementation of the Crime Victims' Rights Act, the General Accountability Office found that 58% of the 243 responding federal crime victims indicated that they were aware of their right to be heard (with an additional 13% indicating that they were not sure about their awareness of this right).[128]

A related difficulty is victims' misperception, misunderstanding, or misrecollection of their rights regarding sentencing. For example, in the Ohio county study, although 90% of the victims who believed that they had completed a victim impact statement had done so, 50% of those who thought that they had not done a victim impact statement had in fact completed one.[129] Researchers in a local New York study found that only 56% of victims in the study who had done a victim impact statement remembered doing so.[130]

Results from the California allocution study suggest reasons that victims choose to exercise and not to exercise their rights to be heard regarding sentencing. The researchers asked victims who were aware of their rights but chose not to exercise them for their reasons: 37% were satisfied with the criminal justice system response without their allocution; 30% thought that their appearance would make no difference; 28% were either too upset, fearful of retaliation, confused, or discouraged to appear; and 5% said that the appearance would have been too costly due to lost wages or expenses required to arrange their appearance. Researchers also asked for the reasons for the exercise of their allocution rights by the 3% of the victims who had done so: 34% wanted to express their feelings to the judge, 32% wanted to perform their "duty," and 26% wanted to achieve a sense of justice or influence the sentence.[131] In the 2008 General Accountability Office study in which less than 10% of responding federal crime victims indicated that they exercised their right to speak at sentencing, the most frequently reported reason for this was the victims' lack of interest in speaking at these proceedings.[132]

Thus, many factors contribute to the sometimes disparate degrees to which victims exercise their right to be heard regarding sentencing. The varied estimates concerning the actual utilization of this right have been mirrored by the varied research results as to the impact of this right on criminal justice system administration and efficiency, sentence outcome, and victim satisfaction. Again, this research confirms neither all of the expectations nor all of the concerns regarding this victim right.

Impact on Criminal Justice System Administration and Efficiency

Initial concerns about the impact of this right on criminal justice system administration and efficiency have largely not been realized. Of course, the introduction of the formal victim impact statement increased the workload of probation personnel who are generally responsible for its preparation as part of the presentence investigation report for the court. The extent of this increased workload has been mitigated, however, by the fact that some information regarding victim loss or impact from the crime was often incorporated in these reports prior to the victim rights requirements.[133]

One survey of states with victim impact laws found that "fiscal impact and administrative burdens [from the implementation of the laws] were uniformly reported as minimal or nonexistent."[134] In a thirty-six-state survey of probation officials, researchers found that almost half said that their victim impact statement responsibilities "posed no problems" for them. Problems mentioned by other respondents included difficulties in obtaining victim cooperation and personnel problems.[135] Perhaps because relatively few victims have taken advantage of allocution rights at sentencing, researchers in the California study found that its effects on criminal justice system workload were "minimal."[136] Thus, it appears, at least at this stage of documented utilization of victim rights to be heard regarding sentencing, there has been no significant impairment of criminal justice system administration and efficiency.[137]

Impact on Sentencing Outcome

One of the areas of greatest expectation *and* concern regarding this victim right has been its potential impact on sentencing outcome. Included in this area have been concerns regarding the types of information victims would convey, and especially whether victims would use this right to seek vengeance or retaliation against offenders. Another area of interest has been the degree to which criminal justice personnel, especially prosecutors and judges, would *listen* to victims' input regarding sentencing. Both of these issues relate directly to the expectations and concerns as to whether sentencing outcomes would change as a result of victim input into the sentencing process. Research results have not conclusively confirmed either these expectations or concerns.

One of the most frequently voiced concerns regarding victim input in sentencing decisions has been the concern that victims would seek vengeance or retaliation or be extremely punitive in their sentencing input. Based on studies primarily conducted during the 1980s, research results in this area, however, have been quite mixed. For example, in a local Ohio study of sexual assault victims, researchers found that approximately 90% of victims assaulted by non-relatives recommended imprisonment sentences. Victim recommendations of incarceration for other offenders varied depending on their relationship to the victim: 83% for acquaintance offenders, 76% for non-parent relatives, and 23% for parents.[138] Researchers in another local Ohio study reported that 60% of felony victims who submitted a victim impact statement requested a sentence of incarceration.[139] In the California study, researchers found that almost half of the victims of felony crimes felt that the offender should be incarcerated. When the small number of victims who had exercised their allocution rights were asked the results they sought through allocution, however, 56% wanted a long or maximum sentence, 15% sought emotional relief, 12% sought restitution, and the remaining 17% sought various other objectives.[140] Researchers in a Brooklyn study found that less than half of the studied victims sought incarceration sentences, with the rest seeking restitution, protection, or a lesser form of punishment.[141]

Finally, still other researchers, in a qualitative study based on presentence interviews with victims for defense attorneys over a number of years, suggested that victims generally express an initial desire for an incarceration sentence for an offender. However, they frequently are willing to revise these recommendations to those involving less severe forms of restraint or alternative community sentences with restitution or treatment when presented with additional sentencing alternatives. Moreover, these researchers also concluded that victims were more willing to consider sentencing alternatives to incarceration as more time elapsed from the occurrence of the crime.[142] Not surprisingly, the above research confirms that victims are not uniformly punitive in their approach to sentencing issues, but that their recommendations regarding punishment vary in individual cases from requests for incarceration to other alternative forms of punishment. In addition, given the fact that individuals in these studies frequently have been the victims of felony and often violent felony crimes, even their recommendations of incarceration sentences for their offenders should not necessarily be viewed as being "punitive."[143]

A second question related to the impact of victim input on sentence outcomes is whether judges and prosecutors *listen* to the victim input. In terms of the preferred format for victim input, survey research has fairly consistently indicated judicial support, in principle, for the use of victim impact statements.[144] There is less consensus as to the usefulness—as opposed to the symbolic value—of victim allocution at the sentencing proceeding itself. For example, researchers determined that most judges in a thirty-six-state survey found all forms of victim input, including victim narratives and oral allocution, "effective means of obtaining useful information."[145] On the other hand, researchers found that the "vast majority" of California presiding judges surveyed thought that an allocution right at sentencing was "unnecessary" because it did not add information to that already contained in the victim impact statement.[146] In terms of the content of victim input, judges in the thirty-six-state survey indicated that they found victim information regarding the financial, physical, and psychological impact of crimes to be the victim information most useful to the sentencing decision. A majority of the judges indicated that victim opinions or recommendations as to the sentence were not useful in the sentencing decision.[147]

Prosecutors also have generally expressed their belief in the usefulness of victim impact information.[148] However, they sometimes view victim impact statements and other formal means of transmission of this information as less useful to them because they duplicate information prosecutors learn through their contact with the victim during the prosecution. For example, in interviews with Bronx prosecutors, researchers found that the majority did not think victim impact statements added substantially to their knowledge of the crime's impact on the victim.[149] Similarly, in an experiment in the Bronx and Brooklyn, checks of prosecutors' case files showed significant numbers of victim impact statements either unopened or not present. Interviews with prosecutors indicated their perception of a lack of not already known information in the victim impact statements, as well as problems in their preparation.[150] It thus appears that, in principle, judges and prosecutors believe that there is utility in victim impact information—although there may be differences of opinion as to the most effective means for victims to transmit this information to them.

Assuming the receptiveness of judges and prosecutors to the use of victim impact information, then the question remains as to its impact on sentencing outcomes. In a thirty-six-state survey conducted in the 1980s, over 80% of responding judges indicated that victim impact statements had either "some" or a "substantial" impact on the type and length of sentences they generally imposed.[151] In the contemporaneous California study of victim allocution, researchers found that 19% of surveyed judges and 70% of prosecutors thought that a victim's allocution sometimes or often increased sentence severity. They also found that 40% of judges and 66% of prosecutors thought it increased the amount of restitution ordered.[152] In the 1995 survey of criminal justice personnel in two "strong" and two "weak" victim rights states, 91% of "strong" state personnel said that the victim impact statement had "some" or "a lot" of effect regarding whether an offender was incarcerated, 47% said that it had such effect concerning the length of sentence given, and 92% said that it had such effect regarding the amount of restitution ordered. In the two "weak" states, 84% of the criminal justice personnel said that the victim impact statement had "some" or "a lot" of effect regarding whether an offender was incarcerated, 38% said that it had such effect concerning the length of sentence given, and 92% said that it had such effect regarding the amount of restitution ordered.[153]

In a 2004–2006 study based on interviews with twenty-two judges and fifteen victim advocates and observations of almost ninety sentencing hearings in domestic violence and sexual assault cases in Minnesota, the study authors concluded that victim impact statements provide a number of benefits, including provision of important information to the court, victim empowerment, impact on the defendant, and humanization of the court process. Although many judges interviewed questioned the actual effect of the impact statements on the sentence imposed (especially in the case of negotiated pleas), they and the victim advocates noted their use in fashioning aspects of the sentence and other positive benefits for the judges and the victims. The study authors identified elements of more persuasive impact statements, including specific details concerning the crime's impact, a balance between objective and emotional insights regarding the crime, an understanding of the justice system's purpose, and a reasonable request for sentencing.[154]

Despite these general survey results regarding victim impact on sentencing outcomes, most research as to specific sentence decision making since the President's Task Force has continued to show that the nature of the charge and the defendant's prior criminal record are the most consistently significant predictors of sentence outcome rather than additional factors of victim input and impact.[155] For example, in a six-site study conducted at the approximate time of the President's Task Force, researchers presented forty-eight judges and over one hundred prosecutors with hypothetical scenarios in several types of cases to determine the impact of various variables on the estimated length of the resulting incarceration sentence. Victim harm variables included the financial, physical, and psychological impact of the crime. These researchers concluded that defendant-related factors were more consistently significant predictors of the length of sentences of incarceration than additional factors of victim harm not already contemplated by the nature of the charge.[156] These results are consistent with those in a contemporaneous local Ohio study of approximately 400 sexual assault victims, in which researchers found that victim recommendations regarding sentence did not have a significant impact on sentencing outcome independently of factors of crime seriousness and prior record.[157]

In a study of an early Brooklyn victim liaison program in the late 1970s that solicited victim input regarding desired sentence outcomes, researchers found that information regarding outcomes desired by victims had a limited effect on case disposition when compared with dispositions in a control group. Although there was some greater increase in orders of restitution and warnings to stay away from victims in the experimental group, most of its victims who experienced financial loss did not receive restitution. There were no significant differences between the experimental and control groups in incarceration sanctions. Court officials and program staff felt that the program had only a "slight effect" on case outcome. This was due in part, however, to the limited discretion that prosecutors sometimes had in disposition recommendations and their unwillingness, in some instances, to incorporate additional victim information in their decision making or to convey it to the court.[158]

In a Bronx study conducted in the late 1980s, almost 300 felony robbery, nonsexual assault, and burglary victims were assigned to one of three experimental groups in which victim impact statements were prepared and given to criminal justice officials, statements were prepared but not disseminated, or no statements were taken. Researchers found that there were no statistically significant differences between the three groups in the types of sentences imposed. They further found that the type and severity of the charge and the defendant's prior convictions were significant influences on the decision to incarcerate, but not the presence of a victim impact statement or an overall victim harm measure. After charge and criminal history were taken into account, overall victim harm and victim impact statements and individual measures of harm played little role in the sentencing decision. There also was no indication that victim impact statements increased the use of special conditions, such as restitution.[159]

An Ohio county study of 500 felony cases conducted in the late 1980s compared cases in which victims had an impact statement, requested a sentence of incarceration, or made oral allocution to those in which victims did not do these things. Researchers found a correlation between victim impact statements and a request for incarceration with the likelihood of a sentence of incarceration (versus probation) and with the length of incarceration sentence given, but found no such correlation regarding oral allocution. In a multivariate analysis, however, while offense severity and prior convictions remained significantly related to sentences of incarceration and their length, only the presence of a victim impact statement remained even modestly related to the incarceration (versus probation) decision.[160]

Explanations given for the absence of greater impact of victim input on sentencing outcomes include the fact that victim impact has often already been reflected in the severity of the conviction offense, one of the factors that is highly predictive of sentence outcome; the masking of some individual changes in sentence outcomes by the aggregation of research data; the increasing presence of guideline or determinate sentencing structures that restrict variances allowed for victim impact or other factors; and the general resistance to change in established norms of criminal justice sentencing decision making.[161] Given the limited effect that victim input has had on sentence outcome, one researcher suggested that requiring victim impact statements and recommendations had only a "placebo value" by creating the "impression that 'something is being done.'" He concluded that victim sentence recommendations have some symbolic and possibly some substantive value in cases in which judges are uncertain regarding a sentencing outcome.[162] After finding that the studied impact statements had "no discernible effect" on sentencing, other researchers noted that their study raised "troubling questions about the viability of impact statements as a vehicle for victims' participation in the court process."[163] Another researcher, however, reached a more positive conclusion after reviewing the relevant literature. She concluded that, although "often the [victim impact statement] and the information it contains are reflected in the charge, the [victim impact statement] may at times provide additional and relevant information that may in turn be used by the judge in meting out a sentence." In addition, the use of victim impact statements had not substituted a "subjective" approach of the victim for the "objective" one required by the law.[164] Once again, in terms of the effect of victim input on sentence outcomes, neither the highest expectations nor the worst fears have been realized.

Impact on Victim Satisfaction

Finally, especially in light of the limited changes in sentence outcome, the impact of this victim right to be heard on victim satisfaction must be considered. At the outset, survey results have varied as to whether victims even believe that their input has affected sentence outcome.[165] As to victims' satisfaction with their right to be heard or increased satisfaction with the resultant sentence outcome, research results are inconclusive. Despite the fact that the 2008 General Accountability Office study of the implementation of the Crime Victims' Rights Act revealed very low levels of victims making oral presentations at sentencing, 51% of the 180 responding victims reported that they were somewhat or very satisfied with the provision of their right to be heard, with an additional 42% having a neutral or no opinion regarding the provision of this right.[166] In a five-state survey of over 350 victims in the 1980s, half were not satisfied with their opportunity to provide input in the sentencing decision.[167] In the 1995 survey, 64% of victims in two "strong" and 51% of victims in two "weak" victim rights states thought that their ability to have input in the case was "adequate" or "more than adequate." Only 46% of "strong" state victims and 37% of "weak" state victims, however, rated the fairness of the sentence as "adequate" or "more than adequate." The most mentioned factor in victims' satisfaction and dissatisfaction with the prosecutor's handling of their cases was the outcome or sentence in the case. Finally, these researchers found a correlation between victim satisfaction and victim belief that their input had had an effect on case outcomes.[168]

In other specific studies, however, the provision of victim input has not been found to result in any significant increase in victims' satisfaction with the specific sentence imposed or with the criminal justice system generally.[169] In the Bronx study, described above, researchers found no significant differences in the experimental and control groups as to their perceptions of various aspects of the prosecution process during interviews taken after the experimental group had completed victim impact statements, but prior to the dispositions in their cases. In fact, the experimental victim impact statement group gave the least positive responses. In interviews following case disposition, there were no significant differences between the groups regarding their perceptions of the court process, their treatment by criminal justice officials, or the case outcome. These researchers therefore noted that their results did not support the argument that victim impact statements are an effective means to increase victim satisfaction with the criminal justice system. They hypothesized that part of the reason may be that many victims do not seek greater participation in the criminal justice process. They suggested additional research to determine the proportion and specific types of victims who want to participate in the process more fully and the means through which *they* want to do so.[170]

The research results in the Bronx study are consistent with those in the Brooklyn study, described previously, in which researchers found no differences in victim satisfaction with case outcome in the experimental victim liaison and control groups.[171] They are also consistent with the results in the California allocution study that found mixed feelings of satisfaction and dissatisfaction among victims who exercised oral allocution rights and no significant differences in satisfaction between victims who exercised allocution rights and those who did not.[172]

Researchers in the Ohio county study, described above, did a companion study of victim satisfaction based on 125 completed surveys from the 500 felony case victims in the general study. They found no significant differences in victim satisfaction with the criminal justice system or the sentence based on the filing of a victim impact statement. They did find that victims' perceptions of unfulfilled expectations from the filing of a victim impact statement resulted in significantly lower satisfaction in these areas. Victim perception of sentence fairness and severity was correlated with satisfaction with the sentence and the criminal justice system. Receipt of restitution also increased perceptions of system satisfaction. Because of the centrality of victim satisfaction with sentence outcomes to their overall satisfaction, these researchers suggested that victim satisfaction with the criminal justice system is an "elusive goal" and that even the most caring system treatment of victims will not prevent their dissatisfaction with the system if they perceive the sentence imposed has been too lenient.[173]

These researchers also concluded that completing a victim impact statement and oral allocution at sentencing did not directly affect victims' distress levels soon after the crime or subsequently, but that they might have an indirect effect on the type of sentence imposed and thus on victims' satisfaction.[174] On a more encouraging note, both the Bronx and Ohio county research reflected that the majority of victims studied, including those who provided victim input at sentencing and those who did not, were at least somewhat satisfied with the outcomes in their cases and the criminal justice system generally.[175]

Conclusion

This review of the victim right to be heard regarding sentencing reveals that there has been an adoption by the federal system and all of the states of some formal means through which eligible victims can provide input regarding sentencing. Reviewing courts have generally upheld this right's implementation in circumstances in which it has not unduly jeopardized defendant rights.

Policy analysts and advocates continue to debate its merits. Although researchers have generally established its acceptable impact on criminal justice administration and efficiency, their research has not clearly established that victims have taken full advantage of their right to be heard regarding sentencing or that this right has had an impact on sentence outcome or victim satisfaction. As a result, the debate as to the nature and effectiveness of this victim right will likely continue.

The Right to Be Heard Regarding Parole

President's Task Force and *New Directions from the Field* Recommendations

Prior to the President's Task Force recommendations, only six states had "open" parole hearings.[176] In its recommendations, the Task Force suggested that parole be abolished and replaced by a system in which the "sentence imposed would be the sentence served."[177] In the absence of the universal adoption of this recommendation, the Task Force recommended legislation to open parole hearings to the public. It criticized the prevailing secrecy in the conduct of parole hearings that had the effect of insulating parole authorities from accountability regarding their parole decision making. The Task Force felt that the potential parolee's, and presumably the parole board's, interest in maintaining the secrecy of parole proceedings must, "on balance, give way to the concern of victims and potential victims for their own safety and the integrity of the system. Opening to public scrutiny the operation of parole boards will go far in helping to restore public confidence in the criminal justice system."[178]

The Task Force also recommended to parole authorities that they allow crime victims or their families or representatives to attend parole hearings and make known the crime's impact on the victim. In the Task Force's view, not only does the crime victim have a valid interest in the outcome of a parole proceeding, but also information about the victim's experience with the offender is relevant to an informed parole decision. The Task Force noted that victims have a "legitimate interest in seeing not only that their attackers are appropriately punished but also that they are not released prematurely to harm others."[179]

The authors of the *New Directions from the Field* study noted the significant expansion of the victim right to be heard in parole proceedings since the President's Task Force *Final Report,* including the fact that 75% of states permitted victims to attend and testify at parole hearings as of 1996. The study authors, however, noted that less 50% of parole hearing cases had victim notification requests filed and only 25% of parole hearings were attended by victims. The study authors therefore not only advocated the adoption of the right to be heard at parole proceedings by the remaining states, but also the adoption by correctional authorities of mechanisms to facilitate victim exercise of this right, such as the greater use of videotaped or videoconference options to minimize victim inconvenience and safety concerns. For victims who choose to attend parole proceedings, the study authors recommended the expansion of procedures, used by 75% of parole agencies, to minimize contact between victims and offenders and otherwise ensure victim safety and support while in prison facilities.[180]

Constitutional and Legislative Response

In the Comprehensive Crime Control Act of 1984, Congress heeded the Task Force's recommendation and abolished parole for federal offenders. Congress replaced federal parole with a period of "supervised release" following an offender's completion of a sentence of incarceration. During his service of the prescribed period of supervised release, the offender is under the jurisdiction of the sentencing court. The period of supervised release is determined by the court at the time of the initial sentencing. Thus, the victim right to be heard regarding federal sentencing, discussed previously in this chapter, would presumably apply to the imposition of supervised release, as well.[181]

The last federal victim rights constitutional amendment proposal introduced in Congress prior to the enactment of the federal statutory Crime Victims' Rights Act in 2004 included a victim right "reasonably" to be heard at public release proceedings.[182] The Act itself includes a victim right to be "reasonably" heard in parole proceedings, presumably regarding federal offenders not affected by the 1984 abolition of federal parole.[183]

In their constitutional provisions, eight states provide victims a right to be heard at important or critical stages of the criminal process or proceedings or generally at criminal justice or public proceedings—all of which could include parole proceedings.[184] An additional eleven states have specific or somewhat more general provisions that could be interpreted to provide a victim right to be heard regarding parole.[185]

In their statutory provisions, virtually every state now grants eligible victims a right to be heard regarding parole decision making—in writing, orally, or both. Provisions regarding this right vary widely in terms of the nature and extent of authorized victim input or whether the nature of such input is specified at all. They also vary according to the procedural prerequisites for the exercise of the right and confidentiality and disclosure requirements concerning its use and content.[186]

At the outset, the victim's right to be heard regarding parole, as most victim participatory rights, is typically available to victims of designated crimes or crime categories only. By their nature, parole decisions generally involve felony offenders which, in some instances, further narrows the categories of eligible victims. Some states impose additional restrictions on crimes for which victims are eligible to be heard in the parole process. For example, Iowa and Maryland restrict their right to be heard regarding parole to victims of "violent" crimes.[187]

Moreover, in the majority of states with a victim right to be heard regarding parole, the right is conditional in some way. The most frequently used conditions are the requirement of a victim request for notification of the parole proceedings or of the opportunity to exercise the right to be heard and the related requirement that crime victims maintain current address information with notifying authorities.[188] A few states condition the right on victim cooperation with criminal justice system authorities.[189]

In terms of the format for victim input regarding parole, most states authorize the victim to give input in oral or written form, or both.[190] In addition, victim impact statements that have been prepared prior to sentencing are often transmitted by the court system to parole authorities.[191] Some states allow a victim to provide input through videotaped statements or via videoconference.[192] Although several states expressly require the parole decision makers to "consider" the prescribed victim input, they generally provide no guidance as to what form such consideration should take.[193]

Unlike the fairly standard procedures for the offering of victim input regarding sentencing, state procedures differ as to when victim input is presented to parole decision makers, i.e., at the parole hearing or in some other forum. They also differ as to whether the offender can be present during oral victim input and whether oral or written victim input is confidential and thus not subject to disclosure to the offender.[194] For example, in California, the victim can appear at the parole hearing itself and express his views "concerning the crime and the person responsible," presumably in the presence of the offender.[195] In Pennsylvania, however, the victim's oral testimony is received and recorded by a hearing examiner who prepares a written report concerning such for inclusion in the parole board's file regarding the offender.[196]

Some states do not specify the content of the victim's input regarding parole at all. Others specify the content broadly, such as Kentucky's allowance of victim comments on "all issues" relating to the prisoner's parole.[197] Other states specify a specific content area, but do not limit victim input to the designated area. For example, Pennsylvania provides that the victim's statement "may include" information concerning the continuing nature and extent of physical, psychological, or emotional harm or trauma from the crime; any lost earnings or ability to work; or the crime's continuing impact on the victim's family.[198] Several states expressly allow a victim to state an opinion regarding the offender and whether he should be released on parole. For example, Colorado gives a victim the right to attend parole proceedings and to "reasonably express his or her views concerning the crime, the offender, and whether or not the offender should be released on parole, and if so released under what conditions."[199]

Most states do not specifically address the effect of a failure to provide a victim's right to be heard regarding parole. A few states expressly provide that the failure to provide a victim the prescribed right to be heard regarding parole does not affect the validity of the parole determination or give rise to any right or cause of action by the victim, or both.[200] A few other states, however, provide express remedies if there has been a failure to obtain the authorized victim input prior to a parole decision.

For example, Arizona allows a victim to seek a re-examination proceeding regarding post-conviction release if there has been a failure to use "reasonable efforts" to provide the victim's right to be heard and if the offender has not been discharged from his sentence.[201] Oklahoma also authorizes a victim to request a reconsideration hearing if parole authorities fail to provide requested notice of the parole hearing at which the victim is allowed to testify. It permits parole authorities to reconsider any previous action taken.[202] Tennessee allows the victim to request a postponement of a parole hearing if it has been scheduled without the required notice to the victim. If the hearing has been held without the required victim notice and the victim submits a written impact statement within fifteen days after the parole decision has been finalized, the board must consider the statement and hold a new hearing if warranted by the impact statement.[203] Finally, in Pennsylvania, if the prescribed victim input has not been obtained prior to the parole hearing and parole decision, the parole board must evaluate the victim information within a reasonable amount of time after its submission. The board must then determine whether the parole decision should be affirmed or modified or whether a rescission hearing should be conducted.[204]

Thus, the crime victim right to be heard regarding parole has been significantly expanded since the President's Task Force recommendations. The expansion of this right is particularly noteworthy in light of the previously "closed" nature of parole decision making. Some of the variations in the provision of this right to be heard from that regarding the sentencing decision reflect the different setting, decisional process, and nature of the parole decision.

Judicial Interpretation

Despite the extensive adoption of this victim right to be heard regarding parole release decisions, it has been the subject of limited judicial interpretation. Construing language in a statute governing authorized presentations at minimum term and parole hearings, the Hawaii Supreme Court concluded that the statute permitted victims to make oral comments at these proceedings. Therefore, the Hawaii parole authorities had not erred when they permitted the mothers of two victims to make oral comments at the offender's minimum term hearing.[205] A Pennsylvania reviewing court examined the state parole board's denial of an offender request for victim impact statements on which it relied in its decision denying him parole. The court concluded that a state statute permitted the parole board to deem all or parts of submitted victim impact information confidential. The reviewing court found no abuse of discretion in the board's determination that these impact statements involving juvenile sexual assault victims should be confidential and thus not disclosed to the offender.[206]

In *State ex rel. Hance v. Arizona Board of Pardons and Paroles*,[207] discussed in Chapter 3, and *Daniels v. Traughber*,[208] victims in Arizona and Tennessee, respectively, were able to obtain reconsideration hearings regarding post-conviction release decisions that had been made without the prescribed notice to them. In the absence of such notice, they were unable to exercise their right to be heard. Moreover, in *Daniels*, the Tennessee appellate court found no due process violation from the rescission of the previously granted, but not yet implemented, parole following a subsequent hearing in which the authorized victim input was received.[209] As noted above, however, Arizona and Tennessee are among the few states providing such a reconsideration hearing remedy.

Even without such a reconsideration remedy, however, the Rhode Island Supreme Court upheld the parole board's rescission of a parole that had been initially authorized without the prescribed victim input in *Yang v. State*.[210] In this case, due to an administrative error, the victims had not been notified and afforded their right to address the parole board. Without hearing from the victims, a parole board subcommittee voted to release the offender to parole. When the notification error became known and prior to the issuance of a parole permit to the offender, the parole board allowed the victims to testify about the violent crime's impact on them. After also hearing from the offender and his attorney, the parole subcommittee rescinded its previous vote granting parole. The board stated that the rescission decision was based on the impact of the crime on the victims' lives. The appellate court found that because the initial parole decision had not yet become final through the issuance of a parole permit, the parole board retained the authority to receive and consider additional information and reconsider its initial parole decision. Thus, the parole board acted properly in rescinding its vote on the offender's parole.[211]

Prisoners have also been unsuccessful in more general challenges to the formal addition of victim input into parole decision making. In *Mosley v. Klincar*,[212] a state prison inmate challenged the denial of his parole request in federal court on the ground that the state's retroactive application of a victim notification provision to his parole proceeding violated the *ex post facto* provision of the United States Constitution. The offender claimed that the notification statute would increase the likelihood that victims would provide input into the parole process which would, in turn, reduce the likelihood of his parole. The Seventh Circuit Court of Appeals court noted that parole authorities had always been able to receive victim input. The contested provision merely required victim notification of the parole hearing, not a change in the criteria for granting parole. The appellate court thus concluded that the offender had failed to establish that the notification provision changed any "substantive" rights in violation of the *ex post facto* clause.[213] In *Johnson v. Rodriguez*,[214] the Fifth Circuit Court of Appeals rejected the offender's equal protection challenge to the Texas parole board's custom of accepting and considering "protest letters" in the parole process from victims and others in addition to the prescribed victim impact statements and comments. The appellate court found that the offender had failed to establish governmental action that improperly distinguished between two groups, a necessary prerequisite for an equal protection claim. The appellate court further found, in any event, that the parole board's practice of receiving information from victims during the parole process furthered victim rights, a legitimate and rational state purpose.[215]

Thus, in the few court decisions concerning the victim right to be heard regarding parole, reviewing courts have construed legislation to uphold the right and have upheld the exercise of the right in the circumstances presented for review.

Implementation and Analysis of the Right

Just as the victim right to be heard regarding parole has been the subject of much less judicial interpretation than the right to be heard regarding sentencing, it has also been the subject of significantly less analysis and empirical research. Those policy advocates and analysts who have addressed this right, however, have raised many of the same issues as have been raised regarding the victim right to be heard regarding sentencing. Their arguments have balanced expectations of victim well-being and satisfaction and more informed parole decision making against concerns about system efficiency and interjection of inappropriate factors into parole decision making.[216]

Some of the policy arguments have had unique aspects when applied to a victim's right to be heard regarding parole. Those arguing the relevance of victim input regarding parole note its usefulness in providing the parole board information regarding the crime that may not be reflected in the inmate's file. They also note the contribution that information regarding the crime's continuing impact may have on the assessment of an inmate's readiness for parole or parole risk. Opponents contend that such information is irrelevant to the paramount question of whether the offender's current behavior makes him an appropriate parole risk and is simply designed to intimidate parole board members into denying parole. In response to these conflicting positions, some analysts have urged legislators to better clarify the content, purpose, and consideration of victim input regarding parole to avoid its misuse.[217]

Some analysts have also noted the increased challenges of victim notification of this right in the context of parole, given individuals' mobility and the possibility of change in address information after the conclusion of the prosecution. Consequently, as seen above, states often give victims the responsibility to maintain current address information with parole authorities to preserve their right to provide parole input. Others question whether the time periods prescribed for victim notification are adequate to enable interested victims to provide input in the context of parole proceedings sometimes in distant locations from the victim's residence. Commentators have also noted that some victims are unlikely to exercise their rights to address parole boards because they fear reprisal from the offenders or simply due to the time and distance often required to attend parole hearings. From the offender's perspective, some commentators have raised due process concerns about the greater tendency in parole proceedings than sentencing proceedings to allow victim input to be offered confidentially or outside the presence of the offender.[218]

The expectations and concerns regarding the impact of this victim right have largely gone unrealized thus far because of the apparent failure of victims to take full advantage of their right to be heard regarding parole. Although often victim impact statements prepared in the trial court are routinely transmitted to correctional authorities, researchers in one state found that victims offered oral or written testimony in only 10% of initial parole consideration cases. Researchers conducting a Pennsylvania study found that in the initial five years after the requirement to allow victim testimony at parole hearings was adopted, victim testimony was offered in 71 initial parole consideration cases in 1987, in 350 such cases in 1989, and in 336 cases in 1991. In the 1989 study year, these 350 cases represented approximately 10% of the initial parole consideration cases the parole board heard.[219] Researchers also conducted a study of the exercise of a California right of allocution at parole hearings in the initial year following its implementation. Due to the application of the state determinate sentencing laws, only offenders serving sentences of life imprisonment received such hearings. At that time, most were serving sentences for murder without a significant likelihood of parole. During the 1983 study period, victims in less than 2% of parole-eligible cases expressed an interest in their allocution rights.[220]

These previous reports of limited victim participation regarding parole proceedings are consistent with the more recent reports of such in the 1995 study of victims in two "strong" and two "weak" victim rights states. Although 86% of surveyed victims said that it was "very important" to them to make a victim impact statement during the offender's parole hearing, only 14% of notified victims in "strong" states and 18% of notified victims in "weak" states attended the hearings in their cases. Of those who said that they were given an opportunity to make a statement at the hearing, 58% of "strong" state victims and 15% of "weak" state victims did so.[221] Although a relatively small number of the attending victims indicated that they were given an opportunity to make a statement at the parole proceeding, 69% of "strong" state criminal justice personnel and 88% of "weak" state personnel stated that victims were allowed to make statements at parole proceedings.[222] In an Alabama study of parole hearings conducted in 1993–1994, 33% of victims in felony cases involving personal injury attended the parole hearings at which there was an opportunity for oral or written victim input.[223]

Had more victims exercised their rights to be heard, however, the limited research that has been conducted suggests that their input potentially could have had an effect on the parole decision outcome. A national survey of parole authorities, reported in 1991, reflected that parole officials in almost every state considered the use of victim impact statements in parole decisions to be important. Parole authorities in twenty-four states indicated that victim input in their parole decisions was "very important," that it was "somewhat important" in six states, and that it was "important" in nineteen states.[224] Similarly, in interviews with parole authorities in thirty-four states in the late 1980s, researchers found that most interviewees indicated that victim statements were either given the same amount of weight as other factors or were given a "great deal" of weight. One interviewee noted that parole denial rises from 40%–50% in the absence of victim statements to 80% when statements are submitted. Most interviewees agreed that personal appearances by victims have a greater effect than written statements.[225] Finally, in the 1995 study, 75% of surveyed criminal justice personnel in the two "strong" states and 100% of personnel in the two "weak" states said that a victim's statement impacts the parole decision.[226]

These survey results regarding the impact of victim input in parole decision making are confirmed by a state study that compared the outcomes of
initial parole consideration cases in which the victim testified with a control group
of cases during a 1989 study period. These researchers compared 100 randomly
selected Pennsylvania parole cases in which oral or written testimony had been
offered with another 100 cases in which no such testimony was offered. In
their victim testimony, significant proportions of victims described the crime's
continuing physical, financial, and psychological impact and their continuing
fear of the offender. In their statements, 73% strongly objected to the offender's
parole release. A third of the victims indicated dissatisfaction with the criminal justice system's handling of their cases, sometimes expressing anger at their
exclusion from earlier stages of the case's processing.[227]

Parole was refused in 43% of cases in which the victim presented oral or
written testimony as opposed to 7% of the control group cases. The difference
in parole refusal rates persisted after researchers took into account the nature
of the crime, the offender's potential for recidivism, and other parole release
variables. Although the parole refusal rate in the control group was consistent
with the state parole guidelines' recommendation of a 10% refusal rate, the
refusal rate exceeded the policy guidelines' recommendations by 33% in the
victim testimony group.[228] In further analysis, the researchers found that the
presence of victim testimony was the most significant variable associated with
parole refusal decisions, even more significant than the inmate's unfavorable
institutional performance, the number of prior convictions, and the fact that
the victim suffered physical injury. Not surprisingly, within the victim testimony
group, a victim's expressed opposition to parole was significantly related to
parole refusal. Because of the significant effect that victim testimony had on
these parole decisions, the researchers urged the authorities to clarify the purposes for which victim input could be considered, to incorporate these purposes
objectively into the parole guideline structure, and to provide safeguards to
assure the reliability of the information conveyed.[229]

The impact of victim participation in parole decision making was also reflected in an Alabama study of 299 parole cases involving personal injury to victims in which victims were notified of parole hearings in 1993–1994. In this
study group, that involved inmates who had been pre-screened by parole authorities to be considered for parole, 57% of inmates were nevertheless denied
parole. In preliminary results from the study, researchers found that written
communications to the parole authorities, above a general threshold of such
communications, had a significant effect on parole decisions and that victim
attendance and oral participation at parole hearings had a greater negative impact on parole decisions than written submissions. In a follow-up study that

assessed the relative impact on parole decision making of various victim-related and non-victim-related factors, the researchers found that the level of victim participation at the parole hearings in comparison to offender participation was the second-strongest predictor (following the senior officer's recommendation) of parole hearing outcome. Their analysis also found that victim allocution and impact statements had significant associations with parole outcomes and that the greater the amount of oral or written input opposing parole, the more likely that parole would be denied.[230]

Another researcher studied the administrative records of a sample of 805 parole-eligible inmates regarding whom parole decisions were made by the New Jersey parole authorities in 2004. This sample included predominantly non-violent offenders (85%, including 54% drug offenders) and was divided between offenders with and without registered victims. Input from victims or non-victims was provided in approximately 22% of the cases. Received input was more frequently provided by victims (53%) than non-victims, more frequently written (69%) than oral, and more frequently negative (58%) than positive. Inmates with registered victims were more likely to receive negative written input from victims, but the quantity, severity, and violent nature of the underlying offense did not significantly affect the likelihood of the provision of input. This researcher found that parole was denied for 64% of inmates with negative input versus parole denial for 38% of inmates without negative input. However, in regression analysis, negative input by victims or non-victims was not a significant predictor of parole release (as opposed to the significant predictors of measures of institutional behavior, crime severity, and criminal history). This researcher did determine that victim input had a slightly greater impact on parole release decisions than non-victim input and that oral input had a greater effect on parole release than written input.[231]

In addition to the impact on parole outcome described by the above-described studies, researchers studying another group of victims who provided oral or written input to the parole board found that they were generally satisfied with their contacts with the criminal justice system. Researchers interviewed forty-one people who had provided or were in the process of providing oral or written input in California parole hearings. Almost all of those interviewed were survivors of murder victims in cases in which the offenders were serving life sentences. A "solid majority" of those interviewed felt that they had been "well served" by the criminal justice agencies. Although their reported satisfaction with the criminal justice system might result from the simple fact of the offenders' convictions and significant sentences, more than half nevertheless felt that the sentences were "too easy." Most were providing input to try to keep the offender in prison by emphasizing the nature and impact of the crime. Following the exercise of their allocution right, some victims expressed a sense of emotional release or satisfaction at fulfilling a perceived duty to the decedent in the murder cases.[232]

Although the empirical research regarding the impact of victim input concerning parole is limited, it suggests the potential for a more significant impact from the exercise of this right to be heard than has been established regarding sentencing. Some higher level of victim satisfaction than that detected regarding victim participation in sentencing might also be present. As in the case of the victim right to be heard regarding sentencing, the right to be heard regarding parole has not been fully utilized by victims.

Conclusion

Thus, in the years since the President's Task Force, the victim right to be heard regarding parole has been significantly expanded. Unlike the previous standard practice in which parole decisions were made behind "closed doors" without any opportunity for victim input, victims now may provide oral or written input, or both, in all federal and state jurisdictions. The limited judicial review of the exercise of this right has generally upheld its application. Finally, unlike the empirical research concerning the right to be heard regarding sentencing, the limited empirical research conducted thus far suggests that this often infrequently exercised victim right may have the potential to have a more significant impact on the parole decisional outcome.

Chapter 7

Remedies for Victim Rights Violations

As reflected in the previous chapters, the federal system and all of the states have ratified constitutional or enacted statutory provisions, or both, granting victims at least some rights of participation in the criminal justice process. As the examination of these provisions and the judicial interpretations of them have reflected, however, the victim rights that have been created are not limitless, especially when they risk conflict with pre-existing offender rights. In addition, available remedies for violations of the specific victim rights are often quite limited.[1]

Despite the numerous action recommendations contained in the President's Task Force *Final Report* concerning the establishment of means through which victims could participate in the criminal justice process, the Task Force was largely silent as to proposed remedies for governmental failure to provide authorized participatory—or other—victim rights.[2] The authors of the *New Directions from the Field* study, however, noted that governmental violations of prescribed victim rights continued to exist. They therefore recommended that victims should have standing and specific remedies to enforce their rights and sanctions should be applied to governmental officials who violate victim rights. They also recommended the establishment of governmental compliance enforcement programs to help facilitate the implementation of victim rights, such as the ombudsman and similar programs initiated in a few states. Finally, the study authors recommended governmental internal procedures to monitor compliance with victim rights, accompanied by public documentation of such and independent audits demonstrating the level of compliance and facilitating improvements.[3]

Although the states have adopted many of the Task Force recommendations concerning victim participatory and other rights, most states have also expressly limited the potential remedies for violations of these rights. A relatively small number of states have provided any express remedies for victim rights violations.[4] In the Crime Victims' Rights Act of 2004, Congress for the first time prescribed certain remedies for violations of victim participatory rights.[5] Prescribed limitations on and remedies for violations of *specific* victim rights have

131

been discussed in the previous chapters. In this chapter, similar federal and state provisions that apply to authorized victim rights *generally* are discussed.

Constitutional and Legislative Action

Federal Provisions

The most frequently used limitations on remedies for victim rights violations are constitutional or statutory provisions that expressly prohibit either any cause of action arising from a rights violation or any challenge to or alteration of the results in a criminal proceeding, or both. The last federal victim rights constitutional amendment proposal introduced in Congress prior to the enactment of the federal statutory Crime Victims' Rights Act in 2004 included a form of both limitations: "Nothing in this article shall be construed to provide grounds for a new trial or to authorize any claim for damages." The proposed amendment also permitted the prescribed rights to be restricted "when and to the degree dictated by a substantial interest in public safety or the administration of criminal justice, or by compelling necessity." The amendment proposal gave the victim or the victim's lawful representative the authority to assert the rights established in the constitutional provision and gave Congress the power to legislatively enforce the rights provisions.[6]

The federal Crime Victim's Rights Act itself has a variety of remedial and enforcement provisions as well as some remedial limitations regarding the prescribed victim rights to reasonable notice, presumptive presence, reasonable hearing, reasonable conferral with the prosecutor, reasonable protection from the accused, freedom from unreasonable delay in the proceedings, full and timely authorized restitution, and treatment with fairness and respect for the victim's dignity and privacy. At the outset, the Act generally requires that the court "shall ensure" that crime victims are provided the prescribed rights in court proceedings regarding the crime and the court shall clearly state on the record the reasons for any decision denying victim relief. The Act also requires federal governmental officials to make their "best efforts" to ensure that crime victims are accorded the prescribed rights. The Act gives the crime victim, or the victim's lawful representative, and the Government's attorney the authority to assert the prescribed rights. The Act also authorizes the Government to assert as error the trial court's denial of any victim right in any appeal from a proceeding to which the right relates. A defendant cannot obtain any form of relief under the Act.[7]

The Act requires that victim rights be asserted initially in the trial court in which a defendant is being prosecuted (or where the crime occurred if no prosecution is in progress). The trial court is required to decide any motion asserting a victim right "forthwith." If the trial court denies the requested relief, the movant may petition the appellate court for a writ of mandamus. The appellate court must decide the application within seventy-two hours after the petition has been filed. The reasons for any appellate denial of relief shall be clearly stated on the record in a written opinion. Trial court proceedings shall not be stayed or continued more than five days for purposes of enforcement of victim rights.[8]

The Act also contains some limitations of the remedial provisions. A failure to afford a prescribed victim right shall not provide a ground for a new trial. A victim motion to re-open a plea or sentence is permitted only if the victim has asserted and been denied the right to be heard before or during the proceeding at issue; the victim has petitioned the appellate court within ten days for a writ of mandamus; and, in the case of a plea, the defendant has not entered a plea to the highest offense charged. Nothing in the Act shall be construed to authorize a cause of action for damages or establish any duty for the breach of which the federal Government or its employees could be held liable for damages. Finally, nothing in the Act shall be construed to "impair" the prosecutorial discretion of the Attorney General or those under his direction.[9]

To facilitate and monitor compliance with the Act, Congress required the Attorney General to promulgate regulations establishing an internal Department of Justice process to receive and investigate complaints regarding the provision of victim rights; to require educational and remedial training and assistance for employees regarding victim rights; and to establish disciplinary sanctions (including termination) for employees who willfully and wantonly fail to comply with the victim rights provisions, with the Attorney General as the final arbiter of any complaint.[10] Congress also required the Administrative Office of the United States Courts to provide annual reports regarding the number of times a right provided in the Act is asserted in a criminal case, the instances in which the requested relief is denied (and the reasons given for the denial), the number of times the prescribed mandamus action is brought, and the result reached in each mandamus action. In addition to appropriations authorizations for federal victim/witness assistance programs and federal and state victim notification systems, Congress authorized the appropriation of $7,000,000 for fiscal year 2005, and $11,000,000 for each of fiscal years 2006–2009 to organizations that provide legal counsel and support services for victims in criminal cases for the enforcement of their rights in federal jurisdictions and states with rights provisions "substantially equivalent" to the federal Act. Congress additionally authorized appropriations for training and technical assistance to states to establish "state-of-the-art" victim rights laws and to design compliance systems. Finally, Congress directed the General Accountability Office to complete a study within four years of the Act's enactment to evaluate the "effect and efficacy" of the Act's implementation on the treatment of federal crime victims.[11]

In response to these provisions in the Act, the Department of Justice revised its Attorney General Guidelines for Victim and Witnesses Assistance in 2005 and established the Office of the Victims' Rights Ombudsman within the Executive Office of the United States Attorneys.[12] The 2008 amendments to the Federal Rules of Criminal Procedure incorporate the Act's provisions regarding assertion of victim rights in the trial court and the prompt resolution thereof, as well as the Act's limitations regarding precluding a rights violation as a ground for a new trial and re-opening a plea or sentence based on the denial of a right to be heard.[13]

State Provisions

In their constitutional provisions, most states limit victim enforcement and remedial provisions in some way. Fifteen states preclude any cause of action due to victim rights violations.[14] Fifteen states prohibit challenges to or changes in the results of proceedings.[15] Ten of these states include both limitations in their constitutional provisions.[16] In fact, the limitations language in the Kansas constitutional provision is lengthier than the language enumerating the authorized victim rights. After providing basic victim rights to be informed of and present at public hearings and to be heard at sentencing and other judicially determined "appropriate" times, to the extent that these rights do not interfere with prescribed rights of the accused, the amendment limits relief in connection with these rights.

> Nothing in this section shall be construed as creating a cause of action for money damages against the state, a county, a municipality, or any of the agencies, instrumentalities, or employees thereof. The legislature may provide for other remedies to ensure adequate enforcement of this section.
>
> Nothing in this section shall be construed to authorize a court to set aside or to void a finding of guilty or not guilty or an acceptance of a plea of guilty or to set aside any sentence imposed or any other final disposition in any criminal case.[17]

Some states include additional remedial limitations in their rights provisions. For example, Maryland, Nevada, and Oregon preclude any stays or continuances of proceedings as a result of victim rights violations or enforcement.[18] Connecticut, Illinois, Louisiana, and Virginia preclude appellate relief based on their rights provisions.[19] Washington expressly states that its rights amendment does not serve as a basis for providing a victim or his representative with court-appointed counsel.[20] A few amendments also state that the failure to provide any of the enumerated victim rights does not provide a basis for an *offender* to seek any relief.[21]

In addition to limitations of relief, some states also provide some remedies for victim rights violations in their constitutional provisions. Nevada authorizes a "person" to "maintain an action to compel a public officer or employee to carry out any duty required by the legislature" pursuant to its rights provision.[22] South Carolina provides that the constitutional victim rights established may be subject to a writ of mandamus to require compliance by any employee or governmental agency or entity responsible for the enforcement of the prescribed rights. It further provides that a "wilful failure" to comply with a writ of mandamus is punishable as contempt.[23] California authorizes the victim, the victim's retained attorney, the victim's lawful representative, or the prosecutor (upon the victim's request) to enforce the prescribed rights in any trial or appellate court with jurisdiction over the case "as a matter of right."[24] Oregon permits a victim or prosecutor (on victim request) to assert the prescribed rights in a pending case, via mandamus if no case is pending, or as otherwise authorized by law.[25] Texas gives the state, through its prosecuting attorney, the right to enforce the enumerated victim rights. It also gives the victim standing to enforce the rights, but does not give the victim standing to "participate as a party in a criminal proceeding or to contest the disposition of any charge."[26]

In addition to or instead of their constitutional provisions, approximately thirty-five states statutorily preclude any civil liability for or cause of action against governmental employees or entities arising from the failure to provide any of the prescribed victim rights.[27] Approximately fifteen states statutorily prohibit any change in criminal justice dispositions due to victim rights violations.[28] Over ten of these states include both limitations on relief in their statutory provisions.[29] Some states also have provisions stating that their victim rights provisions do not give a victim the right to direct the prosecution or that they do not give the victim standing as a party in the prosecution.[30] Thus, the majority of states have some type of limitation of remedy provision as to their authorized victim rights generally or as to a specific right.

Some states, however, in addition to or instead of limiting certain victim remedies, have provided statutory remedies or sanctions for violations of prescribed victim rights. A few states give the state or local prosecutor the general authority or responsibility to assert victim rights or to seek compliance with them.[31] Hawaii permits potential disciplinary action for the failure to provide prescribed victim rights.[32]

At least ten states have provided more specific compliance procedures in their statutes or otherwise. These states have established varying models of victim rights compliance mechanisms with varying powers. These compliance entities generally investigate victim complaints of rights violations and, if substantiated, attempt to resolve them with the non-compliant agency or employee or recommend (or require) procedural changes or training to avoid future complaints. In some states, substantiated rights violations are publicly disclosed in formal reports or otherwise.[33] In Colorado, if the compliance committee is unable to resolve a substantiated complaint, the committee refers the matter to the governor. The governor, in turn, requests the attorney general to file suit to enforce compliance with the victim rights provisions.[34] In Alaska, the victims' advocate has broad investigative powers regarding victim complaints of rights violations, supported by a misdemeanor financial penalty of up to $1,000 for a person who knowingly hinders or refuses to comply with the lawful actions of the victims' advocate. The victims' advocate also has the authority to advocate for a victim's rights in court in an ongoing criminal proceeding (to the extent that the victim would be able to do so).[35] In Wisconsin, the crime victims rights board can issue private or public reprimands for rights violations, seek equitable relief on behalf of crime victims, and bring civil actions to assess a forfeiture of up to $1,000 for intentional failures to provide a prescribed victim right.[36]

Some states allow the victim to directly pursue formal remedies for violations of rights provisions. For example, although South Dakota precludes causes of action based on failures to comply with its rights provisions, it authorizes a victim to file a written allegation of a rights violation with the court with jurisdiction over the criminal matter. The court, in its discretion, may determine whether additional hearings or orders are required to ensure compliance with the rights provisions.[37] North Carolina permits the failure or inability of a person to provide a prescribed victim right to serve as a ground for relief in a mandamus action by a victim, but not in any other criminal or civil proceeding.[38] Maryland gives a victim of violent crime the right to file an application for leave to appeal from an interlocutory or final order denying or failing to consider specified victim rights to notice, presence, hearing, and restitution. The victim's filing of such an application, however, does not stay other proceedings in the criminal case without the consent of all parties.[39] As discussed in the previous chapter, a few states authorize re-examination or reconsideration proceedings as to parole or other post-conviction release proceedings regarding which there have been violations of a victim's participatory rights.[40]

Utah authorizes an action for injunctive relief against a government official who "willfully or wantonly" fails to perform prescribed duties regarding victim rights, as well as against his governmental employer. The state also authorizes the victim, or his representative, to bring an action for declaratory relief or for a writ of mandamus to define or enforce the victim's rights. The victim also has a right to appeal adverse rulings in these actions or on victim motions or requests, provided that no appeal can be a ground for delaying any criminal proceeding. In addition, Utah authorizes a victim to petition to file an amicus brief in any court in any case affecting crime victims. Despite these broader remedial provisions than most states, however, Utah also precludes dismissal of criminal charges, vacations of convictions or guilty pleas, appellate relief from criminal judgments, or causes of action for monetary damages, costs, or attorney's fees based on victim rights or their violations. The state also provides that the prescribed victim rights do not create any victim right to appointed counsel at state expense.[41]

Finally, Arizona authorizes a victim to seek a re-examination proceeding within ten days of a proceeding at which the victim's right was denied (or with leave of court for good cause). Upon a victim's request, the court must hold a re-examination proceeding to consider issues raised by the right's denial, reconsider any decision arising from the proceeding at which the victim's right was not protected (subject to the limitations below), and ensure subsequent protection of the victim's rights. Arizona further grants a victim standing to seek an order, to bring a "special action," or to file an appearance in an appellate proceeding to enforce a prescribed right or to challenge an order denying such a right. Arizona also authorizes a victim to recover damages from a governmental entity for the "intentional, knowing or grossly negligent" violation of prescribed victim rights, subject to existing immunity provisions. As discussed in previous chapters, the state authorizes a victim to seek to re-open a plea or sentence in certain circumstances if the victim's right to be heard was denied before or during the related proceeding. The state also authorizes a re-examination hearing regarding a post-conviction release decision as a remedy for a related rights violation, unless the offender has been discharged from his sentence. Although Arizona has the most extensive remedial provisions for victim rights violations of any state, it also provides, however, that the failure to use "reasonable efforts" to perform a duty or provide a prescribed victim right is not a cause to seek to set aside a conviction after trial or provide grounds for a new trial.[42]

Thus, although most states expressly limit potential remedies for violations of prescribed victim rights in some way, several states—in addition to or instead of such limitations—provide some remedies for victim rights violations.

Judicial Interpretation

State Cases

As described in previous chapters, the lack of or limitations on remedial provisions for violations of prescribed victim rights have generally caused state reviewing courts to deny requested victim relief for rights violations.[43] In the absence of mandatory rights or clear constitutional or statutory enforcement or sanction provisions, some state reviewing courts have characterized victim rights as merely permissive or directory and therefore not judicially enforceable.[44] Other reviewing courts have recognized prescribed victim rights, but not the specific relief that victims have sought.[45] Finally, other reviewing courts have sought to appropriately balance prescribed victim and defendant rights in resolving victim claims for relief.[46]

Of course, as described in previous chapters, some state reviewing courts have upheld relief granted in response to actual or prospective victim rights violations. Appellate courts in Arizona and Tennessee applied the statutory remedy of reconsideration hearings regarding post-conviction release decisions made without the prescribed notice to victims.[47] Even without an express statutory remedy, the Rhode Island Supreme Court and an Alabama appellate court found that parole decisions made without prescribed victim notification or the right to be heard were subject to court review in the circumstances presented.[48] An Illinois appellate court granted court costs to a victim who filed suit to obtain notice of the status of his case after the prosecutor's office failed to respond to his requests for such information.[49] Appellate courts in California and Florida upheld the re-examination of restitution determinations made in the absence of prescribed notice to victims.[50] Finally, the New Jersey Supreme Court upheld the empaneling of a jury from another county rather than granting a venue change in order to facilitate victims' presence at the proceeding, among other factors.[51]

More frequently, however, as described in previous chapters, state reviewing courts have either found that a particular victim right or requested victim remedy does not exist under state law. For example, the Kansas Supreme Court's finding that state law did not require victim notice of judicial parole release hearings led to a subsequent legislative change in the law to expressly include required notification for such hearings.[52] The California Supreme Court's conclusion that no victim notice was legislatively required for a trial court's action to "recall" a previously imposed sentence on an offender and delay his subsequent resentencing[53] was indirectly addressed by the recent amendment and expansion of the state constitutional victim rights provision.[54] In addressing offender objections, the Oregon Supreme Court noted the state's concession that permitting victims to play the decisive role in the decision to accept a plea offer was impermissible under state law.[55] Similarly, a South Carolina appellate court found that victims do not have the right to "veto" a proposed plea agreement under state victim rights laws.[56] After construing the introductory language of the state constitutional victim rights provision that directed the state to treat victims with "fairness, dignity and respect for their privacy," the Wisconsin Supreme Court concluded that this language constituted a "statement of purpose that describes the policies to be promoted by the State and does not provide an enforceable, self-executing right." As such, its asserted violation by a prosecutor did not provide a basis for the private reprimand issued by the state victim rights board to the prosecutor for playing a dramatic 911 tape at the offender's sentencing hearing without prior notice to some of the murder victim's family members.[57]

State reviewing courts have also found that the prescription of a constitutional or statutory victim right does not always guarantee that it will be accompanied by prescribed victim remedies for its violation. In *Lamm v. Nebraska Board of Pardons*,[58] the victims filed a mandamus petition seeking to require the state pardons board to permit them to be heard at the offender's commutation proceeding, a victim right included in the state victim rights constitutional amendment. Although the victims' specific request became moot on other grounds, the Nebraska Supreme Court upheld the trial court's denial and dismissal of the mandamus petition based on its determination that the Nebraska Legislature had not enacted provisions to implement or remedies to enforce the constitutional victim rights provided, as required by the constitutional provision. Because the constitutional provision expressly required legislative action for its implementation and enforcement, the Nebraska Supreme Court concluded that the constitutional provision was not "self-executing." In the absence of legislative implementation or enforcement mechanisms regarding the victim right at issue, the trial court had correctly determined that it could not grant the victims' requested relief and therefore the trial court lacked subject matter jurisdiction regarding their petition.[59] The Nebraska Legislature subsequently enacted legislation stating its "intent" that its statutory rights provisions "shall be construed as enabling" the rights provided in the constitutional victim rights amendment. However, no express remedies are prescribed for rights violations in these statutory provisions.[60]

Even the existence of a remedy for a victim rights violation does not ensure that it will be available when it is asserted by a crime victim. For example, in *Ex parte Littlefield*,[61] the South Carolina Supreme Court noted that victim constitutional rights are expressly enforceable through a writ of mandamus rather than by "direct participation" in the prosecution. In their mandamus action, the petitioners sought to have the defendant's plea set aside because they did not receive sufficient notice of the plea hearing. The South Carolina Supreme Court concluded, however, that the mandamus remedy was not available to these petitioners because the prosecutions in which they had been named as victims had been dismissed on unrelated grounds prior to the plea proceeding. At the time of the plea proceeding, the petitioners were no longer "victims" with rights to notice and attendance at the plea proceeding.[62] Moreover, because the prosecution had been resolved through the defendant's plea and sentencing regarding the outstanding charges, the mandamus remedy could not have compelled the re-opening of the case so that the petitioners could attend the plea proceeding in any event: "A writ of mandamus under the Victims' Bill of Rights is reserved to enforce its provisions, not to re-open a case when a victim is unhappy with its outcome."[63]

State reviewing courts have generally declined to grant victim requests for rights violation relief that involve setting aside completed prosecutions. For example, the highest appellate court in Maryland and a Michigan intermediate appellate court both concluded that state law did not permit a validly imposed sentence to be set aside due to a failure to adequately notify the victim of the proceedings.[64] A Missouri appellate court upheld the defendant's challenge to the trial court's action in setting aside his judgment and sentence due to a violation of the victim's right to be present and heard at the proceedings.[65] Although the Utah Supreme Court found that the victim had properly exercised his prescribed appellate rights to pursue a violation of his right to be heard at a plea proceeding, the reviewing court found that the trial court's "re-opening" of the plea to hear from the victim at the defendant's sentencing before reaffirming the plea and sentencing the defendant remedied the previous rights violation.[66] Because it found that the trial court had adequately honored the victim's right to be heard as described above, the Utah Supreme Court did not address the trial court's additional action of denying the victim motions to set aside the plea, but noted that the "declaration of a misplea" was not a legislatively prescribed remedy for a rights violation and would raise double jeopardy issues.[67]

State reviewing courts have also declined to find that victim rights provisions authorize victims to undertake actions reserved for parties to the prosecution. For example, the Tennessee Supreme Court found that the trial court had erroneously permitted the deceased victim's family and its attorney to participate in hearings regarding a prosecutor's attempt to dismiss a more serious homicide charge in favor of a reduced charge.[68] Consistent with the principle noted by the United States Supreme Court that generally a "private citizen lacks a judicially cognizable interest in the prosecution or nonprosecution of another,"[69] the Colorado Supreme Court concluded that existing state victim rights laws did not give the victim the right to challenge the prosecutor's dismissal motion in the trial court or standing to appeal the court's order granting it.[70] Similarly, the Indiana Supreme Court held that a murder victim's parents lacked standing to intervene and challenge a sentence reduction agreement between the prosecution and defendant.[71] Although finding that a victim right to a prompt disposition of the trial process includes a right to address the trial court when that right is jeopardized, the highest appellate court in Massachusetts held that this victim right did not confer party status or standing on the victim that would authorize her filing a motion to revoke a stay of execution of the defendant's sentence pending his appeal.[72] State appellate courts, including the Arizona and Kentucky Supreme Courts and an Alaska intermediate appellate court, have rejected the notion that victim rights to be heard regarding sentencing or post-conviction relief give victims standing as "aggrieved parties" in the prosecution with rights to petition for relief from or seek appellate review of the merits of courts' sentencing or post-conviction relief decisions.[73] As the Arizona Supreme Court noted, even its more extensive victim rights remedial provisions did "not give the Victim standing to argue before an appellate court that the trial court's ruling in a criminal proceeding was error or to bring the types of action against the defendant that the State can bring."[74]

State reviewing courts have also found that their victim rights provisions do not provide victims a cause of action for damages based on their violation, in the absence of express remedial provisions establishing such.[75] For example, the Rhode Island Supreme Court concluded that, in the absence of legislative or constitutional liability or remedial provisions for rights violations, neither a negligence cause of action nor a constitutional tort accrued when governmental officials failed to notify crime victims of their constitutional and statutory rights.[76] Similarly, an Ohio appellate court held that an express provision in the victim rights statute that prohibited liability based on governmental officials' failure to satisfy its provisions, such as the right to notice of the defendant's release at issue, precluded the victim's suit for damages based on the rights violation. This statutory prohibition of liability and the absence of any common law duty or liability also precluded any related actions based on negligence, recklessness, malice, and wanton disregard for the victim's state law notification right. The appellate court further found that she had failed to establish any federal constitutional right that would support her federal civil rights action based on the notification violation.[77]

An issue related to this discussion of victim rights and remedies is the balance that state legislatures and courts have sought to achieve when victim rights and remedies pose potential conflicts with existing defendant rights and remedies. Some victim participatory rights, such as the rights to notice and to presence at non-testimonial proceedings, do not generally present conflicts with defendant rights. In the area of victim rights of presence at testimonial proceedings, however, most states have made this victim right conditional. This allows a trial court the discretion to exclude a victim from the courtroom in circumstances in which the victim's presence poses undue prejudice to the defendant's rights of confrontation and to a fair trial. In addition, although it is now well-established that victim input regarding sentencing is constitutionally permissible, in principle, trial courts have retained their ability to limit or exclude it if it poses undue prejudice to the defendant's due process rights. Finally, concerns about defendants' double jeopardy rights have been one of the primary reasons for the often express disallowance of rights or remedies that would allow victims to seek to overturn defendants' pleas, convictions, or sentences.[78] Although at least one state has legislatively announced that the state's "victim's rights are paramount to the defendant's rights,"[79] most states leave such balancing of rights to their courts.

The Arizona Supreme Court, the state with arguably the most extensive victim rights provisions, addressed the need for judicial balancing of victim and defendant rights in *State v. Bible*.[80] In finding a prosecutor's references to a homicide victim's rights improper, the reviewing court noted, "It cannot be doubted that victims of crime, and their families, have certain rights. It is equally clear, however, that these rights do not, and cannot, conflict with a defendant's right to a fair trial."[81] Although the court found no fundamental error in the prosecutor's improper remarks suggesting that the jury should consider the victim's rights as well as the defendant's rights, it cautioned that the court, not the jury, was responsible for balancing conflicting rights between the victim and the defendant.[82]

In reaching its holding on this issue, the Arizona Supreme Court cited *State ex rel. Romley v. Superior Court*,[83] a state appellate court ruling, in which a defendant's request for a crime victim's medical records was being resisted pursuant to a state constitutional victim rights provision giving a victim the right to refuse discovery requests from the defendant. In resolving the discovery request issue, the appellate court addressed the conflict between the victim's state constitutional rights and the defendant's state constitutional right to due process.[84] In balancing these constitutional rights, the appellate court noted that due process of law is the "primary and indispensable foundation of individual freedom in our legal system." The appellate court therefore held that "when the defendant's constitutional right to due process conflicts with the Victim's Bill of Rights in a direct manner, such as the facts of this case present, then due process is the superior right." The appellate court also concluded that the state due process rights were congruent with federal constitutional due process rights and that federal due process rights prevail over conflicting state constitutional rights.[85] Although the court remanded the matter for further proceedings, it ruled that the records should be disclosed to the extent necessary to assist in the presentation of the defendant's defense and to effectively cross-examine the victim.[86]

Thus, although generally upholding victims' exercise of prescribed enforcement and remedial provisions, state appellate courts have typically declined to expand such relief provisions beyond their express terms. In addition, state reviewing courts have been reluctant to establish remedies for victims whose rights have been violated in the absence of constitutional or legislative provisions granting such. Finally, state reviewing courts have recognized their responsibility to balance the sometimes conflicting rights of victims and defendants to ensure a fair process.

Federal Cases

Because of the recency of the enactment of the Crime Victims' Rights Act of 2004, the federal courts' interpretation and implementation of its remedial and enforcement provisions are still evolving. As in the state courts and as described in previous chapters, the federal appellate and trial courts have attempted to implement the Act's statutory provisions, but have thus far generally not extended them beyond their express terms.[87] For example, in the federal cases that have addressed asserted victim notification violations, some federal courts have either found no notification violation in the circumstances presented or have been able to fashion adequate remedies for any violations that consequently have not required the granting of requested mandamus relief.[88] Federal courts have acknowledged the Act's legislative presumptions against exclusion of victims at proceedings, but also the Act's provision for limitation of victim presence in appropriate circumstances.[89]

In the only reported case addressing the right to be heard regarding charging decisions, one federal trial judge found that the victim rights to confer with the prosecutor and to be treated with fairness required the prosecutor to consult with the victim regarding a dismissal motion and to report the victim's views to the court in connection with the dismissal motion.[90] Federal courts have upheld victims' rights to reasonably confer with the prosecutor regarding plea agreements and to be reasonably heard in trial court public plea proceedings, but have not extended these rights to include a victim right to control or to veto the plea agreements themselves.[91]

One federal appellate court has held that the victim right to be reasonably heard at sentencing generally includes a right to be *orally* heard by the court (subject to the Act's authorization of reasonable procedures in cases with multiple victims) to carry out the Act's intention that victims be "full participants" in the sentencing proceeding.[92] However, federal courts have denied victim access to requested portions of presentence reports.[93] They have also concluded that the Act does not provide crime victims a basis to utilize the Act's mandamus remedy to appeal a defendant's sentence or to exercise an independent right to appeal a sentence or a rights violation.[94]

In their review of victim mandamus petitions asserting participatory rights violations, federal appellate courts have thus far most often denied requested relief or remanded the proceedings with expressed concerns or instructions for the trial courts rather than grant the requested relief.[95] Federal appellate courts have been divided, however, regarding the appropriate standard of review that they should utilize in examining mandamus petitions filed pursuant to the Act. In *In re W.R. Huff Asset Management*,[96] the Second Circuit Court of Appeals declined to apply the strict review standard typically utilized in mandamus cases. The appellate court noted that the trial court is in a better position than an appellate court to ensure that "reasonable" procedures have been utilized to implement the Act's rights and whether victim relief is warranted under the Act. To implement the right to appellate review of trial court rulings provided by the Act's statutory mandamus remedy, the appellate court adopted an abuse of discretion standard.[97] In *Kenna v. United States District Court*,[98] the Ninth Circuit Court of Appeals determined that the Act's mandamus remedy was a "unique regime that does, in fact, contemplate routine interlocutory review of district court decisions denying rights asserted under the statute." Rather than using the traditional mandamus review standards, the appellate court found that a mandamus writ under the Act must be issued if the trial court's action constitutes an abuse of discretion or legal error.[99]

On the other hand, in *In re Antrobus*,[100] the Tenth Circuit Court of Appeals construed the Act and held that Congress' use of the term "mandamus" to describe its prescribed remedy for review of asserted rights violations required the use of the traditional mandamus review standard. This standard requires the establishment of a "clear and indisputable" right to the mandamus writ, such as those "exceptional" cases involving extreme abuse of discretion or a lack of jurisdiction.[101] The Fifth Circuit Court of Appeals agreed with the Tenth Circuit's analysis and also adopted the traditional mandamus review standard in *In re Dean*.[102] Rather than adopting either the abuse of discretion or the traditional, stricter mandamus review standard, the Fourth Circuit and District of Columbia Courts of Appeals determined that the petitioners before them were not entitled to mandamus relief under either review standard.[103] Although the federal appellate and trial courts' continued interpretation of the Act's remedial and other provisions will establish their actual scope over time, the United States Supreme Court will be required to resolve the conflict in the mandamus review standards that the federal courts utilize in this interpretive process.

Implementation and Analysis

Because so few jurisdictions have remedial provisions for victim rights violations, there has been only limited analysis of the implementation of these provisions. When it enacted the Crime Victims' Rights Act of 2004, Congress directed the General Accountability Office ("GAO") to complete a study within four years of the Act's enactment to evaluate the "effect and efficacy" of the Act's implementation on the treatment of federal crime victims.[104] In its 2008 report, among the items that the GAO examined were the internal victim complaint mechanism established in the Department of Justice pursuant to the Act and the trial and appellate court processes for the assertion of victim rights under the Act.[105]

To coordinate the internal victim complaint mechanism required by the Act, the Department of Justice established the Office of the Victims' Rights Ombudsman within the Executive Office of the United States Attorneys.[106] In its review, the GAO found that 144 written victim complaints were filed with the Ombudsman's office from December 2005 to April 2008. Of the 141 of these complaints that the GAO reviewed, 130 were closed following a preliminary investigation, with 99% of the file closures due to complaint filings that did not involve a federal crime victim or federal crime or that were filed against a non-Department of Justice employee. Following further investigation of the remaining eleven complaints, the Ombudsman determined that none substantiated a Department of Justice employee's failure to comply with the Act's victim rights provisions.[107]

While not independently assessing the reasonableness of the Ombudsman's determinations, the GAO explored potential reasons for the low number of written victim complaints during the study period. Department of Justice officials suggested that the low number of complaints reflected victim satisfaction with governmental efforts to afford victims their rights under the Act, as well as informal efforts to resolve any victim concern prior to it reaching a formal complaint stage. A GAO survey of 248 responding federal victims also revealed a low level of awareness of the complaint procedure: approximately 52% of responding victims stated that they were not aware that they could file a written complaint against Department of Justice employees regarding their rights and an additional 21% could not recall if they were aware of this opportunity. The complaint mechanism is referenced in Department of Justice victim-related materials. A GAO survey of 174 responding victim-witness professionals reflected that most do not routinely personally inform victims of the complaint procedure, absent some expressed victim concern. To strengthen the internal complaint procedure, the GAO recommended efforts to increase victim awareness of the process, ensure the independence and impartiality of investigators examining the complaints, and facilitate victim input in the complaint process.[108] To further strengthen Department of Justice employees' support of prescribed victim rights, the GAO recommended that the Department adopt performance measures to assess progress in this area and incorporate adherence to victim rights requirements in employee work plans and performance appraisals. The Department of Justice generally concurred with these recommendations.[109]

In the period from the Act's enactment through June 2008, the GAO identified forty-three instances in which victims (or prosecutors or victims' attorneys on victims' behalf) presented oral or written motions in the federal trial courts asserting their rights pursuant to the Act. Of the thirty-eight motions in which a decision was based on the Act, approximately 24% filed by a prosecutor on the victim's behalf were granted in full or partially; 8% filed by a victim (or victim's attorney) were granted; 16% filed by a prosecutor were denied; and 52% filed by a victim (or victim's attorney) were denied. During this same period, twenty mandamus petitions were filed that asserted victim rights under the Act (including eight petitions that did not arise out of criminal proceedings). Of the nineteen petitions in which a decision was based on the Act, only two were granted in full or partially.[110] The GAO's findings are fairly consistent with the annual reports of the Administrative Office of the United States Courts to Congress regarding trial and appellate court filings for fiscal years 2005–2007.[111]

Again, without assessing the merits of these court decisions, the GAO explored the reasons for the low number of court filings asserting victim rights. Although victim satisfaction with their treatment, trauma from the crime, and intimidation by the judicial process itself were each mentioned, victim lack of awareness of the court enforcement mechanism was the most frequently cited reason for the low filings. Of the 236 victims responding to the GAO survey regarding this issue, 57% stated that they were not aware of their ability to file a trial court motion to enforce their rights and an additional 20% could not recall if they were aware of this procedure. Information about this process is not included in most Department of Justice victim-related materials or routinely discussed with victims by victim-witness professionals (absent an expressed victim concern). The GAO concluded that the Department of Justice is in a better position than the courts to increase victim awareness of these court procedures and recommended that it expand efforts to do so. The Department agreed to explore this recommendation.[112]

As described previously, at least ten states have victim rights compliance mechanisms with varying powers, including investigation and attempted resolution of victim complaints of rights violations and recommended (or required) procedural changes or training to avoid future complaints.[113] The annual caseloads of these compliance entities varies, depending in part on the range of victim-related compliance services that each offers.[114] For example, in a 2004 report, the Wisconsin Crime Victims Rights Board summarized its activities since its establishment in 1998. In its two-tiered complaint system, most complaints are resolved through communication and mediation in the initial informal phase. For example, from January 2002 through December 2003, the Department of Justice mediator assisted 237 victims with their complaints. Only if the complaint is not resolved in this phase can the victim file a formal complaint to the Board. Since 1998, only ten formal victim complaints have been filed. The Board found probable cause of a rights violation in five cases and no probable cause in three cases. It issued a report and recommendation in one case without a probable cause finding and one case was still pending at the time of the report. Of the five cases in which probable cause was found, the Board issued three private reprimands and two reports and recommendations. One complaint was withdrawn before the Board's final decision. In its report, the Board made general recommendations to law enforcement officers, victim/witness coordinators, and prosecutors to increase and enhance their communication with victims in ways that reflect their respect for and understanding of the victim and the victim's role in the prosecution process under the state victim's rights laws.[115]

This more recent Wisconsin report is consistent with an earlier study of the Colorado, Minnesota, and Wisconsin victim rights compliance mechanisms. From 1993 to 1996, the first four years of the Colorado compliance program, approximately seventy inquiries were received by compliance personnel, with fifteen resulting in substantiated complaints of noncompliance with the state victim rights provisions. Of the 343 cases of alleged noncompliance brought before the Minnesota victim rights ombudsman from 1993 to 1996, 198 were resolved by a quick "assist," often within a few days of the filing of a complaint, or by referral to a more appropriate entity. In fifty-four cases, governmental personnel were found to be in compliance with the victim rights provisions. Complaints were found to be unsubstantiated or unfounded or investigations were discontinued due to victim noncooperation in seventy-two cases. The ombudsman substantiated noncompliance with rights provisions in only nineteen cases that were fully investigated. The Minnesota ombudsman staff sent surveys annually from 1993 to 1996 to victims whose complaints resulted in full-scale investigations and determinations. It found that between 72% and 82% of responding victims were satisfied with compliance services during the survey period. In 1996, the Wisconsin compliance entity attempted to survey the twenty-five victims who had had contact with it and received generally positive feedback from responding victims about the services they had received from the compliance personnel.[116]

On the other hand, the Alaska Office of Victims' Rights, established in 2001, has a broader range of available compliance services than these programs. In its 2008 annual report, this office reported that 353 cases were opened from July 2007 through June 2008. Of the 263 cases that had been resolved by the conclusion of the reporting period, 9% required advice and information only; 46% involved some greater degree of inquiry; 13% resulted in an informal investigation, but were nevertheless resolved through informal means; 2% required a formal investigation; and 30% involved agency staff attorneys' advocacy and argument in court on victims' behalf.[117]

The significant portion of the Alaska compliance office caseload that is devoted to courtroom assistance to victims is consistent with another compliance mechanism that has developed during the last decade—victim rights legal clinics. In 1999, the National Crime Victim Law Institute ("NCVLI") and a Victim Litigation Legal Clinic were established at Lewis & Clark Law School. NCVLI's goal is to protect, enforce, and advance victim rights. Pursuant to a grant from the federal Office for Victims of Crime, NCVLI has established (or expanded) and provided technical assistance to victim litigation clinics in nine states. NCVLI currently funds clinics that provide free legal services to facilitate victim rights in Arizona, Colorado (replacing California, a previous subgrantee), Idaho, Maryland, New Jersey, New Mexico, South Carolina, and Utah. NCVLI works with additional clinics in Ohio and Oklahoma. These clinics have represented over 1,000 victims in efforts to enforce their rights in criminal cases. Under its initial demonstration project grant, NCVLI distributed over $1,800,000 to participating legal clinics between 2003 and 2007. Most of a subsequent Office for Victims of Crime two-year grant of over $4,200,000 will be expended to allow NCVLI to continue its support of the eight clinics currently in its funded network and to establish up to four new clinics. NCVLI also participates as an amicus curiae in certain cases; provides education, training, legal resources, and technical assistance on victim rights to attorneys, victim advocates, victims, and others; maintains a national network of attorneys who are willing to provide pro bono services to victims; and crafts model victim rights law.[118]

It is anticipated that the work initiated by NCVLI to extend legal assistance to victims to enforce their rights will continue to expand. In the Crime Victims' Rights Act of 2004, Congress authorized the appropriation of over $50,000,000 for fiscal years 2005–2009 to organizations that provide legal counsel and support services for victims in criminal cases for the enforcement of their rights in federal jurisdictions and states with rights provisions "substantially equivalent" to the federal Act.[119] Victim rights advocates maintain that the expansion of legal services to victims will significantly enhance their ability to seek enforcement of their rights.[120]

Conclusion

Despite the states' widespread adoption of crime victim rights, enforcement provisions and remedial mechanisms for rights violations remain limited, or even prohibited, in most states. State reviewing courts have generally upheld victims' exercise of prescribed enforcement and remedial provisions, but these courts have typically declined to expand such relief provisions beyond their express terms. State reviewing courts have also recognized their responsibility to balance the sometimes conflicting rights of victims and defendants to ensure a fair process. The federal Crime Victims' Rights Act of 2004 contains more extensive enforcement and remedial provisions than those generally found at the state level. However, the evolving federal court interpretation and implementation of these provisions will ultimately determine their practical scope. Thus far, victims have made only modest use of the existing state and federal enforcement and compliance mechanisms, for reasons ranging from satisfaction with provision of victim rights to lack of knowledge of or assistance in the pursuit of enforcement options. In light of all of the above and as discussed more fully in the concluding chapter, some victim rights scholars seek additional means to more effectively enforce the victim rights that have been established since the President's Task Force on Victims of Crime.[121]

Chapter 8

Restitution

Introduction

When a crime occurs, both society and the crime victim incur a variety of costs. Society generally bears the costs of investigating, prosecuting, and punishing an offender for the crime, as well as providing government-sponsored services to the victim. Society also bears some or all of the costs of victim reimbursement for crime-related losses through private or government-sponsored insurance. Society incurs additional costs of victims' lost productivity as a result of their victimization. Crime victims, however, bear the costs of crime-related property and medical or mental health care losses that are not reimbursed through their own or government-sponsored insurance. They also may incur uncompensated lost workdays or lost school days or housework during their recovery from the crime or in connection with the criminal justice process. In addition, victims may experience pain and suffering or a reduced quality of life as a result of their victimization.[1]

Researchers have attempted to estimate the annual tangible and intangible victim-related costs associated with crime. The most comprehensive such effort was reported in 1996, with estimates based on 1993 cost valuations. Victim-related tangible loss estimates included costs associated with victim medical or mental health care, property loss or damage, lost productivity, victim services, and initial police, fire, or ambulance services to the victim. Intangible costs included those for victim fear, pain, suffering, and lost quality of life. Costs were estimated for the crimes of homicide, sexual and non-sexual assault, child abuse, robbery, arson, burglary, larceny, motor vehicle theft, and drunk driving.[2]

Estimated average losses per victimization ranged from a low of $370 in tangible losses for larceny or attempted larceny, with no additional intangible loss to a high of $1,180,000 in tangible losses for an intoxicated driving fatality with an additional $1,995,000 of associated intangible losses. Component costs varied significantly for the different crimes. For example, 69% of the average $1,400 loss for burglary consisted of property loss with 21% attributed to intangible losses. For the $87,000 estimated loss for each sexual assault, 94% was associated with intangible losses followed by 3% each for mental health care costs and lost productivity and less than 1% for medical care costs. For the approximately $3,000,000 estimated cost per victimization in the homicide categories, intangible losses ranged from 63% to 72% of the totals followed by lost productivity representing 26% to 36% of the total loss.[3]

In the aggregate, these researchers estimated annual tangible victim costs associated with the studied personal crime categories crimes at $105,000,000,000. They estimated an additional $345,000,000,000 of annual intangible costs associated with victims' pain, suffering, and reduced quality of life as a result of these crimes.[4] Other researchers determined that victims of personal fraud incur an additional estimated $40,000,000,000 in losses each year.[5]

Researchers in the general cost analysis study attempted to ascertain how the studied victim-related costs of crime were paid. They estimated that

> insurers pay $45 billion annually due to crime. That's $265 per American adult. Government pays $8 billion annually for restorative and emergency services to victims, plus perhaps one-fourth of the $11 billion in health insurance payments.
>
> Crime victims and their families pay the bill for some crimes, while the public largely pays the bill for others. Taxpayers and insurance purchasers cover almost all the tangible victim costs of arson and drunk driving. They cover $9 billion of the $19 billion in tangible nonservice costs of larceny, burglary, and motor vehicle theft. They cover few of the tangible expenses of other crimes.
>
> Victims pay about $44 billion of the $57 billion in tangible non-service expenses for traditional crimes of violence — murder, rape, robbery, assault, and abuse and neglect. Employers pay almost $5 billion because of these crimes, primarily in their health insurance bills. (This estimate excludes sick leave and disability insurance costs other than workers' compensation.) Government bears the remaining costs through lost tax revenues and Medicare and Medicaid payments.
>
> Crime victim compensation accounts for 38 percent of homeowners' insurance payments and 29 percent of auto insurance payments.[6]

Although private insurance and government-sponsored or societal sources cover a substantial share of the tangible costs of criminal victimization, victims nevertheless must bear the significant remaining loss of any unrecovered tangible costs of crime in addition to most of the intangible costs. Moreover, the victim-related costs of crime described above are even higher currently, as adjusted for inflation, since the 1996 study.

As discussed in Chapter 1, one of the initial goals of the victims' movement was to restore some of the restitutive concepts that characterized the earliest criminal prosecutions in ancient and pre-modern times as well as the earliest prosecutions in this country. Victim rights advocates decried the fact that crime victims should have to suffer financial losses in addition to the other personal losses resulting from criminal victimization.[7] Crime victims' needs for financial recompense were also addressed in the *Final Report* of the President's Task Force on Victims of Crime. In this and the next two chapters, victim financial remedies of restitution, crime victim compensation, and civil suit are discussed.

President's Task Force and *New Directions from the Field* Recommendations

As described in Chapter 1, restitution, i.e., an offender's repayment in kind or extent to a victim suffering loss or injury from a crime, was a central feature of the early victim-centered criminal prosecutions in this country. By the middle of the nineteenth century, however, restitutive damages to the victim were no longer actively pursued in the now government-centered American public prosecution system.[8] Although some penal reformers continued to advocate the use of restitution as a criminal sanction[9] and some American jurisdictions authorized its use as a condition of the developing probation sanction or otherwise,[10] the restitutive sanction was largely ignored in the American criminal justice process until the victims' movement returned attention to the sanction during the 1970s. During this period, several prestigious policy making bodies, such as the American Law Institute and the American Bar Association, also endorsed the expanded use of restitution as a criminal sanction.[11]

Prior to the issuance of the President's Task Force *Final Report*, only eight states had legislation mandating victim restitution as a part of an offender's sentence.[12] Shortly prior to the release of the Task Force *Final Report*, Congress enacted the Victim and Witness Protection Act of 1982 ("VWPA") that expanded the scope of the federal restitution sanction, established restitution as an independent sanction (rather than merely an optional probation condition), encouraged its increased imposition, and fostered improved monitoring and enforcement procedures.[13] To ensure that sentencing judges could address the expanded categories of victim losses compensable through restitution, Congress required the inclusion of a victim impact statement detailing such losses in the presentence report prepared by probation staff for the court.[14]

The VWPA's restitution provisions were much more detailed than those under earlier probation statutes. In cases of bodily injury to a victim, the

VWPA authorized a defendant's payment of the victim's costs regarding physical, psychiatric, and psychological care; necessary physical and occupational therapy and rehabilitation; lost income; and funeral expenses, if applicable. In cases resulting in damage to or loss of property, the VWPA permitted the return of the property or its value. In determining whether to order restitution and its amount, the VWPA required sentencing judges to consider the amount of the victim's loss from the offense, the defendant's financial resources, and the financial needs and earning ability of the defendant and his dependents. An evidentiary resolution of disputes concerning the type or amount of restitution was authorized. Installment payments of restitution were permitted under the VWPA with a maximum period for restitution payment of not later than the end of any probation period, five years after the end of imprisonment, or five years after sentencing in any other case. Both victims and the Government were allowed to enforce a restitution order in the same manner as a civil judgment. A judge was not required to order restitution, however, in instances in which such an order would unduly prolong or complicate the sentencing process.[15] In the materials accompanying the legislation, Congress expressed its intention to restore restitution's priority status in federal sentencing procedures through the VWPA and to serve as an example for the states.[16]

In its restitution recommendations, the President's Task Force adopted and even extended the model of the VWPA's restitution provisions. The Task Force recommended that federal and state executive and legislative authorities propose and enact legislation to "[r]equire restitution in all cases, unless the court provides specific reasons for failing to require it."[17] The Task Force further recommended that prosecutors should facilitate the imposition of restitution and that judicial authorities "should order restitution to the victim in all cases in which the victim has suffered financial loss, unless they state compelling reasons for a contrary ruling on the record."[18] In its commentary to this recommendation, the Task Force stated its recommendation for presumptive restitution was necessary to ensure that offenders were held personally accountable for the victim losses resulting from their crimes, regardless of the other aspects of their criminal sentences.[19] Authorization for victim restitution in the American criminal justice process increased rapidly in the years following the issuance of the Task Force *Final Report* and the enactment of the VWPA.[20]

The authors of the *New Directions from the Field* study noted progress in the adoption of restitution statutes since the *Final Report*. This progress included the enactment of statutes addressing restitution in every state and the adoption of some form of mandatory or presumptive restitution provisions by Congress and twenty-nine states as of 1995. However, the study authors identified much room for improvement in the imposition and collection of restitution for crime victims. The authors noted that restitution remained a significantly underutilized and under-enforced sanction. They reiterated the Task Force recommendation that all states adopt provisions that require full restitution for crime victims for all immediate and expected costs of the crime. In addition, the study authors recommended significant expansion and utilization of mechanisms to enforce court-ordered restitution, including its enforcement through probation, correctional, and parole mechanisms; increased criminal justice resources and use of technology to aid in the collection of restitution; and expanded use of civil mechanisms, such as automatic civil judgments reflecting the restitution award, garnishment, and liens. The study authors described examples of jurisdictions with successful restitution imposition and enforcement models.[21]

Constitutional and Legislative Response

The last federal victim rights constitutional amendment proposal introduced in Congress prior to the enactment of the federal statutory Crime Victims' Rights Act in 2004 included a right to "adjudicative decisions that duly consider the victim's ... just and timely claims to restitution from the offender."[22] Since enacting the statutory restitution provisions of the VWPA in 1982, Congress has continued to expand the federal restitution provisions. In the decade following the enactment of the VWPA, Congress added restitution to the list of factors federal judges must consider in imposing sentence; included restitution as an optional condition of the newly created "supervised release" following imprisonment for a federal crime; and expanded the government's restitution collection and enforcement powers. Congress also clarified and expanded the range of victims eligible for restitution following a defendant's conviction for federal offenses involving schemes, conspiracies, or patterns of criminal activity and regarding convictions requiring restitution as part of a plea agreement. In connection with the Violent Crime Control and Law Enforcement Act of 1994, Congress established mandatory restitution upon an offender's conviction for federal crimes of sexual abuse, sexual exploitation and other abuse of children, domestic violence, and telemarketing fraud.[23]

In addition to these specific offenses, as a result of the Mandatory Victims Restitution Act of 1996, restitution is currently mandatory upon a defendant's conviction for *any* federal violent or property crime in which there is an identifiable victim who has directly and proximately suffered physical injury or pecuniary loss.[24] In cases involving bodily injury to a victim, restitution is authorized for services and devices regarding physical, psychiatric, and psychological care; physical and occupational therapy and rehabilitation; lost income; and funeral expenses, if applicable. Restitution in property cases can include the return of property or its value. Restitution in all cases includes lost income and related expenses associated with a victim's participation in the investigation and prosecution of the underlying crime. The mandatory provisions do not apply to property crimes, however, if the court finds that the number of identifiable victims is so large that restitution is "impracticable" or that the determination of restitution is so complex that it would unduly complicate or prolong the sentencing process such that the burden on the sentencing process outweighs the need to provide restitution.[25]

Upon conviction for other federal crimes, including drug offenses, the imposition of restitution is discretionary. In determining whether to order restitution, the court must consider the amount of victim loss and the defendant's financial resources, needs, and earning ability and that of his dependents. The court may also consider the prolongation of the sentencing process that would result from fashioning a restitution order. In cases in which there is an identifiable victim, restitution is authorized for the same types of losses that are subject to mandatory restitution. In drug cases in which there is no identifiable victim, "community restitution" can be based on the amount of public harm caused by the offense. This type of restitution is distributed for crime victim assistance and drug abuse grants.[26]

In instances in which mandatory or discretionary restitution is imposed, the court "shall order restitution to each victim in the full amount of each victim's losses as determined by the court and without consideration of the economic circumstances of the defendant."[27] In determining the *manner* in which restitution is to be paid, the court considers the defendant's resources, assets, earning potential, and obligations. To assist the court in determining the amount of restitution and the manner of its payment, the probation officer preparing the presentence report includes an accounting of victim losses and information regarding the defendant's economic circumstances. In this connection, the defendant must file an affidavit with the probation officer describing his financial resources, assets, and needs and those of his dependents. Before submitting the report to the court, the probation officer must notify the victim of the restitution calculation and other sentencing-related information, as well as of the victim's ability to submit a separate affidavit detailing the victim's losses. The court must resolve disputes regarding the amount or type of restitution by the preponderance of the evidence, with the burden of demonstrating victim loss on the Government and the burden of demonstrating his financial resources and needs on the defendant.[28]

The court can order lump sum, installment, or in-kind payment of restitution. "Nominal periodic" restitution payments may be ordered in instances
in which the court finds the defendant's financial circumstances "do not allow
the payment of any amount of a restitution order, and do not allow for the
payment of the full amount of a restitution order in the foreseeable future
under any reasonable schedule of payments."[29] A defendant's liability to pay
restitution terminates twenty years from the entry of judgment or release from
imprisonment, whichever is later, or upon the defendant's death. The Attorney General is responsible for the collection of unpaid restitution and is authorized
to use the general means available to enforce civil judgments, such as liens and
garnishment. A victim named in a restitution award can also record an ab-
stract of judgment reflecting the defendant's restitution obligation, which serves
as a lien on the defendant's property as defined by state law. The court can utilize a variety of sanctions upon a defendant's default of his restitution obligations, in appropriate circumstances, including modification or revocation of
probation or supervised release, resentencing, contempt, injunctive relief, and
forced sale of property. The restitution provisions do not create any cause of
action against the federal government or its employees.[30]

In addition to these federal restitution-specific provisions, the Crime Victims' Rights Act of 2004 includes a victim right to "full and timely" restitution,
as authorized by law. The enforcement mechanisms provided in the Act, discussed in the previous chapter, are available to enforce this victim right to
restitution.[31]

Restitution provisions have also been expanded significantly by the states
since the President's Task Force. Twenty of the thirty-three states that have victim rights constitutional amendments include some type of a victim right to
restitution in their provisions.[32] Every state has statutory restitution provisions.[33] Some states include a general right to restitution or to information
about restitution in their statutory lists of victim rights.[34] In addition, most
states have separate restitution statutes, in their victim rights or sentencing
provisions, that authorize restitution as a probation condition or as an independent sentence, or both. Some states also authorize restitution as a parole
or work release condition.[35]

A growing number, representing a majority of the states, use language in their
statutory provisions that creates a presumption that the imposition of restitution is mandatory (at least for certain crimes).[36] For example, upon conviction, Arizona courts must order offenders to make restitution to their victims
"in the full amount of the economic loss" suffered. An offender's economic
circumstances may not be considered in the court's determination of the amount
of restitution, but only as to the manner of its payment.[37] However, other states

that appear to make the imposition of restitution mandatory, authorize courts to require no restitution, or at least less than full restitution, based on a variety of factors unrelated to victim loss, such as an offender's financial circumstances; other factors that render restitution impracticable or unworkable; or extraordinary, compelling, or other reasons the court articulates on the record.[38] In a significant minority of the states, the imposition of restitution is permissive and within the discretion of the sentencing authority.[39]

States vary to some degree in their legislative definitions of the eligible recipients of restitution. For example, Alabama broadly authorizes restitution for any "person whom the court determines has suffered a direct or indirect pecuniary damage as a result of the defendant's criminal activities."[40] Some states expressly identify deceased victims' survivors as eligible restitution recipients.[41] Some states specifically include institutional entities that are direct victims of crime.[42] Other states expressly include reimbursing insurers or victim compensation funds, or both.[43]

Unlike victim participatory rights that are often limited to victims of certain types or categories of crime, states generally permit restitution in both misdemeanor and felony cases involving either violent or property crimes.[44] There is some variation among the states, however, regarding the conviction status of the criminal conduct that can serve as the basis for restitution. Some states restrict restitution to offenses for which an offender has been convicted.[45] Many states, however, expressly authorize restitution regarding uncharged or unconvicted offenses if an offender has admitted to guilt concerning such or has agreed to make restitution for such in a plea agreement. For example, Wyoming defines "criminal activity" for restitution purposes as "any crime for which there is a plea of guilty, nolo contendere or verdict of guilty upon which a judgment of conviction may be rendered and includes any other crime which is admitted by the defendant, whether or not prosecuted."[46] Florida expressly provides that a "plea agreement may contain provisions that order restitution relating to criminal offenses committed by the defendant to which the defendant did not specifically enter a plea."[47]

Although there is some variation in the statutory provisions regarding the types of items for which state victims can recover restitution, most states that expressly address the subject limit recovery to tangible losses. For example, Arkansas' provision allows restitution for a victim's "actual economic loss" from the crime.[48] Oklahoma's provision covers "medical expenses actually incurred, damage to or loss of real and personal property and any other out-of-pocket expenses, including loss of earnings, reasonably incurred as the direct result of the criminal act of the defendant."[49] Some states, including Indiana and Texas, follow the federal model and itemize recoverable tangible losses such as those for property damage or loss, medical care, lost income, and funeral expenses, if any.[50] In addition, some states, such as Idaho, expressly preclude restitution recovery for intangible losses, such as pain and suffering or emotional distress.[51] Some states generally define restitution recovery in terms of the losses that a victim could recover in a civil action against an offender, but most also expressly exclude the types of intangible losses that could potentially be recovered in a civil action. For example, Iowa defines "pecuniary damages" that are recoverable through restitution as "all damages to the extent not paid by an insurer, which a victim could recover against the offender in a civil action arising out of the same facts or event, except punitive damages and damages for pain, suffering, mental anguish, and loss of consortium."[52]

Although they vary in specific details, the state procedural provisions regarding the imposition of restitution are fairly similar to the federal provisions.[53] Courts in most states use information supplied by victims and offenders for presentence reports, as supplemented by information offered at sentencing proceedings, to fashion their restitution orders.[54] In states in which full restitution is not mandatory and in which restitution criteria are specified, courts are usually instructed to consider the victim's loss and the offender's economic circumstances in determining the amount of restitution, if any, and the manner of its payment.[55] Restitution decisions are usually finalized in summary fashion at the sentencing hearing or special restitution hearings. The court generally resolves disputed issues by the preponderance of the evidence, with the government bearing the burden of proof regarding victim-related matters and the offender bearing the burden concerning defendant-related matters.[56] In the majority of states, a restitution order is enforceable in the same manner as a civil judgment.[57] In addition, some states provide specific restitution collection mechanisms, such as restitution liens and wage assignment.[58] Of course, the sentencing judge retains the authority to impose sanctions upon an offender's willful default of his restitution obligations, as do parole authorities, in appropriate cases.[59]

In the states described in Chapter 7 that have specific enforcement provisions for violations of victim rights, presumably these enforcement mechanisms could be pursued in instances in which a victim asserted that the right to restitution had been denied.[60] In fact, Maryland specifically includes a denial of or failure to consider a victim's right to restitution among the rights subject to its right to appeal provision.[61] As previously discussed, however, a relatively small number of states even have such enforcement provisions and many are limited in actual scope. Victims in most states do not have an express mechanism to challenge restitution determinations. This leaves dissatisfied crime victims in the position that is articulated in Wyoming's restitution provisions: "In the event that the victim is not satisfied with the restitution plan approved or modified by the court, the victim's sole and exclusive remedy is a civil action."[62]

Thus, these federal and state provisions reflect a significant re-emergence of restitution as a criminal sanction in the years since the President's Task Force. However, some limitations in the scope and implementation of restitution remain.

Judicial Interpretation

In the years since the President's Task Force *Final Report*, federal and state reviewing courts have addressed defendant challenges both to the structure of their restitution processes and to particular restitution awards made pursuant to them. There have been few opportunities, however, for crime victims to obtain judicial review of restitution awards.

Federal Cases

Following the enactment of the VWPA, federal reviewing courts addressed constitutional challenges to the facial validity of the restitution structure prescribed by it and its subsequent amendments. Constitutional challenges were raised on Fifth, Seventh, and Eighth Amendment grounds. More recent challenges have been raised on Sixth Amendment grounds.[63]

Appellate courts rejected claims that the VWPA's restitution procedures transformed the judicial sentencing proceeding into a "juryless" civil proceeding in violation of the Seventh Amendment. Reviewing courts characterized restitution as a form of punishment that serves recognized punishment goals of deterrence, rehabilitation, and retribution. These courts concluded that the civil aspects of restitution do not transform a criminal sentence into a civil proceeding requiring fact finding by a jury.[64] More recently, federal reviewing courts have held that the United States Supreme Court's holding in *Apprendi v. New Jersey*,[65] that fact finding that increases the maximum penalty for a crime requires a jury determination under the Sixth Amendment, does *not* apply to judicial fact finding involved in a determination of restitution.[66]

Federal reviewing courts rejected Fifth Amendment due process challenges to the VWPA restitution statute. They concluded that considerations required by the restitution statutes, as well as the protections given to each defendant by Federal Rule of Criminal Procedure 32 to challenge presentence information, to make a statement in his own behalf, and to present any information in mitigation of punishment, provide a sufficient basis to ensure a defendant's due process rights regarding restitution ordered at sentencing.[67]

Fifth Amendment equal protection challenges to the VWPA were raised on the ground that it lacked sufficient standards for its imposition and thus would result in impermissible disparate treatment of defendants. Reviewing courts found that the individualized restitution sentences contemplated by the VWPA permissibly required judges to exercise their discretion in this area of sentencing.[68]

Federal reviewing courts also rejected Fifth Amendment equal protection and Eighth Amendment cruel and unusual punishment claims that restitution may not be imposed under the VWPA on defendants who are indigent at sentencing. These courts noted that because the restitution statutes allow an extended period of time within which to satisfy a restitution order, indigence at sentencing is not a bar to restitution. Constitutional concerns would be raised only if a restitution order were enforced at a time when a defendant, through no fault of his own, was unable to comply.[69]

Although the VWPA and its subsequent amendments successfully survived all of the above constitutional challenges, in *Bearden v. Georgia,*[70] the United States Supreme Court addressed the final noted constitutional concern in a state proceeding in which an offender's probation had been revoked due to his inability to pay his restitution and fine. In this case, the offender had timely made his initial restitution and fine payments. The illiterate and indigent offender was unable to complete his payments on time because he lost his job and was unable to secure another one. The trial court revoked his probation due to his failure to complete his payments and sentenced him to a period of incarceration. The offender contended on appeal that his imprisonment for inability to pay his financial obligations violated his equal protection rights. The Supreme Court found that the trial court's *automatic* revocation of the defendant's probation and the resulting sentence of incarceration violated the defendant's due process rights in the absence of the trial court's exploration of the reasons for nonpayment or non-incarceration alternatives.[71]

The initial provisions of the VWPA required the court to consider an offender's employment status, earning ability, financial resources, the willful nature of the offender's nonpayment, and any other circumstances regarding the defendant's ability to pay, before determining whether to revoke probation for nonpayment.[72] Following *Bearden,* however, Congress amended and extended these provisions. Although the court may resentence a defendant who knowingly fails to pay restitution, the court can resentence a defendant to a term of imprisonment only for a willful failure to pay without sufficient bona fide efforts to pay and in the absence of suitable alternative punishments. A defendant cannot be incarcerated under this provision "solely on the basis of inability to make payments because the defendant is indigent."[73]

In addition to resolving facial constitutional challenges to their restitution statutes, federal appellate courts have addressed questions concerning the scope of the statutes, such as the types of victims, victim losses, and offenses covered by the restitution provisions. Significant early federal litigation concerned the VWPA's authorization of restitution to "any victim of the offense" upon a defendant's conviction.[74] Appellate courts differed as to whether this provision permitted courts to require defendants charged with multiple offenses, but actually convicted of fewer offenses, to make restitution for losses related to the other alleged crimes.[75] The Supreme Court resolved the issue, in 1990, by holding that the "language and structure of the [VWPA] make plain Congress' intent to authorize an award of restitution only for the loss caused by the specific conduct that is the basis of the offense of conviction."[76] Soon after this decision, however, Congress clarified and expanded the scope of restitution provisions regarding offenses involving schemes, conspiracies, and patterns of criminal activity, as well as regarding convictions requiring restitution as part of a plea agreement, significantly increasing the number of victims eligible for restitution. The current restitution provisions have not only maintained this expanded restitution coverage, but have also further expanded the statutory definition of "victim" to include representatives for minor, incompetent, incapacitated, or deceased victims and community restitution in certain drug cases in which there is no identifiable victim.[77]

The federal courts have imposed and upheld a wide range of restitution awards for victims. In addition to the human, direct victims eligible for restitution, reviewing courts have found restitution warranted for some indirect human crime victims, such as family members or incidental persons suffering losses as a result of an offender's commission of crimes against direct victims.[78] Appellate courts have also upheld restitution awards to entities directly and sometimes indirectly victimized by defendants.[79] Restitution orders in the millions of dollars have been upheld when supported by evidence of victim loss.[80] In addition to direct losses resulting from a criminal act, reviewing courts have upheld restitution for various ancillary costs associated with the crime, including pre-judgment and post-judgment interest.[81] Reviewing courts, however, have generally not upheld those costs deemed to be consequential damages, such as attorney, accounting, and investigator fees in certain circumstances.[82] Nevertheless, as interpreted by the federal courts, the scope of the federal restitution provisions can be significant.

Although federal courts have generally interpreted their restitution provisions to authorize a wide range of restitution awards for victims, they have not afforded victims many opportunities to challenge restitution rulings that have been made. Federal reviewing courts have found that, under the VWPA's provisions, direct and indirect victims have suffered no "direct injury sufficient to invoke a federal court's jurisdiction to rule on their claim[s]" in circumstances in which they have either been denied requested restitution or previously granted restitution has been rescinded. Unlike the defendant who alone "suffers the direct consequences of a criminal conviction and sentence," victims are "[c]ollateral individuals to the proceeding," without standing to appeal from a restitution ruling[83] or to seek mandamus review of it.[84] These reviewing courts have based their standing conclusions on the language and history of the VWPA restitution provisions: "Nowhere in the statute does Congress suggest that the VWPA was intended to provide victims with a private remedy to sue or appeal restitution decisions, and nothing in the statute's legislative history supports such a reading, either."[85] At least one reviewing court, however, has found victim standing to litigate a trial court's release of a lien entered under the Mandatory Victims Restitution Act in connection with a restitution award.[86]

Thus far, victims attempting to use the mandamus remedy to enforce their right to restitution under the Crime Victims' Rights Act have not been successful in challenging the restitution decisions made in the trial court.[87] For example, the Second Circuit Court of Appeals rejected a mandamus challenge to a settlement agreement in a complex fraud case involving potentially tens of thousands of victims. The appellate court found that the instant case fell under the exceptions to the imposition of mandatory restitution in complex property crime cases, as well as the provision permitting the trial court to adopt "reasonable procedure[s]" to provide the rights prescribed by the Crime Victims' Rights Act in cases involving multiple crime victims. In these circumstances, the reviewing court held that the trial court did not abuse its discretion in approving a settlement agreement that established a $715,000,000 fund for victims rather than undertaking prolonged and uncertain proceedings in an attempt to seek "full" restitution for all crime victims.[88] The Fifth Circuit Court of Appeals upheld the trial court's abatement of the criminal proceedings, vacation of conviction, and declination of the imposition of restitution regarding a defendant who died before his sentencing hearing and while his appeal was pending, finding that the Act's right to restitution was subject to the abatement doctrine.[89]

State Cases

State reviewing courts have followed the federal appellate court examples in rejecting similar constitutional challenges to their restitution provisions.

They have found that restitution serves legitimate punishment purposes, such as rehabilitation, deterrence and protection of the public,[90] as well as the remedial purpose of providing compensation to victims of crime.[91] Despite some of its civil aspects, state reviewing courts have found that no jury is constitutionally required for the determination of restitution.[92] Although state appellate courts have found that defendants are entitled as a matter of due process to counsel and a hearing at which they can contest underlying facts regarding a restitution award, no greater formalities are required beyond those otherwise provided in a defendant's sentencing hearing.[93] State reviewing courts have rejected "excessive fine" and cruel and unusual punishment constitutional challenges regarding the amounts of particular restitution awards in connection with a particular defendant's financial circumstances.[94] They have also rejected equal protection and due process challenges and have upheld the imposition of restitution on offenders with current limited, but future potential ability to pay.[95] Just as the federal appellate courts, they have noted that constitutional issues would be more appropriately addressed to the relationship between an offender's indigence and the enforcement of a restitution order rather than its imposition.[96] Thus, in terms of challenged probation revocations based on a failure to pay restitution, state appellate courts have incorporated the *Bearden* criteria into their reviews of such contested revocations.[97]

Reviewing state courts have generally interpreted their restitution provisions as broadly as the federal courts. State courts have upheld restitution awards to a wide range of direct and indirect human and institutional victims of crime.[98] Individuals directly victimized by crimes ranging from assault and burglary to false swearing and disorderly conduct, have received restitution awards.[99] Humans indirectly victimized by crime have also received restitution in some instances, such as victims' family members or persons whose property was damaged during offenders' commission of crimes against others.[100] Entities directly victimized in crimes ranging from theft or embezzlement to fraudulent receipt of public assistance or other funds, have been awarded restitution.[101] Restitution has sometimes also been granted to indirectly victimized entities, such as direct victims' insurers or employers.[102]

State courts typically grant victims restitution designed to compensate them for direct losses from crime, such as costs of medical treatment in cases of physical injury or those associated with direct property loss.[103] Depending in part on the scope of state restitution provisions, reviewing courts have reached varying results regarding the award of restitution for victims' indirect losses from crime, such as lost income or profits or investigative costs.[104] Most state courts have declined to award restitution for unliquidated damages, such as those for pain and suffering associated with the crime.[105]

As described in previous chapters, state reviewing courts have generally found that crime victims do not have standing to challenge the merits of court orders or judgments,[106] presumably including those concerning restitution. However, at least two state appellate courts have concluded that victims have greater standing rights regarding procedural matters relating to restitution than those recognized regarding other issues. A California appellate court reached its decision in the context of a violation of a victim's rights to notice of and presence and hearing at a "sentencing" proceeding in which the court terminated a previously imposed restitution order. In granting the requested writ of mandate to set aside the termination order, the appellate court distinguished restitution-related matters from other sentencing issues regarding which violations of victim rights might not deprive a court of jurisdiction to proceed: "[A]s to restitution, the notice and right to appear requirements [under state law] are mandatory. If the requirements are not satisfied, the victim may challenge a ruling regarding restitution."[107] Similarly, a Florida appellate court granted a victim's certiorari petition to permit reconsideration of the distribution of restitution awarded to victims at a plea proceeding of which the petitioner victim received insufficient notice. With no opposition from the defendants, the appellate court remanded the restitution order for a hearing with notice to all victims so that the petitioner victim's request for a proportionate division of the restitution could be considered.[108]

Although these decisions were related to procedural rights regarding the restitution decision rather than the merits of the decision itself, they acknowledge a distinction between the victim's interest in restitution and other sentencing issues. Similarly, some courts reviewing their abatement doctrines regarding a defendant's death prior to the completion of a direct appeal have cited the potential extinguishment of a victim's restitution award as a factor in their decisions.[109] Nevertheless, in most states, there is not a mechanism for reviewing courts to consider victim challenges regarding the *merits* of trial judges' restitution orders.[110]

Implementation and Analysis of the Remedy

As the preceding discussion demonstrates, in the years since the President's Task Force on Victims of Crime, victim restitution has re-emerged as an extensively authorized, and often a presumptively required, criminal sanction. Its re-emergence has been actively promoted by those seeking to incorporate a greater range of victim rights in the criminal justice process.[111] The return of restitution has been justified on the ground that its imposition furthers many of the basic aims of the criminal and punishment processes.

On a general level, some theorists advance a restitutive concept of justice or punishment. This approach does not seek to return to the ancient victim-dominated systems of justice, but it does recognize a role for the victim as well as for the government and offender in the pursuit of justice and punishment. In addition to the enforcement of criminal justice as a means to maintain societal law and order and punish individual offenders, it identifies victim restitution as a third element of punishment. Although satisfaction from the conviction and punishment of an offender provides some "spiritual" gratification to a victim, material reparation for injuries or losses suffered as a result of the crime provides a more complete restitutive component of punishment.[112]

Other theorists maintain that restitution furthers most of the existing goals of the criminal justice process, such as rehabilitation, deterrence, and retribution. These theorists suggest that restitution promotes rehabilitative goals of increasing an offender's responsibility and accountability by requiring him to acknowledge the specific harm his act has caused the victim. Through the satisfaction of his restitution obligation, an offender can gain a greater sense of self-worth and accomplishment. Restitution's implicit requirement that an offender recognize the cost of his criminal behavior is also viewed as having a deterrent effect on his future criminal activities and those of others. Finally, by emphasizing the wrongfulness of an offender's conduct and his moral responsibility for it and by seeking to make the victim, as well as society, "whole" through punishment, restitution serves retributive punishment goals.[113]

In addition to these punishment goals, restitution is viewed as promoting several specific objectives of the participants in the criminal justice process. At the most obvious level, if restitution covering a victim's loss is imposed and paid, restitution addresses a victim's economic objectives from the process. This economic redress is also viewed as furthering a victim's psychological recovery from the offense. From an offender's viewpoint, if the punishment goals of restitution are accomplished, it is argued that restitution will result in reduced offender recidivism. Of more immediate "benefit" to an offender, use of restitution is often advocated as an alternative to harsher, and more intrusive, forms of punishment. These offender objectives contribute to the purported larger justice system objective of reduced justice system costs from the use of restitution. More generally, it is argued that use of restitution will enhance the public credibility of the criminal justice system.[114]

The achievement of so many goals and objectives would be a daunting task for any criminal sanction. The challenge of such a task is only made more difficult by the fact that some of the goals and objectives are conflicting so that the priority given to or achievement of one often results in the unfulfillment of another. For example, if victim recovery of loss is perceived to have less importance than offender rehabilitation, restitution may not be imposed or, if imposed, may not be actively enforced if such is deemed unnecessary to achieve rehabilitative goals.[115] Thus, as the following discussion shows, despite the enormous expansion of the constitutional, legislative, and judicial authorization of restitution over the past thirty years, restitution has not been able to achieve many of the goals and objectives identified by its advocates.

Recovery of Victim Economic Loss

As previously indicated, medical, property, and productivity costs associated with criminal victimization are estimated to exceed $100,000,000,000 each year.[116] Victims recover only a fraction of these costs through restitution. This restitution recovery deficit is attributable to many factors. At the outset, restitution is not the only mechanism for the recovery of victim loss. Victims may also obtain recovery through insurance, government-sponsored crime victim compensation, civil suit, and various other means.[117] A victim may also recover his loss from a wrongdoer informally and without the involvement of the criminal justice process, as when a thief returns stolen property and no criminal remedies are pursued by the property owner.[118] With regard to restitution itself, however, it—like all criminal sanctions—is a sanction of limited application. Its imposition requires that a crime be reported and that an offender be apprehended, prosecuted, convicted, and sentenced to pay restitution to the victim. The ultimate recovery of restitution is, of course, dependent on the offender's actual payment of his restitution obligation.

The majority of victims do not receive restitution because they fail to report their victimization to the police. According to the 2008 National Crime Victimization Survey, victims reported approximately 47% of the major violent crimes and 40% of the major property crimes measured by the survey.[119] The absence of a reported crime obviously precludes the prosecution process that could provide victim restitution. Even if a crime is reported to the police, the majority of reported crimes do not result in an arrest and conviction. According to the 2008 Uniform Crime Reports, the clearance rate was only 45.1% for measured violent crimes and 17.4% for measured property offenses.[120] In the 2008 reporting year, approximately 14,006,000 persons were arrested in the over twenty-five crime categories measured.[121] In a typical year, approximately 60% of arrestees are generally prosecuted and convicted of crime.[122] Thus, as a result of this "funneling" effect, and absent required restitution as part of diversionary or other non-dispositional resolutions of criminal cases,[123] generally less than 10% of criminal victimizations are even potentially eligible for restitution by virtue of having reached the conviction and sentencing stage.

Nevertheless, given the widespread support for restitution expressed by leg-islators, judges, practitioners, theorists, and the general public,[124] one would expect a high rate of restitution imposition in cases resulting in a criminal con-viction. Despite this high level of conceptual support and despite the pre-sumptive or even mandatory imposition language of some restitution statutes, restitution continues to be imposed in a minority of state and federal crimi-nal sentences.

The most comprehensive national data regarding the imposition of resti-tution in state courts are contained in biennial studies done by the United States Department of Justice since 1988 regarding felony sentences in state courts. National estimates regarding the imposition of restitution are based on data from a representative sample of counties across the country.[125] These studies reflect that the imposition of restitution rose from a low of 12% of of-fenses for which felons were sentenced in 1988, to a high of 18% in 1994, fol-lowed by a decline back to 12% in 2002, the most recent completed study period regarding this information.[126] In 2002, restitution was imposed in sen-tences for felons in only 21% of property offenses, 11% of violent offenses, 10% of miscellaneous nonviolent offenses, 6% of drug offenses, and 4% of weapons offenses.[127]

Annual data compiled by the United States Sentencing Commission during this period reflect similar trends in the aggregate imposition of restitution in federal courts.[128] In the 1988 reporting year, the Commission reported that restitution was imposed in approximately 9% of cases.[129] This figure rose steadily to a high of approximately 21% in 1995 before declining to approximately 13% in 2008, the most recent reporting year.[130] Unlike in the state courts, however, at least half of the offenders generally sentenced in federal courts are convicted of drug and immigration offenses, offenses that are not as amenable to the imposition of restitution as other offenses. As a result, in 2008, the most recent reporting year, restitution was imposed in approximately 47% of murder/man-slaughter cases, 7% of sexual abuse cases, 75% of robbery cases, 19% of assault cases, 76% of burglary cases, 54% of forgery cases, 62% of larceny cases, 62% of fraud cases, and 82% of embezzlement cases. It was imposed, however, in less than 2% of the drug cases and less than 1% of the immigration cases that were subject to the discretionary imposition of restitution.[131] Although the im-migration and drug offenses reduced the overall percentage of offenses for which restitution was imposed, these data reflect that restitution under the federal *mandatory* restitution provisions regarding violent and property crimes is clearly not being imposed for all federal violent and property crimes.[132]

The gap between legislative mandates and the actual imposition of restitu-tion is further illustrated by the 1995 study that compared the imposition of restitution in two "strong" and two "weak" victim rights states. Contrary to their hypothesis that judges in the "strong" provision states would be more likely to order restitution than those in the "weak" provision states, surveyed victims reported that convicted offenders were ordered to pay restitution in only 22% of the "strong" state cases in which a victim had suffered economic loss as opposed to 42% of such cases in "weak" states.[133] Surveyed criminal justice personnel in the two "strong" states reported, however, that restitution was ordered in 59% of cases, including 83% of the cases in which restitution was requested. "Weak" state criminal justice personnel indicated that restitution was ordered in 53% of cases, including 84% of cases in which it was requested.[134] Although the responses of the criminal justice personnel reflect a significantly smaller "restitution imposition gap" than those of the victims, they also reveal that imposition gaps still remain.

These researchers and others have attempted to ascertain why legislative presumptions and mandates and broad conceptual support for restitution by judges and others involved in the criminal justice process have not resulted in the imposition of restitution for greater portions of eligible victims. One factor often identified as important in the restitution decision is the adequacy of information on which to base a restitution award.[135] In the "strong" and "weak" state study, between 64% and 85% of criminal justice personnel from all of the studied states cited the victim impact statement and presentence report as factors considered in determining victim losses, followed by 36% to 57% who cited consultation with the victim or a separate investigation. In addition to the inability to calculate a victim's loss, between 51% and 69% of the surveyed criminal justice personnel in the "strong" and "weak" states identified several other reasons why judges fail to order restitution: the victim's failure to demonstrate loss or to request restitution, the defendant's inability to pay restitution, and the inappropriateness of restitution in light of other penalties imposed, including incarceration.[136] Other researchers have identified a lack of consensus about the scope of restitution and its implementation and philosophical conflicts about the role of restitution as a punishment sanction as additional impediments to its imposition.[137]

Some researchers have attempted to identify individual and community characteristics that are predictive of the imposition of restitution. In two 2005 studies of restitution decisions in Pennsylvania, researchers found that restitution was ordered more frequently for offenders who committed more serious crimes, female offenders, white offenders, and property offenders in a study involving over 55,000 restitution-eligible cases of offenders sentenced from 1996–1998. A statewide survey of 147 judges, as part of their study, revealed that the judges viewed victim compensation as the most important goal of restitution and primarily relied on victim input and the extent of victim injury to determine restitution. Their study of the effect of a 1995 legislative change to mandatory restitution revealed that the proportion of restitution orders statewide increased from approximately 38% of the approximately 115,000 offenders sentenced in restitution-eligible cases from 1990–1994 to approximately 64% of the approximately 55,000 offenders sentenced in such cases from 1996–1998. This increase, however, was not equal in all counties or for all types of offenses.[138]

In addition to the obstacles to the imposition of restitution, the fact that restitution has been ordered does not automatically mean that the order will cover the full amount of victim losses. Even jurisdictions that ostensibly require that a restitution order cover the full amount of a victim's direct losses from the crime generally authorize extended or nominal payment mechanisms that can indefinitely delay the recovery of restitution. Moreover, in many states, the court is required or permitted to consider an offender's economic circumstances and various other factors in addition to victim loss when determining the amount of restitution ordered.[139] Given the high rate of indigence among offenders[140] and other potential limitations on restitution, restitution orders often do not cover all of the victim's direct losses from the crime in those instances in which restitution is imposed.[141]

Finally, a victim's ultimate recovery of whatever amount of restitution is imposed is totally dependent on the offender's compliance with the restitution order. Restitution in the average case is generally for a relatively modest sum. A national study of felons on probation, based on a representative sample of counties, reflected that the average restitution order imposed was $3,368 per probationer.[142] An earlier national study, in which fourteen restitution programs reported information, found that all except one of the programs reported an average amount of restitution ordered per case of $500 or less.[143] Despite these seemingly obtainable sums, achieving offender compliance with a restitution order remains a challenge.

In a national study of seventy-five restitution programs, conducted in 1988, restitution program directors reported an average of 67% of offenders fully paid their restitution obligations. When researchers performed more standardized compliance analyses at four of the program sites, however, they determined that only 42% of the offenders made full restitution payment within two years of the restitution award.[144] Researchers in an earlier national study of twenty-two programs reported compliance rates for individual programs ranging from 23% to 100% of cases.[145] An even earlier study of eleven restitution programs reported an average compliance rate of 74%.[146] In the 1995 four-state study, only 37% of "strong" state victims and 43% of "weak" state victims reported receiving any of the restitution ordered. This compares with the criminal justice personnel who reported that at least some of the ordered restitution was collected in 58% of "strong" state cases and 52% of "weak" state cases. Personnel in all states estimated that approximately 47% of the restitution ordered was collected.[147] The federal General Accountability Office reported outstanding criminal debt associated with unpaid restitution in federal cases at approximately $17,000,000,000 as of 2002 and a debt collection rate of less than 10%.[148] Thus, many of the victims who survive all of the above steps in the criminal process and ultimately obtain a restitution award never recover the full amount of the restitution ordered.

Restitution compliance remains a challenge despite the availability of a wide range of enforcement mechanisms and sanctions. Obstacles to restitution compliance that have been identified include lack of clarity in the court's restitution order, lack of enforcement priority and role conflict in the criminal justice personnel entrusted with restitution compliance, lack of adequate collection procedures to increase the efficiency of restitution collection, and perceived or actual offender indigence or lack of employment skills that inhibit compliance and resulting enforcement sanctions.[149] Some jurisdictions are experimenting with automated collection systems, restitution-specific enforcement units, and other innovative strategies to increase offender compliance with restitution orders.[150]

Several studies have also been conducted to better understand the factors contributing to offender compliance with these orders. Not surprisingly, researchers conducting a national study of restitution programs in the late 1980s found that those that considered an offender's economic circumstances regarding the imposition of restitution had higher restitution payment compliance rates than those that did not. These researchers found that 71% of offenders fully complied with restitution orders in jurisdictions that considered offenders' financial circumstances versus 55% of offenders in jurisdictions that did not.[151]

In a 1992 local study of eighty-two federal probationers, however, 52% of the surveyed offenders indicated that payment of their restitution (or fine) obligation did not pose a specific hardship for them. For 71% of the offenders, payment came from their employment salaries, with 11% of offenders each relying on social benefit programs or loans for payment of their obligations. Even some offenders for whom restitution payment was a hardship, indicated their capacity to make the payments if they perceived the justice system was "serious" about the fulfillment of their obligations.[152]

These researchers also found that reinforcement of the offender's awareness of the court's "seriousness" about restitution compliance before a significant period of delinquency is established is important. They found that offenders' concerns about consequences of nonpayment of their financial obligations diminished over time. At the time of sentencing, 67% of the probationers believed that they would be sent to prison if they failed to comply with their financial obligations—based either on their understanding of the law or the judge's statements at sentencing. The researchers also found a higher probability of full satisfaction of their payment obligations if the probationers made their first payment within thirty days of the court's order. Yet, although 45% of the probationers thought that their probation officer would report a subsequent payment default, only 15% believed that the officer would recommend incarceration to the court based on the default and almost 37% believed that their probation officer only expected them to make a good faith effort to pay their obligations or did not even expect them to make full payment.[153]

Researchers have found that there is no single optimal way to address delinquencies in restitution compliance. Researchers, in a 1980s Chicago study of 223 probationers convicted primarily of property and minor violent offenses and ordered to pay a mean amount of restitution of $500, sent delinquency and warning letters to an experimental group of the offenders who had paid 10% or less of the restitution ordered and had made no payments for three consecutive months or longer prior to the study. A follow-up letter was sent four months after the beginning of the study. The offenders in the control group received no correspondence. The proportionate increase in the percentage of restitution paid during the thirteen-month study period was measured. The researchers found that the notification procedure "significantly increased" restitution payment. In terms of cost effectiveness, $38.75 in defaulted payments was realized for every dollar spent on processing and mailing the delinquency and warning letters.[154]

Researchers in an early 1990s Brooklyn study of 449 misdemeanor probationers convicted of a variety of offenses and ordered to pay a median amount of restitution of $263 used three compliance techniques in their study. The maximum enforcement group received initial invoices and payment schedules, monthly reminder letters, and follow-up phone calls in cases of delinquency. They also were subject to efforts to return their cases to the court's docket and additional demands for payment after any three-month period of delinquency in payment. The moderate enforcement level included all of the above measures except the follow-up telephone calls. The minimum enforcement group received only an initial demand for payment within the required time frame and a second payment demand and warning a month prior to the return of the case to the court's docket in instances of delinquency. Offenders in the maximum and moderate enforcement groups paid their restitution obligations at higher rates at intermediate measurement points in the study. By the end of the approximately one-year study period, however, offenders in *all* groups had paid between 50% and 60% of the total amount owed, with no significant compliance differences between the enforcement groups.[155]

Although these studies suggest the benefits of correctional efforts to address restitution payment delinquencies, they also reveal that no single approach is always more effective than another. Explaining the differing responses to differing techniques, in part, is related research addressing offender characteristics that appear to predict restitution compliance. One researcher in a local study identified factors most predictive of restitution *nonpayment*: offender unemployment, sentences of probation for a drug or burglary offense, restitution orders in a higher than average amount, and a greater number of prior arrests and probations.[156] Consistent with these findings, in the Chicago study described above, the delinquency warning letters had greater impact on the probationers who had jobs and those with fewer arrests and prior probations.[157]

In a two-site study in Brooklyn and Minneapolis in the late 1980s, researchers found that a variety of factors generally were *not* predictive of restitution compliance: the nature of the underlying crime, other aspects of the offender's sentence, and aspects of the restitution order (i.e., its size, length of time for payment, and installment or other method of payment). On the other hand, in both sites, certain offender community ties predicted restitution compliance: offender employment, school enrollment, and stable residence in Minneapolis and school enrollment in Brooklyn. In Brooklyn, where other offender criminal justice information was available, researchers found that the absence of other criminal cases pending was a good predictor of restitution payment. They also found that offenders with felony convictions and outstanding warrants were less likely to pay restitution.[158] Researchers in a 1994 Pittsburgh study found that female offenders and offenders who were rearrested during the payment period were less likely to pay restitution, but those whose victims were business entities were more likely to make their restitution payments.[159] Researchers in a 2005 meta-analysis found that offenders in restorative justice programs had substantially higher restitution compliance rates than other offenders.[160] This research suggests that by considering the offender characteristics that indicate higher risks of restitution nonpayment, correctional personnel can customize their enforcement strategies to achieve higher restitution compliance.[161]

Nevertheless, despite the extensive legislative and judicial authorization of restitution, it is clear that significant progress remains to be made in achieving the objective of victim recovery of economic loss through the imposition and collection of restitution.

Recovery of Victim Psychological Loss and Victim Satisfaction

Victims' inability to obtain full restitution for losses suffered as a result of crime can impede not only their economic recovery, but also their psychological recovery from crime and overall satisfaction with the criminal justice process. Researchers found that the receipt of partial or full restitution was related to victims' reduced levels of distress during the study period approximately two years after their victimization, as well as to the victims' satisfaction with their offenders' sentence and the criminal justice system. This research was based on a survey of 125 victims whose felony cases were prosecuted in an Ohio county between 1985 and 1988. The survey assessed measures of victim distress and various factors that might increase or decrease it. These researchers also found that receipt of restitution was significantly associated with victims' satisfaction with their offenders' sentences and with the criminal justice system. They found that receipt of restitution decreased the likelihood that a victim would believe the sentence imposed was too lenient. In turn, victim perception of sentence fairness was the chief variable influencing victim satisfaction with the sentence imposed. Satisfaction with the sentence played a major role in determining victims' satisfaction with the criminal justice system.[162]

These results are consistent with another researcher's findings that 61% of surveyed victims selected restitution as the fairest form of punishment in their cases. In this survey of approximately 150 victims from nineteen restitution programs across the country in the late 1970s, more victims selected restitution as the fairest form of punishment in their cases than incarceration (23%), community service (9%), probation (6%), and personal service restitution (1%).[163]

Although researchers found the above positive results associated with restitution, they have also cautioned about the negative impact on victim satisfaction resulting from unfulfilled expectations regarding offenders' sentences. In terms of incomplete or delayed restitution payments, some observers maintain that such payments are nevertheless valuable for victims because they defray some of the costs associated with the crime and provide psychological benefit through a restoration of at least some degree of fairness and equity to the victim. Others contend that incomplete or delayed restitution provides insufficient economic benefit to victims and produces a negative psychological effect by keeping the victimization experience "alive" or producing a second victimization by the offender from the victim's unfulfilled expectations regarding restitution.[164]

These latter conclusions are consistent with research findings of significant levels of victim dissatisfaction with restitution awards and compliance. In the late 1970s national study described above, researchers found that only 55% of the victims studied viewed the restitution amount as fair and only 44% reported that they were satisfied with the overall treatment their offenders received.[165] In a late 1980s survey of approximately 200 violent and property crime victims associated with four well-regarded restitution programs across the country and in which the median restitution award was $249, researchers found only 56% of victims were "very" or "somewhat" satisfied with the size of their restitution awards and that only 44% felt that the awards fully covered their losses. An even smaller number, 37%, were satisfied with the timeliness of their restitution payments and only 33% were satisfied with the amount of restitution actually received. Victims also expressed significant dissatisfaction with the treatment they received from criminal justice personnel before and after the restitution award, especially regarding restitution collection.[166]

These researchers found, in multivariate analysis, that the best predictors of victims' satisfaction with restitution were the percentage of the award actually paid and whether the award covered the victims' losses. Of these two factors, the variable addressing offender compliance with the restitution award was the single best predictor of victim satisfaction with restitution. Interestingly, in bivariate analysis, neither the amount of restitution awarded nor the length of time the offender was given to pay or actually took to pay the restitution was correlated with victim satisfaction with restitution.[167]

The researchers also found that factors related to keeping the victim informed about restitution and giving the victim the name of a contact person were also significant predictors of victim satisfaction with restitution.[168] In a follow-up experiment in Brooklyn, researchers increased the amount of restitution-related information provided to victims in an experimental group. Although these victims generally reported being better informed about the restitution process than the control group victims, there was virtually no difference between the experimental and control groups regarding satisfaction with the amount of restitution awarded and received and with the speed of the recovery of restitution. Victims in both groups suggested improvements in the coverage and enforcement of restitution.[169]

Thus, recovery of victim economic loss appears to be inextricably linked to victim recovery of psychological loss, as well as to victim satisfaction with the sentence and with the criminal justice system itself. As a result, it also appears that victim satisfaction will not significantly increase until the imposition and collection of restitution increases.[170]

Reduced System Intrusiveness and Offender Recidivism

Restitution objectives often associated with offenders are the ostensible reduction in criminal justice system intrusiveness from the imposition of restitution and the purported reduction in recidivism among, and hence rehabilitation of, offenders subject to restitution orders. Of course, recidivism reduction and offender rehabilitation also benefit the criminal justice system and the general public. As of yet, these objectives have not been clearly established.[171]

Perhaps because restitution is most frequently imposed in connection with probationary sentences, it is often perceived as an alternative to and thus a less intrusive sanction than incarceration. This perception would be accurate, however, only if offenders who are ordered to pay restitution would otherwise have received sentences of incarceration—a result that has not been established by corroborative research. Instead, the level of system intrusiveness resulting from the imposition of restitution is more appropriately compared to that associated with non-restitutive community sentences. In this comparison, there is clearly as much or more system intrusiveness associated with a restitutive sanction than exists with other community sentences.[172] Offenders with restitutive sentences are subject to a variety of enforcement mechanisms, from liens and garnishment to probation extensions. Some research indicates that they are more likely to have their community sentences revoked for technical violations than otherwise similar offenders.[173] Finally, the local study of federal probationers revealed that the majority of them perceived that restitution was imposed to achieve retributive punishment rather than rehabilitation or other goals. Almost half of the probationers felt that its imposition resulted in significant hardship or severe deprivation for them.[174] It thus seems doubtful that restitution achieves the offender objective of reduced system intrusiveness.

Likewise, research has not established that a restitutive sentence results in reduced recidivism. A review of six studies, reported in 1992, did not indicate significant recidivism reduction among offenders receiving restitutive sentences. After an extensive search of the literature from 1975 to 1992, this researcher identified six studies of the effects of a restitutive sentence on recidivism in adult offenders that had adequate comparison groups in their analyses. All of the studies were completed prior to 1984. Two of the studies used total sample sizes of less than 40 offenders. Some of the study settings involved confounding factors such as residential placement or more intensive supervision. Some of the studies had research design problems that diminished the importance of their research findings. While noting these limitations, this researcher reviewed the studies' results.[175]

In some of the studies, fewer offenders receiving restitutive sentences were rearrested than the "control" offenders, but small sample sizes and other con-

founding factors prevented the research results from reaching statistical significance. In a very small residential program study, 16% of the restitution experimental group offenders had parole violations for new crimes versus 50%
of the control group offenders. In a larger subsequent study of the same program, 6% of the experimental group were returned to prison for a new court
commitment as opposed to 24% of the control group. In two other studies,
the rearrest or new crime violation rates were close for both groups. In another small sample study, 74% of the experimental group versus 50% of the
control group were rearrested. The final study also found higher recidivism
rates for the experimental group offenders.[176] A study not included in the review reported that 87% of offenders successfully participating in a restitution
shelter program were rearrested within eighteen months of release from the
program.[177] It has been suggested that the obligation to pay restitution might
influence an offender to commit new crimes to obtain funds to pay his restitution obligation, but there is no empirical evidence to support this suggestion.[178]
Finally, the reviewed studies also revealed higher reincarceration rates based on
technical violations of their community sentences for offenders with restitutive sentences. For example, in one study, 40% of the experimental group offenders were returned to prison for technical violations versus 10% of the
control group offenders.[179]

On a more positive note, one study did conclude that an offender's actual
payment of restitution—as opposed to merely being ordered to pay restitution—was "strongly and positively" related to probation success, with success based on factors unrelated to noncompliance with the restitution order.
The researcher in this study found that probationers who were not ordered
to pay restitution and those who did not fully comply with their restitution
orders were about equally likely to fail on probation, excluding factors based
solely on noncompliance with the restitution order. These offenders were
also likely to fail on probation at "considerably higher" rates than those offenders who fully paid their restitution orders.[180] This finding is consistent with
the comparative review of studies regarding the effect of restitution on juvenile offenders in which the reviewing researcher found that the most promising research result was in a study in which the researcher found that
restitution program completion was most strongly correlated with reduced
recidivism.[181]

The positive effect of restitution payment completion was also found in the
1994 Pittsburgh area study of 127 restitution orders with a mean amount of $1,642
and a median amount of $315. In this sample, 48% of the defendants fully
paid their restitution, 36% paid some of the ordered restitution, and 16% paid
none of the restitution. Of those defendants who paid a portion of their resti-

tution, 69% (or 25% of the total sample) paid less than half of the restitution ordered. The researchers conducted logistic regression analyses to examine the effects of payment on rearrest.[182]

They found that males, members of minorities, and younger people were more likely to be rearrested, regardless of their payment of restitution. The variable reflecting the presence or absence of restitution payment did not have a statistically significant predictive effect regarding rearrest. The variable reflecting the *percentage* of restitution paid, however, did have a significant negative relationship to rearrest. The researchers interpreted this result to indicate that "restitution may reduce recidivism, but its effectiveness is largely a function of how much of the ordered amount is paid." The researchers also found that those who paid restitution were less likely to be rearrested even when they controlled for the potential reciprocal effect of rearrest on the ability to pay restitution. The researchers further found that the effect that restitution payment had on reduced recidivism was far stronger among married persons and somewhat stronger among employed and older individuals, suggesting that these factors of community integration influence the effectiveness of the restitution sanction. In addition, the significant effect that the variable of the amount of time allotted for payment had on rearrest suggested "the more time probationers have to pay restitution, the less likely they are to be rearrested." The researchers speculated that the increase in time might make the restitution sanction seem "more reasonable and more fair" and thus decrease offenders' defiance of the law. Contrary to their findings regarding restitution payment, the researchers found that fine payment had little or no effect on recidivism in their sample.[183]

The researchers summarized the policy implications of their study. They emphasized the importance of restitution payment rather than restitution imposition to their reduced recidivism findings. The requirement of restitution in circumstances in which payment is not realistic or the enforcement of restitution payment is not a priority would not likely produce similar reduced recidivism results. Consequently, they characterized the possibilities for restitution as "promising but uncertain," with its effectiveness likely "only if offenders understand its reparative intent and if they have reasonable opportunities to pay the ordered amounts." They cautioned that restitution is not a "panacea for reducing crime," but that its careful application could provide an effective way for offenders to compensate victims.[184] Thus, although the imposition of restitution itself has not yet been authoritatively shown to reduce offender recidivism, there are at least some promising findings regarding the positive effect of restitution payment completion on offender recidivism that bear further exploration.

Reduced System Costs and Enhanced System Credibility

In addition to the criminal justice system and societal benefit of reduced offender recidivism, it has been suggested that restitution results in reduced system costs and enhanced system credibility. As seen in the preceding section, reduced offender recidivism from the imposition of restitution has not yet been conclusively established. The achievement of the other criminal justice system objectives also cannot be substantiated at this time.[185]

The reduction of criminal justice system costs has been identified as an objective of restitution. As when this objective is identified regarding any sanction, it omits the relevant inquiry, i.e., cost reduction as compared to what alternative sanction? *If* restitution is imposed on an offender who would otherwise have been sentenced to a period of incarceration *and* that offender completes his restitution obligation in the community without the imposition of any incarceration in the process of enforcing the obligation, then few would deny that restitution is a less costly sanction than the incarceration sentence that the offender would have otherwise received. Rather than being used as an alternative to a sentence of incarceration, however, restitution is generally imposed *in addition* to the sometimes numerous other sanctions accompanying a community sentence or a sentence of incarceration.[186]

As a result, the costs of investigating the victim's loss, determining the restitution amount, monitoring the offender's compliance, and seeking enforcement of the restitution obligation typically represent additional system costs associated with the imposition of restitution rather than reduced costs.[187] For example, cost projections associated with the enactment of the federal mandatory restitution provisions estimated that the provisions would result in 10,000–20,000 additional restitution orders annually and that implementation costs would be $30,000,000 annually.[188] Recent federal Government Accountability Office studies have documented increased and costly burdens on the federal restitution compliance mechanisms resulting from the mandatory provisions.[189] Research also suggests that restitution program participation may increase an offender's length of contact with the criminal justice system, resulting in still other additional system costs. Moreover, given the greater likelihood of revocation of community sentences for technical violations experienced by offenders with restitution obligations suggested by existing research, ultimate incarceration costs may sometimes be added to the costs associated with restitution.[190]

Some jurisdictions, however, are experimenting with mechanisms to use restitution as a true alternative to a more costly sanction. For example, in the federal system, restitution may be imposed "in lieu of any other penalty" in

misdemeanor cases.[191] Use of this alternative would still require system monitoring and enforcement of restitution collection, but would presumably save
the cost of more general probation supervision or initial incarceration.[192] Some
states authorize residential placement at "restitution centers" for purportedly
otherwise prison-bound offenders at which they can pay off their restitution
and other financial obligations in a less restrictive and less expensive incarceration environment than prison.[193]

In response to such potentially less costly restitution-focused punishments,
some theorists maintain that restitution should not be the sole punishment
for a crime because it cannot fulfill all the purposes of punishment.[194] On the
other hand, some restitution advocates contend that system cost reduction
should not be a desired objective of restitution. They maintain that any increased costs related to the pursuit of restitution are justified by its other benefits to the victim, offender, and criminal justice system.[195] Despite these varying
points of view, at least at this stage of restitution implementation, the stated
objective of reduced system costs has not been achieved.

The achievement of the restitution objective of enhanced criminal justice system credibility is perhaps the most difficult to meaningfully assess. One might measure enhanced system credibility by the degree to which restitution has achieved
its other goals and objectives. As the preceding discussion has indicated, restitution has not yet fulfilled its sometimes conflicting goals and objectives and thus
would not have achieved greater system credibility under this approach. Another,
more immediate, way to measure this objective is to judge enhanced system credibility by the degree to which victims *and* offenders can perceive the restitution
process as fair—despite any dissatisfaction that either might have with its ultimate
outcome. A restitution process that is fair to both victims and offenders should
clearly identify the types of losses that are subject to recovery through restitution
and the circumstances in which such can be recovered; provide a meaningful opportunity to accurately identify the subject losses and any other factors relevant
to the restitution determination; offer a reasonable mechanism to resolve disputes as to the imposition of restitution; and provide realistic means to achieve
compliance.[196] Complicating the development of a fair restitution process is its need
to reincorporate victim-centered objectives in an otherwise offender-focused
criminal justice system, that requires what has been characterized as the "pursuit
of compensatory justice in a punitive system."[197] As evidenced by the literally
hundreds of laws enacted and judicial opinions written, as well as the countless
legal and policy analyses of them, determined attempts are being made to achieve
a fair restitution process. Further progress in this area ultimately should enable
restitution to better achieve more of its other goals and objectives and, in turn,
bring more credibility to the criminal justice system that implements it.

Conclusion

The role of restitution in the American criminal justice process has undergone many transformations—from its ascendancy in early American proceedings to its virtual elimination as a sanction for almost two hundred years to its significant return in the years following the President's Task Force on Victims of Crime. The federal system and every state have adopted constitutional provisions, legislation, or both, requiring or facilitating expanded use of restitution. Reviewing courts have generally given supportive interpretations to these restitution provisions. Nevertheless, although significant progress has been made in the restoration of the restitution sanction in the last thirty years, restitution has not been able to achieve many of the often conflicting or unrealistic goals and objectives identified for it.

Researchers and commentators have offered various suggestions for the improved utilization of restitution. Some advocate that consideration of offender ability to pay is an essential component in the determination of a fair and realistic restitution order and that increased collection and enforcement efforts are essential to restitution compliance.[198] Others maintain that full and mandatory restitution for immediate and expected crime-related costs, including pain and suffering, is necessary,[199] along with the enhanced enforcement mechanisms required to achieve offender compliance.[200] Still others provide more detailed prescriptions for the entire restitution process, including a clearer definition of its goals and objectives.[201] Whichever of these approaches or combination of the approaches is taken, a clearer articulation of restitution's goals and objectives and the commitment of necessary resources to pursue them can only aid the implementation of the renewed restitution sanction. Otherwise, the sanction risks misuse or worse, nonuse, a result benefitting neither victims, offenders, nor society.[202]

Chapter 9

Crime Victim Compensation

Introduction

Unlike restitution, discussed in Chapter 8, that contemplates an offender's repayment to a victim for losses suffered as a result of an offense, crime victim compensation provides government compensation to a victim in circumstances in which a victim has not received or will not receive recompense from an offender or another source for crime-related losses. Just as regarding restitution, crime victim compensation has ancient roots. In instances in which an offender was not apprehended or could not or would not pay restitution, some ancient societies recognized a role for the government to assist the victim in recovering his crime-related losses.[1] Most trace the modern return of crime victim compensation to the efforts of British reformer Margery Fry beginning in the 1950s that culminated in the establishment of the first major contemporary program in New Zealand in 1963 followed by one in Great Britain in 1964.[2]

In this country, California established the first victim compensation program in 1965. By 1980, approximately thirty states had established such programs. The American compensation programs were generally structured so that the government was the "payer of last resort" for certain crime victim losses that were not compensated through other means.[3] Many identify the rapid development of these victim compensation programs as a major contributing factor in the evolving victims' movement in the 1970s.[4]

These initial state programs, however, varied considerably. Philosophically, some programs treated victim compensation as a social welfare program for disadvantaged victims, others as an entitlement due to innocent victims, and others as a means to increase victim cooperation with the criminal justice system. These early programs typically shared the characteristics of small size, limited funding, restrictive eligibility requirements, and poor visibility.[5]

For example, in 1980, the majority of the states' compensation staffs included ten or fewer members. State compensation program budgets ranged from a low of less than $100,000 in Nebraska to a high of over $6,000,000 in New York.

State programs were generally funded from general revenues; offender sur-charges, fines, or costs; or a combination of both. Most programs were limited to victims of specified violent crimes or more generally to victims who had suf-fered personal injury or death as a result of crime. To further narrow the pool of eligible recipients, most programs had at least some additional eligibility re-quirements, such as reporting of the crime and filing of the compensation ap-plication within certain time limits, minimum loss levels, or financial means testing. Most programs also had specified ineligibility criteria, such as for victims who contributed to their victimization or those who were related to their offenders. As a result of these restrictions, between 1978 and 1980, only 38% of compen-sation applications were approved for assistance. Moreover, the awards granted to successful applicants were often restricted to otherwise uncompensated med-ical expenses, lost earnings or support, and funeral and burial expenses. Most states also had maximum award limits, usually ranging from $10,000 to $25,000. The average award granted in 1980, however, was just over $3,200. In addition to these compensation recovery challenges, the low visibility of many of these early programs often resulted in very small proportions of potentially eligible victims even applying for compensation.[6]

President's Task Force and *New Directions from the Field* Recommendations

By the time that the President's Task Force on Victims of Crime convened in 1982, over thirty states had established crime victim compensation pro-grams.[7] Thus, unlike many areas it addressed, the Task Force was trying to en-hance an already widely adopted victim remedy rather than to promote the initiation of a newly fashioned approach. Nevertheless, as the above descrip-tion indicates, many states had not yet established victim compensation pro-grams and significant grounds for improvement remained in those state programs that had been implemented in the years prior to the Task Force work.

At the outset, the Task Force stated that financial compensation for losses that victims suffer as a result of violent crime must be an "integral part" of the federal and state governmental response to these citizens. The Task Force rec-ognized the limitations of restitution and personal insurance in addressing these losses. It further noted the deficiencies of many of the existing state vic-tim compensation programs, many of which problems were tied directly or indirectly to the acquisition of adequate funding. In particular, the Task Force criticized certain state eligibility limitations, such as minimum loss require-ments, victim relationship with offender restrictions, residency requirements, and limitations on certain classes of compensable losses. Most of these specific limitations, as well as others, flowed from the funding challenges faced by most programs.[8]

To address these funding challenges that existing and potential compensation programs faced, the Task Force recommended that Congress enact legislation to provide federal funding to assist state compensation programs. With such federal funding assistance, not only could the state compensation programs service the needs of federal crime victims within their jurisdictions, but they could also expand and improve services to their state crime victims. To this end, the Task Force proposed the establishment of a Crime Victim's Assistance Fund. This fund would be composed primarily of federal offenders' fines and forfeitures, as well as a new special assessment levied on all convicted federal offenders. Half of the funds generated would be distributed to existing or subsequently established state compensation programs meeting federal guidelines for receipt of funds, with the remaining half reserved for victim and witness assistance programs.[9]

To ensure state commitment to victim compensation, each participating state would be awarded a proportionate share of available funds based on the amount of compensation it awarded in the previous year. In addition, no state could receive more than 10% of its total awards for the previous year from the federal fund. To address some of the deficiencies in existing programs, the Task Force recommended that participating state programs would have to provide compensation to eligible victims of both state and federal crimes occurring in a jurisdiction, regardless of the victim's state of residency, and would have to provide compensation for psychological counseling.[10] To improve the visibility of these programs, the Task Force also recommended federal and state legislative and executive action regarding the provision of information to victims concerning compensation for "out-of-pocket" losses.[11]

By the time of the *New Directions from the Field* study, all fifty states were operating crime victim compensation programs and some progress had been made regarding compensation processing and payments. The federal legislation recommended by the President's Task Force had been enacted in 1984 and federal funding for victim compensation had even been expanded beyond that recommended by the Task Force. Victim compensation claims had increased due to greater visibility of compensation programs and other victim services and expansion of victim rights laws. However, gaps in compensation coverage still remained as well as the need to expand the visibility of and access to compensation programs.[12]

The authors of the *New Directions from the Field* study recommended continued efforts to reduce the barriers to and increase the scope of victim compensation. To reduce barriers to victim compensation, the study authors recommended eliminating or extending required time periods for reporting the crime beyond the most frequently imposed requirement of within seventy-two hours of the crime. They also recommended eliminating or extending required time limits regarding filing compensation claims beyond the most frequently imposed requirement of within one year of the crime. The study authors advocated expanded outreach efforts to inform victims about victim compensation, especially regarding special and underserved populations. Although all programs provided some degree of coverage for medical expenses, mental health counseling, lost wages/support, and funeral expenses (if applicable), the study authors recommended increased mental health benefits and increased medical benefits for victims of catastrophic injury. They advocated that compensation claims be processed within 90–150 days. The study authors also recommended increased development of funding sources for compensation programs and expanded training for and coordination between compensation and other victim-related personnel.[13]

Constitutional and Legislative Response

Crime victim compensation is not addressed in the last federal victim rights constitutional amendment introduced in Congress prior to the enactment of the federal statutory Crime Victims' Rights Act in 2004 or in the Act itself.[14] Although Congressional proposals for federal involvement in the provision of crime victim compensation were introduced as early as 1965,[15] it was not until two years after the President's Task Force *Final Report* that Congress took action on these proposals. In the Victims of Crime Act of 1984 ("VOCA"), Congress followed many of the Task Force's recommendations. It established a federal Crime Victims Fund, primarily consisting of not otherwise committed federal offender fines and forfeited bail bonds and collateral, as well as a special assessment of $50 from all convicted federal felony offenders and $25 from all convicted federal misdemeanants. Half of the funds deposited each year were to be available for grants to state victim compensation programs and the remaining half would support victim assistance programs.[16]

Assuming the availability of sufficient deposits in the Fund, eligible compensation programs could receive 35% of the amounts they awarded in the preceding fiscal year for non-property damages. To be eligible for the federal funds, state programs had to provide compensation funds to eligible victims of state and federal crimes committed within their jurisdictions, regardless of the residency of the victims. They had to provide compensation to victims and survivors for medical expenses attributable to physical injury from eligible crimes, including mental health counseling and care expenses; lost wages attributable to such physical injury; and funeral expenses resulting from a death caused by such crimes. Participating programs had to promote "cooperation" by victims with the reasonable requests of law enforcement authorities. They also had to certify that the federal funds received would not "supplant" state funds otherwise available for victim compensation and provide other information and assurances as reasonably required by the Attorney General.[17]

Currently, the Crime Victims Fund is primarily funded from the same sources as at its creation, but the special assessments have been raised to $100 for convicted individual felony offenders and restructured for different classes of federal misdemeanants. After certain designated victim-related annual expenditures, 47.5% of the collected funds remaining in the Fund (up to a Congressionally designated cap) are now annually disbursed to the states for crime victim compensation.[18] If sufficient sums are available in the Fund, grants can now be 60% of amounts awarded by each participating state in the preceding fiscal year for non-property damage. In addition to the initial program eligibility criteria, participating programs must at least provide compensation to victims and survivors of victims of criminal violence, including drunk driving and domestic violence, as a result of which victims suffer personal injury or death.[19] All fifty state compensation programs currently meet the VOCA eligibility requirements and serve victims of federal and state crimes committed in their jurisdictions.[20] To assist victims of federal crimes learn about compensation, federal executive branch employees must inform victims of "relief" to which they may be entitled and the manner to obtain such relief.[21]

Only two states refer to victim compensation in their victim rights constitutional provisions. Rhode Island's amendment states that crime victims "shall be entitled to receive, from the perpetrator of the crime, financial compensation for any injury or loss caused by the perpetrator of the crime, and shall receive such other compensation as the state may provide."[22] Wisconsin simply includes "compensation" among the "privileges and protections as provided by law" that crime victims in the state have.[23] Although a few states provide a statutory victim right to compensation itself,[24] most states that address the matter provide only a right to notification or information about victim compensation.[25] Some of these states also expressly provide that the failure to give such notification does not establish a cause of action or affect any of the time periods required regarding the compensation process.[26]

In terms of their substantive statutory victim compensation provisions, the VOCA requirements provide a certain base of uniformity among the states. Beyond this common foundation, there is still considerable variation among the states regarding the state compensation programs' funding sources, eligibility requirements, benefits, and procedural processes.[27]

In terms of funding for compensation programs, all states are currently eligible to receive and do receive annual VOCA grants. Since the introduction of VOCA funding, there has been a declining use of state general revenue funds to support victim compensation programs. Less than fifteen states currently use general revenue sources to contribute to their compensation programs. Most states rely on offender sources, such as special assessments, fees, or fines, for the bulk of their non-VOCA funding. The special assessments, usually imposed on all convicted offenders, are generally for a relatively modest sum. On the other hand, some states authorize assessments that can range as high as several thousand dollars.[28]

Generally, only victims of specifically identified violent crimes or victims who have suffered personal injury or death as a result of crime are eligible for victim compensation. Some compensation benefits are also typically available to certain family members of eligible victims or others with a recognized connection to an eligible victim.[29] In addition to this general eligibility limitation, every state has supplemental eligibility criteria. In recent years, many states have shown increasing flexibility in administering their eligibility criteria. For example, as required by VOCA, all states promote victim cooperation with law enforcement authorities, generally or in more specific ways. In this connection, virtually every state requires the victim to report the crime to law enforcement authorities within a specified period of time. Although the most frequently specified time period is seventy-two hours, many states have longer deadlines and most states permit the reporting requirement to be extended or waived for good cause.[30] Similarly, although the most common application filing deadline is one year following the crime, many states have longer deadlines and many allow good cause extensions or waivers of the deadline.[31]

States also typically permit the reduction or denial of a compensation claim in circumstances in which a claimant has been injured while committing a crime or has contributed to the misconduct causing the victimization.[32] Although prohibited by VOCA from automatically excluding family members or cohabitants of the offender from compensation, many states do exclude such persons or others to the extent necessary to prevent unjust enrichment of an offender, as permitted by VOCA.[33] Less than fifteen states currently require claimants to satisfy a minimum loss requirement, usually of $200 or less.[34] A small number of states currently limit compensation awards to those claimants demonstrating financial hardship or satisfying a financial means test.[35]

In terms of recoverable losses, all state compensation programs are structured to be "payers of last resort." Compensable losses are considered to be those that have not been or cannot be readily recovered from other sources, such as private insurance, worker's compensation or other employee benefits, or other governmental programs, such as Social Security, Medicare, or Medicaid. Unrecovered losses, such as from restitution or civil litigation, are often compensable, with provisions for victim reimbursement to the compensation fund upon their recovery or subrogation of the victim's claim to the governmental authorities, usually to the extent necessary to prevent double recovery by a victim.[36]

Virtually all states have maximum benefits caps, most often between $10,000 and $25,000, for aggregate losses resulting from a crime. Approximately fifteen states have higher maximum caps, at least in specified circumstances.[37] Included in these states are California and Texas, the two most populous states, in which compensation award caps are $70,000 and $50,000, respectively.[38] Washington has a $150,000 maximum allowance for medical expenses and New York has no maximum benefit for medical expenses.[39] In addition to the overall maximum benefit caps, states often have individual caps for certain categories of compensable losses. Some states have supplemental benefit provisions in cases of catastrophic or permanent injury resulting from the crime.[40]

Most states authorize compensation for categories of losses in addition to the medical expenses, mental health counseling and care, lost wages, and funeral expenses required by VOCA. States generally cover not only lost wages, but also lost support, at least for dependents of homicide victims. Approximately thirty-five states can grant limited emergency awards for certain otherwise compensable costs. Approximately thirty states or more also allow claims for designated rehabilitation, crime scene clean-up, transportation, or attorney expenses. Approximately half of the states permit claims for moving or relocation expenses related to the victimization.[41] Only a few states permit recovery for property-related losses[42] or for pain and suffering losses.[43]

Procedurally, victims file their compensation applications in the state in which their victimization occurred, regardless of their own residency. There is no requirement that an offender be apprehended or convicted prior to the filing of an application or the receipt of compensation. In most states, applications are processed by administrative personnel affiliated with a statewide executive or administrative entity or comprising an independent statewide entity. In most states, initial compensation decisions are made by professional compensation staff or by boards or commissions associated with the administrative entities. Regardless of the initial decision maker, a majority of states authorize an administrative appeal of the initial compensation decision or a subsequent appeal to a court, with varying degrees of judicial review authorized, or both.[44]

Thus, crime victim compensation has been not only one of the earliest adopted of the modern crime victim rights and remedies, but also, in many ways, the most extensively adopted one. As the above description indicates, however, property crime victims and even many violent crime victims are generally not eligible for victim compensation. Moreover, as to eligible victims, the extent of coverage can vary significantly from state to state.

Judicial Interpretation

Because crime victim compensation has generally been administered through state compensation systems, its judicial interpretation has also primarily been through the state courts. Moreover, because victim compensation is delivered primarily through administratively based systems, its judicial interpretation has been somewhat more limited than that regarding court-based remedies, such as restitution. Nevertheless, the interpretive decisions that have been rendered provide a "flavor" of the scope of crime victim compensation in operation.[45]

In interpreting their statutory compensation provisions, reviewing courts have generally made clear that there is no victim "right" to compensation, but only an expectation.[46] They have further indicated that victim compensation is not the equivalent of a tort claim and is not intended to remedy all of a victim's damages as a result of a crime.[47] Nevertheless, reviewing courts have also recognized that their compensation statutes are remedial statutes that are entitled to a "liberal" construction, with doubt resolved in favor of a victim.[48]

Reviewing courts have sometimes been called upon to determine a claimant's eligibility for victim status under compensation statutes. In most instances, claimants have either clearly suffered personal injury or death as a result of crime—or not. In unusual cases, however, reviewing courts must construe compensation statutes to determine victim eligibility. For example, reviewing courts have held that individuals who have taken a fatal overdose of drugs, attempted suicide, or experienced the "tense" divorce of their parents are not victims for purposes of their compensation statutes.[49] Although property crimes themselves are usually not covered under compensation statutes, reviewing courts have held that persons who suffered physical or emotional injury during or as a result of a burglary could be eligible victims, as could a person who was injured in a car accident with a stolen vehicle.[50] One reviewing court even granted victim status to a person who had been injured by a bite from a dog that was not under reasonable control, as required by statute.[51]

Courts have also been called upon to determine whether certain victims have complied with reporting of the crime and cooperation with law enforcement requirements for eligibility. For example, a report of a crime to a 911 operator and another victim's report to a local children services board have been found to be adequate for compensation eligibility.[52] In addition, a victim's mental impairment and another victim's fear for safety have been found to be "good cause" justifications for reporting the crime to officials after the expiration of the statutory time periods.[53] Courts have found that victims' refusals to give police officers necessary information and to appear at trial represent failures to cooperate with law enforcement that bar compensation eligibility.[54] Courts have reached mixed results, however, regarding whether victims' decisions not to prosecute or to dismiss a filed suit constitute a failure to cooperate with law enforcement authorities that would bar the victims from compensation.[55]

Although most claims for compensation are fairly straightforward in terms of coverage under compensation statutes, courts must sometimes address unusual compensation requests. For example, in examining a sexual assault victim's claim for compensation, a reviewing court found that her relocation airfare was a justified "economic loss" following the crime, but not her education loan expense, furniture costs, and travel expenses incurred due to her relocation.[56] Another reviewing court found that costs associated with a sexual assault victim's home security measures were a justified expense under the applicable compensation statute.[57] In evaluating claims for lost earnings as a result of crime, most reviewing courts have required that the claimant actually be employed at the time of the crime, rather than simply employable, to recover such losses.[58] There is usually not a specific standard regarding the type of eligible employment, however, as illustrated by one court's approval of lost earnings for an unlicensed hairdresser.[59] Although almost all states expressly or implicitly preclude compensation for unliquidated pain and suffering losses, states and reviewing courts have sometimes recognized that pain and suffering may result in compensable economic losses, such as regarding mental health care expenses.[60] In the few states that allow victim compensation for pain and suffering resulting from the crime itself, reviewing courts have upheld justified compensation awards for such.[61]

In reviewing procedural claims regarding compensation, courts have generally found that the claimant has the burden of proof to establish the claim for compensation, usually by a preponderance of the evidence when a standard of proof is stated.[62] Based on their statutory procedures or otherwise, however, some courts have found that a victim does not have the burden of proof to disprove the criteria that preclude victim eligibility for compensation.[63] Depending on the procedures prescribed by statute, courts have reached mixed results regarding whether a hearing on a compensation claim is required.[64]

Again based on the prescribed statutory procedures, the scope of judicial review of the generally administratively rendered compensation decisions has
varied.[65]

In addition to victim suits regarding compensation awards, some reviewing courts have also addressed offender challenges to special assessments, imposed in conjunction with offenders' convictions and subsequently contributed
to state compensation funds. The United States Supreme Court rejected a federal offender's claim that the federal special assessment was an unconstitutional violation of the "origination" clause regarding revenue bills.[66] Other
federal appellate courts rejected due process, equal protection, and other constitutional challenges to the federal special assessment system.[67] State courts
have also rejected constitutional challenges to assessments on due process and
equal protection grounds.[68] State reviewing courts have generally upheld the
specific special assessments that have been levied, as long as state procedural
requirements for their imposition have been followed.[69]

Thus, again, reviewing courts have generally upheld the compensation structures and awards as legislatively prescribed. They have not, however, typically
attempted to extend the compensation programs beyond their legislatively imposed limits.

Implementation and Analysis of the Remedy

The universal adoption of crime victim compensation by the states and the
significant infusion of federal VOCA funds would suggest that victim compensation has reached its maximum potential as a victim remedy. Research
has indicated, however, that despite the rapid expansion of compensation programs over the past forty-five years, much work remains to be done to maximize the potential of this crime victim remedy. Of course, defining "success"
for victim compensation depends, in part, on defining the goals or underlying philosophy of this remedy.

At least three different rationales have been advanced for crime victim compensation, each of which can have some impact on compensation program
characteristics and goals. One approach to compensation utilizes a "social contract" theory that views compensation as an obligation of the state due to its
failure to protect the victim from crime after having undertaken the responsibility of maintaining public order and safety. Program characteristics that are
consistent with this approach are those eligibility requirements that restrict
compensation to "innocent" or "worthy" victims, such as those who have reported the crime to and cooperated with law enforcement authorities and who

have not engaged in or contributed to the criminal conduct underlying their victimization. A second rationale for victim compensation is a "social welfare" approach that extends general governmental welfare policies to innocent crime victims suffering deprivation resulting from their victimization. Program characteristics consistent with this approach include collateral source restrictions, financial means tests or financial hardship limitations, and minimum loss requirements that restrict compensation to those most in need. A final rationale for victim compensation is as a political tool to win public and victim support for the criminal justice system and greater cooperation in crime prevention and prosecution. The reporting and cooperation requirements are consistent with this approach. As a practical matter, most programs integrate a combination of these rationales into their implemented programs.[70]

As with most crime victim rights and remedies, crime victim compensation has its detractors as well as its advocates. Some opponents of victim compensation challenge the necessity and advisability of this program. They contend that most victim losses from crime are small and can be adequately addressed through victims' private insurance or already existing general governmental insurance or assistance programs. To the extent that these sources do not adequately provide for victims' financial losses, reimbursement should come directly from the offender through restitution or civil suit rather than from the government. Ensuring the financial responsibility and obligation of the individual offender is preferable to these critics to diffusing this responsibility through collective assessments of all offenders or provision of general revenue support for victim compensation.[71] Other critics challenge the manner in which crime victim compensation has been implemented. They regard victim compensation as merely a "symbolic" program designed only to make a public statement about victim loss and suffering rather than to accomplish the instrumental goals of financial recompense to victims and improvement of the criminal justice system.[72] Although these criticisms have not prevented the widespread adoption of crime victim compensation in this country, they and the above rationales advanced in support of victim compensation should be remembered as the effectiveness of victim compensation is reviewed in the remainder of this section.

Utilization of the Remedy

The most basic objective of crime victim compensation is the provision of financial compensation to victims of violent crime. To gain some perspective on the fulfillment of this objective, it is useful to examine the progress that has been made in achieving it. In 1988, thirty-eight surveyed compensation programs received over 92,000 claims and made awards in approximately 65,800 of them. The awards from these surveyed states represented over $125,000,000 in payments to victims, with a median average award of $2,600.[73] In 1998, the fifty states (and two additional covered federal jurisdictions) received 162,509 new claims. During the year, 117,486 claims were approved and 47,201 were denied. In 1998, $265,522,894 was awarded to 117,704 victims and the average compensation award was approximately $2,256.[74] In 2008, the fifty states (and three additional federal jurisdictions) received 180,933 new claims; approved as eligible 178,061 claims; and denied or closed 59,129 claims. In 2008, 151,643 claims were paid, representing $431,904,585 in payments, or an average payment of approximately $2,848.[75] This comparison of time periods reflects an increase in the overall number of compensation applications, number of approved claims, and amount of monetary awards made, with average awards remaining below $3,000 throughout the reporting periods.

Although there has been some increase in overall compensation applications, the number of such applications reflects one of the major concerns about the effectiveness of crime victim compensation, i.e., the limited utilization of this victim remedy. At the outset, by definition, crime victim compensation is generally restricted to the approximately 20% of victims who suffer personal injury or death from crime. Moreover, some studies of the utilization of victim compensation prior to the mid-1980s reflected that only approximately 2% or less of violent crime victims even applied for compensation, with an obviously smaller percentage actually receiving compensation.[76]

National studies conducted in the late 1980s reflected a higher compensation application rate among violent crime victims. One research team compared national violent crime data primarily for 1987–1988 with data regarding the number of compensation claims and awards made during this period in the thirty-nine programs for which data were available. These researchers concluded that nationally an average of 6% of reported violent crime victims requested compensation, with almost 4% (or approximately 64% of the applicants) actually receiving compensation. On a state-by-state basis, the percentage of reported violent crime victims who filed compensation applications ranged from approximately 31% in Colorado and Montana to approximately 1% in Illinois and Louisiana.[77]

Other researchers using 1987 national violent crime data and compensation claim application data from approximately forty programs used a different approach to estimate the compensation utilization rate. These researchers began with the estimated number of reported violent crimes for which victim compensation is most frequently available and regarding which compensation is most often awarded. They reduced these crime figures by an estimated proportion of such crimes in which victims would be ineligible for compensation due to the most common eligibility exclusions, such as victim contributory misconduct and the availability of private insurance coverage. Using the most restrictive eligibility exclusion assumptions, these researchers estimated that 45% of these potentially *eligible* violent crime victims had applied for victim compensation nationally. Using alternative and broader victim eligibility assumptions, the researchers concluded that 22% of eligible victims had filed compensation applications during this late 1980s time period.[78]

A survey of 969 responding victims of reported violent felony crimes whose cases reached final disposition in 1997 was conducted in Texas. Almost 28% of the victims who responded to the survey said that they had applied for victim compensation. Of the multiple reasons given by the responding victims who said that they had not applied for compensation, almost 43% said that they were not aware of the compensation program; over 20% said that they had no expenses resulting from their victimization; approximately 13% said that they were not eligible for compensation; over 11% indicated that they did not understand the compensation program; approximately 10% said that their insurance paid their expenses; and approximately 17% gave miscellaneous other reasons for not applying for compensation.[79] Many of the reasons given by a significant portion of the responding victims for not applying for compensation establish that they would indeed not have been eligible for compensation had they filed an application. Nevertheless, the remaining explanations, such as lack of awareness and lack of understanding of the compensation program, indicate that the compensation program is not reaching significant portions of potentially eligible victims.

Researchers have attempted to identify characteristics of victims who are more likely to apply for compensation and those who are not. In a 1999 national survey of victim compensation program administrators, 85% of fifty-two administrators indicated that there were certain categories of victims who apply for compensation less frequently than expected based on known victimization rates. Approximately 50% or more of these administrators included victims of domestic violence, elder abuse, adult sexual assault, and child physical and sexual assault in this "under-applying" group. Over 50% of these administrators identified lack of knowledge of compensation, embarrassment, fear of retaliation by the offender, and crime reporting requirements as reasons for the less frequent than expected applications. In this survey, 65% of the program administrators indicated that certain demographic and other groups under-utilized compensation. At least 50% of these administrators included remote and rural residents and non-English speakers in this category and almost 50% identified racial and ethnic minorities.[80]

In a companion six-state survey of 452 compensation claimants whose claims were primarily decided in 1999–2000, these researchers compared the demographic and offense characteristics of the victims who filed compensation claims against victim characteristics in national victimization data. Regarding applicable claimants, they found that victims of homicide and sexual assault filed claims at higher rates than the national victimization rates for these offenses; physical assault claims were lower than the national victimization rates; and robbery claims rates were generally comparable to the national victimization rates. In this sample, compensation claimants were older, more female, and less likely to be racial or ethnic minorities than applicable crime victims generally.[81]

These researchers suggested that the differences between type of crime compensation claim filing and victimization data may be due, in part, to the greater likelihood of compensable expenses associated with the crimes with higher claims rates than the national victimization rates. They also suggested that the demographic characteristic differences may be due to a variety of factors, including eligibility criteria and outreach strategies.[82] Nevertheless, although progress has been made in extending the reach of crime victim compensation to those victims who are potentially eligible for it, substantial work remains to be done.

With regard to those victims who do file claims for compensation, some progress has been made regarding the compensation claims programs and process. As indicated previously, a number of states have increased maximum compensation benefit caps, adopted greater flexibility in the implementation of eligibility restrictions, and increased the types of losses for which compensation is available.[83] Through the use of automation and other efficiencies, claims processing time has been reduced. In 1997, the nationwide average number of weeks between the filing of a claim, its determination, and payment to a victim was twenty-nine weeks and the median time was eighteen weeks. In the 1999 nationwide survey of compensation administrators, the largest percentage (46%) identified claim verification as the task taking the most time in the claim process.[84] These processing times can be compared to the twelve to twenty-one week processing time advocated by the authors of the *New Directions from the Field* study.[85] In fiscal year 1997, claims approval rates ranged from 41% to 93% in the individual states, with a nationwide average approval rate of 68%. The reasons most frequently cited for claim denial in the 1999 program administrator survey were contributory conduct by the victim (an average of 28% of denials), ineligible crimes or losses (16%), incomplete paperwork or missed deadlines (16%), and expenses paid by collateral sources (15%).[86] As previously described, the nationwide average compensation payment has generally remained below $3,000.[87] Some factors that continue to constrain greater progress in the utilization of crime victim compensation are the low visibility of the remedy and limited program staff and funding.

Low Visibility of the Remedy

The low visibility of many victim compensation programs has been noted as an obstacle to the effectiveness of this remedy since the establishment of the earliest compensation programs. Researchers frequently cited lack of information about compensation programs generally and about how to access them as significant deficiencies of early compensation programs. Some researchers suggested that programs' low visibility was an intentional strategy to restrict the number of applications, especially regarding early programs with limited staffs and funding.[88] By the time of the late 1980s national studies, compensation programs' limited visibility was still identified as a problem. In a survey of almost forty state victim compensation program officials, only ten said that victims in their states were adequately informed about their compensation programs. The officials indicated that compensation information directed to known victims was more effective than that directed to the general public. More specifically, they ranked information delivery by police as the most important, followed by victim assistance personnel, hospital or emergency room personnel, and prosecutors.[89]

Consistent with these findings, a majority of states have included information about victim compensation among the information that law enforcement officers or prosecutors or both are required to provide to crime victims.[90] Nevertheless, the 1997 Texas study revealed that approximately 37% of the responding violent crime victims said that no one informed them of the compensation program. This figure contrasts with the overall 76% of 641 responding criminal justice and victim services personnel who indicated that they routinely inform victims about compensation, including almost 99% of responding prosecutor victim services personnel and over 80% of responding police officer crime victim liaisons.[91]

In a separate 1997 study of Texas law enforcement officers, however, only 25% of approximately 1,900 respondents indicated that they "almost always" advised crime victims about compensation—even though they are statutorily required to do so. Moreover, almost 38% of responding officers rated their performance in referring victims to agencies that can help them apply for compensation as "poor," with an additional 35% rating their performance as "fair." Although higher performance ratings were given by police administrators, prosecutors, and victim-specific police and prosecutor personnel, police officers are usually the first and sometimes the only criminal justice personnel with whom victims have contact and therefore their role in delivery of information about compensation is critical. These researchers identified factors that contributed to police delivery of compensation information, including institutional support for the advising function and knowledge about compensation.[92]

In the 1999 nationwide survey of compensation administrators, respondents identified external and internal factors contributing to the limited visibility of the compensation remedy. When asked the three most frequent ways that victims learn about compensation, administrators most often identified prosecutors' offices (30%) and police (25%). Although 65% of administrators indicated that police are statutorily required to inform victims about compensation, 72% of administrators said that police actually did so about half of the time or less. Internally, at least 50% of administrators engaged in outreach through brochures in victim services agencies, notification cards for distribution by police and victim service providers, training for related personnel, and toll-free phone numbers for victims. Less than 50% of administrators used special outreach efforts or materials for non-English speakers, provided applications on the Internet, or provided information through non-victim-related avenues, such as schools or churches.[93]

Reflecting the continuing challenge of compensation program visibility, in the six-state survey of 452 victims with compensation claims primarily decided in 1999–2000, 88% said that they did not know about the compensation program before their victimization. These claimants stated that they were most often informed about compensation by a victim advocate or hotline operator (33%) or police (23%). Of those claimants who were not previously aware of victim compensation, 53% indicated that they were informed of it within a week or less after the crime and 22% were informed two to four weeks after the crime.[94] In a 2002–2003 Maryland survey of 104 victims who were presumptively eligible to file compensation claims, only 29% indicated awareness of the compensation program. Of those victims who were aware of compensation, they were most often informed of it by police and victim service providers. Researchers determined that victims with physical injuries were more likely to be informed of compensation than victims without such injuries. Victim demographic characteristics (age, race, gender, and income level) and the existence of out-of-pocket expenses did not affect the likelihood that these victims were aware of compensation.[95]

Of course, awareness of victim compensation does not automatically translate into the filing of a compensation claim. In the Maryland study, of the thirty victims who indicated awareness of compensation, 70% chose not to file a compensation claim, most often citing low or no expenses incurred

(38%).[96] In an attempt to determine whether outreach and assistance in filing compensation claims could mitigate compensation filing disparities for disadvantaged crime victims, researchers in a 2008 California study found that these efforts increased the likelihood of filing for compensation for younger, less educated, and homeless victims, but had no such effect regarding gender, ethnicity, type of crime, or other victim characteristics.[97] Thus, these studies indicate that lack of visibility and information dissemination about victim compensation is still a problem. Although information dissemination does not always result in the filing of a compensation claim, it is obviously a necessary first step to the utilization of victim compensation.

Limited Program Staff and Funding

Most victim compensation programs also continue to experience the challenges of small staffs or limited funding or both, problems that have characterized these programs since their initiation. As of 1980, one research team found that nineteen of twenty-five responding state compensation programs had staffs of ten members or less.[98] By the late 1980s, thirty of forty-two responding compensation programs reported full- and part-time staffs of ten persons or less. Of the 564 total compensation employees from the forty-two reporting states, 45% were investigators, 41% were clerical employees, and 14% were employed in other professional capacities.[99] Currently, three-fourths of the states operate with compensation staffs of twelve or fewer employees. Only ten states employ more than thirty compensation staff members.[100] To supplement their efforts and to counteract the distancing effect that the centralized administration of most compensation programs potentially has on claimants, most states rely on local police, prosecution, or other victim services personnel to assist victims in the compensation claims process.[101] In fact, to encourage such supplemental assistance, programs receiving VOCA victim assistance grants must assist potential compensation recipients in seeking such benefits, as part of their services.[102]

In most states, however, the final compensation claim investigation and decision making processes are administered by a centralized compensation entity.[103] In the late 1980s national survey of state compensation program administrators, half of the respondents said that funding for program administration was inadequate. In this connection, administrative costs represented an average of 16% of thirty-one responding states' total budgets, with individual state percentages ranging from approximately 3% to 31%. Moreover, in identifying program weaknesses, the most frequent responses involved problems caused by lack of adequate staffing, such as backlogs in processing time and time-related deficiencies in the quality of staff work. Limited staffing also precluded other important compensation activities, such as outreach to increase compensation utilization, services to special populations, and the development of structured training and decision making processes.[104] Despite these identified staffing-related problems and despite the amendment of VOCA in 1994 to allow up to 5% of VOCA compensation grant funds to be used for the administration of state compensation programs,[105] small compensation staff sizes remain the rule rather than the exception, thereby diminishing the potential effectiveness of the compensation remedy.

The limited funding that hampers the administration of state compensation programs also restricts the compensation awards that state programs can make. In the late 1980s national survey of compensation program administrators, eighteen of forty state respondents said that their resources were not sufficient to pay deserved compensation benefits to the existing number of claimants.[106] Of course, many of the compensation eligibility exclusions and maximum benefit caps can be traced to the limited funds available for compensation awards.[107] Some of these restrictions have been relaxed somewhat since state programs have shifted to greater reliance on offender-generated funds than those appropriated from state general revenue sources. Offender-based revenues are not unlimited, however, and many state programs are also expanding their efforts to increase compensation fund revenues through more aggressive exercise of their subrogation rights.[108]

Although compensation funding is likely to always be a matter of great concern, some of the funding crises that plagued compensation programs in their earlier years, as the number of compensation claims escalated, subsided somewhat as compensation claims stabilized in many states. Moreover, in addition to expanding their funding mechanisms, many states undertook efforts to control costs through greater use of technological aids or otherwise.[109] As a result, in the 1999 nationwide survey of compensation program administrators, 81% indicated that they had sufficient funds to pay all eligible claims, including 67% who said that their revenues exceeded their immediate payout needs. Some states used these excess funds to expand their compensation coverage or build up their reserves or both.[110] Similarly, the federal Crime Victims Fund experienced an unusually large cash infusion from 1996–2004 due to twelve exceptionally large corporate defendant fines, representing $2,300,000,000 or 35% of the total of $6,700,000,000 deposited in the Fund from 1985–2004. Rather than annually distribute all of the funds received, beginning in fiscal year 2000, Congress imposed an annual distribution cap for the Crime Victims Fund, placing any excess revenues received in reserve.[111]

Unfortunately, in recent years, annual outflows from the Crime Victims Fund have exceeded inflows and this reserve has been tapped to meet the annual Fund obligations to the states. If this trend continues, it will potentially impact the federal funding available for victim compensation. Proposals to increase the stability of the Fund include expansion of revenue sources and increased federal debt collection.[112] Moreover, as states have faced budget crises in recent years, legislatures regarding one-fourth of compensation programs have taken away funds from these programs for use in funding other programs. This legislative action particularly affects compensation programs funded through general revenue sources, but it also places at risk reserves established by other compensation programs. Also contributing to the recent strains on compensation program revenues are potential increased claim expenditures due to increases in violent crime and crime-related costs.[113] Thus, adequate funding remains a challenge for some compensation programs. Moreover, even compensation programs with sufficient current revenues to meet their claims obligations must strategically plan to accommodate changes in their revenue sources and demands.

Victim Cooperation and Satisfaction

Perhaps as the means to increase victim access to compensation improve, through expanded program visibility, staff size, and funding, other measures of compensation program effectiveness will improve as well. When victim compensation programs were established, it was anticipated that their existence would increase crime victim participation in and satisfaction with the criminal justice system. Indeed, crime reporting and victim cooperation eligibility requirements are part of virtually every state compensation program.[114] Research regarding early compensation programs explored the impact of victim compensation on crime reporting, the crime and conviction rates, and victim satisfaction.

Researchers conducting a series of studies in the 1970s hypothesized that the existence of a crime victim compensation program would lead to an increased rate of violent crime reported to the police as well as to increased clearance and conviction rates. Using official crime statistics regarding crimes reported to the police from four states with compensation programs and ten states without such programs, however, these researchers could not substantiate a causal relationship between the existence of a compensation program and a violent crime rate change. In another study using self-reported victimization data from twenty-six cities, the researchers also found that the presence of a compensation program did not result in an increase in violent crime reporting. Companion studies in Canada also failed to establish increases in violent crime clearance or conviction rates in areas with crime victim compensation programs.[115]

In addition to the above measures of the relationship between victim compensation and victim cooperation with the criminal justice process, research has also been conducted regarding whether the receipt of compensation fosters future cooperation with the criminal justice system. Researchers studied 121 persons who were awarded compensation in Florida in 1979 and 77 who were denied compensation that year. Survey respondents were asked, based on their experiences in the cases on which their compensation claims were based, whether they would be willing to cooperate in the future with the compensation commission, the police, the prosecutor, and the judge. Compensated victims generally and some segments of the uncompensated victims were more likely to cooperate with the compensation commission in the future. No category of victims, however, was significantly more likely to cooperate in the future with the police, prosecutor, or judge.[116]

In the Florida study, respondents were also asked about their degree of satisfaction regarding how the compensation commission, police, prosecutor, and judge handled their cases. Researchers found that receipt of compensation had a significant positive effect on victim satisfaction with the compensation commission, but not with the police, prosecutor, or judge. They established this positive satisfaction effect regarding victims receiving compensation generally and for all demographic subgroups of compensated victims. In terms of compensated victim satisfaction with the other justice system representatives, only the subgroup of minority victims had a significantly more positive satisfaction level with the police.[117]

Researchers conducting a study in New York and New Jersey in the late 1970s also failed to establish a positive relationship between victim compensation and victim cooperation or satisfaction with the criminal justice system. These researchers surveyed almost 350 violent crime victims in Brooklyn and Newark, including those who had received compensation, had been denied compensation, and had never applied for compensation. At the outset, they found that less than 1% of violent crime victims applied for compensation and that only 35% of the applicants received awards. In addition, 80% of those receiving awards were not satisfied with their awards. Three-fourths of all applicants indicated that they would not apply for compensation again. Specific complaints were made about compensation process delays, outcomes, expenses, inconveniences, eligibility requirements, and administrative treatment.[118]

Both claimant and nonclaimant victims expressed dissatisfaction with their involvement in and treatment by the criminal justice system generally and law enforcement officials specifically, as well as with their criminal case outcomes. They expressed little willingness to participate in future programs or to cooperate with law enforcement authorities, government officials, or the compensation board. Generally, these researchers found claimants did not have better attitudes regarding these issues than nonclaimants and, in fact, had worse attitudes due to their overall dissatisfaction with the compensation process and awards. Positive outcomes in satisfaction and cooperation were limited to the subset of compensation awardees who received what they considered to be adequate compensation awards.[119]

More recent research has revealed higher levels of satisfaction with the compensation process and outcomes, but confirms the importance of the compensation award in claimants' overall level of satisfaction. In the six-state survey of 452 victims whose claims were primarily decided in 1999–2000, 78% of the responding victims said both that their claim was paid in a reasonable amount of time and that the payment decision was fair and reasonable. Constructing a satisfaction scale ranging from twelve to twenty-four based on responses to particular questions related to the compensation experience, researchers found that the median satisfaction level of surveyed claimants was 22.7 and the average was 21.8. Following regression analyses, the researchers found that the claimants with the most positive perceptions of the compensation process had their claims processed more quickly and with more expenses paid and were white females.[120]

In a similar Maryland survey of 104 victims whose compensation claims were decided in 2001–2002, 75% of responding claimants said that the claim payment decision was fair and reasonable. However, 52% of responding claimants said that the payment decision was not made in a reasonable amount of time. In the satisfaction scale that ranged from ten to thirty (based on responses to individual questions), the median satisfaction score was 25 and the average was 24.4. In multivariate analyses, claimants' satisfaction increased as more of their expenses were paid through compensation and as they had to pay less themselves, but case processing time was not significantly associated with claimant satisfaction in the Maryland study. Perhaps increasing the claimant satisfaction level is the fact that 93% of the surveyed claimants received payment for all requested expenses and 4% received partial payments, with a median compensation payment of $4,772 and an average payment of $9,872, well above the national average compensation award.[121]

Thus, based on early research, victim compensation itself has not yet been demonstrated to result in significant increases in cooperation with the criminal justice system beyond the cooperation required for compensation eligibility in the case generating the compensation claim. Research does indicate, however, that victims' satisfaction with their compensation awards is associated with increased victim satisfaction and cooperation. This research finding simply reinforces the significance of the primary goal of victim compensation, i.e., to provide meaningful financial recompense to victims of violent crime.

Conclusion

Crime victim compensation has been not only one of the earliest, but also one of the most extensively adopted of the modern crime victim rights and remedies. As conceived and implemented, it is a limited remedy—primarily providing restricted funds for otherwise uncompensated expenses to eligible victims who suffer personal injury or death from crime. Although progress has been made in the expansion of access to victim compensation, work remains to be done to address the continuing challenges of small compensation program size and poor visibility and to ensure adequate sources of funding.

Chapter 10

Civil Litigation

Introduction

As indicated previously in this text, the earliest "criminal" proceedings in primitive times were conducted between the alleged offender and the victim and had the goal of exacting appropriate restitutive or retributive remedies. This victim-focused system of redress continued in Western law until approximately the eleventh century after which the government gradually replaced the victim as the primary party-in-interest. This shift in litigants also resulted in a shift in the primary outcomes of the criminal litigation. Fines paid to the government and capital, corporal, and other forms of punishment soon accompanied and often replaced previous requirements of restitution to crime victims. Over time, the pursuit of restitution was largely transferred to private litigation initiated by the victim against the offender in the separate "civil" justice system.[1] A similar evolution with similar results occurred in this country as a government-centered public police and prosecution system emerged following the American Revolution from the victim-centered system widely utilized during the colonial era.[2]

Although the pursuit of victim recompense through civil litigation was available, it was not widely used in this country prior to the victims' movement. The victims' movement focused attention on victims' unmet need to be "made whole" from their crime-related losses—through restitution in the criminal prosecution, crime victim compensation, and, in appropriate cases, civil litigation. In addition to private and government- and employer-sponsored insurance and benefits, these remedies represent a "package" of potential financial relief for victims from crime-related losses. Each remedy has its own advantages and disadvantages, in terms of eligible victims and losses as well as ease and likelihood of recovery. Although it remains the least used of victims' financial remedies, the utilization of civil litigation has definitely increased in the years since the emergence of the victims' movement.[3]

With regard to civil litigation, an offender's commission of a crime often gives rise not only to a criminal prosecution by the government, but also to a civil cause of action based on the law of torts, or civil or private wrongs, that a crime victim can pursue in the civil justice system. The law of torts includes both intentional acts and those resulting from negligence. Depending on the circumstances of the crime, a victim, as plaintiff in a civil suit, may sue an offender-defendant based on an intentional tort cause of action, such as assault, battery, false imprisonment, infliction of mental or emotional distress, trespass, or conversion of property. A crime victim may also be able to sue a non-offender third person who did not intentionally participate in the crime, but whose negligence permitted the crime to occur. The primary relief sought in either instance is the recovery of monetary damages for losses suffered as a result of the crime. In some instances, these damages can include recovery for certain intangible losses, such as regarding generalized pain and suffering from the crime, and punitive or punishment damages for especially outrageous non-negligent acts.[4]

The causes of action described above are based on common law concepts of civil liability. In addition to these theories of relief, most jurisdictions have established additional statutory causes of action relevant to proceedings based on the commission of crime. For example, all states have established "wrongful death" causes of action to address wrongful or negligent acts that cause death, including intentional acts, such as crimes.[5] Thus, the crime victim considering a civil lawsuit has a variety of common law and statutorily created causes of action that may be applicable to the case.

The President's Task Force on Victims of Crime did not make any action recommendations regarding the victim remedy of civil litigation. The greater visibility the Task Force gave to all crime victim issues, however, certainly contributed to the increased use of civil litigation by crime victims and to the establishment of some of the crime-specific statutory causes of action that facilitate it. The authors of the *New Directions from the Field* study noted initial efforts to identify and support attorneys with expertise to represent crime victims in civil litigation, the most prominent of which was the Carrington Victims' Litigation Project of the National Center for Victims of Crime (providing the impetus for the current National Crime Victim Bar Association). The study authors recommended the development of wider expertise in civil litigation remedies for crime victims by attorneys, broader dissemination of information about these remedies to crime victims and professionals in the criminal justice system, and expansion of laws that establish civil remedies for criminal violations.[6] The remainder of this chapter reviews the development of this civil litigation remedy for crime victims.

Constitutional and Legislative Action

Civil litigation is not addressed in the last federal victim rights constitutional amendment introduced in Congress prior to the enactment of the federal statutory Crime Victims' Rights Act in 2004 or in the Act itself.[7] Nevertheless, crime victims can seek civil relief in the federal court system in a variety of circumstances. Crime victims can assert common law intentional or negligent tort or statutory wrongful death causes of action in federal courts, pursuant to these courts' "diversity of citizenship" jurisdiction, if the victim resides in a different state from all of the defendants being sued and the victim's damages claims exceed $75,000.[8] Crime victims can also bring suit in federal courts pursuant to the courts' "federal question" jurisdiction if their suit arises under the federal Constitution or laws.[9] For example, Congress has provided civil remedies for certain discriminatory actions that could potentially be utilized by victims of certain bias-based actions or "hate" crimes.[10] In an attempt to provide relief in this area, Congress established a federal civil cause of action for compensatory and punitive damages and other forms of relief for victims of federal or state felony crimes of violence "motivated by gender."[11] However, the United States Supreme Court found that Congress had exceeded the scope of its federal legislative authority in enacting this provision and thus found the law unconstitutional.[12]

In addition to these specific civil remedies, a victim may use the more general civil statutory remedy prescribed for certain torts committed by federal personnel.[13] Additional remedies are provided for violations of federal constitutional and statutory law "under color" of state law or action against direct wrongdoers or eligible third parties whose actions or inaction directly contributes to a crime or other covered act by the primary wrongdoer.[14] Such "§ 1983" civil suits for deprivation of rights have been permitted, in appropriate circumstances, against state and local officials sued in their individual capacities, private individuals and entities acting under color of state law, and local governmental entities.[15]

At the state level, civil litigation is also not addressed in the constitutional or statutory victim rights provisions. Nevertheless, crime victims can pursue civil remedies in state courts through means similar to those available in federal courts. Many of the criminal acts committed by offenders have parallel common law intentional tort causes of action. The intentional torts of assault, battery, false imprisonment, infliction of mental or emotional distress, trespass to land, and trespass to or conversion of personal property can serve as the basis of a victim's civil suit against a defendant who has committed a variety of criminal offenses. Through such a civil suit, a crime victim can seek to recover damages from the defendant for losses suffered as a result of the crime. Such losses generally include those for actual and projected future lost earnings and medical care, property loss, and pain and suffering, as well as puni-tive or punishment damages in more extreme circumstances. Of course, a de-fendant in a civil suit can assert a variety of defenses to liability, some of which are similar to those available in a criminal action, such as consent, necessity, self-defense, and defense of others.[16]

In addition to these common law intentional tort suits against a wrongdoer, all states have statutory "wrongful death" causes of action that can be brought by a homicide victim's surviving relatives or estate against a defendant whose intentional or negligent act resulted in the victim's death. In such suits, the party bringing the action can seek recovery of damages for losses suffered as a result of the victim's death. These losses often include funeral expenses, as well as loss of the victim's support, services, and contributions, such as the victim's lost future earnings or replacement costs for the victim's services. Some state statutes also include "survival" causes of action that permit the victim's estate to pursue causes of action the victim had accrued at his death as a result of his injuries. In these actions, the victim's estate can usually seek recovery of losses such as the victim's medical expenses, pain and suffering, and lost earnings following the crime or wrongful act.[17]

Common law also provided another civil cause of action—negligence—that crime victims have primarily used against third persons whose actions or inaction has contributed to the crime committed by the direct wrongdoer. A victim's recovery in a negligence suit requires the establishment of a defen-dant's duty of care to the victim, his breach of such duty, and a resulting in-jury to the victim that resulted in damages. Crime victims have brought third-party negligence actions for failure to prevent or contribution to the commission of a crime against a wide range of defendants, including law en-forcement and correctional officers and related governmental entities; com-mon carriers, innkeepers, landlords, and victims' employers and schools with control of the locations at which crimes have occurred; and criminals' parents, employers, and psychiatrists. With the exception of punitive damages, gener-ally the same types of losses can be recovered in a negligence action as in an intentional tort action. Negligence-based defenses include a victim's contrib-utory or comparative negligence or assumption of the risk.[18]

In addition to these more generalized civil causes of action, some states have statutorily created civil causes of action regarding specific crimes. For exam-ple, some states have such causes of action regarding theft, receiving stolen property, or other property offenses. These provisions often permit recovery of two or three times a victim's actual property loss.[19] Some states have estab-lished specific parallel civil causes of action regarding sexual offenses and stalk-ing.[20] Some states have also extended their statutes of limitations regarding suits based on sexual assaults of minors.[21] Finally, a majority of states have established civil causes of action based on the infliction of personal injury or property damage due to bias against or hatred of a person's racial or ethnic background, religion, or other protected characteristics.[22]

To assist crime victims obtain a financial recovery in civil suits against criminal defendants, the federal government and over forty states enacted laws that require an offender to place in escrow for a period of years certain profits obtained as a result of the commission of the crime, especially profits generated by the sale of information about the crime to the media through book contracts or for film portrayals. These laws are often called "Son of Sam" laws because they follow the model of the first such law enacted in New York in connection with a serial killer who identified himself as the "Son of Sam." New York legislators were concerned that the offender would profit by "selling his story" to the media at the expense of his victims.[23] Although New York's statute was subsequently declared unconstitutional by the United States Supreme Court on First Amendment grounds,[24] the federal system and the majority of states have retained their anti-profit laws or revised them to address the Court's concerns, in order to provide this potential source of recovery for crime victims pursuing civil litigation.[25]

Judicial Interpretation

As indicated in the previous section, the commission of a crime can give rise to a variety of civil causes of action. In this section, illustrative federal and state cases will be described to provide a sense of the types of circumstances that can result in a direct or third party defendant's civil liability and the types of issues that might arise in such civil litigation.

Intentional Tort and Related Direct Actions

Common law intentional tort suits against direct wrongdoers can be based on a variety of types of criminal conduct. For example, a plaintiff prevailed in a false imprisonment and assault suit after mistakenly driving his car onto ranch land and destroying a portion of a fence. In a resulting altercation over removal of the car and payment for the fence, the defendants prevented a wrecker from removing the plaintiff's car and grabbed, held, and struck the plaintiff. The appellate court upheld a damage award of over $150,000, primarily consisting of damages for mental anguish and pain and suffering accompanying a resulting eye injury.[26] In an intentional tort suit based on a drive-by shooting into a group of suspected rival gang members as a result of which the plaintiff was struck by several shotgun pellets and permanently lost his vision in one eye, the appellate court upheld a compensatory damage award of over $300,000 and a punitive damage award of $100,000.[27] In a suit based on the sexual battery of a twelve-year-old girl by a man with whom the plaintiff and her family were living, the appellate court upheld a damage award including $12,000 for future counseling expenses, $25,000 for past and future pain and suffering, and $185,000 in punitive damages.[28]

Statutory civil causes of action based on criminal or quasi-criminal conduct can be brought by themselves or in combination with common law causes of action. For example, the parents of a foreign exchange student, who was killed by a homeowner when the student mistakenly thought that a Halloween party he had come to attend was at the homeowner's house, recovered over $650,000 in a statutory wrongful death and survival action against the homeowner. The court determined that the shooting, that occurred after the student had mistakenly approached the homeowner's house and did not respond to the owner's command to "freeze," was intentional and was not justified.[29] An appellate court also upheld an approximately $4,000,000 damage award, including approximately $2,500,000 for funeral expenses and pain and suffering, in a wrongful death suit brought by the decedent's widow, personally and as administrator of his estate, against an intoxicated driver who crashed her car into the decedent's motorcycle and later entered a guilty plea to vehicular homicide.[30] In a case in which a man engaged in a series of acts to provoke his former wife to commit suicide before murdering her himself, the reviewing court upheld a damage award of over $4,800,000 in a wrongful death and intentional infliction of emotional distress case brought by her estate. The court found that the damage award was appropriate under the state's enhanced compensatory damages provisions based on his murder conviction and was not otherwise excessive based on the cruel and premeditated nature of the murder.[31]

Suits brought under hate or bias-based statutory authorization are often combined with common law intentional tort causes of action. After the defendants, members of an informal group that sometimes espoused threatening action toward minorities, burned a cross on the yard and threw a brick through the window of a primarily African-American household, the family members successfully sued the defendants pursuant to federal laws prohibiting discrimination regarding property and housing, a state law addressing hate crimes, and common law intentional infliction of emotional distress and trespass actions.[32] A waitress successfully sued her former supervisor and employer for sexual harassment under the federal gender discrimination laws as well as for the sexual assault and battery common law actions that resulted in the harassment.[33] An African-American man, who was the only minority patron in a skating rink owned by the defendants who had made racially derogatory remarks in the past, was asked to leave the skating floor and see the owners in the "back room." Feeling threatened and intimidated, the plaintiff declined to comply and remained seated in the public area. In response to a call from one of the owners, a sheriff's deputy, who had previously worked for the rink owners, forcibly ejected the plaintiff from the rink and ultimately transported him to the county jail where he was held overnight. The plaintiff brought a combination of actions against the rink owners and the deputy. He prevailed in his state racially motivated intimidation and harassment action against the rink owners and his federal § 1983 civil rights action and common law actions for false arrest and imprisonment and assault and battery against the deputy sheriff.[34]

Intentional tort actions based on criminal or quasi-criminal conduct sometimes involve special proof issues. For example, if a civil defendant has already been criminally convicted of the same conduct on which the intentional tort action is based, the defendant is often precluded by collateral estoppel principles from relitigating the factual issues underlying the conviction in the civil action. Illustrating this principle is the appellate court's conclusion that the defendant's admission, in connection with his guilty plea for attempted murder, that he shot at the plaintiff in an attempt to kill her established the elements of his liability for assault and battery in the plaintiff's subsequent civil suit against him.[35] On the other hand, a defendant's acquittal in a criminal trial based on the higher standard of proof required does not preclude a subsequent civil suit based on the same conduct and measured by the lower civil standard of proof.[36] If the civil suit precedes a criminal prosecution, a defendant's assertion of his privilege against self-incrimination in the civil suit to avoid providing information that might incriminate him in a subsequent criminal prosecution may result in the defendant's inability to affirmatively defend himself in the civil litigation or to present affirmative claims. Moreover, if the civil suit follows the conclusion of the criminal prosecution or the defendant is otherwise immune from prosecution, no privilege against self-incrimination is available to him in the civil proceeding.[37]

Intentional tort or related statutory actions sometimes also involve special issues regarding damages. Compensatory damages in such suits can generally include damages for past and future tangible and intangible losses related to the defendant's conduct. Plaintiffs can seek compensation for established past and reasonably projected future medical expenses, property losses, actual and reasonably projected future lost wages or earnings, and similar tangible losses. In addition, damages for such intangible losses as mental anguish and pain and suffering can generally be recovered even though such losses are not amenable to easy quantification.[38] As one court noted regarding mental anguish damages, "[o]nce the existence of some amount of mental anguish has been established, the incalculable quantity cannot logically be refuted or shown to be factually insufficient because there are no objective facts to calibrate measurement."[39] Similarly, the punitive damages that are usually available in an intentional tort action are not subject to precise calculation. Such damages are designed to punish wrongdoing rather than compensate the claimant for specific losses. The determination of these damages is generally entrusted to the discretion of the fact finder, subject to a review for excessiveness. Factors considered by reviewing courts include the egregious nature of the act or malicious intent and the relationship to the award of compensatory damages.[40]

Illustrating these principles, one court upheld a compensatory damage award of over $300,000 and a punitive damage award of $100,000 in a tort action arising out of a drive-by shooting by a seventeen-year-old defendant and a companion as a result of which the victim sustained permanent vision loss in one eye. Although the defendant had already received a twenty-seven-year prison sentence in the related criminal case, the reviewing court found that the punitive damage award was not unreasonable and that the defendant would have earning potential to satisfy it upon his release from prison.[41] Another reviewing court upheld a compensatory damage award of $20,000 and a punitive damage award of $350,000 in a tort action arising out of a battery of a woman by her husband with whom she was engaged in an acrimonious divorce action. The husband had also been convicted of criminal battery for the beating, fined $10,000, and sentenced to five years in prison. In light of the nature of the attack on the victim and the injuries sustained, the reviewing court found that the punitive damage award that was over seventeen times the amount of the compensatory damage award was not excessive.[42] On the other hand, another reviewing court found that the jury's award of $650,000 in punitive damages in an assault and battery case in which the jury had awarded $200,000 in compensatory damages was excessive and motivated by passion. The appellate court ordered a new trial on the issue of punitive damages unless the plaintiff agreed to a reduced punitive damage award of $400,000.[43]

A final aspect of damages that involves special issues regarding intentional torts is the plaintiff victim's ability to recover damages from the defendant's insurer. Homeowner's and other types of insurance often have coverage exclusion provisions concerning losses from an insured's intentional act in which the resulting injury was also intended or could be expected. In such cases, a victim plaintiff may be limited to a recovery only from the defendant and not his insurer.[44] For example, in a wrongful death action, the victim's parents sued the defendant who participated in an armed robbery in which the victim was shot and killed and also sued the defendant's parents' homeowner's insurance issuer. The insurance policy contained a coverage exclusion for bodily injury "expected or intended" by the insured. Although the defendant was the getaway car driver in the robbery and did not shoot the victim, the reviewing court found that the defendant was aware that his co-defendant planned to use a loaded gun to carry out the armed robbery. The appellate court further found that "some type of bodily injury is so substantially certain to occur during the commission of an armed robbery that the law will infer an intent to injure on behalf of the insured actor without regard to his claimed intent." The court therefore found that the insurance carrier had no liability pursuant to the coverage exclusion.[45] Thus, in intentional tort cases, insurance coverage exclusion provisions may restrict the victim plaintiff's choice of potential defendants.

Third Party Actions

Although the number of direct civil actions against offenders has grown in the years since the President's Task Force on Victims of Crime, the number and types of victim third party actions arising out of criminal conduct have expanded even more significantly.[46] Victims primarily bring such actions based on theories of negligent conduct by third parties that permits the criminal conduct to occur. In some instances, accompanying statutory causes of action against third parties may be available.

Facilitating such actions are principles of liability articulated in the Restatement of Torts, promulgated by the prestigious American Law Institute ("ALI") as an "orderly statement of the general common law of the United States."[47] After first stating the general principle that an actor's realization that his action is necessary "for another's aid or protection does not of itself impose upon him a duty to take such action," the ALI identifies a number of exceptions to this principle in which certain actors do have an affirmative duty to act with reasonable care to aid or protect others.[48] One such exception addresses "special relations" that create an affirmative duty to use reasonable care to aid or protect others in the relationship against an "unreasonable risk of physical harm." Such special relationships include those between common carriers and their passengers, innkeepers and their guests, possessors of land open to the public and their invitees, those who take custody of others and those in their custody, and employers and their employees.[49]

Similarly, although there is no general duty to control another's conduct to prevent him from causing physical harm to a third person, some special relationships can impose such a duty to exercise reasonable care to control the conduct of another to avoid unreasonable risks of harm to others. In instances in which they have reason to know of their ability, necessity, and opportunity to control, parents, employers, and possessors of land or chattels can have such duties of control with regard to their children, employees, and licensees, respectively. In addition, those who take charge of persons with dangerous propensities may also have such a duty to exercise reasonable care to control their conduct to prevent them from doing harm to others.[50] Finally, certain duties to aid others may be created by the inadequate performance of an undertaking by an actor that places another at risk of harm.[51]

Although these Restatement principles are not binding on any court, the ALI represents that they are the "product of expert opinion and ... the expression of the law by the legal profession" and thus are a "correct statement of the general law" in this country.[52] Significantly, these principles simply recognize a duty of reasonable care in certain third parties in specified circumstances—the first step in establishing negligence liability. To prevail in a negligence action, victim plaintiffs must also establish a breach of such a duty with resulting injuries and damages. Illustrative cases reflect the application of these principles in the expanding area of third party liability in suits brought by crime victims.[53]

Special Relationships Creating Duties of Reasonable Care

The special relationship of care between a common carrier and its passengers was recognized long before its acknowledgment in the Restatement principles.[54] The passenger's purchase of a ticket has generally been deemed to include the carrier's provision of safe transport and thus protection from intentional acts of the carrier's employees and from third persons whose actions the carrier could have reasonably anticipated or prevented.[55] These principles are still recognized as reflected in an appellate court's upholding of a jury's finding of negligence against a transit authority for significant injuries suffered by a bus passenger as a result of an assault by two unruly bus passengers. The injured passenger alleged that the bus driver was negligent in failing to follow the transit authority's safety directives, including those about ejecting disruptive passengers or summoning aid, in the ten minutes of the assailants' threatening conduct leading up to the assault. In light of the carrier's special relationship with its passengers and its duty to protect its passengers from foreseeable harm arising from the criminal conduct of others, the appellate court upheld the jury's conclusion that the bus driver's inaction proximately caused the victim plaintiff's injuries by the other passengers.[56]

Innkeepers have also been deemed to have a special relationship with their guests that gives rise to a duty to exercise reasonable care for their guests' safety and protection of their belongings. In addition to actions concerning conduct by innkeepers' employees, allegations of innkeeper negligence concerning crimes committed by non-employee third persons may involve inadequate security measures or personnel, inadequate response to similar crimes in the area, or failure to take appropriate action regarding suspicious persons on the premises.[57] In one of the more prominent of the early contemporary suits in this area, entertainer Connie Francis brought suit against the motel in which she was staying after she was assaulted by an intruder who entered her room through a door with faulty locks. The court upheld the jury's verdict awarding her $2,500,000 for the resulting loss of earnings, pain, suffering, mental anguish, and humiliation.[58]

On the other hand, courts have also maintained that innkeepers are not insurers of their guests' safety and their duty to their guests is limited to reasonable care to maintain the premises in a reasonably safe condition under the circumstances presented. In this connection, a trial court dismissed a negligence action by a guest against the motel in which she was brutally raped, robbed, and assaulted when armed intruders forced their way into her room after her husband opened the room door in response to their knock. The court found that the motel's security program, design, lighting, locking mechanisms, and warning system were reasonable, especially in light of the absence of personal crimes on the premises prior to the incident.[59]

Other business owners also have been deemed to have a duty of reasonable care to their business invitees to reasonably warn them of or protect them from foreseeable physical harm by third persons.[60] For example, an appellate court upheld a jury verdict finding that a shopping center was negligent regarding the degree of security provided in the center's parking lot in which the plaintiff was attacked and robbed. Although the shopping center had security personnel in the parking lot, the evidence supported the jury's finding that the security provided was inadequate in light of the high number of reported criminal incidents in the vicinity, the usual seasonal increase in criminal incidents, and the comparative security practices of other malls.[61] Again, however, business owners are not insurers of their patrons' safety. Another appellate court upheld a judgment in favor of a shopping center regarding a patron who was shot while attempting to leave a tenant night club. Although the center had previously obtained private security services in the center's common areas at the tenant's request in response to numerous crimes committed in the club, it was not obligated to provide security in the club where the patron was shot nor did evidence suggest that the security provided in the common areas was inadequate. The assailant had not engaged in previous acts outside the club that would have alerted security personnel that those inside the club were in danger.[62]

Bar owners are subject to the same principles of liability as other business owners in terms of their reasonable supervision, care, or control of their business premises. These business owners' sale of alcohol, however, may create additional aspects of common law negligence liability or statutory liability under "dramshop" provisions.[63] Illustrating the general principle, an appellate court upheld a jury's verdict in favor of a plaintiff in his suit against a bar for negligence that contributed to his shooting in the bar parking lot following an altercation that began in the bar between the plaintiff's current and former girlfriends. During the altercation, the bar bouncers had refused the plaintiff's requests for help and had taken no action to end the altercation. The reviewing court found that the bar was on notice that the plaintiff was in danger. The court further found that the harm to the plaintiff was foreseeable in light of two previous shootings in the bar parking lot not long before this shooting. Finally, the appellate court concluded that a reasonable jury could have found that the bar did not take reasonable steps to prevent the plaintiff's injury.[64]

On the other hand, a reviewing court found that summary judgment should have been granted to a bar owner on negligence and dramshop claims arising out of the sexual assault and murder of a bar patron by another patron after both had left the bar. The appellate court found that the bar's general reputation for fighting; the consumption of large amounts of alcohol by the victim and offender; the fact that the offender made advances toward the victim at the bar; knowledge of a bar waitress that the offender's sexual drive increased when he was intoxicated; and knowledge by one or more of the bartenders on duty that the offender carried a gun did not establish the bar's knowledge of the offender's propensity to commit sexual assault or murder so as to establish a duty to protect the victim from the offender's subsequent intentional criminal acts. Similarly, a bar employee's request that the offender take the obviously intoxicated victim out of the bar did not establish the bar's intent to provide for her safety. Finally, with regard to the bar's liability under the state's dramshop provisions, the appellate court found that even if the bar had improperly served alcohol to the visibly intoxicated offender, his intoxication was not the proximate cause of his subsequent intentional act of sexual assault and murder, as required for liability under the statute.[65]

Although traditionally landlords were not deemed to have a duty to protect tenants from criminal activities on their premises, there has been an increasing trend in recent years to recognize a landlord duty to exercise reasonable care to protect tenants against foreseeable criminal acts of third persons at their residences. In instances in which such a duty has been recognized, it has been based on a variety of theories including a landlord's affirmative negligent acts, implied warranty of habitability, voluntary assumption of responsibility for security, failure to disclose latent defects in the premises, express or implied contract to maintain the premises in a safe condition, a general duty to maintain common areas in a safe condition, and various statutory duties. Reviewing courts have examined residential and commercial tenants' claims regarding landlords' failure to adequately physically secure their premises, to provide adequate security personnel, to warn tenants regarding known risks of harm, and similar claims.[66]

One of the first major cases recognizing a landlord's duty to protect tenants from the criminal acts of others on their premises was *Kline v. 1500 Massachusetts Avenue Apartment Corporation*,[67] decided in 1970. In *Kline*, a tenant brought suit against her landlord based on the landlord's failure to provide adequate security to protect her from the foreseeable robbery and assault she suffered in the common hallway of her apartment building. Reversing the trial court, the appellate court acknowledged a landlord's duty to take reasonable steps to protect tenants from foreseeable criminal acts of others on their premises. In recognizing such a landlord duty, the appellate court analogized the modern urban, multiple unit apartment complex to the traditional multi-room inn regarding which traditional duties of care were recognized between innkeepers and their guests. Although landlords were not obligated to be insurers of their tenants' safety, they were obligated to take reasonable steps to guard against predictable risks of intruders and thereby minimize foreseeable risks to their tenants. In this case, the appellate court also recognized the landlord's implied contractual obligation to provide protective measures within its reasonable capacity. The appellate court concluded that the landlord had not maintained a standard of reasonable care due to its deficient provision of security in the face of known risks and increasing actual occurrences of crime on its premises and particularly in the common areas of the premises that were peculiarly under its control.[68]

Still, as in other areas in which a duty of care has been recognized, landlords are obligated only to provide a level of reasonable care to their tenants under the applicable circumstances. For example, an appellate court upheld the grant of summary judgment in favor of the landlord in a suit brought by a tenant who had been raped and robbed in her apartment parking garage. The reviewing court found that previous incidents of property crimes, such as theft and vandalism, in the parking garage had not been of a nature to put the landlord on notice of the risk that a violent sexual crime might occur on the premises. In reviewing the location, nature, and extent of the previous criminal conduct, the reviewing court found that it was insufficient to raise a factual issue regarding whether the instant assault on the tenant was reasonably foreseeable. In the absence of other evidence supporting the foreseeability of the violent attack on the tenant, she could not maintain her suit that alleged the landlord had failed to safely maintain the premises.[69]

Courts have also recognized certain duties of reasonable care concerning employers with regard to their employees in the work place[70] and schools with regard to students at school.[71] Over sixty years ago, the United States Supreme Court concluded that an employer had a duty to make "reasonable provision" against a foreseeable danger of intentional or criminal misconduct on the work premises on which its employee was required to work. By recognizing such a duty, the Court allowed the employee to proceed with her negligence claim in which she contended that her employer was aware of conditions at her work site that placed her at risk for the assault that she suffered.[72] In the context of the school-student relationship, some courts have recognized schools' duty to take reasonable care to protect minor students from the criminal acts of other students or third persons on the school premises that students are required to attend, as well as to provide a general duty of supervision to students placed in their care. One reviewing court found a similar duty of care between a university and an adult student who was robbed and assaulted at an off-campus mandatory internship site that had been approved by the university. The court found that the university had a "duty to exercise reasonable care in assigning her to an internship site, including the duty to warn her of foreseeable and unreasonable risks of injury."[73]

Crime victim plaintiffs have also attempted to assert a special relationship between them and police or other governmental agents or entities that would create a duty of reasonable care or protection from the criminal acts of third persons.[74] At the outset, such suits are often precluded by common law or statutory concepts of absolute or qualified sovereign immunity. Even when sovereign immunity does not completely bar suit against a governmental entity or agent, it will still often restrict suit to those instances in which the governmental defendant was exercising a ministerial or proprietary rather than a discretionary or governmental function.[75] Moreover, even if suit against a governmental party is not precluded or limited on immunity grounds, courts have generally maintained that governmental bodies, and their agents, are not insurers of the public safety and that duties of protection owed to the public in general do not give rise to individual duties of protection to specific citizens, absent special circumstances establishing a special relationship and duty of care.[76] Although a detailed discussion of the interpretation of sovereign immunity is beyond the scope of this text, illustrative cases representing the courts' interpretation of a special relationship between certain governmental defendants and victims are presented.

The United States Supreme Court examined the existence of this special relationship in a federal civil rights action based on a minor plaintiff's alleged deprivation of his due process liberty rights by a local social service entity and its employees resulting from their failure to protect him from the actions of and ultimate severe assault by his abusive father. The Court found that "nothing in the language of the Due Process Clause itself requires the State to protect the life, liberty, and property of its citizens against invasion by private actors" and thus a "State's failure to protect an individual against private violence simply does not constitute a violation of the Due Process Clause."[77] The Court also found that the social service workers' prior efforts to address the abuse in the minor's home did not establish a special relationship between them that would create a federal *constitutional* duty of the state to protect him. Although the state's voluntary undertaking of protection of the minor might give rise to a duty of protection under state tort law, it did not create such a duty of protection under the due process provision.[78]

The Supreme Court more recently held that the statutory and judicial language requiring the police to enforce a restraining order did not remove all police discretion in such enforcement. As a result, the woman who had obtained a restraining order against her estranged husband did not have a protectable property interest sufficient to support her due process claim against the town when police failed to undertake sufficient action to enforce the restraining order and her estranged husband killed their three children.[79] This holding, however, contrasts with a state supreme court's interpretation that its domestic violence statutes created a special relationship triggering a sheriff's duty to protect a domestic violence victim by notifying her of her statutory rights, seizing a weapon used in a domestic violence situation, and/or arresting the abuser prior to the abuser's subsequent use of the weapon to murder his wife. The sheriff's negligent violation of these protective statutes designed to protect the victim supported the jury's award of damages of $358,000.[80]

Victim plaintiffs seeking to assert the existence of a special relationship between them and police and related governmental entities and agents under state law have had mixed results. For example, a reviewing court rejected the plaintiff victims' claim, in their negligence suit, that a special relationship and resulting duty of care were established between them and defendant local police officers and their employers. Over a three-week period, in response to the plaintiffs' repeated expressions of concern about their safety after reporting the commission of a sexual assault by a relative on their minor daughter and their attempts to facilitate the offender's arrest, police officers sought to minimize their safety concerns and took steps to effect the offender's arrest, including notifying him of the arrest warrant once it was issued. Before the offender was arrested, he broke into the victims' home and attacked them so severely that the daughter died. In these circumstances, however, the appellate court found that there were neither affirmative acts by the police causing the injuries nor specific promises or representations by the officers that would create justifiable reliance so as to establish a special relationship between them.[81]

On the other hand, another reviewing court did find the existence of a special relationship between police and a teenaged homicide witness who was threatened and ultimately murdered prior to giving testimony in the offender's case. In the plaintiff's negligent wrongful death action against a police officer and the city, the reviewing court found that by isolating and elevating the importance of the victim's incriminating testimony, the police officer had placed her in a position of clearly foreseeable danger and he thus had a duty to warn her of the resulting danger that was not otherwise readily discoverable by her. Instead, the officer lulled her into a false sense of security regarding the danger to her from her involvement in the prosecution. Due to its conclusion that the evidence supported a finding of a duty to warn based on creation of peril, as well as a duty of care based on the officer's request for the victim's assistance in the case, the reviewing court reversed the trial court's granting of the defendants' motion for nonsuit and allowed the action to proceed.[82]

As these cases illustrate, there is no clear definition of the circumstances in which police or related governmental defendants will be deemed to have entered into a special relationship with and undertaken a consequent special duty of protection regarding an individual citizen. A finding of such a special relationship becomes more likely, the more specific a promise of protection to an individual citizen against harm from a particular offender is or the more the government actor's conduct can be construed to create circumstances of peril for the victim from the ultimate offender.[83] Again, however, the finding of a special relationship and thus a duty of reasonable care in these, as in all of the above circumstances, simply provides the initial step in a determination of liability based on the breach of the duty with resulting injuries and damages.

Duty to Control or to Warn of the Conduct of Others

In addition to the above special relationships that establish a duty of reasonable care between classes of persons and others who are victimized by the criminal conduct of third persons, there are other special relationships between persons and the wrongdoers themselves that establish a duty to control or to warn others of the wrongdoers' conduct. Such special relationships have been recognized in certain instances regarding parents and their minor children, employers and their employees, certain mental health care professionals and their patients, and governmental parties and offenders subject to their control. The duty of reasonable care arising from these special relationships is generally one to control the other's conduct so as to prevent intentional harm or unreasonable risk of physical harm to others in circumstances in which the person has the ability to exercise such control and should know of the necessity and opportunity for exercising it.[84]

Courts have considered whether parents are liable, under negligence theories, in circumstances in which they have failed to control the reasonably foreseeable tortious conduct of their minor children that has resulted in harm to others, as well as in circumstances in which parents have entrusted or made accessible an instrumentality that a minor child has used to harm another.[85] For example, an appellate court upheld a grant of summary judgment in favor of defendant parents in a case alleging their negligent supervision of their son who shot a police officer while the son was committing a burglary. The reviewing court found that the parents' knowledge of their son's prior burglary and other property crimes, his possession of Ninja weapons and books, his sneaking out of the house at night in a Ninja costume, and his ongoing psychological counseling were insufficient to put the parents on notice that their son might engage in a violent offense. In the absence of such notice, the parents could not be held liable for negligent supervision in failing to exercise reasonable care to avoid the son's act of violence.[86] On the other hand, a reviewing court reversed a grant of summary judgment in favor of a father whose minor son had taken a handgun from his father's locked storage container and subsequently used it to shoot and kill another youth after a verbal altercation. In light of the disputed testimony regarding the father's knowledge and consent regarding his son's access to the weapon and the foreseeability of the son's conduct due to his other recent misconduct, the reviewing court found that factual issues concerning the father's liability for the shooting remained to be resolved.[87]

In addition to common law liability theories, some states have enacted statutes that impose varying degrees of parental liability for the tortious conduct of minor children.[88] In this connection, a reviewing court upheld a recovery against defendant parents of $50,000, consisting of $2,500 for each of twenty sexual contacts between their minor son and a minor girl, under the state parental liability law.[89]

Crime victim plaintiffs have also sought to impose liability on employers for the crimes of their employees under several theories. In instances in which the employee's act has been committed within the scope of employment or was arguably incidental to his employment, plaintiffs have sought to impose vicarious liability on the employer under a respondeat superior theory. Because intentional or criminal acts are less likely to be committed within the scope of an employee's employment, victim plaintiffs have also sought to impose employer liability under theories of negligent hiring, training, or supervision of the offending employee.[90]

In a suit illustrating various theories of employer liability for an employee's conduct, a plaintiff victim sued a store on a respondeat superior theory for false imprisonment, assault, and battery by its assistant manager, as well as for its own negligent or wanton supervision and training of the employee. The victim plaintiff alleged that the employee had improperly detained her based on a false accusation of shoplifting and had subsequently forced her to perform fellatio on him to avoid the employee's filing a criminal charge against her. The reviewing court upheld the jury's finding of the employer's respondeat superior liability for the employee's false imprisonment of the plaintiff. It also, however, upheld the trial court's grant of a directed verdict in favor of the employer regarding the assault and battery claims, finding that they were outside the scope of the employee's employment. Based on the employer's failure to adequately train the employee regarding the proper methods to detain and question suspected shoplifters and its failure to adequately investigate or take action regarding a previous complaint of improper sexual harassment against the employee, the reviewing court upheld the jury's finding of employer liability due to its negligent and wanton supervision and training of the employee.[91]

Third party suits have also been brought against mental health professionals and institutions, both for their negligent discharge from psychiatric institutions of patients who subsequently injure others or for their failure to warn victims who are specifically threatened by their patients.[92] Because mental health treatment and discharge decisions involve often difficult issues of professional judgment, liability in negligent discharge suits is generally limited to those circumstances in which mental health personnel or their institutions have been grossly negligent in their discharge decision and the patient's resulting criminal conduct was reasonably foreseeable.[93] The first major case recognizing third party liability for a mental health professional's failure to warn a victim of harm threatened by a patient was *Tarasoff v. Regents of the University of California*,[94] decided in 1976, that involved a patient's threat to kill a specific victim that was communicated to the offender's psychotherapist and the patient's subsequent murder of his intended victim. The reviewing court recognized a duty of reasonable care to an intended victim by a therapist who determines or reasonably should determine that his patient represents a serious threat of violence to the intended victim. The reviewing court further found that the discharge of such a duty of care could include warning the intended victim of the threatened violence, notifying the police, or taking other reasonably necessary steps under the circumstances to protect the intended victim from the threatened danger.[95]

Questions of judgment, discretion, causation, and sovereign immunity from suit have restricted plaintiff crime victims' attempts to sue parole authorities for their negligence in paroling offenders who subsequently victimize others while on parole.[96] Even in those instances in which reviewing courts have recognized an actionable duty of care regarding parole release decisions, they have recognized the difficulties inherent in the parole release decision. For example, one reviewing court defined the applicable standard of care as the avoidance of grossly negligent or reckless release of a "highly dangerous" prisoner. The breach of such a standard could result from a release despite an entire record reflecting a prisoner's violent propensities without any reasonable basis for a belief that the prisoner had changed while incarcerated, but not from a record in which the evidence is conflicting or contradictory.[97] In addition to the restriction of parole board liability under state law, the United States Supreme Court has held that a murder by a parolee five months after his parole release was too remote a consequence of the release decision to constitute a deprivation of life by state action for purposes of a federal civil rights suit under the circumstances presented.[98] Although third party suits based on a negligent governmental release from custody decision are limited, there has been somewhat of a greater recognition of the potential for liability for the negligent supervision of a parolee or probationer who victimizes another while in the community.[99]

Implementation and Analysis of the Remedy

As the preceding section indicates, crime victims have increasingly utilized the remedy of civil litigation against their direct wrongdoers and negligent third parties in the years since the President's Task Force on Victims of Crime. Reflecting this trend, the National Crime Victim Bar Association has collected a data base with over 11,000 summaries of crime victim litigation cases.[100] Crime victim recoveries in the hundreds of thousands, and even millions, of dollars in such suits are no longer uncommon.[101] These facts, however, do not mean that civil litigation is a viable remedy for most crime victims. In this connection, its significant advantages must be weighed against its substantial disadvantages.[102]

Procedurally, civil suits have certain advantages for the crime victim litigant over criminal prosecutions. For example, a lower standard of proof is required of the victim plaintiff in a civil suit than that required of the prosecutor in a criminal proceeding. In order to prevail in a civil suit, the victim need establish his claim only by the preponderance of the evidence, i.e., the greater weight of the credible evidence. In criminal trials, the prosecutor must establish proof beyond a reasonable doubt to obtain a criminal conviction. In addition, unlike in criminal trials, civil trial juries can generally determine liability based on a non-unanimous jury finding. Finally, crime victims can recover a much wider range of damages in a civil suit than is possible through restitution or crime victim compensation. Recovery for intangible losses, such as pain and suffering and mental anguish, is typically permissible, as is recovery of punitive or punishment damages in actions involving non-negligent conduct.[103]

The opportunity for the crime victim to control the civil suit, as opposed to the victim's more limited role in the criminal prosecution, is often cited as an advantage of civil litigation. The victim's control of all aspects of the civil litigation can help counteract the loss of control a victim often experiences during the crime itself and sometimes during the prosecution as well. This regaining of control can help rebuild the crime victim's sense of empowerment and aid in the healing process. Regardless of the extent of the monetary recovery from a civil suit, a finding of defendant liability can serve as a personal vindication for the crime victim.[104]

Crime victims also can view their civil suits as a means to deter a direct offender's future criminal conduct. The imposition of a significant monetary judgment may have a greater deterrent effect on some offenders than a sentence of incarceration. Third party suits can also be means to achieve corrective action for negligent conduct that has contributed to the commission of a crime and to aid in the prevention of future crimes. Monetary judgments may encourage those with special relationships with potential crime victims, such as landlords and business owners, and those with special relationships with potential offenders, such as parents and employers, to undertake additional efforts to exercise their duties of reasonable care to prevent foreseeable harm to others.[105] In addition, third party suits have been used by some crime victims to achieve larger aims of social policy, as when they are brought against groups that have incited or negligently contributed to violent acts by their employees or followers, such as those brought against Ku Klux Klan groups, and result in substantial monetary judgments that can impair the viability of the defendant organization.[106]

Balanced against the significant benefits of civil litigation are its accompanying difficulties. The challenges of pursuing civil litigation against a direct wrongdoer outweigh the advantages for most crime victims. At the outset, pursuit of civil litigation obviously requires a victim's knowledge of the offender's identity. Such litigation is not even an option in circumstances in which a crime has been committed by a stranger and no suspect has been arrested. Even when the identity of the offender is known to the victim, either because the crime has been committed by a non-stranger or a suspect has been arrested, most offenders lack adequate resources to ever satisfy a significant monetary judgment.[107] In this connection, the "Son of Sam" laws, adopted in the federal system and a majority of the states to establish escrow accounts for any offender profits resulting from the crime, have been rarely used and are a largely irrelevant source of financial recovery for crime victims.[108]

Compounding the limited likelihood of financial recovery from most direct wrongdoers is the fact that the crime victim is responsible for bearing the costs of retaining counsel to bring the civil suit and for other costs of litigation. Even in circumstances in which a victim can defer the payment of attorney fees through a contingency fee or recovery-sharing arrangement, the victim plaintiff nevertheless usually remains responsible for other pretrial costs of the litigation. Thus, if a victim plaintiff does not obtain a judgment against a direct wrongdoer or the wrongdoer cannot satisfy the judgment obtained, the civil litigation may actually result in a *negative* financial recovery for the victim.[109]

In addition to the financial costs of the litigation, the crime victim litigant may also be subject to much more extensive pretrial and trial inquiries into a wider range of aspects of the victim's life than would be permissible in a criminal prosecution. For example, if a victim is seeking recovery for pain and suffering or mental anguish resulting from a crime, a defendant may seek to probe aspects of the victim's mental health before and after the crime. Broader procedural rules regarding pretrial discovery and expanded concepts of relevance in such civil suits would facilitate these more extensive inquiries and perhaps more "revictimization" than the crime victim would experience through the criminal prosecution. Moreover, it generally takes a longer time to resolve civil litigation than criminal litigation and thus the financial and emotional costs of the litigation to the victim last for a longer period of time.[110]

Of course, crime victims' likelihood of financial recovery from third party defendants is much greater than from direct wrongdoers. However, the costs and adversarial nature of litigation against these more formidable adversaries is also likely to be greatly increased. In addition, proof of a third party's negligence or other liability is often more difficult to establish than that of the direct wrongdoer. Moreover, suits against some potential governmental third party defendants are limited or barred by immunity doctrines.[111]

Thus, despite its benefits, the significant challenges of civil litigation have precluded its pursuit by most crime victims. Because of these challenges, some commentators have suggested expanding the scope of criminal restitution to include recovery for unliquidated damages, such as pain and suffering, in appropriate cases.[112] Others have proposed adoption of a variation of some European justice systems in which victims could bring their civil suits in conjunction with government-initiated criminal prosecutions.[113] Neither of these proposals seems likely to achieve widespread adoption in the near future.

Conclusion

In the years since the President's Task Force on Victims of Crime, crime victims have increasingly utilized civil litigation against direct wrongdoers and third parties to obtain financial and personal recovery for losses suffered as a result of crime. Although the challenges inherent in such litigation make it likely that civil litigation will be pursued by a relatively small proportion of crime victims, such litigation nevertheless represents an important option for crime victims seeking to be "made whole" from their crime-related losses.

Chapter 11

The Future of Crime Victim Rights and Remedies

Introduction

Although the victims' movement had evolved steadily throughout the 1970s, the modern era of crime victim rights and remedies was still in its infancy when President Ronald Reagan convened the President's Task Force on Victims of Crime in 1982.[1] In this connection, there was limited federal legislation in the area. Only two states required victim notification of crucial developments in the criminal proceedings, one state authorized victim input into key prosecutorial decisions, eight states required a victim impact statement at sentencing, three states authorized victim allocution at sentencing, and six states allowed victims and other members of the public to attend parole hearings. Although thirty-seven states had some form of victim compensation program, many of these were not functioning at an optimal level. Only eight states required victim restitution as part of an offender's sentence and seven states provided funds for services to all crime victims. Just four states had any kind of comprehensive laws that included multiple victim rights provisions.[2]

In its *Final Report*, the President's Task Force provided an action plan addressed to the federal and state executive, legislative, and judicial branches and criminal justice system entities, and to others involved in crime victim service delivery. In its over sixty specific action recommendations, the Task Force proposed mechanisms to expand crime victim access to and participation in the criminal justice process, as well as to enhance crime victim services.[3] In the almost thirty years since the issuance of the *Final Report*, the legislative, judicial, and research response to the Task Force recommendations has dramatically transformed the status of victim rights and remedies in this country.

Over thirty states have ratified constitutional amendments that contain crime victim "bills of rights" or other victim-related provisions[4] and proposals for a federal victim rights constitutional amendment have been introduced in Congress.[5] It has been estimated that there are over 27,000 federal and state statutes that directly or indirectly affect crime victim rights and interests.[6] More specifically, the federal government and the majority of states have constitutional or legislative provisions, or both, that require crime victim notification of important events and actions in the criminal justice process and allow, to varying degrees, crime victim presence and hearing at critical stages of the criminal justice process. The federal government and all of the states have statutory victim compensation programs, as well as restitution provisions that authorize restitution as a probation condition or as an independent sentence, or both. Opportunities for victim civil litigation against offenders and others have been enhanced by statute and practice.[7]

The breadth of the expansion of crime victim rights and remedies in the years since the President's Task Force on Victims of Crime might cause one to conclude that work on the Task Force recommendations has been largely completed. In fact, substantial responsive executive, legislative, judicial, and criminal justice system action has been undertaken on most of the applicable Task Force recommendations. Few would deny that significant progress has been made. Nevertheless, as discussed throughout this text, the actual extent of the progress, and the optimal scope of crime victim rights and remedies, remain matters of some debate. Not surprisingly, therefore, views as to the future course of victim rights and remedies vary considerably. A sampling of such views will be briefly discussed here.

Visions of the Future

As a result of their 1995 study of crime victims, local criminal justice and victim services personnel, and state officials in two states with "strong" victim rights provisions and two states with "weak" provisions concerning rights to notice, presence, hearing, and restitution, the researchers concluded that implementation of victim rights is a "linear process," consisting of a chain of events and behaviors occurring in the context of the larger criminal justice system. They identified the essential links in the chain as the "passage of strong laws; education regarding crime victims' rights; resources to implement rights; and enhancing motivation and/or allowing for the enforcement of victims' rights."[8]

More specifically, they concluded that the passage of strong victim rights laws is an essential first step in ensuring the provision of crime victim rights, as reflected by the generally higher degree of rights implementation in the "strong" states versus the "weak" states in their study.[9] The existence of victim rights provisions is meaningless, however, unless criminal justice personnel entrusted with their implementation and crime victims themselves are aware of and educated about the laws. The next crucial link is the availability of resources to carry out the laws. These researchers found that surveyed local personnel and state officials most frequently cited resource limitations as the reason that they were unable to implement victim rights provisions. These researchers noted that resource limitations could result from an actual resource deficiency or from the low priority given to the implementation of victim rights. The former possibility could be addressed by the use of an information tracking and accounting system to help officials better maximize existing resources toward the more efficient implementation of victim rights. The latter possibility could be addressed by better education regarding the importance of victim rights with a resulting potentially higher funding priority given to such.[10]

Finally, these researchers stressed the importance of the motivation of criminal justice personnel to implement victim rights and remedies. At the outset, these researchers suggested better mechanisms to track official compliance with victim rights responsibilities. Such a tracking mechanism is an important means to improve rights implementation, adjust resource allocations, and identify official failure or refusal to implement victim rights. To "motivate" criminal justice officials who refuse to implement victim rights, these researchers proposed giving victims some means to enforce their rights. In this regard, almost half of surveyed local criminal justice and victim service personnel favored giving victims a right to bring disciplinary proceedings against officials to enforce their rights, with smaller percentages favoring the availability of a civil action for damages or declaratory or injunctive relief.[11] Thus, by starting with a base of "strong" victim rights laws and providing the education, resources, and motivation necessary for their implementation, these researchers concluded that greater implementation of crime victim rights and remedies could be achieved.[12]

Several of these themes were also reflected in the study that resulted in *New Directions from the Field: Victims' Rights and Services for the 21st Century*[13] in 1998. The study authors noted areas of progress since the President's Task Force, but also identified areas of needed improvement regarding victim rights and services. They compiled over 250 recommendations based on input from over 1,000 crime victims, criminal justice practitioners, and professionals involved in victim service delivery. These action recommendations, addressed to the governmental entities and professions that come in contact with crime victims, were synthesized into five global challenges for responding to crime victims in the years ahead: to enact and enforce consistent, fundamental crime victim rights; to provide access to comprehensive, quality victim services; to ensure that those involved in the justice system and victim service delivery receive comprehensive training regarding victim issues; to support, improve, and replicate promising practices regarding victim rights and services; and to ensure that crime victims play a central role in the nation's response to crime and victimization.[14]

The study authors' specific recommendations regarding crime victim rights and remedies have been noted throughout this text. In this connection, they proposed additional efforts to fulfill the original action recommendations of the President's Task Force, such as ways to improve victim access to and utilization of financial remedies. Based on the lessons learned in the years following the issuance of the *Final Report*, the study authors also suggested refinement and expansion of some Task Force recommendations, such as an expanded federal victim rights constitutional amendment proposal; more explicit and broader victim rights to notice, presence, and hearing; and recognition of victim standing and other mechanisms to enforce granted rights.[15]

More recently, one leading victim rights scholar has suggested a "third wave" of victim rights following the first wave of the enactment of statutory victim rights and the second wave of the adoption of constitutional victim rights by over thirty states. Although noteworthy accomplishments, this scholar suggests that these rights are often illusory for several reasons. For example, some degree of governmental discretion is often incorporated into the provision of these victim rights that hinders or precludes victim standing to assert rights violations, or victim standing is expressly limited or precluded. Effective remedies for the violation of victim rights are either expressly precluded or limited. Meaningful appellate review of victim rights violations is impaired due to the inability to assert a rights violation in a timely fashion that avoids problems of ripeness and mootness, as well as the express limitations on appellate review of rights violations or the provision of solely discretionary appellate or writ review.[16]

To overcome these obstacles and actually make victim rights meaningful, this scholar proposes a "third wave" of victim rights in which victims have standing to assert rights violations, an effective remedy, and appellate review as a matter of right. Although he proposes a federal victim rights constitutional amendment as the best way to achieve these goals nationally, he notes the difficulty of such an undertaking and identifies alternative means for states to achieve the goals. To facilitate victim standing to assert rights violations, states need to convert any discretionary victim rights in their statutes or constitutional provisions to mandatory, self-enabling rights; to narrowly define and provide mechanisms for review of any exceptions to mandatory provisions; and/or to explicitly grant victims standing to seek redress for rights violations.[17]

Regarding remedies for rights violations, this scholar characterizes as inferior remedies those remedies meant to compensate victims for rights violations (e.g., civil suits, injunctions, or administrative or disciplinary actions) and notes their limited effectiveness and availability. On the other hand, superior remedies permit victims to exercise their rights following a rights violation and consist of voiding the result and requiring reconsideration. This scholar urges states to eliminate the widely adopted constitutional and statutory provisions that prohibit or limit the remedy of voiding and reconsideration based on a victim rights violation and to authorize this "superior" remedy for the violation. He notes that many of the current prohibitions are based on concerns about the defendant's double jeopardy rights. While such concerns might preclude the voiding of a trial based on a violation of the victim right to attend, they should not affect the voiding of any pretrial rulings or actions involving victim rights. Moreover, the denial of a mandatory victim right to be heard at a plea or sentencing proceeding should be analogized to a similar deprivation for a defendant or the government that would permit voiding of the proceeding and reconsideration of the result following the provision of the violated right, without a violation of the double jeopardy principles.[18]

Finally, this scholar proposes a *nondiscretionary* writ of mandamus to provide meaningful appellate review of victim rights violations. To avoid problems of ripeness or mootness in the appellate assertion of victim rights violations, he proposes that issues regarding the assertion of victim rights be addressed prior to trial to permit time for interlocutory appellate review, if necessary.[19]

This scholar notes that Congress provided a model for many of these "third wave" proposals in the Crime Victims' Rights Act of 2004. In fact, the Act was designed to provide such a model to the states. Moreover, Congress authorized accompanying grants for five years following the Act's enactment for training and technical assistance to states to update their victim rights laws and to design compliance systems, as well as for legal counsel and support for victims to enforce their rights in states with "substantially equivalent" laws to the federal Act. Rather than continuing the effort to enact a federal victim rights constitutional amendment (that actually lacked sufficient Congressional support for adoption at that time), advocates of the amendment agreed to defer their efforts for at least the next five years to review the impact of the federal statutory efforts on the further development of victim rights and remedies at the state level.[20]

Five years since the enactment of the Crime Victims' Rights Act have now elapsed. Whatever the assessment of the progress that states have made regarding the development of their victim rights provisions, it is anticipated that advocacy and opposition regarding a federal victim rights constitutional amendment will re-emerge at some point. Both the President's Task Force and the *New Directions from the Field* authors recommended the adoption of a federal victim rights constitutional amendment.[21] In addition to the deficiencies of the current victim rights laws described above, proponents of a victim rights amendment have contended that only a federal constitutional amendment can achieve the uniform provision of the enumerated victim rights in this country, and that it is essential to the enforcement of such rights. They have also maintained that the statutory victim rights provisions in the federal system and every state and even the constitutional provisions in now thirty-three states are inadequate to secure victim rights because they remain "subservient" to defendants' federal constitutional rights. They contend, therefore, that a federal victim rights constitutional amendment is required to achieve a "balance" between the rights of victims and defendants.[22]

At the outset, however, although the last version of the proposed federal victim rights constitutional amendment prior to the adoption of the Crime Victims' Rights Act in 2004 includes the major participatory rights to notice, presence, and hearing regarding the criminal justice process, restitution, and certain other rights *and* gives victims authority to assert the granted rights and Congress power to enforce them, the proposal also contains many of the limitations of the state provisions. In this connection, the proposed rights are restricted to only certain eligible victims, i.e., victims of violent crime. Some of the proposed rights are limited to their "reasonable" provision rather than stated in absolute terms. Moreover, any of the prescribed rights can be restricted "when and to the degree dictated by a substantial interest in public safety or the administration of criminal justice, or by compelling necessity." The proposed amendment does not provide grounds for a new trial and does not authorize a claim for damages. Thus, despite work on this amendment proposal since it was first introduced in 1996, the last significant version of the proposed federal victim rights amendment contains many of the limitations found in the state provisions.[23]

Moreover, opponents of a federal constitutional victim rights provision contend that such a provision is a constitutionally inappropriate, potentially counterproductive, and ultimately unnecessary means to secure greater enforcement of the thousands of already existing federal and state statutory and state constitutional victim rights provisions. They also deny that any lack of enforcement of victim rights has been the product of an "imbalance" between defendant and victim rights.[24] One scholar has suggested that any lack of enforcement of victim rights is most likely the result of lack of resources and personnel rather than malevolence or indifference toward victim rights. He suggests that the provision of greater enabling resources and the use of administrative sanctions, in the rare instances when such are appropriate, would achieve greater enforcement of crime victim rights than a largely symbolic federal constitutional amendment.[25] Thus, when the debate over a federal victim rights constitutional amendment resumes, it will include not only whether to have such an amendment, but, if so, what provisions should be included in it.

All of the above recommendations suggest enhancements of the existing criminal justice system to obtain resulting enhancements of victim rights and remedies. Others, however, have suggested that alternatives to the existing justice system must be explored that are more responsive to crime victim needs. "Restorative justice" is the term that has been applied to a variety of such alternative proposals. Included in this evolving concept are existing approaches found in victim impact statements and panels, restitution, and community service, as well as expanded use of victim-offender mediation or other forms of alternative dispute resolution. These proposals share the common principles that the government, victim, offender, and community should be included in an integrated effort to resolve a criminal episode and achieve public safety. The goals of this approach are to repair the harm caused to the victim and the community by the crime and to hold the offender accountable for the harm and for aiding in its repair. In many ways, restorative justice principles incorporate approaches of the ancient victim-centered justice systems.[26]

Whether viewed as associated with a restorative justice approach or not, there has been an increasing use of strategies associated with the restorative justice concept. As discussed in Chapter 8, judges are increasingly imposing restitution as part of offenders' sentences. Similarly, community service is a frequent component of community-based sentences. There are currently almost 300 victim-offender mediation programs in this country, primarily used to resolve property or minor assault cases.[27] Advocates of such mediation programs believe that they result in increased victim satisfaction and reduced fear of revictimization and increased offender accountability. In addition, they can divert minor cases from the formal justice process and reduce disposition time and incarceration use and costs. Critics raise concerns about the absence of procedural and substantive due process in the programs, outcome disparity, and the inappropriateness of the approach for many victims and offenders and regarding many crimes.[28] Even the most ardent proponents of restorative justice do not anticipate the dismantling of the existing criminal justice system and the substitution of a restorative justice system in the near future. Nevertheless, they do believe that more restorative justice principles can be incorporated into the existing system and that appropriate cases can be diverted for disposition through a restorative justice model.[29]

Conclusion

Whatever one's views are as to the future of crime victim rights and remedies, few could deny that significant progress has been made in restoring a role for crime victims in the American criminal justice process in the years since the President's Task Force on Victims of Crime. Unlike the situation existing prior to the Task Force work, crime victims now have much greater means to have access to and provide input into the criminal justice process and have expanded remedies to be "made whole" from harm caused by their victimization. These newly created or expanded rights and remedies by no means restore the early victim-centered model of criminal prosecution, but they do provide an opportunity for greater victim participation in and recompense from the criminal justice process.

The crime victim rights and remedies described in this text have been adopted against a backdrop of great expectations *and* concerns about their impact on the criminal justice process, both of which have been largely unrealized as the empirical research in this text has shown. With almost thirty years of federal and state legislative and judicial experience with the implementation of these expanded victim rights and remedies, it is perhaps an appropriate time for jurisdictions to assess the status of available rights and remedies and modify or clarify the provisions as necessary to achieve their intended purposes. The range of legislative and judicial approaches described in this text, as well as the research and policy evaluations of them, can help inform such an assessment. Moreover, jurisdictions should review the adequacy and effectiveness of their implementation of established victim rights and remedies.

The relevant current focus should be to ensure that crime victim rights and remedies are appropriate and meaningful in the context of the varied individual and societal interests involved in criminal prosecutions. Criminal proceedings must be fair for all of those with an interest in them, including the victim, the defendant, the prosecuting authority, and society as a whole. In this connection, crime victim rights and remedies can form part of that universally sought goal of achieving justice in criminal proceedings in this country.

Appendix 1

President's Task Force on Victims of Crime Action Recommendations

Proposed Executive and Legislative Action at the Federal and State Levels

Recommendations for Federal and State Action

1. Legislation should be proposed and enacted to ensure that addresses of victims and witnesses are not made public or available to the defense, absent a clear need as determined by the court.
2. Legislation should be proposed and enacted to ensure that designated victim counseling is legally privileged and not subject to defense discovery or subpoena.
3. Legislation should be proposed and enacted to ensure that hearsay is admissible and sufficient in preliminary hearings, so that victims need not testify in person.
4. Legislation should be proposed and enacted to amend the bail laws to accomplish the following:
   a. Allow courts to deny bail to persons found by clear and convincing evidence to present a danger to the community;
   b. Give the prosecution the right to expedited appeal of adverse bail determinations, analogous to the right presently held by the defendant;

    c. Codify existing case law defining the authority of the court to detain defendants as to whom no conditions of release are adequate to ensure appearance at trial;

    d. Reverse, in the case of serious crimes, any standard that presumptively favors release of convicted persons awaiting sentence or appealing their convictions;

    e. Require defendants to refrain from criminal activity as a mandatory condition of release; and

    f. Provide penalties for failing to appear while released on bond or personal recognizance that are more closely proportionate to the penalties for the offense with which the defendant was originally charged.

5. Legislation should be proposed and enacted to abolish the exclusionary rule as it applies to Fourth Amendment issues.

6. Legislation should be proposed and enacted to open parole release hearings to the public.

7. Legislation should be proposed and enacted to abolish parole and limit judicial discretion in sentencing.

8. Legislation should be proposed and enacted to require that school officials report violent offenses against students or teachers, or the possession of weapons or narcotics on school grounds. The knowing failure to make such a report to the police, or deterring others from doing so, should be designated a misdemeanor.

9. Legislation should be proposed and enacted to make available to businesses and organizations the sexual assault, child molestation, and pornography arrest records of prospective and present employees whose work will bring them in regular contact with children.

10. Legislation should be proposed and enacted to accomplish the following:

    a. Require victim impact statements at sentencing;

    b. Provide for the protection of victims and witnesses from intimidation;

    c. Require restitution in all cases, unless the court provides specific reasons for failing to require it;

    d. Develop and implement guidelines for the fair treatment of crime victims and witnesses; and

    e. Prohibit a criminal from making any profit from the sale of the story of his crime. Any proceeds should be used to provide full restitution to his victims, pay the expenses of his prosecution, and finally, assist the crime victim compensation fund.

11. Legislation should be proposed and enacted to establish or expand employee assistance programs for victims of crime employed by government.

12. Legislation should be proposed and enacted to ensure that sexual assault victims are not required to assume the cost of physical examinations and materials used to obtain evidence.

Proposed Federal Action

1. Congress should enact legislation to provide federal funding to assist state crime victim compensation programs.

2. Congress should enact legislation to provide federal funding, reasonably matched by local revenues, to assist in the operation of federal, state, local, and private nonprofit victim/witness assistance agencies that make comprehensive assistance available to all victims of crime.

3. The federal government should establish a federally based resource center for victim and witness assistance.

4. The President should establish a task force to study the serious problem of violence within the family, including violence against children, spouse abuse, and abuse of the elderly, and to review and evaluate national, state, and local efforts to address this problem.

5. A study should be commissioned at the federal level to evaluate the juvenile justice system from the perspective of the victim.

6. The Task Force endorses the principle of accountability for gross negligence of parole board officials in releasing into the community dangerous criminals who then injure others. A study should be commissioned at the federal level to determine how, and under what circumstances, this principle of accountability should be implemented.

Proposed Action for Criminal Justice System Agencies

Recommendations for Police

1. Police departments should develop and implement training programs to ensure that police officers are:
   a. Sensitive to the needs of victims; and
   b. Informed, knowledgeable, and supportive of the existing local services and programs for victims.
2. Police departments should establish procedures for the prompt photographing and return of property to victims (with the prosecutor's approval).
3. Police departments should establish procedures to ensure that victims of violent crime are periodically informed of the status and closing of investigations.
4. Police officers should give a high priority to investigating witnesses' reports of threats or intimidation and should forward these reports to the prosecutor.

Recommendations for Prosecutors

1. Prosecutors should assume ultimate responsibility for informing victims of the status of a case from the time of the initial charging decision to determinations of parole.
2. Prosecutors have an obligation to bring to the attention of the court the views of victims of violent crime on bail decisions, continuances, plea bargains, dismissals, sentencing, and restitution. They should establish procedures to ensure that such victims are given the opportunity to make their views on these matters known.
3. Prosecutors should charge and pursue to the fullest extent of the law defendants who harass, threaten, injure, or otherwise attempt to intimidate or retaliate against victims or witnesses.
4. Prosecutors should strongly discourage case continuances. When such delays are necessary, procedures should be established to ensure that cases are continued to dates agreeable to victims and witnesses, that those dates are secured in

advance whenever possible, and that the reasons for the continuances are adequately explained.

5. Prosecutors' offices should use a victim and witness on-call system.

6. Prosecutors' offices should establish procedures to ensure the prompt return of victims' property, absent a need for the actual evidence in court.

7. Prosecutors' offices should establish and maintain direct liaison with victim/witness units and other victim service agencies.

8. Prosecutors must recognize the profound impact that crimes of sexual violence have on both child and adult victims and their families.

Recommendations for the Judiciary

1. It should be mandatory that judges at both the trial and appellate level participate in a training program addressing the needs and legal interests of crime victims.

2. Judges should allow victims and witnesses to be on call for court proceedings.

3. Judges or their court administrators should establish separate waiting rooms for prosecution and defense witnesses.

4. When ruling on requests for continuances, judges should give the same weight to the interests of victims and witnesses as that given to the interests of defendants. Further, judges should explain the basis for such rulings on the record.

5. Judges should bear their share of responsibility for reducing court congestion by ensuring that all participants fully and responsibly utilize court time.

6. Judges should allow for, and give appropriate weight to, input at sentencing from victims of violent crime.

7. Judges should order restitution to the victim in all cases in which the victim has suffered financial loss, unless they state compelling reasons for a contrary ruling on the record.

8. Judges should allow the victim and a member of the victim's family to attend the trial, even if identified as witnesses, absent a compelling need to the contrary.

9. Judges should give substantial weight to the victim's interest in speedy return of property before trial in ruling on the admissibility of photographs of that property.

10. Judges should recognize the profound impact that sexual molestation of children has on victims and their families and treat it as a crime that should result in punishment, with treatment available when appropriate.

Recommendations for Parole Boards

1. Parole boards should notify victims of crime and their families in advance of parole hearings, if names and addresses have been previously provided by these individuals.
2. Parole boards should allow victims of crime, their families, or their representatives to attend parole hearings and make known the effect of the offender's crime on them.
3. Parole boards should take whatever steps are necessary to ensure that parolees charged with a crime while on parole are immediately returned to custody and kept there until the case is adjudicated.
4. Parole boards should not apply the exclusionary rule to parole revocation hearings.

Recommendations for Other Organizations

Recommendations for Hospitals

1. Hospitals should establish and implement training programs for hospital personnel to sensitize them to the needs of victims of violent crimes, especially the elderly and those who have been sexually assaulted.
2. Hospitals should provide emergency medical assistance to victims of violent crime without regard to their ability to pay, and collect payments from state victim compensation programs.
3. Hospitals should provide emergency room crisis counseling to victims of crime and their families.
4. Hospitals should encourage and develop direct liaison with all victim assistance and social service agencies.
5. Hospitals should develop, in consultation with prosecuting agencies, a standardized rape kit for proper collection of physical evidence, and develop a procedure to ensure proper stor-

age and maintenance of such evidence until it is released to the appropriate agency.

Recommendations for the Ministry

1. The ministry should recognize and address the needs of crime victims.
2. The ministry should develop both seminary and in-service training on the criminal justice system, the needs of victims, and ways to restore victims' spiritual and material health.

Recommendations for the Bar

1. All attorneys should recognize that they have an obligation, as officers of the court, to make certain that the justice system deals fairly with all participants in criminal litigation.
2. Prosecutors in particular should recognize their obligation to be active members of the bar at the local, state, and national levels and to represent the often unspoken needs and interests of victims.
3. Those who organize formal bar committees to deal with issues arising in the criminal justice system should ensure that the members of such groups represent a balance between opposing parties in criminal litigation.

Recommendations for Schools

1. School authorities should develop and require compliance with guidelines for prompt reporting of violent crimes committed in schools, crimes committed against school personnel, and the possession of weapons or narcotics.
2. School authorities should check the arrest and conviction records for sexual assault, child molestation, or pornography offenses of anyone applying for work in a school, including anyone doing contract work involving regular proximity to students, and make submission to such a check a precondition for employment.
3. Educators should develop and provide courses on the problems, needs, and legal interests of victims of crime.

4. School authorities should be mindful of their responsibility to make students aware of how they can avoid being victimized by crime.

Recommendations for the Mental Health Community

1. The mental health community should develop and provide immediate and long-term psychological treatment programs for victims of crime and their families.
2. The mental health community should establish training programs that will enable practitioners to treat crime victims and their families.
3. The mental health community should study the immediate and long-term psychological effects of criminal victimization.
4. The mental health community should work with public agencies, victim compensation boards, and private insurers to make psychological treatment readily available to crime victims and their families.
5. The mental health community should establish and maintain direct liaison with other victim service agencies.

Recommendations for the Private Sector

1. Businesses should authorize paid administrative leave for employees who must miss work because of injuries sustained in a violent crime, and for employees who must attend court hearings.
2. Businesses should establish employee assistance programs for victims of crime.
3. Creditors should make liberal allowances for persons who are unable to make timely payments because of recent victimization.
4. The private sector should encourage private contributions of money and other support to victim service agencies, whether public or private.

A Proposed Amendment to the Constitution

(to add the italicized language to the Sixth Amendment to the United States Constitution):

In all criminal prosecutions the accused shall enjoy the right to a speedy and public trial, by an impartial jury of the State and district wherein the crime shall have been committed, which district shall have been previously ascertained by law, and to be informed of the nature and cause of the accusation; to be confronted with the witnesses against him; to have compulsory process for obtaining witnesses in his favor and to have the Assistance of Counsel for his defense. *Likewise, the victim, in every criminal prosecution shall have the right to be present and to be heard at all critical stages of judicial proceedings.*

Appendix 2

Proposed Federal Victim Rights Constitutional Amendment

Senate Joint Resolution 1

(Introduced January 7, 2003[1])

SECTION 1. The rights of victims of violent crime, being capable of protection without denying the constitutional rights of those accused of victimizing them, are hereby established and shall not be denied by any State or the United States and may be restricted only as provided in this article.

SECTION 2. A victim of violent crime shall have the right to reasonable and timely notice of any public proceeding involving the crime and of any release or escape of the accused; the rights not to be excluded from such public proceeding and reasonably to be heard at public release, plea, sentencing, reprieve, and pardon proceedings; and the right to adjudicative decisions that duly consider the victim's safety, interest in avoiding unreasonable delay, and just and timely claims to restitution from the offender. These rights shall not be restricted except when and to the degree dictated by a substantial interest in public safety or the administration of criminal justice, or by compelling necessity.

SECTION 3. Nothing in this article shall be construed to provide grounds for a new trial or to authorize any claim for damages. Only the victim or the victim's lawful representative may assert the rights es-

---

1. A proposed federal victim rights constitutional amendment was first introduced in Congress in 1996. In this appendix, the last Senate version of the proposed amendment prior to the enactment of the federal statutory Crime Victims' Rights Act in 2004 is presented. Companion joint resolutions with identical text were introduced in the House of Representatives (H.R.J. Res. 10; H.R.J. Res. 48). Although a Senate committee approved this proposed amendment, neither the full Senate nor House of Representatives voted on it.

tablished by this article, and no person accused of the crime may obtain any form of relief hereunder.

SECTION 4. Congress shall have power to enforce by appropriate legislation the provisions of this article. Nothing in this article shall affect the President's authority to grant reprieves or pardons.

SECTION 5. This article shall be inoperative unless it has been ratified as an amendment to the Constitution by the legislatures of three-fourths of the several States within 7 years from the date of its submission to the States by the Congress. This article shall take effect on the 180th day after the date of its ratification.

Appendix 3

State Victim Rights Constitutional Provisions

Alabama
(Article I, §6.01; 1994[1])

Crime Victims; Rights

(a) Crime victims, as defined by law or their lawful representatives, including the next of kin of homicide victims, are entitled to the right to be informed, to be present, and to be heard when authorized, at all crucial stages of criminal proceedings, to the extent that these rights do not interfere with the constitutional rights of the person accused of committing the crime.

(b) Nothing in this amendment or in any enabling statute adopted pursuant to this amendment shall be construed as creating a cause of action against the state or any of its agencies, officials, employees, or political subdivisions. The Legislature may from time to time enact enabling legislation to carry out and implement this amendment.

Alaska
(Article I, §§12, 24; 1994)

Section 12. Criminal Administration. Excessive bail shall not be required, nor excessive fines imposed, nor cruel and unusual punishments inflicted. Criminal administration shall be based upon the following: the need for protecting the public, community condemnation of the offender, the rights of victims of crimes, restitution from the offender, and the principle of reformation.

Section 24. Rights of Crime Victims. Crime victims, as defined by law, shall have the following rights as provided by law: the right to be reasonably protected from the accused through the imposition of appropriate bail or condi-

---

1. The year stated reflects the year of voter approval of the amendment.

247

tions of release by the court; the right to confer with the prosecution; the right to be treated with dignity, respect, and fairness during all phases of the criminal and juvenile justice process; the right to timely disposition of the case following the arrest of the accused; the right to obtain information about and be allowed to be present at all criminal or juvenile proceedings where the accused has the right to be present; the right to be allowed to be heard, upon request, at sentencing, before or after conviction or juvenile adjudication, and at any proceeding where the accused's release from custody is considered; the right to restitution from the accused; and the right to be informed, upon request, of the accused's escape or release from custody before or after conviction or juvenile adjudication.

Arizona

(Article 2, §2.1; 1990)

Victims' Bill of Rights

(A) To preserve and protect victims' rights to justice and due process, a victim of crime has a right:

1. To be treated with fairness, respect, and dignity, and to be free from intimidation, harassment, or abuse, throughout the criminal justice process.

2. To be informed, upon request, when the accused or convicted person is released from custody or has escaped.

3. To be present at and, upon request, to be informed of all criminal proceedings where the defendant has the right to be present.

4. To be heard at any proceeding involving a post-arrest release decision, a negotiated plea, and sentencing.

5. To refuse an interview, deposition, or other discovery request by the defendant, the defendant's attorney, or other person acting on behalf of the defendant.

6. To confer with the prosecution, after the crime against the victim has been charged, before trial or before any disposition of the case and to be informed of the disposition.

7. To read pre-sentence reports relating to the crime against the victim when they are available to the defendant.

8. To receive prompt restitution from the person or persons convicted of the criminal conduct that caused the victim's loss or injury.

9. To be heard at any proceeding when any post-conviction release from confinement is being considered.

10. To a speedy trial or disposition and prompt and final conclusion of the case after the conviction and sentence.

11. To have all rules governing criminal procedure and the admissibility of evidence in all criminal proceedings protect victims' rights and to have these rules be subject to amendment or repeal by the legislature to ensure the protection of these rights.

12. To be informed of victims' constitutional rights.

(B) A victim's exercise of any right granted by this section shall not be grounds for dismissing any criminal proceeding or setting aside any conviction or sentence.

(C) "Victim" means a person against whom the criminal offense has been committed or, if the person is killed or incapacitated, the person's spouse, parent, child or other lawful representative, except if the person is in custody for an offense or is the accused.

(D) The legislature, or the people by initiative or referendum, have the authority to enact substantive and procedural laws to define, implement, preserve and protect the rights guaranteed to victims by this section, including the authority to extend any of these rights to juvenile proceedings.

(E) The enumeration in the constitution of certain rights for victims shall not be construed to deny or disparage others granted by the legislature or retained by victims.

California

(Article 1, § 28; 1982, 2008)

(a) The People of the State of California find and declare all of the following:

(1) Criminal activity has a serious impact on the citizens of California. The rights of victims of crime and their families in criminal prosecutions are a subject of grave statewide concern.

(2) Victims of crime are entitled to have the criminal justice system view criminal acts as serious threats to the safety and welfare of the people of California. The enactment of comprehensive provisions and laws ensuring a bill of rights for victims of crime, including safeguards in the criminal justice system fully protecting those rights and ensuring that crime victims are treated with respect and dignity, is a matter of high public importance. California's victims of crime are largely dependent upon the proper functioning of government, upon the criminal justice system and upon the expeditious enforcement of the rights of victims of crime described herein, in order to protect the public safety

and to secure justice when the public safety has been compromised by criminal activity.

(3) The rights of victims pervade the criminal justice system. These rights include personally held and enforceable rights described in paragraphs (1) through (17) of subdivision (b).

(4) The rights of victims also include broader shared collective rights that are held in common with all of the People of the State of California and that are enforceable through the enactment of laws and through good-faith efforts and actions of California's elected, appointed, and publicly employed officials. These rights encompass the expectation shared with all of the people of California that persons who commit felonious acts causing injury to innocent victims will be appropriately and thoroughly investigated, appropriately detained in custody, brought before the courts of California even if arrested outside the State, tried by the courts in a timely manner, sentenced, and sufficiently punished so that the public safety is protected and encouraged as a goal of highest importance.

(5) Victims of crime have a collectively shared right to expect that persons convicted of committing criminal acts are sufficiently punished in both the manner and the length of the sentences imposed by the courts of the State of California. This right includes the right to expect that the punitive and deterrent effect of custodial sentences imposed by the courts will not be undercut or diminished by the granting of rights and privileges to prisoners that are not required by any provision of the United States Constitution or by the laws of this State to be granted to any person incarcerated in a penal or other custodial facility in this State as a punishment or correction for the commission of a crime.

(6) Victims of crime are entitled to finality in their criminal cases. Lengthy appeals and other post-judgment proceedings that challenge criminal convictions, frequent and difficult parole hearings that threaten to release criminal offenders, and the ongoing threat that the sentences of criminal wrongdoers will be reduced, prolong the suffering of crime victims for many years after the crimes themselves have been perpetrated. This prolonged suffering of crime victims and their families must come to an end.

(7) Finally, the People find and declare that the right to public safety extends to public and private primary, elementary, junior high, and senior high school, and community college, California State University, University of California, and private college and university campuses, where students and staff have the right to be safe and secure in their persons.

(8) To accomplish the goals it is necessary that the laws of California relating to the criminal justice process be amended in order to protect the legitimate rights of victims of crime.

(b) In order to preserve and protect a victim's rights to justice and due process, a victim shall be entitled to the following rights:

(1) To be treated with fairness and respect for his or her privacy and dignity, and to be free from intimidation, harassment, and abuse, throughout the criminal or juvenile justice process.

(2) To be reasonably protected from the defendant and persons acting on behalf of the defendant.

(3) To have the safety of the victim and the victim's family considered in fixing the amount of bail and release conditions for the defendant.

(4) To prevent the disclosure of confidential information or records to the defendant, the defendant's attorney, or any other person acting on behalf of the defendant, which could be used to locate or harass the victim or the victim's family or which disclose confidential communications made in the course of medical or counseling treatment, or which are otherwise privileged or confidential by law.

(5) To refuse an interview, deposition, or discovery request by the defendant, the defendant's attorney, or any other person acting on behalf of the defendant, and to set reasonable conditions on the conduct of any such interview to which the victim consents.

(6) To reasonable notice of and to reasonably confer with the prosecuting agency, upon request, regarding, the arrest of the defendant if known by the prosecutor, the charges filed, the determination whether to extradite the defendant, and, upon request, to be notified of and informed before any pretrial disposition of the case.

(7) To reasonable notice of all public proceedings, including delinquency proceedings, upon request, at which the defendant and the prosecutor are entitled to be present and of all parole or other post-conviction release proceedings, and to be present at all such proceedings.

(8) To be heard, upon request, at any proceeding, including any delinquency proceeding, involving a post-arrest release decision, plea, sentencing, post-conviction release decision, or any proceeding in which a right of the victim is at issue.

(9) To a speedy trial and a prompt and final conclusion of the case and any related post-judgment proceedings.

(10) To provide information to a probation department official conducting a pre-sentence investigation concerning the impact of the offense on the victim and the victim's family and any sentencing recommendations before the sentencing of the defendant.

(11) To receive, upon request, the pre-sentence report when available to the defendant, except for those portions made confidential by law.

(12) To be informed, upon request, of the conviction, sentence, place and time of incarceration, or other disposition of the defendant, the scheduled release date of the defendant, and the release of or the escape by the defendant from custody.

(13) To restitution.

(A) It is the unequivocal intention of the People of the State of California that all persons who suffer losses as a result of criminal activity shall have the right to seek and secure restitution from the persons convicted of the crimes causing the losses they suffer.

(B) Restitution shall be ordered from the convicted wrongdoer in every case, regardless of the sentence or disposition imposed, in which a crime victim suffers a loss.

(C) All monetary payments, monies, and property collected from any person who has been ordered to make restitution shall be first applied to pay the amounts ordered as restitution to the victim.

(14) To the prompt return of property when no longer needed as evidence.

(15) To be informed of all parole procedures, to participate in the parole process, to provide information to the parole authority to be considered before the parole of the offender, and to be notified, upon request, of the parole or other release of the offender.

(16) To have the safety of the victim, the victim's family, and the general public considered before any parole or other post-judgment release decision is made.

(17) To be informed of the rights enumerated in paragraphs (1) through (16).

(c) (1) A victim, the retained attorney of a victim, a lawful representative of the victim, or the prosecuting attorney upon request of the victim, may enforce the rights enumerated in subdivision (b) in any trial or appellate court with jurisdiction over the case as a matter of right. The court shall act promptly on such a request.

(2) This section does not create any cause of action for compensation or damages against the State, any political subdivision of the State, any officer, employee, or agent of the State or of any of its political subdivisions, or any officer or employee of the court.

(d) The granting of these rights to victims shall not be construed to deny or disparage other rights possessed by victims. The court in its discretion may extend the right to be heard at sentencing to any person harmed by the defendant. The parole authority shall extend the right to be heard at a parole hearing to any person harmed by the offender.

(e) As used in this section, a "victim" is a person who suffers direct or threatened physical, psychological, or financial harm as a result of the commission or attempted commission of a crime or delinquent act. The term "victim" also includes the person's spouse, parents, children, siblings, or guardian, and includes a lawful representative of a crime victim who is deceased, a minor, or physically or psychologically incapacitated. The term "victim" does not include a person in custody for an offense, the accused, or a person whom the court finds would not act in the best interests of a minor victim.

(f) In addition to the enumerated rights provided in subdivision (b) that are personally enforceable by victims as provided in subdivision (c), victims of crime have additional rights that are shared with all of the People of the State of California. These collectively held rights include, but are not limited to, the following:

(1) Right to Safe Schools. All students and staff of public primary, elementary, junior high, and senior high schools, and community colleges, colleges, and universities have the inalienable right to attend campuses which are safe, secure and peaceful.

(2) Right to Truth-in-Evidence. Except as provided by statute hereafter enacted by a two-thirds vote of the membership in each house of the Legislature, relevant evidence shall not be excluded in any criminal proceeding, including pretrial and postconviction motions and hearings, or in any trial or hearing of a juvenile for a criminal offense, whether heard in juvenile or adult court. Nothing in this section shall affect any existing statutory rule of evidence relating to privilege or hearsay, or Evidence Code Sections 352, 782 or 1103. Nothing in this section shall affect any existing statutory or constitutional right of the press.

(3) Public Safety Bail. A person may be released on bail by sufficient sureties, except for capital crimes when the facts are evident or the presumption great. Excessive bail may not be required. In setting, reducing or denying bail, the judge or magistrate shall take into consideration the protection of the public, the safety of the victim, the seriousness of the offense charged, the previous criminal record of the defendant, and the probability of his or her appearing at the trial or hearing of the case. Public safety and the safety of the victim shall be the primary considerations.

A person may be released on his or her own recognizance in the court's discretion, subject to the same factors considered in setting bail.

Before any person arrested for a serious felony may be released on bail, a hearing may be held before the magistrate or judge, and the prosecuting attorney and the victim shall be given notice and reasonable opportunity to be heard on the matter.

When a judge or magistrate grants or denies bail or release on a person's own recognizance, the reasons for that decision shall be stated in the record and included in the court's minutes.

(4) Use of Prior Convictions. Any prior felony conviction of any person in any criminal proceeding, whether adult or juvenile, shall subsequently be used without limitation for purposes of impeachment or enhancement of sentence in any criminal proceeding. When a prior felony conviction is an element of any felony offense, it shall be proven to the trier of fact in open court.

(5) Truth in Sentencing. Sentences that are individually imposed upon convicted criminal wrongdoers based upon the facts and circumstances surrounding their cases shall be carried out in compliance with the courts' sentencing orders, and shall not be substantially diminished by early release policies intended to alleviate overcrowding in custodial facilities. The legislative branch shall ensure sufficient funding to adequately house inmates for the full terms of their sentences, except for statutorily authorized credits which reduce those sentences.

(6) Reform of the parole process. The current process for parole hearings is excessive, especially in cases in which the defendant has been convicted of murder. The parole hearing process must be reformed for the benefit of crime victims.

(g) As used in this article, the term "serious felony" is any crime defined in subdivision (c) of Section 1192.7 of the Penal Code, or any successor statute.

Colorado

(Article 2, § 16a; 1992)

Rights of crime victims

Any person who is a victim of a criminal act, or such person's designee, legal guardian, or surviving immediate family members if such person is deceased, shall have the right to be heard when relevant, informed, and present at all critical stages of the criminal justice process. All terminology, including the term "critical stages", shall be defined by the general assembly.

Connecticut
(Article I, § 8; 1996)

[a. deals with rights of the accused.]

b. In all criminal prosecutions, a victim, as the general assembly may define by law, shall have the following rights: (1) The right to be treated with fairness and respect throughout the criminal justice process; (2) the right to timely disposition of the case following arrest of the accused, provided no right of the accused is abridged; (3) the right to be reasonably protected from the accused throughout the criminal justice process; (4) the right to notification of court proceedings; (5) the right to attend the trial and all other court proceedings the accused has the right to attend, unless such person is to testify and the court determines that such person's testimony would be materially affected if such person hears other testimony; (6) the right to communicate with the prosecution; (7) the right to object to or support any plea agreement entered into by the accused and the prosecution and to make a statement to the court prior to the acceptance by the court of the plea of guilty or nolo contendere by the accused; (8) the right to make a statement to the court at sentencing; (9) the right to restitution which shall be enforceable in the same manner as any other cause of action or as otherwise provided by law; and (10) the right to information about the arrest, conviction, sentence, imprisonment and release of the accused. The general assembly shall provide by law for the enforcement of this subsection. Nothing in this subsection or in any law enacted pursuant to this subsection shall be construed as creating a basis for vacating a conviction or ground for appellate relief in any criminal case.

Florida
(Article 1, § 16; 1988)

Rights of accused and of victims

[(a) deals with rights of the accused.]

(b) Victims of crime or their lawful representatives, including the next of kin of homicide victims, are entitled to the right to be informed, to be present, and to be heard when relevant, at all crucial stages of criminal proceedings, to the extent that these rights do not interfere with the constitutional rights of the accused.

Idaho

(Article I, § 22; 1994)

Rights of crime victims.—A crime victim, as defined by statute, has the following rights:

(1) To be treated with fairness, respect, dignity and privacy throughout the criminal justice process.

(2) To timely disposition of the case.

(3) To prior notification of trial court, appellate and parole proceedings and, upon request, to information about the sentence, incarceration and release of the defendant.

(4) To be present at all criminal justice proceedings.

(5) To communicate with the prosecution.

(6) To be heard, upon request, at all criminal justice proceedings considering a plea of guilty, sentencing, incarceration or release of the defendant, unless manifest injustice would result.

(7) To restitution, as provided by law, from the person committing the offense that caused the victim's loss.

(8) To refuse an interview, ex parte contact, or other request by the defendant, or any other person acting on behalf of the defendant, unless such request is authorized by law.

(9) To read presentence reports relating to the crime.

(10) To the same rights in juvenile proceedings, where the offense is a felony if committed by an adult, as guaranteed in this section, provided that access to the social history report shall be determined by statute.

Nothing in this section shall be construed to authorize a court to dismiss a case, to set aside or void a finding of guilt or an acceptance of a plea of guilty, or to obtain appellate, habeas corpus, or other relief from any criminal judgment, for a violation of the provisions of this section; nor be construed as creating a cause of action for money damages, costs or attorney fees against the state, a county, a municipality, any agency, instrumentality or person; nor be construed as limiting any rights for victims previously conferred by statute. This section shall be self-enacting. The legislature shall have the power to enact laws to define, implement, preserve, and expand the rights guaranteed to victims in the provisions of this section.

Illinois

(Article 1, §8.1; 1992)

Crime Victim's Rights

(a) Crime victims, as defined by law, shall have the following rights as provided by law:

(1) The right to be treated with fairness and respect for their dignity and privacy throughout the criminal justice process.

(2) The right to notification of court proceedings.

(3) The right to communicate with the prosecution.

(4) The right to make a statement to the court at sentencing.

(5) The right to information about the conviction, sentence, imprisonment, and release of the accused.

(6) The right to timely disposition of the case following the arrest of the accused.

(7) The right to be reasonably protected from the accused throughout the criminal justice process.

(8) The right to be present at the trial and all other court proceedings on the same basis as the accused, unless the victim is to testify and the court determines that the victim's testimony would be materially affected if the victim hears other testimony at the trial.

(9) The right to have present at all court proceedings, subject to the rules of evidence, an advocate or other support person of the victim's choice.

(10) The right to restitution.

(b) The General Assembly may provide by law for the enforcement of this Section.

(c) The General Assembly may provide for an assessment against convicted defendants to pay for crime victims' rights.

(d) Nothing in this Section or in any law enacted under this Section shall be construed as creating a basis for vacating a conviction or a ground for appellate relief in any criminal case.

Indiana

(Article 1, §13; 1996)

[(a) deals with rights of the accused]

(b) Victims of crime, as defined by law, shall have the right to be treated with fairness, dignity, and respect throughout the criminal justice process; and, as defined by law, to be informed of and present during public hearings and to confer with the prosecution, to the extent that exercising these rights does not infringe upon the constitutional rights of the accused.

Kansas

(Article 15, §15; 1992)

Victims' rights. (a) Victims of crime, as defined by law, shall be entitled to certain basic rights, including the right to be informed of and to be present at public hearings, as defined by law, of the criminal justice process, and to be heard at sentencing or at any other time deemed appropriate by the court, to the extent that these rights do not interfere with the constitutional or statutory rights of the accused.

(b) Nothing in this section shall be construed as creating a cause of action for money damages against the state, a county, a municipality, or any of the agencies, instrumentalities, or employees thereof. The legislature may provide for other remedies to ensure adequate enforcement of this section.

(c) Nothing in this section shall be construed to authorize a court to set aside or to void a finding of guilty or not guilty or an acceptance of a plea of guilty or to set aside any sentence imposed or any other final disposition in any criminal case.

Louisiana

(Article 1, §25; 1998)

Rights of a Victim

Any person who is a victim of crime shall be treated with fairness, dignity, and respect, and shall be informed of the rights accorded under this Section. As defined by law, a victim of crime shall have the right to reasonable notice and to be present and heard during all critical stages of preconviction and postconviction proceedings; the right to be informed upon the release from custody or the escape of the accused or the offender; the right to confer with the prosecution prior to final disposition of the case; the right to refuse to be interviewed by the accused or a representative of the accused; the right to review and comment upon the presentence report prior to imposition of sentence; the right to seek restitution; and the right to a reasonably prompt conclusion of the case. The legislature shall enact laws to implement this Section. The evidentiary and procedural laws of this state shall be interpreted in a manner consistent with this Section.

Nothing in this Section shall be construed to inure to the benefit of an accused or to confer upon any person the right to appeal or seek supervisory review of any judicial decision made in a criminal proceeding. Nothing in this Section shall be the basis for an award of costs or attorney fees, for the appointment of counsel for a victim, or for any cause of action for compensation or damages against the state of Louisiana, a political subdivision, a public agency, or a court, or any officer, employee, or agent thereof. Remedies to enforce the rights enumerated in this Section shall be provided by law.

Maryland
(Article 47; 1994)

Rights of victim of crime.

(a) A victim of crime shall be treated by agents of the State with dignity, respect, and sensitivity during all phases of the criminal justice process.

(b) In a case originating by indictment or information filed in a circuit court, a victim of crime shall have the right to be informed of the rights established in this Article and, upon request and if practicable, to be notified of, to attend, and to be heard at a criminal justice proceeding, as these rights are implemented and the terms "crime", "criminal justice proceeding", and "victim" are specified by law.

(c) Nothing in this Article permits any civil cause of action for monetary damages for violation of any of its provisions or authorizes a victim of crime to take any action to stay a criminal justice proceeding.

Michigan
(Article 1, §24; 1988)

Rights of crime victims; enforcement; assessment against convicted defendants

(1) Crime victims, as defined by law, shall have the following rights, as provided by law:

The right to be treated with fairness and respect for their dignity and privacy throughout the criminal justice process.

The right to timely disposition of the case following arrest of the accused.

The right to be reasonably protected from the accused throughout the criminal justice process.

The right to notification of court proceedings.

The right to attend trial and all other court proceedings the accused has the right to attend.

The right to confer with the prosecution.

The right to make a statement to the court at sentencing.

The right to restitution.

The right to information about the conviction, sentence, imprisonment, and release of the accused.

(2) The legislature may provide by law for the enforcement of this section.

(3) The legislature may provide for an assessment against convicted defendants to pay for crime victims' rights.

Mississippi

(Article 3, § 26A; 1998)

Victims' rights; construction of provisions; legislative authority

(1) Victims of crime, as defined by law, shall have the right to be treated with fairness, dignity and respect throughout the criminal justice process; and to be informed, to be present and to be heard, when authorized by law, during public hearings.

(2) Nothing in this section shall provide grounds for the accused or convicted offender to obtain any form of relief nor shall this section impair the constitutional rights of the accused. Nothing in this section or any enabling statute shall be construed as creating a cause of action for damages against the state or any of its agencies, officials, employees or political subdivisions.

(3) The Legislature shall have the authority to enact substantive and procedural laws to define, implement, preserve and protect the rights guaranteed to victims by this section.

Missouri

(Article 1, § 32; 1992)

Crime victims' rights

1. Crime victims, as defined by law, shall have the following rights, as defined by law:

(1) The right to be present at all criminal justice proceedings at which the defendant has such right, including juvenile proceedings where the offense would have been a felony if committed by an adult;

(2) Upon request of the victim, the right to be informed of and heard at guilty pleas, bail hearings, sentencings, probation revocation hearings, and

parole hearings, unless in the determination of the court the interests of justice require otherwise;

(3) The right to be informed of trials and preliminary hearings;

(4) The right to restitution, which shall be enforceable in the same manner as any other civil cause of action, or as otherwise provided by law;

(5) The right to the speedy disposition and appellate review of their cases, provided that nothing in this subdivision shall prevent the defendant from having sufficient time to prepare his defense;

(6) The right to reasonable protection from the defendant or any person acting on behalf of the defendant;

(7) The right to information concerning the escape of an accused from custody or confinement, the defendant's release and scheduling of the defendant's release from incarceration; and

(8) The right to information about how the criminal justice system works, the rights and the availability of services, and upon request of the victim the right to information about the crime.

2. Notwithstanding section 20 of article I of this Constitution, upon a showing that the defendant poses a danger to a crime victim, the community, or any other person, the court may deny bail or may impose special conditions which the defendant and surety must guarantee.

3. Nothing in this section shall be construed as creating a cause of action for money damages against the state, a county, a municipality, or any of the agencies, instrumentalities, or employees provided that the General Assembly may, by statutory enactment, reverse, modify, or supercede any judicial decision or rule arising from any cause of action brought pursuant to this section.

4. Nothing in this section shall be construed to authorize a court to set aside or to void a finding of guilt, or an acceptance of a plea of guilty in any criminal case.

5. The general assembly shall [have] power to enforce this section by appropriate legislation.

Montana

(Article II, § 28; 1998)

Criminal justice policy—rights of the convicted.

(1) Laws for the punishment of crime shall be founded on the principles of prevention, reformation, public safety, and restitution for victims.

(2) Full rights are restored by termination of state supervision for any offense against the state.

Nebraska

(Article I, § 28; 1996)

Crime victims; rights enumerated; effect; Legislature; duties.

(1) A victim of a crime, as shall be defined by law, or his or her guardian or representative shall have: The right to be informed of all criminal court proceedings; the right to be present at trial unless the trial court finds sequestration necessary for a fair trial for the defendant; and the right to be informed of, be present at, and make an oral or written statement at sentencing, parole, pardon, commutation, and conditional release proceedings. This enumeration of certain rights for crime victims shall not be construed to impair or deny others provided by law or retained by crime victims.

(2) The Legislature shall provide by law for the implementation of the rights granted in this section. There shall be no remedies other than as specifically provided by the Legislature for the enforcement of the rights granted by this section.

(3) Nothing in this section shall constitute a basis for error in favor of a defendant in any criminal proceeding, a basis for providing standing to participate as a party to any criminal proceeding, or a basis to contest the disposition of any charge.

Nevada

(Article 1, § 8; 1996)

[1. deals with rights of the accused.]

2. The legislature shall provide by law for the rights of victims of crime, personally or through a representative, to be:

(a) Informed, upon written request, of the status or disposition of a criminal proceeding at any stage of the proceeding;

(b) Present at all public hearings involving the critical stages of a criminal proceeding; and

(c) Heard at all proceedings for the sentencing or release of a convicted person after trial.

3. Except as otherwise provided in subsection 4, no person may maintain an action against the state or any public officer or employee for damages or injunctive, declaratory or other legal or equitable relief on behalf of a victim

of a crime as a result of a violation of any statute enacted by the legislature pursuant to subsection 2. No such violation authorizes setting aside a conviction or sentence or continuing or postponing a criminal proceeding.

4. A person may maintain an action to compel a public officer or employee to carry out any duty required by the legislature pursuant to subsection 2.

[5. and 6. deal with due process and the prohibition of "taking" of private property without just compensation, respectively.]

New Jersey
(Article 1, §22; 1991)
Rights of victims of crimes

A victim of a crime shall be treated with fairness, compassion and respect by the criminal justice system. A victim of a crime shall not be denied the right to be present at public judicial proceedings except when, prior to completing testimony as a witness, the victim is properly sequestered in accordance with law or the Rules Governing the Courts of the State of New Jersey. A victim of crime shall be entitled to those rights and remedies as may be provided by the Legislature. For the purposes of this paragraph, "victim of a crime" means: a) a person who has suffered physical or psychological injury or has incurred loss of or damage to personal or real property as a result of a crime or an incident involving another person operating a motor vehicle while under the influence of drugs or alcohol, and b) the spouse, parent, legal guardian, grandparent, child or sibling of the decedent in the case of a criminal homicide.

New Mexico
(Article II, §24; 1992)
Victim's Rights

A. A victim of arson resulting in bodily injury, aggravated arson, aggravated assault, aggravated battery, dangerous use of explosives, negligent use of a deadly weapon, murder, voluntary manslaughter, involuntary manslaughter, kidnapping, criminal sexual penetration, criminal sexual contact of a minor, homicide by vehicle, great bodily injury by vehicle or abandonment or abuse of a child or that victim's representative shall have the following rights as provided by law:

(1) the right to be treated with fairness and respect for the victim's dignity and privacy throughout the criminal justice process;

(2) the right to timely disposition of the case;

(3) the right to be reasonably protected from the accused throughout the criminal justice process;

(4) the right to notification of court proceedings;

(5) the right to attend all public court proceedings the accused has the right to attend;

(6) the right to confer with the prosecution;

(7) the right to make a statement to the court at sentencing and at any post-sentencing hearings for the accused;

(8) the right to restitution from the person convicted of the criminal conduct that caused the victim's loss or injury;

(9) the right to information about the conviction, sentencing, imprisonment, escape or release of the accused;

(10) the right to have the prosecuting attorney notify the victim's employer, if requested by the victim, of the necessity of the victim's cooperation and testimony in a court proceeding that may necessitate the absence of the victim from work for good cause; and

(11) the right to promptly receive any property belonging to the victim that is being held for evidentiary purposes by a law enforcement agency or the prosecuting attorney, unless there are compelling evidentiary reasons for retention of the victim's property.

B. A person accused or convicted of a crime against a victim shall have no standing to object to any failure by any person to comply with the provisions of Subsection A of Section 24 of Article 2 of the constitution of New Mexico.

C. The provisions of this amendment shall not take effect until the legislature enacts laws to implement this amendment.

North Carolina
(Article I, §37; 1996)

Rights of victims of crime.

(1) *Basic rights.* Victims of crime, as prescribed by law, shall be entitled to the following basic rights:

(a) The right as prescribed by law to be informed of and to be present at court proceedings of the accused.

(b) The right to be heard at sentencing of the accused in a manner prescribed by law, and at other times as prescribed by law or deemed appropriate by the court.

(c) The right as prescribed by law to receive restitution.

(d) The right as prescribed by law to be given information about the crime, how the criminal justice system works, the rights of victims, and the availability of services for victims.

(e) The right as prescribed by law to receive information about the conviction or final disposition and sentence of the accused.

(f) The right as prescribed by law to receive notification of escape, release, proposed parole or pardon of the accused, or notice of a reprieve or commutation of the accused's sentence.

(g) The right as prescribed by law to present their views and concerns to the Governor or agency considering any action that could result in the release of the accused, prior to such action becoming effective.

(h) The right as prescribed by law to confer with the prosecution.

(2) *No money damages; other enforcement.* Nothing in this section shall be construed as creating a claim for money damages against the State, a county, a municipality, or any of the agencies, instrumentalities, or employees thereof. The General Assembly may provide for other remedies to ensure adequate enforcement of this section.

(3) *No ground for relief in criminal case.* The failure or inability of any person to provide a right or service provided under this section may not be used by a defendant in a criminal case, an inmate, or any other accused as a ground for relief in any trial, appeal, postconviction litigation, habeas corpus, civil action, or any similar criminal or civil proceeding.

Ohio
(Article I, § 10a; 1994)

Rights of victims of crime.

Victims of criminal offenses shall be accorded fairness, dignity, and respect in the criminal justice process, and, as the general assembly shall define and provide by law, shall be accorded rights to reasonable and appropriate notice, information, access, and protection and to a meaningful role in the criminal justice process. This section does not confer upon any person a right to appeal or modify any decision in a criminal proceeding, does not abridge any other right guaranteed by the Constitution of the United States or this constitution, and does not create any cause of action for compensation or damages against the state, any political subdivision of the state, any officer, employee, or agent of the state or of any political subdivision, or any officer of the court.

Oklahoma
(Article 2, §34; 1996)
Rights of Victims

A. To preserve and protect the rights of victims to justice and due process, and ensure that victims are treated with fairness, respect and dignity, and are free from intimidation, harassment, or abuse, throughout the criminal justice process, any victim or family member of a victim of a crime has the right to know the status of the investigation and prosecution of the criminal case, including all proceedings wherein a disposition of a case is likely to occur, and where plea negotiations may occur. The victim or family member of a victim of a crime has the right to know the location of the defendant following an arrest, during a prosecution of the criminal case, during a sentence to probation or confinement, and when there is any release or escape of the defendant from confinement. The victim or family member of a victim of crime has a right to be present at any proceeding where the defendant has a right to be present, to be heard at any sentencing or parole hearing, to be awarded restitution by the convicted person for damages or losses as determined and ordered by the court, and to be informed by the state of the constitutional rights of the victim.

B. An exercise of any right by a victim or family member of a victim or the failure to provide a victim or family member of a victim any right granted by this section shall not be grounds for dismissing any criminal proceeding or setting aside any conviction or sentence.

C. The Legislature, or the people by initiative or referendum, has the authority to enact substantive and procedural laws to define, implement, preserve and protect the rights guaranteed to victims by this section, including the authority to extend any of these rights to juvenile proceedings and if enacted by the Legislature, youthful offender proceedings.

D. The enumeration in the Constitution of certain rights for victims shall not be construed to deny or disparage other rights granted by the Legislature or retained by victims.

Oregon
(Article I, §§ 42, 43; 1999,[2] 2008)
Section 42. Rights of victim in criminal prosecutions and juvenile court delinquency proceedings.

---

2. A previous version of this amendment was ratified in 1996, but it was subsequently declared unconstitutional by the Oregon Supreme Court in *Armatta v. Kitzhaber*, 959 P.2d 49 (Or. 1998), due to its inclusion of several distinct amendments in one provision.

(1) To preserve and protect the right of crime victims to justice, to ensure crime victims a meaningful role in the criminal and juvenile justice systems, to accord crime victims due dignity and respect and to ensure that criminal and juvenile court delinquency proceedings are conducted to seek the truth as to the defendant's innocence or guilt, and also to ensure that a fair balance is struck between the rights of crime victims and the rights of criminal defendants in the course and conduct of criminal and juvenile court delinquency proceedings, the following rights are hereby granted to victims in all prosecutions for crimes and in juvenile court delinquency proceedings:

(a) The right to be present at and, upon specific request, to be informed in advance of any critical stage of the proceedings held in open court when the defendant will be present, and to be heard at the pretrial release hearing and the sentencing or juvenile court delinquency disposition;

(b) The right, upon request, to obtain information about the conviction, sentence, imprisonment, criminal history and future release from physical custody of the criminal defendant or convicted criminal and equivalent information regarding the alleged youth offender or youth offender;

(c) The right to refuse an interview, deposition or other discovery request by the criminal defendant or other person acting on behalf of the criminal defendant provided, however, that nothing in this paragraph shall restrict any other constitutional right of the defendant to discovery against the state;

(d) The right to receive prompt restitution from the convicted criminal who caused the victim's loss or injury;

(e) The right to have a copy of a transcript of any court proceeding in open court, if one is otherwise prepared;

(f) The right to be consulted, upon request, regarding plea negotiations involving any violent felony; and

(g) The right to be informed of these rights as soon as practicable.

(2) This section applies to all criminal and juvenile court delinquency proceedings pending or commenced on or after the effective date of this section. Nothing in this section reduces a criminal defendant's rights under the Constitution of the United States. Except as otherwise specifically provided, this section supersedes any conflicting section of this Constitution. Nothing in this section is intended to create any cause of action for compensation or damages nor may this section be used to invalidate an accusatory instrument, conviction or adjudication or otherwise terminate any criminal or juvenile delinquency proceedings at any point after the case is commenced or on appeal.

Except as otherwise provided in subsections (3) and (4) of this section, nothing in this section may be used to invalidate a ruling of a court or to suspend any criminal or juvenile delinquency proceedings at any point after the case is commenced.

(3)(a) Every victim described in paragraph (c) of subsection (6) of this section shall have remedy by due course of law for violation of a right established in this section.

(b) A victim may assert a claim for a right established in this section in a pending case, by a mandamus proceeding if no case is pending or as otherwise provided by law.

(c) The Legislative Assembly may provide by law for further effectuation of the provisions of this subsection, including authorization for expedited and interlocutory consideration of claims for relief and the establishment of reasonable limitations on the time allowed for bringing such claims.

(d) No claim for a right established in this section shall suspend a criminal or juvenile delinquency proceeding if such a suspension would violate a right of a criminal defendant guaranteed by this Constitution or the Constitution of the United States.

(4) Upon the victim's request, the prosecuting attorney, in the attorney's discretion, may assert and enforce a right established in this section.

(5) Upon the filing by the prosecuting attorney of an affidavit setting forth cause, a court shall suspend the rights established in this section in any case involving organized crime or victims who are minors.

(6) As used in this section:

(a) "Convicted criminal" includes a youth offender in juvenile court delinquency proceedings.

(b) "Criminal defendant" includes an alleged youth offender in juvenile court delinquency proceedings.

(c) "Victim" means any person determined by the prosecuting attorney or the court to have suffered direct financial, psychological or physical harm as a result of a crime and, in the case of a victim who is a minor, the legal guardian of the minor.

(d) "Violent felony" means a felony in which there was actual or threatened serious physical injury to a victim or a felony sexual offense.

(7) In the event that no person has been determined to be a victim of the crime, the people of Oregon, represented by the prosecuting attorney, are con-

sidered to be the victims. In no event is it intended that the criminal defendant be considered the victim.

Section 43. Rights of victim and public to protection from accused person during criminal proceedings; denial of pretrial release.

(1) To ensure that a fair balance is struck between the rights of crime victims and the rights of criminal defendants in the course and conduct of criminal proceedings, the following rights are hereby granted to victims in all prosecutions for crimes:

(a) The right to be reasonably protected from the criminal defendant or the convicted criminal throughout the criminal justice process and from the alleged youth offender or youth offender throughout the juvenile delinquency proceedings.

(b) The right to have decisions by the court regarding the pretrial release of a criminal defendant based upon the principle of reasonable protection of the victim and the public, as well as the likelihood that the criminal defendant will appear for trial. Murder, aggravated murder and treason shall not be bailable when the proof is evident or the presumption strong that the person is guilty. Other violent felonies shall not be bailable when a court has determined there is probable cause to believe the criminal defendant committed the crime, and the court finds, by clear and convincing evidence, that there is danger of physical injury or sexual victimization to the victim or members of the public by the criminal defendant while on release.

(2) This section applies to proceedings pending or commenced on or after the effective date of this section. Nothing in this section abridges any right of the criminal defendant guaranteed by the Constitution of the United States, including the rights to be represented by counsel, have counsel appointed if indigent, testify, present witnesses, cross-examine witnesses or present information at the release hearing. Nothing in this section creates any cause of action for compensation or damages nor may this section be used to invalidate an accusatory instrument, conviction or adjudication or otherwise terminate any criminal or juvenile delinquency proceeding at any point after the case is commenced or on appeal. Except as otherwise provided in paragraph (b) of subsection (4) of this section and in subsection (5) of this section, nothing in this section may be used to invalidate a ruling of a court or to suspend any criminal or juvenile delinquency proceedings at any point after the case is commenced. Except as otherwise specifically provided, this section supersedes any conflicting section of this Constitution.

(3) As used in this section:

(a) "Victim" means any person determined by the prosecuting attorney or the court to have suffered direct financial, psychological or physical harm as a result of a crime and, in the case of a victim who is a minor, the legal guardian of the minor.

(b) "Violent felony" means a felony in which there was actual or threatened serious physical injury to a victim or a felony sexual offense.

(4)(a) The prosecuting attorney is the party authorized to assert the rights of the victim and the public established by this section.

(b) Upon the victim's request, the prosecuting attorney, in the attorney's discretion, may assert and enforce a right established in this section.

(5)(a) Every victim described in paragraph (a) of subsection (3) of this section shall have remedy by due course of law for violation of a right established in this section.

(b) A victim may assert a claim for a right established in this section in a pending case, by a mandamus proceeding if no case is pending or as otherwise provided by law.

(c) The Legislative Assembly may provide by law for further effectuation of the provisions of this subsection, including authorization for expedited and interlocutory consideration of claims for relief and the establishment of reasonable limitations on the time allowed for bringing such claims.

(d) No claim for a right established in this section shall suspend a criminal or juvenile delinquency proceeding if such a suspension would violate a right of a criminal defendant or alleged youth offender guaranteed by this Constitution or the Constitution of the United States.

(6) In the event that no person has been determined to be a victim of the crime, the people of Oregon, represented by the prosecuting attorney, are considered to be the victims. In no event is it intended that the criminal defendant be considered the victim.

Rhode Island

(Article 1, § 23; 1986)

Rights of victims of crime.—A victim of crime shall, as a matter of right, be treated by agents of the state with dignity, respect and sensitivity during all phases of the criminal justice process. Such person shall be entitled to receive, from the perpetrator of the crime, financial compensation for any injury or loss caused by the perpetrator of the crime, and shall receive such other compensation as the state may provide. Before sentencing, a victim shall have the right to address the court regarding the impact which the perpetrator's conduct has had upon the victim.

South Carolina
(Article I, §24; 1996)

(A) To preserve and protect victims' rights to justice and due process regardless of race, sex, age, religion, or economic status, victims of crime have the right to:

(1) be treated with fairness, respect, and dignity, and to be free from intimidation, harassment, or abuse, throughout the criminal and juvenile justice process, and informed of the victim's constitutional rights, provided by statute;

(2) be reasonably informed when the accused or convicted person is arrested, released from custody, or has escaped;

(3) be informed of and present at any criminal proceedings which are dispositive of the charges where the defendant has the right to be present;

(4) be reasonably informed of and be allowed to submit either a written or oral statement at all hearings affecting bond or bail;

(5) be heard at any proceeding involving a post-arrest release decision, a plea, or sentencing;

(6) be reasonably protected from the accused or persons acting on his behalf throughout the criminal justice process;

(7) confer with the prosecution, after the crime against the victim has been charged, before the trial or before any disposition and informed of the disposition;

(8) have reasonable access after the conclusion of the criminal investigation to all documents relating to the crime against the victim before trial;

(9) receive prompt and full restitution from the person or persons convicted of the criminal conduct that caused the victim's loss or injury including both adult and juvenile offenders;

(10) be informed of any proceeding when any post-conviction action is being considered, and be present at any post-conviction hearing involving a post-conviction release decision;

(11) a reasonable disposition and prompt and final conclusion of the case;

(12) have all rules governing criminal procedure and the admissibility of evidence in all criminal proceedings protect victims' rights and have these rules subject to amendment or repeal by the legislature to ensure protection of these rights.

(B) Nothing in this section creates a civil cause of action on behalf of any person against any public employee, public agency, the State, or any agency responsible for the enforcement of rights and provision of services contained in this section. The rights created in this section may be subject to a writ of mandamus, to be issued by any justice of the Supreme Court or circuit court judge to require compliance by any public employee, public agency, the State, or any agency responsible for the enforcement of the rights and provisions of these services contained in this section, and a wilful failure to comply with a writ of mandamus is punishable as contempt.

(C) For purposes of this section:

(1) A victim's exercise of any right granted by this section is not grounds for dismissing any criminal proceeding or setting aside any conviction or sentence.

(2) "Victim" means a person who suffers direct or threatened physical, psychological, or financial harm as the result of the commission or attempted commission of a crime against him. The term "victim" also includes the person's spouse, parent, child, or lawful representative of a crime victim who is deceased, who is a minor or who is incompetent or who was a homicide victim or who is physically or psychologically incapacitated.

(3) The General Assembly has the authority to enact substantive and procedural laws to define, implement, preserve, and protect the rights guaranteed to victims by this section, including the authority to extend any of these rights to juvenile proceedings.

(4) The enumeration in the Constitution of certain rights for victims shall not be construed to deny or disparage others granted by the General Assembly or retained by victims.

Tennessee

(Article I, § 35; 1998)

Rights of victims of crimes. — To preserve and protect the rights of victims of crime to justice and due process, victims shall be entitled to the following basic rights:

1. The right to confer with the prosecution.

2. The right to be free from intimidation, harassment and abuse throughout the criminal justice system.

3. The right to be present at all proceedings where the defendant has the right to be present.

4. The right to be heard, when relevant, at all critical stages of the criminal justice process as defined by the General Assembly.

5. The right to be informed of all proceedings, and of the release, transfer or escape of the accused or convicted person.

6. The right to a speedy trial or disposition and a prompt and final conclusion of the case after conviction or sentence.

7. The right to restitution from the offender.

8. The right to be informed of each of the rights established for victims.

The general assembly has the authority to enact substantive and procedural laws to define, implement, preserve and protect the rights guaranteed to victims by this section.

Texas

(Article 1, § 30; 1989)

Rights of crime victims

(a) A crime victim has the following rights:

(1) the right to be treated with fairness and with respect for the victim's dignity and privacy throughout the criminal justice process; and

(2) the right to be reasonably protected from the accused throughout the criminal justice process.

(b) On the request of a crime victim, the crime victim has the following rights:

(1) the right to notification of court proceedings;

(2) the right to be present at all public court proceedings related to the offense, unless the victim is to testify and the court determines that the victim's testimony would be materially affected if the victim hears other testimony at the trial;

(3) the right to confer with a representative of the prosecutor's office;

(4) the right to restitution; and

(5) the right to information about the conviction, sentence, imprisonment, and release of the accused.

(c) The legislature may enact laws to define the term "victim" and to enforce these and other rights of crime victims.

(d) The state, through its prosecuting attorney, has the right to enforce the rights of crime victims.

(e) The legislature may enact laws to provide that a judge, attorney for the state, peace officer, or law enforcement agency is not liable for a failure or inability to provide a right enumerated in this section. The failure or inability of any person to provide a right or service enumerated in this section may not be used by a defendant in a criminal case as a ground for appeal or post-conviction writ of habeas corpus. A victim or guardian or legal representative of a victim has standing to enforce the rights enumerated in this section but does not have standing to participate as a party in a criminal proceeding or to contest the disposition of any charge.

Utah

(Article I, § 28; 1994)

Declaration of the rights of crime victims.

(1) To preserve and protect victims' rights to justice and due process, victims of crimes have these rights, as defined by law:

(a) To be treated with fairness, respect, and dignity, and to be free from harassment and abuse throughout the criminal justice process;

(b) Upon request, to be informed of, be present at, and to be heard at important criminal justice hearings related to the victim, either in person or through a lawful representative, once a criminal information or indictment charging a crime has been publicly filed in court; and

(c) To have a sentencing judge, for the purpose of imposing an appropriate sentence, receive and consider, without evidentiary limitation, reliable information concerning the background, character, and conduct of a person convicted of an offense except that this subsection does not apply to capital cases or situations involving privileges.

(2) Nothing in this section shall be construed as creating a cause of action for money damages, costs, or attorney's fees, or for dismissing any criminal charge, or relief from any criminal judgment.

(3) The provisions of this section shall extend to all felony crimes and such other crimes or acts, including juvenile offenses, as the Legislature may provide.

(4) The Legislature shall have the power to enforce and define this section by statute.

Virginia

(Article I, § 8-A; 1996)

Rights of victims of crime. — That in criminal prosecutions, the victim shall be accorded fairness, dignity and respect by the officers, employees and agents of the Commonwealth and its political subdivisions and officers of the courts and, as the General Assembly may define and provide by law, may be accorded rights to reasonable and appropriate notice, information, restitution, protection, and access to a meaningful role in the criminal justice process. These rights may include, but not be limited to, the following:

1. The right to protection from further harm or reprisal through the imposition of appropriate bail and conditions of release;

2. The right to be treated with respect, dignity and fairness at all stages of the criminal justice system;

3. The right to address the circuit court at the time sentence is imposed;

4. The right to receive timely notification of judicial proceedings;

5. The right to restitution;

6. The right to be advised of release from custody or escape of the offender, whether before or after disposition; and

7. The right to confer with the prosecution.

This section does not confer upon any person a right to appeal or modify any decision in a criminal proceeding, does not abridge any other right guaranteed by the Constitution of the United States or this Constitution, and does not create any cause of action for compensation or damages against the Commonwealth or any of its political subdivisions, any officer, employee or agent of the Commonwealth or any of its political subdivisions, or any officer of the court.

Washington

(Article 1, § 35; 1989)

Rights of Crime Victims

Effective law enforcement depends on cooperation from victims of crime. To ensure victims a meaningful role in the criminal justice system and to accord them due dignity and respect, victims of crime are hereby granted the following basic and fundamental rights.

Upon notifying the prosecuting attorney, a victim of a crime charged as a felony shall have the right to be informed of and, subject to the discretion of the individual presiding over the trial or court proceedings, attend trial and all other court proceedings the defendant has the right to attend, and to make a statement at sentencing and at any proceeding where the defendant's release is considered, subject to the same rules of procedure which govern the defendant's rights. In the event the victim is deceased, incompetent, a minor, or otherwise unavailable, the prosecuting attorney may identify a representative to appear to exercise the victim's rights. This provision shall not constitute a basis for error in favor of a defendant in a criminal proceeding nor a basis for providing a victim or the victim's representative with court appointed counsel.

Wisconsin

(Article 1, § 9m; 1993)

Victims of crime

This state shall treat crime victims, as defined by law, with fairness, dignity and respect for their privacy. This state shall ensure that crime victims have all of the following privileges and protections as provided by law: timely disposition of the case; the opportunity to attend court proceedings unless the trial court finds sequestration is necessary to a fair trial for the defendant; reasonable protection from the accused throughout the criminal justice process; notification of court proceedings; the opportunity to confer with the prosecution; the opportunity to make a statement to the court at disposition; restitution; compensation; and information about the outcome of the case and the release of the accused. The legislature shall provide remedies for the violation of this section. Nothing in this section, or in any statute enacted pursuant to this section, shall limit any right of the accused which may be provided by law.

Notes

Notes for Chapter 1

1. Michael R. Rand, U.S. Dep't of Justice, Criminal Victimization, 2008, at 1 (2009).

2. Federal Bureau of Investigation, U.S. Dep't of Justice, Crime in the United States, 2008, at Table 1 (2009), *available at* http://www.fbi.gov/ucr/cius2008/data/table_01.html.

3. *See, e.g.,* Ted. R. Miller et al., U.S. Dep't of Justice, Victim Costs and Consequences: A New Look 1 (1996); David A. Anderson, *The Aggregate Burden of Crime,* 42 J.L. & Econ. 611 (1999); Debbie Deem et al., *Victims of Financial Crime, in* Victims of Crime 125 (Robert C. Davis et al. eds., 3d ed. 2007); Richard M. Titus et al., *Victimization of Persons by Fraud,* 41 Crime & Delinq. 54 (1995)

4. Anderson, *supra* note 3, at 624–29.

5. Miller et al., *supra* note 3, at 9–17.

6. *See generally* William F. Mcdonald, *Towards a Bicentennial Revolution in Criminal Justice: The Return of the Victim,* 13 Am. Crim. L. Rev. 649 (1976).

7. *See* A.S. Diamond, Primitive Law 277–330 (2d ed. 1950); Stephen Schafer, Victimology: The Victim and His Criminal 5–11 (1977); Harold J. Berman, *The Background of the Western Legal Tradition in the Folklaw of the Peoples of Europe,* 45 U. Chi. L. Rev. 553 (1978); Richard E. Laster, *Criminal Restitution: A Survey of Its Past History and An Analysis of Its Present Usefulness,* 5 U. Rich. L. Rev. 71, 71–75 (1970); Marvin E. Wolfgang, *Victim Compensation in Crimes of Personal Violence,* 50 Minn. L. Rev. 223, 223–26 (1965). *See generally* A.S. Diamond, Primitive Law Past and Present (1971).

8. *See* Diamond, *supra* note 7, at 22–45, 85–133, 277–330.

9. *Exodus* 21:23–25.

10. *Exodus* 21: 18–19. *See* Chilperic Edwards, The Hammurabi Code and the Sinaitic Legislation (reissued 1971).

11. *See* Berman, *supra* note 7, at 556–59; Laster, *supra* note 7, at 71–75; Wolfgang, *supra* note 7, at 224–25.

12. *See* Berman, *supra* note 7, at 557, 575–76.

13. *See* Berman, *supra* note 7, at 567–86; Laster, *supra* note 7, at 74–75. *See generally* Frederick Pollock & Frederic William Maitland, The History of English Law before the Time of Edward I (2d ed. 1959).

14. *See* Diamond, *supra* note 7, at 277–330; Berman, *supra* note 7, at 574–75; Laster, *supra* note 7, at 79.

15. *See* Diamond, *supra* note 7, at 277–330; Laster, *supra* note 7, at 75–80; Wolfgang, *supra* note 7, at 228–29.

16. *See* Laster, *supra* note 7, at 79–80.

17. *See* Stephen Schafer, Compensation and Restitution to Victims of Crime 7 (2d ed. 1970); Richard C. Boldt, *Restitution, Criminal Law, and the Ideology of Individuality*, 77 J. Crim. L. & Criminology 969, 985 (1986); Laster, *supra* note 7, at 75–80; Note, *Victim Restitution in the Criminal Process: A Procedural Analysis*, 97 Harv. L. Rev. 931, 933–34 (1984).

18. *See* Juan Cardenas, *The Crime Victim in the Prosecutorial Process*, 9 Harv. J. L. & Pub. Pol'y 357, 366–68 (1986); Deborah P. Kelly, *Victims*, 34 Wayne L. Rev. 69, 82–83 (1987); McDonald, *supra* note 6, at 651–53.

19. *See* Cardenas, *supra* note 18, at 366–68; McDonald, *supra* note 6, at 651–53.

20. *See* Cardenas, *supra* note 18, at 368; McDonald, *supra* note 6, at 654.

21. *See* Cardenas, *supra* note 18, at 369; McDonald, *supra* note 6, at 654–56. *See generally* Cesare Beccaria, Essay on Crimes and Punishments (1764).

22. *See* Cardenas, *supra* note 18, at 368–69; McDonald, *supra* note 6, at 653–54.

23. *See* Douglas E. Beloof & Paul G. Cassell, *The Crime Victim's Right to Attend the Trial: The Reascendant National Consensus*, 9 Lewis & Clark L. Rev. 481, 484–93 (2005);Cardenas, *supra* note 18, at 369–71; McDonald, *supra* note 6, at 654–68; *cf.* Erin Ann O'Hara, *Victim Participation in the Criminal Process*, 13 J.L. & Pol'y 229, 235–36 (2005).

24. *See* Schafer, *supra* note 17, at 9–11; Alan T. Harland, *Monetary Remedies for the Victims of Crime: Assessing the Role of the Criminal Courts*, 30 UCLA L. Rev. 52, 57 (1982).

25. *See* Cardenas, *supra* note 18, at 369; McDonald, *supra* note 6, at 654–56.

26. *See* William G. Doerner & Steven P. Lab, Victimology 3–7 (5th ed. 2008); Schafer, *supra* note 7, at 33–41. *See generally* Hans von Hentig, The Criminal and his Victim: Studies in the Sociobiology of Crime (1948); Beniamin Mendelsohn, *The Victimology*, Etudes Internationales De Psycho-Sociologie Criminelle, July 1956, at 23; Hans von Hentig, *Remarks on the Interaction of Perpetrator and Victim*, 31 J. Crim. L., Criminology & Police Sci. 303 (1941).

27. *See, e.g.*, Doerner & Lab, *supra* note 26, at 8–17; From Crime Policy to Victim Policy: Reorienting the Justice System (Ezzat A. Fattah ed., 1986); Michael J. Hindelang et al., Victims of Personal Crime: An Empirical Foundation for a Theory of Personal Victimization (1978); R.I. Mawby & S. Walklate, Critical Victimology 7–22 (1994); Perspectives on Crime Victims (Burt Galaway & Joe Hudson eds., 1981); Schafer, *supra* note 7, at 41–97; Victimology (Israel Drapkin & Emilio Viano eds., 1974); *Symposium on Victimization and Victimology*, 72 J. Crim. L. & Criminology 704 (1981); Emilio Viano, *Victimology: The Development of a New Perspective*, 8(1–2) Victimology 17 (1983); Marvin E. Wolfgang & Simon I. Singer, *Victim Categories of Crime*, 69 J. Crim. L. & Criminology 379 (1978).

28. *See, e.g.*, Lynne N. Henderson, *The Wrongs of Victim's Rights*, 37 Stan. L. Rev. 937, 953–66 (1985); Robert F. Kidd & Ellen F. Chayet, *Why Do Victims Fail to Report? The Psychology of Criminal Victimization*, 40 J. Soc. Issues 39 (1984); Dean G. Kilpatrick & Randy K. Otto, *Constitutionally Guaranteed Participation in Criminal Justice Proceedings for Victims: Potential Effects on Psychological Functioning*, 34 Wayne L. Rev. 7, 9–20, 26 (1987). *See generally* Pamela Tontodonato & Edna Erez, *Crime, Punishment, and Victim Distress*, 3 Int'l Rev. Victimology 33, 34–36 (1994).

29. *See, e.g.*, Criminal Justice and the Victim (William F. McDonald ed., 1976); Josephine Gittler, *Expanding the Role of the Victim in a Criminal Action: An Overview of Issues and Problems*, 11 Pepp. L. Rev. 117, 135–78 (1984); Deborah P. Kelly, *Victims' Perceptions of Criminal Justice*, 11 Pepp. L. Rev. 15 (1984); Kilpatrick & Otto, *supra* note 28, at 22–28; *cf., e.g.*, Leslie Sebba, Third Parties: Victims and the Criminal Justice Sys-

TEM (1996); Ezzat A. Fattah, *Toward a Victim Policy Aimed at Healing, Not Suffering, in* VIC-TIMS OF CRIME 257 (Robert C. Davis et al. eds., 2d ed. 1997); Henderson, *supra* note 28, at 986–1012.

30. *See* DOERNER & LAB, *supra* note 26, at 17–19; Frank Carrington & George Nicholson, *The Victims' Movement: An Idea Whose Time Has Come*, 11 PEPP. L. REV. 1, 1–5 (1984); Marlene A. Young, *Victim Rights and Services: A Modern Saga, in* VICTIMS OF CRIME, *supra* note 29, at 194, 195. *See generally* THE PRESIDENT'S COMMISSION ON LAW ENFORCEMENT AND ADMINISTRATION OF JUSTICE, TASK FORCE REPORT: CRIME AND ITS IMPACT—AN ASSESSMENT (1967).

31. *See* DOERNER & LAB, *supra* note 26, at 19; Young, *supra* note 30, at 195.

32. *See* Young, *supra* note 30, at 196.

33. *See* Carrington & Nicholson, *supra* note 30, at 2, 5–6 & n.17; LeRoy L. Lamborn, *Victim Participation in the Criminal Justice Process: The Proposals for a Constitutional Amendment*, 34 WAYNE L. REV. 125, 131 n.35 (1987); Young, *supra* note 30, at 196–97.

34. *See* Carrington & Nicholson, *supra* note 30, at 1–6; Young, *supra* note 30, at 195–97.

35. *See* Young, *supra* note 30, at 195–97.

36. *See* DOERNER & LAB, *supra* note 26, at 34–43.

37. Young, *supra* note 30, at 197.

38. *See, e.g.*, Robert Elias, *Community Control, Criminal Justice and Victim Services, in* FROM CRIME POLICY TO VICTIM POLICY, *supra* note 27, at 290; Ezzat A. Fattah, *From Crime Policy to Victim Policy: The Need for a Fundamental Policy Change, in* VICTIMS OF CRIME AND THE VICTIMIZATION PROCESS, at 75, 80–83 (Marilyn McShane & Frank P. Williams III eds., 1997); Fattah, *supra* note 29, at 268–69.

39. *See, e.g.*, Fattah, *supra* note 29, at 262–70; Henderson, *supra* note 28, 961–66, 986–1012; Christopher R. Goddu, Comment, *Victims' "Rights" or a Fair Trial Wronged?*, 41 BUFF. L. REV. 245 (1993). *But see, e.g.*, Andrew J. Karmen, *Who's Against Victims' Rights? The Nature of the Opposition to Pro-Victim Initiatives in Criminal Justice*, 8 ST. JOHN'S J. LEGAL COMMENT. 157 (1992).

40. *See, e.g.*, Fattah, *supra* note 29, at 261–63; Henderson, *supra* note 28, at 942–53, 966–86. *See generally* ROBERT ELIAS, VICTIMS STILL: THE POLITICAL MANIPULATION OF CRIME VICTIMS (1993); FRANK J. WEED, CERTAINTY OF JUSTICE: REFORM IN THE CRIME VICTIM MOVEMENT (1995); Ezzat A. Fattah, *Prologue: On Some Visible and Hidden Dangers of Victim Movements, in* FROM CRIME POLICY TO VICTIM POLICY, *supra* note 27, at 1.

41. *See generally* George Nicholson, *Victims' Rights, Remedies, and Resources: A Maturing Presence in American Jurisprudence*, 23 PAC. L.J. 815 (1992); *Victims' Rights Symposium*, 11 PEPP. L. REV. 1 (1984).

42. *See* Carrington & Nicholson, *supra* note 30, at 7; Young, *supra* note 30, at 197–98.

43. *See* PRESIDENT'S TASK FORCE ON VICTIMS OF CRIME, FINAL REPORT ii–iii (1982); Carrington & Nicholson, *supra* note 30, at 7; Young, *supra* note 30, at 198.

44. *See* PRESIDENT'S TASK FORCE ON VICTIMS OF CRIME, *supra* note 43.

45. *Id.* at 114; *see* Lamborn, *supra* note 33, at 172–200.

46. *See* PRESIDENT'S TASK FORCE ON VICTIMS OF CRIME, *supra* note 43, at 33, 60–66, 76–78, 80, 83–84.

47. *See* OFFICE OF JUSTICE PROGRAMS, U.S. DEP'T OF JUSTICE, FOUR YEARS LATER: A REPORT ON THE PRESIDENT'S TASK FORCE ON VICTIMS OF CRIME 4–5 (1986).

48. *See* DAVID BEATTY ET AL., NATIONAL VICTIM CENTER, STATUTORY AND CONSTITUTIONAL PROTECTION OF VICTIMS' RIGHTS: IMPLEMENTATION AND IMPACT ON CRIME VIC-

TIMS 6 (1996); OFFICE FOR VICTIMS OF CRIME, U.S. DEP'T OF JUSTICE, NEW DIRECTIONS FROM THE FIELD: VICTIMS' RIGHTS AND SERVICES FOR THE 21ST CENTURY ix (1998).

49. *See generally* S. REP. No. 106-254, at 57–60 (2000); OFFICE FOR VICTIMS OF CRIME, U.S. DEP'T OF JUSTICE, ATTORNEY GENERAL GUIDELINES FOR VICTIM AND WITNESS ASSISTANCE (2005); U.S. GOVERNMENT ACCOUNTABILITY OFFICE, CRIME VICTIMS' RIGHTS ACT: INCREASING AWARENESS, MODIFYING THE COMPLAINT PROCESS, AND ENHANCING COMPLIANCE MONITORING WILL IMPROVE IMPLEMENTATION OF THE ACT 113–16 (2008); Peggy M. Tobolowsky, *"Constitutionalizing" Crime Victim Rights*, 33 CRIM. L. BULL. 395, 397–405 (1997).

50. *See generally* S. REP. No. 108-191 (2003); S. REP. No. 106-254 (2000); OFFICE FOR VICTIMS OF CRIME, *supra* note 48, at 9–12; PRESIDENT'S TASK FORCE ON VICTIMS OF CRIME, *supra* note 43, at 114–15; Symposium, *Crime Victims' Rights in the Twenty-First Century*, 1999 UTAH L. REV. 285 (1999); Symposium, *Perspectives on Proposals for a Constitutional Amendment Providing Victim Participation in the Criminal Justice System*, 34 WAYNE L. REV. 1 (1987); Tobolowsky, *supra* note 49; Victoria Schwartz, Recent Development, *The Victims' Right Amendment*, 42 HARV. J. ON LEGIS. 525 (2005); National Victims' Constitutional Amendment Passage, http://www.nvcap.org (last visited Oct. 4, 2008).

51. *See* 18 U.S.C.A. § 3771 (West Supp. 2009); 42 U.S.C.A. § 10603d–e (West 2005); Crime Victims' Rights Act of 2004, Pub. L. No. 108-405, Title I, §§ 103–104, 118 Stat. 2260, 2264–65 (2004); Fed. R. Crim. P. 1, 12.1, 17, 18, 32, 60; OFFICE FOR VICTIMS OF CRIME, *supra* note 49; *see* David E. Aaronson, *New Rights and Remedies: The Federal Crime Victims' Rights Act of 2004*, 28 PACE L. REV. 623 (2008); Russell P. Butler, *What Practitioners and Judges Need to Know Regarding Crime Victims' Participatory Rights in Federal Sentencing Proceedings*, 19 FED. SENT'G REP. 21 (2006); Paul G. Cassell, *Treating Crime Victims Fairly: Integrating Victims into the Federal Rules of Criminal Procedure*, 2007 UTAH L. REV. 861 (2007); U.S. Courts, Proposed Amendments to the Federal Rules of Criminal Procedure (effective Dec. 1, 2008), http://www.uscourts.gov/rules/supct0408.html (last visited Jan. 2, 2009) (including the amendments to the federal rules and related reports).

52. *See generally* National Center for Victims of Crime, VictimLaw, http://www.victim-law.info/victimlaw/ (last visited Jan. 1, 2009); National Conference of State Legislatures, Victims' Rights Laws in the States, http://www.ncsl.org (last visited Jan. 1, 2009).

53. As of the end of 2008, thirty-three states have victim-related constitutional amendments. *See* ALA. CONST. art. I, § 6.01; ALASKA CONST. art. I, §§ 12, 24; ARIZ. CONST. art. 2, § 2.1; CAL. CONST. art. 1, § 28; COLO. CONST. art. 2, § 16a; CONN. CONST. art. I, § 8; FLA. CONST. art. 1, § 16; IDAHO CONST. art. I, § 22; ILL. CONST. art. 1, § 8.1; IND. CONST. art. 1, § 13; KAN. CONST. art. 15, § 15; LA. CONST. art. 1, § 25; MD. CONST. art. 47; MICH. CONST. art. 1, § 24; MISS. CONST. art. 3, § 26A; MO. CONST. art. 1, § 32; MONT. CONST. art. II, § 28; NEB. CONST. art. I, § 28; NEV. CONST. art. 1, § 8; N.J. CONST. art. 1, § 22; N.M. CONST. art. II, § 24; N.C. CONST. art. I, § 37; OHIO CONST. art. I, § 10a; OKLA. CONST. art. 2, § 34; OR. CONST. art. I, §§ 42, 43; R.I. CONST. art. 1, § 23; S.C. CONST. art. I, § 24; TENN. CONST. art. I, § 35; TEX. CONST. art. 1, § 30; UTAH CONST. art. I, § 28; VA. CONST. art. I, § 8-A; WASH. CONST. art. 1, § 35; WIS. CONST. art. 1, § 9 m. *See generally* App. 3.

54. *See, e.g.,* Edna Erez & Julian Roberts, *Victim Participation in the Criminal Justice System, in* VICTIMS OF CRIME, *supra* note 3, at 277; Susan Howley & Carol Dorris, *Legal Rights for Crime Victims in the Criminal Justice System, in* VICTIMS OF CRIME, *supra* note 3, at 299; Deborah P. Kelly & Edna Erez, *Victim Participation in the Criminal Justice System, in* VICTIMS OF CRIME, *supra* note 29, at 231; David L. Roland, *Progress in the Victim Reform Movement: No Longer the "Forgotten Victim,"* 17 PEPP. L. REV. 35 (1989); Barbara E. Smith &

Susan W. Hillenbrand, *Making Victims Whole Again: Restitution, Victim-Offender Reconciliation Programs, and Compensation, in* VICTIMS OF CRIME, *supra* note 29, at 245; Young, *supra* note 30, at 198–200; Karyn Ellen Polito, Note, *The Rights of Crime Victims in the Criminal Justice System: Is Justice Blind to the Victims of Crime?*, 16 NEW ENG. J. ON CRIM. & VIC. CONFINEMENT 241 (1990). *See generally* DOUGLAS E. BELOOF ET AL., VICTIMS IN CRIMINAL PROCEDURE (2d ed. 2006); Jay M. Zitter, Annotation, *Validity, Construction, and Application of State Constitutional or Statutory Victims' Bill of Rights,* 91 A.L.R. 5th 343 (2001); National Center for Victims of Crime, *supra* note 52; National Conference of State Legislatures, *supra* note 52; Office for Victims of Crime, Crime Victims' Rights in America: A Historical Overview, http://www.ojp.usdoj.gov/ovc/ncvrw/2006/pdf/landmarks.pdf (last visited Dec. 26, 2008).

55. *See generally* OFFICE FOR VICTIMS OF CRIME, *supra* note 48.

56. With the exception of the chapter on civil suits by crime victims, this text examines only crime victim rights and remedies afforded through the criminal justice system. As such, it does not address other victim remedies, such as private insurance. *See* SUSAN KISS SARNOFF, PAYING FOR CRIME: THE POLICIES AND POSSIBILITIES OF CRIME VICTIM REIMBURSEMENT (1996). Moreover, this text does not address the separate rights provisions for victims of juvenile offenders which some states have. *See, e.g.,* ARIZ. REV. STAT. ANN. § 8-381 (2007). Finally, this text primarily examines the expansion of crime victim rights in the United States rather than the renewal of interest in crime victims which has taken place internationally. *See* UNITED NATIONS, DECLARATION OF BASIC PRINCIPLES OF JUSTICE FOR VICTIMS OF CRIME AND ABUSE OF POWER (1985); Matti Joutsen, *Victim Participation in Proceedings and Sentencing in Europe,* 3 INT'L REV. VICTIMOLOGY 57 (1994); Matti Joutsen, *Listening to the Victim: The Victim's Role in European Criminal Justice Systems,* 34 WAYNE L. REV. 95 (1987); Mike Maguire & Joanna Shapland, *Provision for Victims in an International Context, in* VICTIMS OF CRIME, *supra* note 29, at 211; Young, *supra* note 30, at 199.

Notes for Chapter 2

1. *See* PRESIDENT'S TASK FORCE ON VICTIMS OF CRIME, FINAL REPORT 2–13, 33, 60–66, 76–78, 80, 83–84, 114 (1982).

2. *See generally* Peggy M. Tobolowsky, *Victim Participation in the Criminal Justice Process: Fifteen Years After the President's Task Force on Victims of Crime,* 25 NEW ENG. J. ON CRIM. & CIV. CONFINEMENT 21 (1999); National Center for Victims of Crime, VictimLaw, http://www.victimlaw.info/victimlaw/ (last visited Jan. 1, 2009); National Conference of State Legislatures, Victims' Rights Laws in the States, http://www.ncsl.org (last visited Jan. 1, 2009).

3. As of the end of 2008, thirty-three states have victim-related constitutional amendments. *See* ALA. CONST. art. I, § 6.01; ALASKA CONST. art. I, §§ 12, 24; ARIZ. CONST. art. 2, § 2.1; CAL. CONST. art. 1, § 28; COLO. CONST. art. 2, § 16a; CONN. CONST. art. I, § 8; FLA. CONST. art. 1, § 16; IDAHO CONST. art. I, § 22; ILL. CONST. art. 1, § 8.1; IND. CONST. art. 1, § 13; KAN. CONST. art. 15, § 15; LA. CONST. art. 1, § 25; MD. CONST. art. 47; MICH. CONST. art. 1, § 24; MISS. CONST. art. 3, § 26A; MO. CONST. art. 1, § 32; MONT. CONST. art. II, § 28; NEB. CONST. art. I, § 28; NEV. CONST. art. 1, § 8; N.J. CONST. art. 1, § 22; N.M. CONST. art. II, § 24; N.C. CONST. art. I, § 37; OHIO CONST. art. I, § 10a; OKLA. CONST. art. 2, § 34; OR. CONST. art. I, §§ 42, 43; R.I. CONST. art. 1, § 23; S.C. CONST. art. 1, § 24; TENN.

CONST. art. I, §35; TEX. CONST. art. 1, §30; UTAH CONST. art. I, §28; VA. CONST. art. I, §8-A; WASH. CONST. art. 1, §35; WIS. CONST. art. 1, §9 m. *See generally* App. 3.

4. *See* S.J. Res. 1, 108th Cong. (2003); H.R.J. Res. 48, 108th Cong. (2003); H.R.J. Res. 10, 108th Cong. (2003). *See generally* S. REP. No. 108-191 (2003); OFFICE FOR VICTIMS OF CRIME, U.S. DEP'T OF JUSTICE, NEW DIRECTIONS FROM THE FIELD: VICTIMS' RIGHTS AND SERVICES FOR THE 21ST CENTURY 9–12 (1998); Victoria Schwartz, Recent Development, *The Victims' Right Amendment*, 42 HARV. J. ON LEGIS. 525 (2005); National Victims' Constitutional Amendment Passage, http://www.nvcap.org (last visited Oct. 4, 2008).

5. *See* PRESIDENT'S TASK FORCE ON VICTIMS OF CRIME, *supra* note 1, at 72, 83.

6. S.J. Res. 1, 108th Cong. (2003); H.R.J. Res. 48, 108th Cong. (2003); H.R.J. Res. 10, 108th Cong. (2003).

7. 18 U.S.C.A. §3771 (West Supp. 2009); *cf.* 42 U.S.C.A. §10607 (West 2005) (defining a crime victim in the statute governing provision of services); Andrew Nash, *Victims By Definition*, 85 WASH. U. L. REV. 1419 (2008) (discussing the absence of a definition of victim in the Federal Sentencing Guidelines).

8. Fed. R. Crim. P. 1.

9. *E.g.*, ALASKA CONST. art. I, §24; IND. CONST. art. 1, §13; WIS. CONST. art. 1, §9m.

10. CONN. CONST. art. I, §8.

11. *E.g.*, ALA. CONST. art. I, §6.01; FLA. CONST. art. 1, §16.

12. CAL. CONST. art. 1, §28; *cf.* ARIZ. CONST. art. 2, §2.1; N.J. CONST. art. 1, §22; S.C. CONST. art. I, §24 (including detailed definitions).

13. *See* OR. CONST. art. I, §42.

14. *See generally* National Conference of State Legislatures, *supra* note 2.

15. *E.g.*, KAN. STAT. ANN. §74-7333 (2002).

16. *E.g.*, COLO. REV. STAT. ANN. §24-4.1-302 (West 2008); FLA. STAT. ANN. §960.001 (West Supp. 2008); KY. REV. STAT. ANN. §421.500 (LexisNexis 2005); N.H. REV. STAT. ANN. §21-M:8-k (LexisNexis 2008).

17. *E.g.*, W. VA. CODE ANN. §61-11A-6 (LexisNexis 2005) (notice to the victim and one member of the immediate family).

18. *E.g.*, ALA. CODE §15-23-60 (LexisNexis 1995); UTAH CODE ANN. §77-38-2 (Supp. 2007).

19. State v. Roscoe, 912 P.2d 1297 (Ariz. 1996) (en banc); *cf.* Patterson v. Mahoney, No. 1 CA-SA 08-0263, 2008 WL 5255322 (Ariz Ct. App. Dec. 18, 2008) (finding the definition of "victim" in the victim rights statute that included the decedent's siblings superseded the definition in the procedural rule that did not include the siblings for purposes of applying the witness exclusion rule).

20. Knapp v. Martone, 823 P.2d 685 (Ariz. 1992) (en banc).

21. State *ex rel.* Romley v. Superior Court, 909 P.2d 476 (Ariz. Ct. App. 1995).

22. *Ex parte* Littlefield, 540 S.E.2d 81 (S.C. 2000); *cf.* ARIZ. REV. STAT. ANN. §13-4402.01 (Supp. 2007) (authorizing victims in charges dismissed pursuant to a plea bargain to retain victim rights as though the charges had not been dismissed).

23. State v. Stauffer, 58 P.3d 33 (Ariz. Ct. App. 2002).

24. Stapleford v. Houghton, 917 P.2d 703 (Ariz. 1996).

25. *See, e.g.*, State v. David G.K., 632 N.W.2d 123 (Wis. Ct. App. 2001).

26. *See, e.g.*, Lynn v. Reinstein, 68 P.3d 412 (Ariz. 2003) (allowing victim impact evidence, but not sentencing recommendation).

27. Wallace v. State, 486 N.E.2d 445 (Ind. 1985).

28. *See* State v. Superior Court, 922 P.2d 927 (Ariz. Ct. App. 1996).

29. United States v. Turner, 367 F. Supp. 2d 319, 326–27, 329–31 (E.D.N.Y 2005); *cf.* Saum v. Widnall, 912 F. Supp. 1384, 1396 (D. Colo. 1996), *dismissed on other grounds*, 959 F. Supp. 1310 (D. Colo. 1997) (finding that victim status for a military cadet depended on whether the cadet could establish the presence or need for a federal criminal investigation).

30. United States v. Sharp, 463 F. Supp. 2d 556, 561 n.11, 568 (E.D. Va. 2006); *see* Office for Victims of Crime, U.S. Dep't of Justice, Attorney General Guidelines for Victim and Witness Assistance 9 (2005) (interpreting victim status to apply regarding charged offenses); *cf.* United States v. Merkosky, No. 1:02cr-0168-01, 2008 U.S. Dist. LEXIS 29968 (N.D. Ohio Apr. 11, 2008) (finding no victim status for a convicted offender alleging impropriety in the handling of his prosecution); Searcy v. Paletz, C/A No. 6:07-1389-GRA-WMC, 2007 U.S. Dist. LEXIS 46682 (D.S.C. June 27, 2007) (finding no victim status for an inmate whose assault allegations against another inmate did not result in a criminal prosecution).

31. *See* United States v. BP Products North America, Cr. No. H-07-434, 2008 U.S. Dist. LEXIS 12893, at *36–*37 (S.D. Tex. Feb. 21, 2008); United States v. Ingrassia, CR 04-0455, 2005 U.S. Dist. LEXIS 27817, at *52–*56 (E.D.N.Y. Sept. 7, 2005).

32. *See* 18 U.S.C.A. § 3771 (West Supp. 2009).

33. *See In re* Stewart, No. 08-16753, 2008 WL 5265344 (11th Cir. Dec. 19, 2008).

34. *See In re* Antrobus, 519 F.3d 1123 (10th Cir. 2008); *see also In re* Jane Doe, 264 Fed. Appx. 260 (4th Cir. 2007) (unpublished opinion) (finding an absence of direct and proximate harm from the charged illegal misbranding of a drug to a person who alleged she became addicted to the drug and therefore no victim status under the restitution statute or the Act).

35. *See generally* National Conference of State Legislatures, *supra* note 2.

36. *See* President's Task Force on Victims of Crime, *supra* note 1, at 72.

37. Office for Victims of Crime, *supra* note 4, at 25.

38. S.J. Res. 1, 108th Cong. (2003); H.R.J. Res. 48, 108th Cong. (2003); H.R.J. Res. 10, 108th Cong. (2003).

39. *See* 18 U.S.C.A. § 3771 (West Supp. 2009).

40. *See,.e.g.*, Colo. Const. art. 2, § 16a; Ill. Const. art. 1, § 8.1; Mo. Const. art. 1, § 32; Va. Const. art. I, § 8-A.

41. Cal. Const. art. 1, § 28; Fla. Const. art. 1, § 16; N.M. Const. art. II, § 24; N.J. Const. art. 1, § 22; Or. Const. art. I, § 42; R.I. Const. art. 1, § 23; S.C. Const. art. I, § 24; Utah Const. art. I, § 28; Wash. Const. art. 1, § 35.

42. Idaho Code § 19-5306 (2004); *see also, e.g.*, Ariz. Rev. Stat. Ann. § 13-4401 (Supp. 2007); Ohio Rev. Code Ann. § 2930.01 (LexisNexis Supp. 2008); Utah Code Ann. § 77-38-5 (2003).

43. Ala. Code § 15-23-60 (LexisNexis 1995); *see also, e.g.*, 725 Ill. Comp. Stat. Ann. 120/3 (West Supp. 2008); Miss. Code Ann. § 99-43-3 (West 2006); Tex. Code Crim. Proc. Ann. art. 56.01 (Vernon Supp. 2008).

44. *See* Del. Code Ann. tit. 11, § 9401 (2007); *see also, e.g.*, Colo. Rev. Stat. Ann. § 24-4.1-302 (West 2008); N.M. Stat. Ann. § 31-26-3 (LexisNexis Supp. 2008).

45. *See* W. Va. Code Ann. §§ 61-11A-2, -6, -8 (LexisNexis 2005); *see also, e.g.*, Alaska Stat. §§ 12.61.010, .015 (2006); Cal. Penal Code §§ 679.01, .03, .04 (West 1999 & Supp. 2008); Iowa Code Ann. §§ 915.10, .18 (West 2003 & Supp. 2008); Kan. Stat. Ann. §§ 22–3727 (2007), 74–7333 (2002); Mass. Ann. Laws ch. 258B, §§ 1, 3 (LexisNexis 2004); ch. 279, § 4B (LexisNexis 2002); Tenn. Code Ann. § 40-38-103 (2006).

46. *See, e.g.*, N.J. Stat. Ann. § 52:4B-36, -37 (West Supp. 2008).

47. *See, e.g.,* Ark. Code Ann. § 16-90-1109 (2006); Mich. Comp. Laws Ann. §§ 780.756, .763 (West 2007); Tex. Code Crim. Proc. Ann. art. 56.02 (Vernon Supp. 2008).

48. *See, e.g.,* R.I. Gen. Laws § 12-28-3 (Supp. 2007).

49. State *ex rel.* Thomas v. Klein, 150 P.3d 778 (Ariz. Ct. App. 2007).

50. 18 U.S.C.A. § 3771 (West Supp. 2008).

51. *See* Chad Trulson, *Victims' Rights and Services: Eligibility, Exclusion, and Victim Worth,* 4 Criminology & Pub. Pol'y 399 (2005). *See generally* Douglas E. Beloof et al., Victims in Criminal Procedure 49–109 (2d ed. 2006).

Notes for Chapter 3

1. *See* President's Task Force on Victims of Crime, Final Report 33–34, 60–61, 64, 83–84 (1982).

2. *See* Office for Victims of Crime, U.S. Dep't of Justice, New Directions from the Field: Victims' Rights and Services for the 21st Century 23–24, 61–62, 104 (1998).

3. *See generally* 18 U.S.C.A. § 3771 (West Supp. 2009); National Center for Victims of Crime, VictimLaw, http://www.victimlaw.info/victimlaw/ (last visited Jan. 1, 2009); National Conference of State Legislatures, Victims' Rights Laws in the States, http://www.ncsl.org (last visited Jan. 1, 2009).

4. S.J. Res. 1, 108th Cong. (2003); H.R.J. Res. 48, 108th Cong. (2003); H.R.J. Res. 10, 108th Cong. (2003). *See generally* S. Rep. No. 108–191 (2003).

5. 18 U.S.C.A. § 3771 (West Supp. 2009).

6. *See* Ariz. Const. art. 2, § 2.1; Cal. Const. art. 1, § 28; La. Const. art. 1, § 25; Md. Const. art. 47; Mo. Const. art. 1, § 32; N.C. Const. art. I, § 37; Okla. Const. art. 2, § 34; Or. Const. art. I, § 42; S.C. Const. art. I, § 24; Tenn. Const. art. I, § 35.

7. *See, e.g.,* Ala. Code § 15-23-62 (LexisNexis 1995); Cal. Penal Code § 679.02 (West 1999); Ga. Code Ann. § 17-17-6 (West 2003); Ohio Rev. Code Ann. § 2930.04 (LexisNexis 2006); Wyo. Stat. Ann. § 1-40-204 (2007).

8. *See, e.g.,* Del. Code Ann. tit. 11, § 9411 (2007); Iowa Code Ann. § 915.12 (West Supp. 2008); Minn. Stat. Ann. § 611A.02 (West 2003); N.M. Stat. Ann. § 31-26-9 (LexisNexis Supp. 2008); Tex. Code Crim. Proc. Ann. art. 56.08 (Vernon 2006).

9. *See, e.g.,* Del. Code Ann. tit. 11, §§ 9410, 9411 (2007); Ohio Rev. Code Ann. §§ 2930.04, .06 (LexisNexis 2006).

10. *See, e.g.,* Conn. Gen. Stat. § 54-203 (2007); R.I. Gen. Laws § 12-28-9 (2002).

11. *See, e.g.,* Ariz. Rev. Stat. Ann. § 13-4438 (Supp. 2007); *see also* Fla. Stat. Ann. § 960.021 (West 2006) (permitting posters on courtroom doors with the prescribed rights as an alternative to courtroom announcements).

12. *See* National Center for Victims of Crime, *supra* note 3; National Conference of State Legislatures, *supra* note 3.

13. 875 P.2d 824 (Ariz. Ct. App. 1993).

14. *See id.* at 826, 829, 830.

15. *See id.* at 826–27.

16. *See id.* at 829–30.

17. *Id.* at 830 (citation omitted).

18. *See id.* at 831–32; *cf.* United States v. Rubin, 558 F. Supp. 2d 411, 428 (E.D.N.Y. 2008) (finding a violation of the victims' right to notification of rights, but no violation of their substantive rights that would warrant relief for this past violation).

19. *See* U.S GOVERNMENT ACCOUNTABILITY OFFICE, CRIME VICTIMS' RIGHTS ACT: INCREASING AWARENESS, MODIFYING THE COMPLAINT PROCESS, AND ENHANCING COMPLIANCE MONITORING WILL IMPROVE IMPLEMENTATION OF THE ACT 48–49, 81–83, 97–100 (2008).

20. *See* Jim Sinclair, *Partners for Justice: Crime Victims and State Policymakers in the Northeast Join Together for System Change,* 3 THE CRIME VICTIMS REPORT 17, 17–18, 26 (1999).

21. *See* DAVID BEATTY ET AL., NATIONAL VICTIM CENTER, STATUTORY AND CONSTITUTIONAL PROTECTION OF VICTIMS' RIGHTS: IMPLEMENTATION AND IMPACT ON CRIME VICTIMS 9–34 (1996); *see also* DEAN G. KILPATRICK ET AL., U.S. DEP'T OF JUSTICE, THE RIGHTS OF CRIME VICTIMS—DOES LEGAL PROTECTION MAKE A DIFFERENCE? (1998). *But see* S. REP. NO. 106-254, at 62 (2000).

22. *See* EDWIN VILLMOARE & VIRGINIA V. NETO, U.S. DEP'T OF JUSTICE, VICTIM APPEARANCES AT SENTENCING HEARINGS UNDER THE CALIFORNIA VICTIMS' BILL OF RIGHTS 42 (1987).

23. *See* BEATTY ET AL., *supra* note 21, at 80–81, 97.

24. *See id.* at 58–63.

25. *See* OFFICE OF JUSTICE PROGRAMS, U.S. DEP'T OF JUSTICE, FOUR YEARS LATER: A REPORT ON THE PRESIDENT'S TASK FORCE ON VICTIMS OF CRIME 4 (1986).

26. *See* PRESIDENT'S TASK FORCE ON VICTIMS OF CRIME, *supra* note 1, at 33–34, 60–61.

27. *See id.* at 33–34, 64.

28. *See id.* at 18, 83–84.

29. *See* OFFICE FOR VICTIMS OF CRIME, *supra* note 2, at 12–14, 63, 82–83, 133–36.

30. *See generally* 18 U.S.C.A. § 3771 (West Supp. 2009); National Center for Victims of Crime, *supra* note 3; National Conference of State Legislatures, *supra* note 3.

31. S.J. Res. 1, 108th Cong. (2003); H.R.J. Res. 48, 108th Cong. (2003); H.R.J. Res. 10, 108th Cong. (2003).

32. 18 U.S.C.A. § 3771 (West Supp. 2009).

33. Fed. R. Crim. P. 60.

34. 42 U.S.C.A. § 10607 (West 2005).

35. ALA. CONST. art. I, § 6.01; ALASKA CONST. art. I, §§ 12, 24; ARIZ. CONST. art. 2, § 2.1; CAL. CONST. art. 1, § 28; COLO. CONST. art. 2, § 16a; CONN. CONST. art. I, § 8; FLA. CONST. art. 1, § 16; IDAHO CONST. art. I, § 22; ILL. CONST. art. 1, § 8.1; IND. CONST. art. 1, § 13; KAN. CONST. art.15, § 15; LA. CONST. art. 1, § 25; MD. CONST. art. 47; MICH. CONST. art. 1, § 24; MISS. CONST. art. 3, § 26A; MO. CONST. art. 1, § 32; NEB. CONST. art. I, § 28; N.M. CONST. art. II, § 24; N.C. CONST. art. I, § 37; OHIO CONST. art. I, § 10a; OKLA. CONST. art. 2, § 34; OR. CONST. art. I, § 42; S.C. CONST. art. I, § 24; TENN. CONST. art. I, § 35; TEX. CONST. art. 1, § 30; UTAH CONST. art. I, § 28; VA. CONST. art. I, § 8-A; WASH. CONST. art. 1, § 35; WIS. CONST. art. 1, § 9 m.

36. CAL. CONST. art. 1, § 28; IDAHO CONST. art. I, § 22; MO. CONST. art. 1, § 32; NEB. CONST. art. I, § 28; S.C. CONST. art. I, § 24.

37. IDAHO CONST. art. I, § 22.

38. MO. CONST. art. 1, § 32.

39. *See* ALASKA CONST. art. I, § 24; ARIZ. CONST. art. 2, § 2.1; CAL. CONST. art. 1, § 28; CONN. CONST. art. I, § 8; IDAHO CONST. art. I, § 22; ILL. CONST. art. 1, § 8.1; LA. CONST. art.1, § 25; MICH. CONST. art. 1, § 24; MO. CONST. art. 1, § 32; NEV. CONST. art. 1, § 8; N.M. CONST. art. II, § 24; N.C. CONST. art. I, § 37; OKLA. CONST. art. 2, § 34; OR. CONST.

art. I, §42; S.C. Const. art. I, §24; Tenn. Const. art. I, §35; Tex. Const. art. 1, §30; Va. Const. art. I, §8-A; Wis. Const. art. 1, §9m.

40. *See* Cal. Const. art. 1, §28; Conn. Const. art. I, §8; Idaho Const. art. I, §22; Ill. Const. art. 1, §8.1; Mich. Const. art. 1, §24; Nev. Const. art. 1, §8; N.M. Const. art. II, §24; N.C. Const. art. I, §37; Okla. Const. art. 2, §34; Or. Const. art. I, §42; Tex. Const. art. 1, §30; Wis. Const. art. 1, §9m.

41. *See generally* National Center for Victims of Crime, *supra* note 3; National Conference of State Legislatures, *supra* note 3.

42. *See, e.g.,* Colo. Rev. Stat. Ann. §§24-4.1-302, -302.5 (West 2008); Fla. Stat. Ann. §960.001 (West Supp. 2008).

43. *See, e.g.,* Mich. Comp. Laws Ann. §780.756 (West 2007); Tenn. Code Ann. §40-38-103 (2006); Va. Code Ann. §19.2-11.01 (Supp. 2007).

44. *See, e.g.,* Ga. Code Ann. §17-17-5 (West 2003); Ky. Rev. Stat. Ann. §421.500 (LexisNexis 2005); Mo. Ann. Stat. §595.209 (West Supp. 2008); N.Y. Exec. Law §646 (McKinney Supp. 2008).

45. *See, e.g.,* Ala. Code §§15-23-60, -63 (LexisNexis 1995); Conn. Gen. Stat. §51-286e (2007); Iowa Code Ann. §915.13 (West Supp. 2008); Mont. Code Ann. §46-24-203 (2007).

46. *See, e.g.,* Del. Code Ann. tit. 11, §9411 (2007); Me. Rev. Stat. Ann. tit. 17-A, §1172 (2006); N.J. Stat. Ann. §52:4B-44 (West Supp. 2008); Wash. Rev. Code Ann. §7.69.030 (West 2007).

47. *See, e.g.,* Cal. Penal Code §679.02 (West 1999); La. Rev. Stat. Ann. §46:1844 (Supp. 2008); W. Va. Code Ann. §61-11A-6 (LexisNexis 2005).

48. *See, e.g.,* 725 Ill. Comp. Stat. Ann. 120/4.5 (West Supp. 2008); Mass. Ann. Laws ch. 258B, §3 (LexisNexis 2004); Utah Code Ann. §§77-38-2, -3 (2003 & Supp. 2007).

49. *See, e.g.,* Colo. Rev. Stat. Ann. §24-4.1-302 (West 2008); Idaho Code Ann. §19-5306 (2004).

50. *See, e.g.,* Ky. Rev. Stat. Ann. §421.500 (LexisNexis 2005); La. Rev. Stat. Ann. §46:1844 (Supp. 2008); N.D. Cent. Code §12.1-34-02 (Supp.2007); R.I. Gen. Laws §12-28-3 (Supp.2007).

51. *See, e.g.,* Ala. Code §15-23-75 (LexisNexis 1995); Ohio Rev. Code Ann. §2930.12 (LexisNexis 2006); Wash. Rev. Code Ann. §7.69.030 (West 2007).

52. *See, e.g.,* Haw. Rev. Stat. Ann. §801D-4 (LexisNexis 2007); N.J. Stat. Ann. §52:4B-44 (West Supp. 2008); Okla. Stat. Ann. tit. 19, §215.33 (West Supp. 2008); S.D. Codified Laws §23A-28C-1 (Supp. 2008); W. Va. Code Ann. §61-11A-6 (LexisNexis 2005).

53. *See, e.g.,* Nev. Rev. Stat. Ann. §213.130 (LexisNexis Supp. 2007); N.C. Gen. Stat. §15A-825 (2007); 18 Pa. Stat. Ann §11.201 (West Supp. 2008).

54. *See, e.g.,* Idaho Code Ann. §19-5306 (2004); Mo. Stat. Ann. §595.209 (West Supp. 2008).

55. *See, e.g.,* Ga. Code Ann. §17-17-7 (West 2003); Ohio Rev. Code Ann. §2930.04 (LexisNexis 2006); Wyo. Stat. Ann. §1-40-204 (2007).

56. *See, e.g.,* Ark. Code Ann. §16-90-1109 (2006); Cal. Penal Code §679.02 (West 1999); 725 Ill. Comp. Stat. Ann. 120/4.5 (West Supp. 2008); N.J. Stat. Ann. §52:4B-44 (West Supp. 2008); Wyo. Stat. Ann. §1-40-203 (2007).

57. *See, e.g.,* Ariz. Rev. Stat. Ann. §13-4417 (2001); Colo. Rev. Stat. Ann. §24-4.1-303 (West 2008); Mo. Stat. Ann. §595.209 (West Supp. 2008).

58. *See, e.g.,* N.M. Stat. Ann. §31-26-5 (LexisNexis 2000); R.I. Gen. Laws §12-28-3 (Supp. 2007).

59. *See, e.g.*, FLA. STAT. ANN. §960.001 (West Supp. 2008); MICH. COMP. LAWS ANN. §780.756 (West 2007); N.Y. EXEC. LAW §646-a (McKinney Supp. 2008). *But see, e.g.*, IDAHO CODE ANN. §19-5306 (2004).

60. *See* ARIZ. REV. STAT. ANN. §§13-4405 to -4417 (2001 & Supp. 2007); CAL. PENAL CODE §679.02 (West 1999). *See generally* Susan E. Gegan & Nicholas Ernesto Rodriguez, Note, *Victims' Roles in the Criminal Justice System: A Fallacy of Victim Empowerment*, 8 ST. JOHN'S J. LEGAL COMMENT. 225, 244–47 (1992).

61. *See, e.g.*, VA. CODE ANN. §19.2-11.01 (Supp. 2007); WASH. REV. CODE ANN. §7.69.030 (West 2007).

62. *See* National Victim Notification Network (VINE), http://www.appriss.com/VINE.html, http://www.vinelink.com (last visited Jan. 2, 2009) (describing the system used by a majority of states regarding inmate custody status); United States Department of Justice Victim Notification System, http://www.usdoj.gov/criminal/vns/ (last visited Jan. 3, 2009) (describing the federal automated notification system regarding court events and outcomes and offender custody status).

63. *See, e.g.*, TENN. CODE ANN. §40-38-118 (2006); Susan Howley & Carol Dorris, *Legal Rights for Crime Victims in the Criminal Justice System*, *in* VICTIMS OF CRIME 299, 301 (Robert C. Davis et al. eds., 3d ed. 2007).

64. *See* Crime Victims' Rights Act of 2004, Pub. L. No. 108-405, Title I, §§103–104, 118 Stat. 2260, 2264–65 (2004); 42 U.S.C.A. §10603e (West 2005) (permitting additional grants pursuant to the crime victim assistance grant program). *But see* United States v. Ingrassia, CR 04-0455, 2005 U.S. Dist. LEXIS 27817, at *42–*43 (E.D.N.Y. Sept. 7, 2005) (noting Congress' failure to actually appropriate the initial $2,000,000 authorized for the federal automated notification system).

65. *See* OFFICE FOR VICTIMS OF CRIME, *supra* note 2, at 14.

66. 18 U.S.C.A. §3771 (West Supp. 2009); 42 U.S.C.A. §10607 (West 2005); Fed. R. Crim. P. 60.

67. GA. CODE ANN. §§17-17-15 (West 2003), 42-1-11 (West 2008).

68. ME. REV. STAT. ANN. tit. 17-A, §1175 (Supp. 2008).

69. *See* LA. REV. STAT. ANN. §46:1844 (Supp. 2008); *cf.* S.C. CODE ANN. §16-3-1525 (2003 & Supp. 2007).

70. *See* ARIZ. REV. STAT. ANN. §13-4436 (Supp. 2007); Ariz. R. Crim. P. 39.

71. *See* ARIZ. REV. STAT. ANN. §13-4436 (Supp. 2007); HAW. REV. STAT. ANN. §706-670.5 (LexisNexis 2007); OKLA. STAT. ANN. tit. 57, §332.2 (West 2004); TENN. CODE ANN. §40-28-505 (2006).

72. 874 P.2d 1183 (Kan. 1994).

73. *See id.* at 1184, 1187.

74. *Id.* at 1184–88; *cf.* State v. Sims, 887 P.2d 72 (Kan. 1994).

75. *See* KAN. STAT. ANN. §74-7335 (Pamp.2007).

76. 807 P.2d 1063 (Cal. 1991) (in bank).

77. *See id.* at 1064–68; *cf.* People v. Superior Court *ex rel.* Thompson, 202 Cal. Rptr. 585 (Cal. Ct. App. 1984) (finding that, even assuming a notification rights violation, California law provided no enforcement or remedy mechanism that would permit the requested relief to vacate the sentence).

78. *See* CAL. CONST. art. 1, §28.

79. 523 N.W.2d 640 (Mich. Ct. App. 1994).

80. *See id.* at 641–44.

81. 948 A.2d 30 (Md. 2008).

82. *See id.* at 38–42, 44–52.

83. *Id.* at 52; *see* Lopez-Sanchez v. State, 879 A.2d 695 (Md. 2005); Cianos v. State, 659 A.2d 291 (Md. 1995); Lodowski v. State 490 A.2d 1228 (Md. 1985), *vacated on other grounds*, 475 U.S. 1078 (1986); Lamb v. Kontgias, 901 A.2d 860 (Md. Ct. Spec. App. 2006).

84. 715 A.2d 580 (R.I. 1998).

85. *See id.* at 582–83.

86. *See id.* at 584–85.

87. *See id.* at 586–87.

88. *Id.* at 595–96 (citations omitted). *But see id.* at 601–03 (Flanders, J. dissenting).

89. 521 N.E.2d 98 (Ill. App. Ct. 1987).

90. *See id.* at 99–100.

91. 237 Cal. Rptr. 5 (Cal. Ct. App. 1987).

92. *See id.* at 6–7; *cf.* People v. Superior Court *ex rel.* Thompson, 202 Cal. Rptr. 585 (Cal. Ct. App. 1984).

93. 829 So. 2d 946 (Fla. Dist. Ct. App. 2002).

94. *See id.* at 947–48.

95. 802 So. 2d 242 (Ala. Civ. App. 2001).

96. *See id.* at 243, 245, 247–48.

97. 926 A.2d 328 (N.J. 2007).

98. *See id.* at 334–35.

99. 18 U.S.C.A. §3771 (West Supp. 2008).

100. 409 F.3d 555 (2d Cir. 2005).

101. *See id.* at 559–60.

102. *Id.* at 560–64; *cf.* United States v. Rubin, 558 F. Supp. 2d 411 (E.D.N.Y. 2008) (finding no actual violation of the notification rights provisions); United States v. Stokes, No. 3:06-00204, 2007 WL 1849846 (M.D. Tenn. June 22, 2007) (finding use of proxy and publication notification permissible in a case with 35,000 estimated victims).

103. 367 F. Supp. 2d 319 (E.D.N.Y. 2005).

104. *See id.* at 320–21, 324

105. CR 04-0455, 2005 U.S. Dist. LEXIS 27817 (E.D.N.Y. Sept. 7, 2005).

106. *See id.; cf.* United States v. Saltsman, No. 07-CR-641, 2007 U.S. Dist. LEXIS 87044 (E.D.N.Y. Nov. 27, 2007) (finding that notice by publication and then through a web site with case status information was reasonable in a case involving tens of thousands of potential victims).

107. 527 F.3d 391 (5th Cir. 2008) (per curiam); *see* United States v. BP Products North America, Cr. No. H-07-434, 2008 U.S. Dist. LEXIS 12893 (S.D. Tex. Feb. 21, 2008) (trial court decision).

108. *See Dean*, 527 F.3d at 392–93.

109. *See id.* at 394–96.

110. 963 F.2d 1296 (9th Cir. 1992).

111. *See id.* at 1298–1301; *cf.* Jackson v. Henderson, No. 3:05-0677, 2006 U.S. Dist. LEXIS 63066 (M.D. Tenn. Aug. 31, 2006) (finding no federal civil rights violation based on alleged violation of state notice provisions).

112. *See* Office for Victims of Crime, *supra* note 2, at 74, 123, 125.

113. *See* William G. Doerner & Steven P. Lab, Victimology 270–71 (2d ed. 1998).

114. *See* CAROLINE LARSEN & DOUGLAS L. YEARWOOD, NORTH CAROLINA GOVERNOR'S CRIME COMMISSION, NOTIFYING AND INFORMING VICTIMS OF CRIME: AN EVALUATION OF NORTH CAROLINA'S SAVAN SYSTEM 1–17 (2004), *available at* http://www.ncgccd.org/PDFs/pubs/SAVAN.pdf.

115. *See* U.S. GENERAL ACCOUNTABILITY OFFICE, *supra* note 19, at 83–84, 97–100.

116. *See* LARSEN & YEARWOOD, *supra* note 114, at 17–19; *see also* Howley & Dorris, *supra* note 63, at 311 (describing notification rates in additional state studies).

117. *See* Sinclair, *supra* note 20, at 17–18, 26–27.

118. *See* BEATTY ET AL., *supra* note 21, at 9–30, 41–42.

119. *See id.* at 31–34.

120. *See id.* at 77–82, 84–85, 89, 97, 125–42.

121. *See id.* at 44, 49–58.

122. *See* JOLENE C. HERNON & BRIAN FORST, U.S. DEP'T OF JUSTICE, THE CRIMINAL JUSTICE RESPONSE TO VICTIM HARM 10, 45, 62 (1984).

123. *See* Deborah P. Kelly, *Delivering Legal Services to Victims: An Evaluation and Prescription*, 9 JUST. SYS. J. 62, 64–65, 73–77 (1984).

124. *See* Robert C. Davis et al., *Expanding the Victim's Role in the Criminal Court Dispositional Process: The Results of an Experiment*, 75 J. CRIM. L. & CRIMINOLOGY 491, 493, 495, 497–98 (1984).

125. *See* John Hagan, *Victims Before the Law: A Study of Victim Involvement in the Criminal Justice Process*, 73 J. CRIM. L. & CRIMINOLOGY 317, 319–20, 324–25, 327–28 (1982).

126. *See* Pamela Tontodonato & Edna Erez, *Crime, Punishment, and Victim Distress*, 3 INT'L REV. VICTIMOLOGY 33, 37–38, 40–48 (1994).

127. *See* BEATTY ET AL., *supra* note 21, at 148.

Notes for Chapter 4

1. *See generally* Douglas E. Beloof & Paul G. Cassell, *The Crime Victim's Right to Attend the Trial: The Reascendant National Consensus*, 9 LEWIS & CLARK L. REV. 481, 484–503 (2005); LeRoy L. Lamborn, *Victim Participation in the Criminal Justice Process: The Proposals for a Constitutional Amendment*, 34 WAYNE L. REV. 125, 140–43, 153–60 (1987).

2. *See* U.S. CONST. amends. I, VI; Press-Enterprise Co. v. Superior Court, 464 U.S. 501 (1984); Globe Newspaper Co. v. Superior Court, 457 U.S. 596 (1982); Lamborn, *supra* note 1, at 140–41.

3. *Globe Newspaper Co.*, 457 U.S. at 606.

4. *See* Lamborn, *supra* note 1, at 153–54.

5. *See id.* at 154–60; *see also* Beloof & Cassell, *supra* note 1, at 484–503.

6. *See* Beloof & Cassell, *supra* note 1, at 494–503; Lamborn, *supra* note 1, at 153–61.

7. *See* OFFICE OF JUSTICE PROGRAMS, U.S. DEP'T OF JUSTICE, FOUR YEARS LATER: A REPORT ON THE PRESIDENT'S TASK FORCE ON VICTIMS OF CRIME 4 (1986).

8. PRESIDENT'S TASK FORCE ON VICTIMS OF CRIME, FINAL REPORT 114 (1982) (emphasis added); *see* Beloof & Cassell, *supra* note 1, at 502–04; Lamborn, *supra* note 1, at 185–87, 193–200.

9. PRESIDENT'S TASK FORCE ON VICTIMS OF CRIME, *supra* note 8, at 80.

10. *Id.*

11. *Id.* at 72, 80 (emphasis added).

12. *Id.* at 83–84.

13. *See* Office for Victims of Crime, U.S. Dep't of Justice, New Directions from the Field: Victims' Rights and Services for the 21st Century 15, 25–26, 106–07, 138–39 (1998).

14. S.J. Res. 1, 108th Cong. (2003); H.R.J. Res. 48, 108th Cong. (2003); H.R.J. Res. 10, 108th Cong. (2003); *see* S. Rep. No. 108-191 (2003); Beloof & Cassell, *supra* note 1, at 517–19; Robert P. Mosteller, Essay, *Victims' Rights and the Constitution: Moving from Guaranteeing Participatory Rights to Benefiting the Prosecution*, 29 St. Mary's L.J. 1053, 1058 (1998).

15. 42 U.S.C.A. § 10606 (repealed 2004, as reflected in West 2005).

16. *See* 143 Cong. Rec. S2507-09 (daily ed. Mar. 19, 1997); 143 Cong. Rec. H1048-52 (daily ed. Mar. 18, 1997); Beloof & Cassell, *supra* note 1, at 514–17.

17. *See* 42 U.S.C.A. § 10608 (West 2005).

18. *See* 18 U.S.C.A. § 3510 (West 2000); S. Rep. No. 105-409, at 56 (1998); Roslyn K. Myers, *Victim Rights Clarification Act of 1997 Affects Victim Bill of Rights Act, Violent Crime Control Act, and Rule of Evidence*, 1 The Crime Victims Report 17 (1997).

19. Fed. R. Evid. 615 (emphasis added).

20. 18 U.S.C.A. § 3771 (West Supp. 2009); Fed. R. Crim. P. 60; Beloof & Cassell, *supra* note 1, at 519–20.

21. *See generally* National Center for Victims of Crime, VictimLaw, http://www.victimlaw.info/victimlaw/ (last visited Jan. 1, 2009); National Conference of State Legislatures, Victims' Rights Laws in the States, http://www.ncsl.org (last visited Jan. 1, 2009); *cf.* Beloof & Cassell, *supra* note 1, at 504–14 (describing victims' right to attend trial).

22. *See* Peggy M. Tobolowsky,*"Constitutionalizing" Crime Victim Rights*, 33 Crim. L. Bull. 395, 418–19 (1997). *See generally* App. 3.

23. *See* Mont. Const. art. II, § 28; Ohio Const. art. I, § 10a.

24. *See* Conn. Const. art. I, § 8; Ill. Const. art. 1, § 8.1; Mich. Const. art. 1, § 24; Neb. Const. art. I, § 28; N.J. Const. art. 1, § 22; N.M. Const. art. II, § 24; N.C. Const. art. I, § 37; Or. Const. art. I, § 42 Tex. Const. art. 1, § 30; Wash. Const. art. 1, § 35; Wis. Const. art. 1, § 9m; *cf.* R.I. Const. art. 1, § 23; Va. Const. art. I, § 8-A (including a victim right to address the court at or regarding sentence and implicitly including a right to be present there).

25. Ill. Const. art. 1, § 8.1.

26. *See* Ala. Const. art. I, § 6.01; Alaska Const. art. I, § 24; Ariz. Const. art. 2, § 2.1; Cal. Const. art. 1, § 28; Colo. Const. art. 2, § 16a; Fla. Const. art. 1, § 16; Idaho Const. art. I, § 22; Ind. Const. art. 1, § 13; Kan. Const. art. 15, § 15; La. Const. art. 1, § 25; Md. Const. art. 47; Miss. Const. art. 3 § 26A; Mo. Const. art. 1, § 32; Nev. Const. art. 1, § 8; Okla. Const. art. 2, § 34; S.C. Const. art. I, § 24; Tenn. Const. art. I, § 35; Utah Const. art. I, § 28;

27. *See* Cal. Const. art. 1, § 28; Neb. Const. art. I, § 28; S.C. Const. art. I, § 24.

28. *See* Idaho Code Ann. § 19-5306 (2004); S.C. Code Ann. §§ 16-3-1515, -1525, -1535 (2003 & Supp. 2007); Utah Code Ann. § 77-38-4 (2003).

29. *See* Alaska Stat. § 12.61.010 (2006); Mo. Ann. Stat. § 595.209 (West Supp. 2008); N.H. Rev. Stat. Ann. § 21-M:8-k (LexisNexis 2008); N.M. Stat. Ann. § 31-26-4 (LexisNexis 2000).

30. *See* La. Code Evid. Ann. art. 615 (2006); Ariz. R. Crim. P. 9.3; Ark. R. Evid. 616; Utah R. Evid. 615.

31. *See* Ala. Const. art. I, § 6.01; Ala. Code §§ 15-14-50 to -57 (LexisNexis1995).

32. *See, e.g.,* COLO. REV. STAT. ANN. §§ 24-4.1-302, -302.5, -303 (West 2008); OHIO REV. CODE ANN. § 2930.09 (LexisNexis 2006).

33. *See, e.g.,* DEL. CODE ANN. tit. 11, §§ 3512, 9407 (2007); OKLA. STAT. ANN. tit. 12, § 2615 (West 2009).

34. *See, e.g.,* S.D. CODIFIED LAWS § 19-14-29 (2004); WASH. REV. CODE ANN. § 7.69.030 (West 2007).

35. *See* CAL. EVID. CODE § 777 (West 1995); CAL. PENAL CODE § 1102.6 (West 2004).

36. *See, e.g.,* IOWA CODE ANN. § 915.21 (West 2003); W. VA. CODE ANN. § 61-11A-2 (LexisNexis 2005).

37. *See, e.g.,* DEL. CODE ANN. tit. 11, § 9407 (2007); MASS. ANN. LAWS ch. 258B, § 3 (LexisNexis 2004); OKLA. STAT. ANN. tit. 12, § 2615 (West 2009); WYO. STAT. ANN. § 1-40-206 (2007).

38. *See, e.g.,* ALASKA STAT. § 33.16.120 (2006); IOWA CODE ANN. § 915.18 (West 2003); S.C. CODE ANN. § 16-3-1560 (2003); W. VA. CODE ANN. § 62-12-23 (LexisNexis Supp. 2008); Maureen McLeod, *Getting Free: Victim Participation in Parole Board Decisions,* 4 CRIM JUST. 12, 14–15 (1989).

39. *See, e.g.,* DEL. CODE ANN. tit. 11, § 4361 (2007); LA. REV. STAT. ANN. § 46:1844 (Supp. 2008).

40. *See* ALA. CODE §§ 15-14-57, 15-23-76 (LexisNexis 1995); CONN. GEN. STAT. § 54-85c (2007); GA. CODE ANN. § 24-9-61.1 (West 2003); UTAH CODE ANN. § 77-38-10 (2003).

41. *See* ARIZ. REV. STAT. ANN. § 13-4436 (Supp. 2007); OKLA. STAT. ANN. tit. 57, § 332.2 (West 2004); TENN. CODE ANN. § 40-28-505 (2006).

42. *See, e.g.,* COLO. REV. STAT. ANN. § 24-4.1-302.5 (West 2008); DEL. CODE ANN. tit. 11, § 9409 (2007); LA. REV. STAT. ANN. § 46:1844 (Supp. 2008); MASS. ANN. LAWS ch. 258B, § 3 (LexisNexis 2004); S.C. CODE ANN. § 16-3-1550 (2003); UTAH CODE ANN. § 77-37-3 (Supp. 2007). *See generally* National Conference of State Legislatures, *supra* note 21.

43. MICH. COMP. LAWS ANN. § 780.762 (West 2007); MINN. STAT. ANN. § 611A.036 (West Supp. 2008).

44. *See generally* Beloof & Cassell, *supra* note 1, at 527–34; Jay M. Zitter, Annotation, *Validity, Construction, and Application of State Constitutional or Statutory Victims' Bill of Rights,* 91 A.L.R. 5th 343, 399–407 (2001).

45. 737 A.2d 55 (N.J. 1999).

46. *Id.* at 74–76. In another ruling supporting a victim's right to be present, a Colorado appellate court disapproved of the trial court's exclusion from the courtroom of the deceased victim's father following his testimony and found that the state constitutional and statutory victim rights provisions took precedence over the state witness exclusion rule here. People v. Coney, 98 P.3d 930, 935 (Colo. Ct. App. 2004).

47. 233 S.W.3d 796 (Mo. Ct. App. 2007).

48. *Id.* at 797–99; *see also* People v. Pfeiffer, 523 N.W.2d 640 (Mich. Ct. App. 1994) (reaching a similar conclusion regarding trial court's resentencing of the defendant; described in Chapter 3).

49. 720 S.W.2d 301 (Ark. 1986).

50. *See id.* at 303; *cf.* State v. Schoening, 770 So. 2d 762 (La. 2000) (finding that the trial court improperly declared sua sponte that the state's victim exemption from the witness exclusion rule was unconstitutional).

51. 975 P.2d 75 (Ariz. 1999).

52. *See id.* at 92.

53. 922 P.2d 30 (Utah Ct. App. 1996).

54. *See id.* at 32–35; *see also, e.g.,* Robinson v. State, 896 S.W.2d 442, 443 (Ark. Ct. App. 1995); Sireci v. State, 587 So. 2d 450, 454 (Fla. 1991); Cain v. State, 758 So. 2d 1257 (Fla. Dist. Ct. App. 2000); Watts v. State, 406 S.E.2d 562, 564 (Ga. Ct. App. 1991); Wheeler v. State, 596 A.2d 78, 86–89 (Md. Ct. Spec. App. 1991); State v. Cosey, 873 P.2d 1177, 1180–81 (Utah Ct. App. 1994); State v. Rangel, 866 P.2d 607, 609–13 (Utah Ct. App. 1993); *cf.* Carey v. Musladin, 549 U.S. 70 (2006); Overstreet v. State, 877 N.E.2d 144 (Ind. 2007) (regarding the wearing of buttons in the courtroom with the victim's image).

55. 787 S.W.2d 516 (Tex. App. 1990).

56. *See id.* at 524; *cf.* State v. Heath, 957 P.2d 449, 471–72 (Kan. 1998) (finding abuse of discretion in allowing the deceased victim's mother and a potential suspect to remain in the courtroom throughout the trial, but no prejudice to the defendant in this case in light of her testimony and hence no reversible error); State v. Williams, 960 A.2d 805 (N.J. Super. Ct. App. Div. 2008) (finding no error in permitting the victim who remained in the courtroom following his testimony to be recalled to make a voice identification after hearing the defendant's voice in court).

57. 893 S.W.2d 324 (Ark. 1995).

58. *See id.* at 325–26.

59. 913 S.W.2d 288 (Ark. 1996).

60. *See id.* at 290.

61. *See* Mask v. State, 869 S.W.2d 1 (Ark. 1993).

62. Hall v. State, 579 So. 2d 329, 330–31 (Fla. Dist. Ct. App. 1991).

63. *See* Fuselier v. State, 468 So. 2d 45, 52–53 (Miss. 1985). *But see* Commonwealth v. Carbone, 574 A.2d 584, 590 n.8 (Pa.), *modified,* 585 A.2d 445 (Pa. 1990). *See generally* Jay M. Zitter, Annotation, *Emotional Manifestations by Victim or Family of Victim During Criminal Trial as Ground for Reversal, New Trial, or Mistrial,* 31 A.L.R. 4th 229 (1984).

64. *See, e.g.,* McGowan v. State, CR-95-1775, 2003 Ala. Crim. App. LEXIS 314 (Ala. Crim. App. Dec. 12, 2003); Grimsley v. State, 678 So. 2d 1197, 1210 (Ala. Crim. App. 1996). *See generally* Christopher R. Goddu, Comment, *Victims' "Rights" or a Fair Trial Wronged?,* 41 Buff. L. Rev. 245 (1993); Sonja A. Soehnel, Annotation, *Propriety and Prejudicial Effect of Permitting Nonparty to be Seated at Counsel Table,* 87 A.L.R.3d 238 (1978). On a related issue, reviewing courts have generally upheld the application of statutes permitting support persons to accompany a victim in court or during testimony. *See, e.g.,* People v. Johns, 65 Cal. Rptr.2d 434, 436–38 (Cal. Ct. App. 1997); People v. Patten, 12 Cal. Rptr.2d 284, 287–94 (Cal. Ct. App. 1992). *But cf.* Commonwealth v. Harris, 567 N.E.2d 899, 905–06 (Mass. 1991). *See generally* Goddu, *supra*; Carol A. Crocca, Annotation, *Propriety and Prejudicial Effect of Third Party Accompanying or Rendering Support to Witness During Testimony,* 82 A.L.R. 4th 1038 (1990).

65. Miller v. State, 648 N.E.2d 1208 (Ind. Ct. App. 1995).

66. 106 F.3d 325 (10th Cir. 1997).

67. *See id.* at 328–33.

68. *Id.* at 334–36; *cf.* Saum v. Widnall, 912 F. Supp. 1384, 1395–96 (D. Colo. 1996), *dismissed on other grounds,* 959 F. Supp. 1310 (D. Colo. 1997).

69. *See* 18 U.S.C.A. §3510 (West 2000).

70. See 18 U.S.C.A. §3771 (West Supp. 2008).

71. 362 F. Supp. 2d 1043 (N.D. Iowa 2005).

72. *See id.* at 1053–56.

73. 425 F. Supp. 2d 948 (N.D. Iowa 2006).

74. *See id.*

75. 453 F.3d 1137 (9th Cir. 2006) (per curiam).

76. *Id.* at 1138–40.

77. 367 F. Supp. 2d 319 (E.D.N.Y. 2005).

78. *Id.* at 333; *see* Beloof & Cassell, *supra* note 1, at 518–19

79. 428 F.3d 1300 (10th Cir. 2005).

80. *See id.* at 1314–15; *cf.* United States v. Edwards, No. 06-11643, 2008 WL 1932136 (11th Cir. May 5, 2008) (finding no abuse of discretion in the denial of the defendant's motion to sequester victim-witnesses in his trial and rejecting the defendant's contention that he had a constitutional right to exclude witnesses from the courtroom).

81. 486 F.3d 13 (1st Cir. 2007).

82. *See id.* at 46–47.

83. *See* U.S. GOVERNMENT ACCOUNTABILITY OFFICE, CRIME VICTIMS' RIGHTS ACT: INCREASING AWARENESS, MODIFYING THE COMPLAINT PROCESS, AND ENHANCING COMPLIANCE MONITORING WILL IMPROVE IMPLEMENTATION OF THE ACT 13, 86, 101 (2008).

84. *See* Edna Erez & Pamela Tontodonato, *Victim Participation in Sentencing and Satisfaction with Justice,* 9 JUST. Q. 393, 400 & n.3 (1992); *cf.* Anne M. Heinz & Wayne A. Kerstetter, *Pretrial Settlement Conference: Evaluation of a Reform in Plea Bargaining,* 13 LAW & SOCIETY REV. 349, 356–57 (1979) (finding approximately one-third of invited victims attended experimental settlement conferences).

85. *See* Maureen McLeod, *An Examination of the Victim's Role at Sentencing: Results of a Survey of Probation Administrators,* 71 JUDICATURE 162, 162–65 (1987).

86. *See* DAVID BEATTY ET AL., NATIONAL VICTIM CENTER, STATUTORY AND CONSTITUTIONAL PROTECTION OF VICTIMS' RIGHTS: IMPLEMENTATION AND IMPACT ON CRIME VICTIMS 9–30, 34–35, 87–88 (1996); *see also* DEAN G. KILPATRICK ET AL., U.S. DEP'T OF JUSTICE, THE RIGHTS OF CRIME VICTIMS—DOES LEGAL PROTECTION MAKE A DIFFERENCE? (1998).

87. *See* John Hagan, *Victims Before the Law: A Study of Victim Involvement in the Criminal Justice Process,* 73 J. CRIM. L. & CRIMINOLOGY 317 (1982).

88. *See* Erez & Tontodonato, *supra* note 84, at 397–99, 402–03; Edna Erez & Pamela Tontodonato, *The Effect of Victim Participation in Sentencing on Sentence Outcome,* 28 CRIMINOLOGY 451, 455, 460–67 (1990).

89. *See* Pamela Tontodonato & Edna Erez, *Crime, Punishment, and Victim Distress,* 3 INT'L REV. VICTIMOLOGY 33, 37, 40, 42–51 (1994).

90. *See* Ken Eikenberry, *Victims of Crime/Victims of Justice,* 34 WAYNE L. REV. 29, 38–47 (1987). *But see* Robert P. Mosteller, Essay, *Victims' Rights and the United States Constitution: An Effort to Recast the Battle in Criminal Litigation,* 85 GEO. L.J. 1691, 1698–1702 (1997). *See generally* DOUGLAS E. BELOOF ET AL., VICTIMS IN CRIMINAL PROCEDURE 529–65 (2d ed. 2006).

Notes for Chapter 5

1. *See generally* Edna Erez & Julian Roberts, *Victim Participation in the Criminal Justice System, in* VICTIMS OF CRIME 277 (Robert C. Davis et al. eds., 3d ed. 2007).

2. *See* MICHAEL R. RAND, U.S. DEP'T OF JUSTICE, CRIMINAL VICTIMIZATION, 2008, at 6–7 (2009).

3. *See* Juan Cardenas, *The Crime Victim in the Prosecutorial Process,* 9 HARV. J. L. & PUB. POL'Y 357 (1986); Sarah N. Welling, *Victims in the Criminal Process: A Utilitarian Analysis of Victim Participation in the Charging Decision,* 30 ARIZ. L. REV. 85 (1988); Herbert B.

Chermside Jr., Annotation, *Power of Private Citizen to Institute Criminal Proceedings Without Authorization or Approval by Prosecuting Attorney*, 66 A.L.R. 3d 732 (1975); *cf.* Douglas E. Beloof & Paul G. Cassell, *The Crime Victim's Right to Attend the Trial: The Reascendant National Consensus*, 9 Lewis & Clark L. Rev. 481, 484–503 (2005).

4. *See* Donald J. Hall, *The Role of the Victim in the Prosecution and Disposition of a Criminal Case*, 28 Vand. L. Rev. 931, 946–53 (1975).

5. *See* Welling, *supra* note 3, at 94–113.

6. *See* Office of Justice Programs, U.S. Dep't of Justice, Four Years Later: A Report on the President's Task Force on Victims of Crime 4 (1986).

7. President's Task Force on Victims of Crime, Final Report 33–34, 64–66 (1982).

8. *Id.* at 114; *see* LeRoy L. Lamborn, *Victim Participation in the Criminal Justice Process: The Proposals for a Constitutional Amendment*, 34 Wayne L. Rev. 125, 187–200 (1987).

9. *See* Office for Victims of Crime, U.S. Dep't of Justice, New Directions from the Field: Victims' Rights and Services for the 21st Century 15–17, 88 (1998).

10. *See generally* Douglas E. Beloof et al., Victims in Criminal Procedure 259–378, 453–76 (2d ed. 2006); National Center for Victims of Crime, VictimLaw, http://www.victimlaw.info/victimlaw/ (last visited Jan. 1, 2009); National Conference of State Legislatures, Victims' Rights Laws in the States, http://www.ncsl.org (last visited Jan. 1, 2009).

11. *See* S.J. Res. 1, 108th Cong. (2003); H.R.J. Res. 48, 108th Cong. (2003); H.R.J. Res. 10, 108th Cong. (2003).

12. 18 U.S.C.A. §3771 (West Supp. 2009).

13. *See* Office for Victims of Crime, U.S. Dep't of Justice, Attorney General Guidelines for Victim and Witness Assistance 29–30 (2005).

14. *See* Alaska Const. art. I, §24; Conn. Const. art. I, §8; Idaho Const. art. I, §22; Ill. Const. art. 1, §8.1; Ind. Const. art. 1, §13; Mich. Const. art. 1, §24; N.M. Const. art. II, §24; N.C. Const. art. I, §37; Tenn. Const. art. I, §35; Tex. Const. art. 1, §30; Va. Const. art. I, §8-A; Wis. Const. art. 1, §9m.

15. *See* Ariz. Const. art. 2, §2.1; Cal. Const. art. 1, §28; La. Const. art. 1, §25; S.C. Const. art. I, §24.

16. *See* Ala. Const. art. I, §6.01; Colo. Const. art. 2, §16a; Fla. Const. art. 1, §16; La. Const. art. 1, §25; Md. Const. art. 47; Miss. Const. art. 3, §26A; Tenn. Const. art. I, §35; Utah Const. art. I, §28; *cf.* Kan. Const. art. 15, §15; N.C. Const. art. I, §37; Wis. Const. art. 1, §9m.

17. *See, e.g.*, N. M. Stat. Ann. §31-26-4 (LexisNexis 2000).

18. *See* Ariz. Rev. Stat. Ann. §§13-4408, -4419 (2001); N.J. Stat. Ann. §§52:4B–36, -44 (West Supp. 2008).

19. *See* Ky. Rev. Stat. Ann. §421.500 (LexisNexis 2005); La. Rev. Stat. Ann. §46:1844 (Supp. 2008); 18 Pa. Stat. Ann. §11.201 (West Supp. 2008); *see also, e.g.*, Ala. Code §15-23-64 (LexisNexis 1995); Mont. Code Ann. §46-24-104 (2007); W. Va. Code Ann. §61-11A-6 (LexisNexis 2005).

20. *See, e.g.*, Ariz. Rev. Stat. Ann. §13-4419 (2001); Mass. Ann. Laws ch. 258B, §3 (LexisNexis 2004).

21. *See, e.g.*, Del. Code Ann. tit. 11, §9405 (2007); N.Y. Exec. Law §642 (McKinney Supp. 2008); Ohio Rev. Code Ann. §2930.06 (LexisNexis 2006); Tenn. Code Ann. §40-38-114 (2006).

22. *See generally* National Center for Victims of Crime, *supra* note 10; National Conference of State Legislatures, *supra* note 10.

23. *See generally* BELOOF ET AL., *supra* note 10, at 225–378, 453–76; Richard L. Aynes, *Constitutional Considerations: Government Responsibility and the Right Not to be a Victim*, 11 PEPP. L. REV. 63, 97–107 (1984); Abraham S. Goldstein, *Defining the Role of the Victim in Criminal Prosecution*, 52 MISS. L.J. 515, 558–59 (1982); Welling, *supra* note 3, at 85; Andrew Sidman, Comment, *The Outmoded Concept of Private Prosecution*, 25 AM. U. L. REV. 754 (1976).

24. *See* COLO. REV. STAT. ANN. § 16-5-209 (West 2006); *see also* KAN. STAT. ANN. § 22-2301 (2007).

25. *See* WIS. STAT. ANN. §§ 968.02, .26 (West 2007). *See generally* Chermside, *supra* note 3.

26. *See* BELOOF ET AL., *supra* note 10, at 335–77; *cf.* Peter L. Davis, *Rodney King and the Decriminalization of Police Brutality in America: Direct and Judicial Access to the Grand Jury as Remedies for Victims of Police Brutality When the Prosecutor Declines to Prosecute*, 53 MD. L. REV. 271 (1994).

27. *See, e.g.*, KAN STAT. ANN. § 19-717 (2007). *See generally* BELOOF ET AL., *supra* note 10, at 554–65; John D. Bessler, *The Public Interest and the Unconstitutionality of Private Prosecutors*, 47 ARK. L. REV. 511 (1994); Cardenas, *supra* note 3, at 372–84; Hall, *supra* note 4, at 974–78; Sidman, *supra* note 23.

28. *See* Welling, *supra* note 3, at 95–98; *cf.* Donald G. Gifford, *Equal Protection and the Prosecutor's Charging Decision: Enforcing an Ideal*, 49 GEO. WASH. L. REV. 659 (1981).

29. *See* Wayte v. United States, 470 U.S. 598, 607–08 (1985); Inmates of Attica Correctional Facility v. Rockefeller, 477 F.2d 375 (2d Cir. 1973).

30. 410 U.S. 614 (1973).

31. *Id.* at 619; *see id.* at 614–16, 618.

32. *See id.* at 614–16, 618–19; *see also* Taylor v. Newton Division of District Court Department, 622 N.E.2d 261, 262 (Mass. 1993); Susan Bandes, *Victim Standing*, 1999 UTAH L. REV. 331, 343–47 (1999); Welling, *supra* note 3, at 98–102; *cf.* Leeke v. Timmerman, 454 U.S. 83, 86–87 (1981).

33. *See* Hall, *supra* note 4, at 968–72; Welling, *supra* note 3, at 102–05.

34. 214 S.W.3d 442 (Tenn. 2007).

35. *See id.* at 445–47, 453–54.

36. *Compare* Salt Lake City v. Johnson, 959 P.2d 1022 (Utah Ct. App. 1998), *with* People v. Williams, 625 N.W.2d 132 (Mich. Ct. App. 2001).

37. 888 P.2d 256 (Colo. 1995) (en banc).

38. *See id.* at 257.

39. *Id.* at 258–59 n.7.

40. *See id.* at 258–59.

41. *See id.* at 258 n.5.

42. 675 P.2d 300 (Colo. 1984) (en banc).

43. *Id.* at 303 & n.4.

44. Moody v. Larsen, 802 P.2d 1169, 1174 (Colo. Ct. App. 1990).

45. 441 N.W.2d 696 (Wis. 1989).

46. *See id.* at 698–704.

47. *See* State *ex rel.* Unnamed Petitioner v. Circuit Court for Walworth County, 458 N.W.2d 575 (Wis. Ct. App. 1990).

48. *See* Gavcus v. Maroney, 377 N.W.2d 200 (Wis. Ct. App. 1985).

49. 565 A.2d 764 (Pa. 1989).

50. *See id.* at 766–68.

51. Commonwealth v. Pritchard, 596 A.2d 827, 833 (Pa. Super. Ct. 1991) (citations omitted). *See generally* Chermside, *supra* note 3.

52. 678 P.2d 146 (Kan. 1984).

53. *See id.* at 148–53.

54. *See generally* Beloof et al., *supra* note 10, at 554–65; Cardenas, *supra* note 3, at 372–84; Sidman, *supra* note 22, at 765–73.

55. *See, e.g.*, East v. Johnson, 123 F.3d 235 (5th Cir. 1997); East v. Scott, 55 F.3d 996 (5th Cir. 1995); Person v. Miller, 854 F.2d 656 (4th Cir. 1988); Woods v. Linahan, 648 F.2d 973 (5th Cir. 1981); *cf.* State v. Kinder, 701 F. Supp. 486 (D.N.J. 1988) (upholding state private prosecution procedure in minor municipal court matter).

56. 481 U.S. 787 (1986).

57. *See id.* at 789–92, 805, 806, 807, 814; *see* Bessler, *supra* note 26.

58. 458 F. Supp. 2d 1271 (D. Utah 2006).

59. *See id.* at 1272–73.

60. *See* David Beatty et al., National Victim Center, Statutory and Constitutional Protection of Victims' Rights: Implementation and Impact on Crime Victims 42 (1996); *see also* Dean G. Kilpatrick et al., U.S. Dep't of Justice, The Rights of Crime Victims—Does Legal Protection Make a Difference? (1998).

61. *See* Wendy J. Murphy, *Massachusetts Initiates Victim "Miranda" Law*, 3 The Crime Victims Report 50, 58 (1999); Jim Sinclair, *Partners for Justice: Crime Victims and State Policymakers in the Northeast Join Together for System Change*, 3 The Crime Victims Report 17 (1999).

62. U.S. Government Accountability Office, Crime Victims' Rights Act: Increasing Awareness, Modifying the Complaint Process, and Enhancing Compliance Monitoring Will Improve Implementation of the Act 83–84 (2008).

63. Beatty et al., *supra* note 60, at 86.

64. *See* William G. Doerner & Steven P. Lab, Victimology 270–71 (2d ed. 1998).

65. *See* Jolene C. Hernon & Brian Forst, U.S. Dep't of Justice, The Criminal Justice Response to Victim Harm 13, 26–32 (1984); *cf.* Hall, *supra* note 4, at 948–53.

66. John W. Stickels et al., *Elected Texas District and County Attorneys' Perceptions of Crime Victim Involvement in Criminal Prosecutions*, 14 Tex. Wesleyan L. Rev. 1, 15–18 (2007).

67. Welling, *supra* note 3, at 93–94, 114–17; *see also* Hall, *supra* note 4, at 980–85.

68. *See* Goldstein, *supra* note 23, at 554–58.

69. *See* Aynes, *supra* note 23, at 97–107; Douglas Evan Beloof, *The Third Model of Criminal Process: The Victim Participation Model*, 1999 Utah L. Rev. 289, 313–17 (1999); Gifford, *supra* note 28, at 716–17; Josephine Gittler, *Expanding the Role of the Victim in a Criminal Action: An Overview of Issues and Problems*, 11 Pepp. L. Rev. 117, 161–63 (1984); Paul S. Hudson, *The Crime Victim and the Criminal Justice System: Time for a Change*, 11 Pepp. L. Rev. 23, 58–59 (1984).

70. *See, e.g.*, George P. Fletcher, With Justice for Some: Victims' Rights in Criminal Trials 193–97, 248–50 (1995); Cardenas, *supra* note 3, at 392–98; Peter L. Davis, *The Crime Victim's "Right" to a Criminal Prosecution: A Proposed Model Statute for the Governance of Private Criminal Prosecutions*, 38 DePaul L. Rev. 329 (1989); Gittler, *supra* note 69, at 160–61; Goldstein, *supra* note 23, at 558–60; *cf.* United States v. Cheung, 952 F. Supp. 148 (E.D.N.Y. 1997). *But see, e.g.*, Bessler, *supra* note 27; Hall, *supra* note 4, at 974–78, 984; Sidman, *supra* note 23, at 773–94.

71. *See generally* Beloof et al., *supra* note 10, at 476–97; National Center for Victims of Crime, *supra* note 10; National Conference of State Legislatures, *supra* note 10.

72. *See, e.g.*, Samuel Walker, Sense and Nonsense about Crime and Drugs 168 (6th ed. 2006); Gittler, *supra* note 69, at 164 & n.141.

73. *See* Office of Justice Programs, *supra* note 6, at 4.

74. *See* President's Task Force on Victims of Crime, *supra* note 7, at 33–34, 66.

75. *Id.* at 65.

76. *Id.* at 114; *see* Lamborn, *supra* note 8, at 187–200.

77. *See* Office for Victims of Crime, *supra* note 9, at 15–17, 86–87, 108–09.

78. *See* S.J. Res. 1, 108th Cong. (2003); H.R.J. Res. 48, 108th Cong. (2003); H.R.J. Res. 10, 108th Cong. (2003).

79. 18 U.S.C.A. §3771 (West Supp. 2009).

80. Fed. R. Crim. P. 60; *see* U.S. Courts, Proposed Amendments to the Federal Rules of Criminal Procedure (effective Dec. 1, 2008), http://www.uscourts.gov/rules/ supct0408.html (last visited Jan. 2, 2009) (including the amendments to the federal rules and related reports); *cf.* Fed. R. Crim. P. 11 (permitting the court to defer acceptance or rejection of certain plea agreements until after receipt of the presentence report).

81. *See* Office for Victims of Crime, *supra* note 13, at 29–30.

82. *See* Alaska Const. art. I, §24; Ariz. Const. art. 2, §2.1; Cal. Const. art. 1, §28; Conn. Const. art. I, §8; Idaho Const. art. I, §22; Ill. Const. art. 1, §8.1; Ind. Const. art. 1, §13; La. Const. art. 1, §25; Mich. Const. art. 1, §24; N.M. Const. art. II, §24; N.C. Const. art. I, §37; Or. Const. art. I, §42; S.C. Const. art. I, §24; Tenn. Const. art. I, §35; Tex. Const. art. 1, §30; Va. Const. art. I, §8-A; Wis. Const. art. 1, §9m.

83. *See* Ala. Const. art. I, §6.1; Colo. Const. art. 2, §16a; Fla. Const. art. 1, §16; La. Const. art. 1, §25; Md. Const. art. 47; Miss. Const. art. 3, §26A; Tenn. Const. art. I, §35; Utah Const. art. I, §28; *cf.* Kan. Const. art. 15, §15; N.C. Const. art. I, §37.

84. *See* Ariz. Const. art. 2, §2.1; Cal. Const. art. 1, §28; Conn. Const. art. I, §8; Idaho Const. art. I, §22; Mo. Const. art. 1, §32; S.C. Const. art. I, §24; Wis. Const. art. 1, §9m.

85. *Compare, e.g.*, Ga. Code Ann. §17-17-11 (West 2003) (providing specific consultation right regarding plea negotiations), *with, e.g.*, N. M. Stat. Ann. §31-26-4 (LexisNexis 2000) (providing general right to confer). *See generally* National Center for Victims of Crime, *supra* note 10; National Conference of State Legislatures, *supra* note 10.

86. *See, e.g.*, Cal. Penal Code §679.02 (West 1999); Tenn. Code Ann. §40-38-103 (2006); Tex. Code Crim. Proc. Ann. art. 56.08 (Vernon 2006)

87. *See, e.g.*, Ark. Code Ann. §16-21-106 (Supp. 2007); Haw. Rev. Stat. Ann. §801D-4 (LexisNexis 2007); Ky. Rev. Stat. Ann. §421.500 (LexisNexis 2005); Vt. Stat. Ann. tit. 13, §5321 (Supp. 2007).

88. *See, e.g.*, 725 Ill. Comp. Stat. Ann. 120/4.5 (West Supp. 2008); Mich. Comp. Laws Ann. §780.756 (West 2007); W. Va. Code Ann. §61-11A-6 (LexisNexis 2005).

89. *See* Fla. Stat. Ann. §960.001 (West Supp. 2008).

90. *See* 18 Pa. Stat. Ann. §11.201 (West Supp. 2008).

91. *See* N.J. Stat. Ann. §52:4B-44 (West Supp. 2008).

92. *See, e.g.*, Ala. Code §15-23-71 (LexisNexis 1995); Me. Rev. Stat. Ann. tit. 17-A, §1173 (2006); Wash. Rev. Code Ann. §9.94A.431 (West 2003).

93. *See* S.D. Codified Laws §§23A-7-8, -9 (2004).

94. *See* Ohio Rev. Code Ann. §2930.06 (LexisNexis 2006).

95. *See* Ariz. Rev. Stat. Ann. §§13-4419, -4423 (2001).

96. *See, e.g.*, Alaska Stat. §12.61.015 (2006); La. Rev. Stat. Ann. §46:1844 (Supp. 2008).

97. *See, e.g.*, Colo. Rev. Stat. Ann. § 24-4.1-303 (West 2008); Wash. Rev. Code Ann. § 9.94A.421 (West 2003).

98. *See, e.g.*, Ark. Code Ann. § 16-21-106 (Supp. 2007); Del. Code Ann. tit. 11, § 9405 (2007); N.Y. Exec. Law § 642 (McKinney Supp. 2008); Ohio Rev. Code Ann. § 2930.06 (LexisNexis 2006).

99. *See* Ariz. Rev. Stat. Ann. § 13-4419 (2001).

100. *See, e.g.*, Colo. Rev. Stat. Ann. § 24-4.1-302.5 (West 2008); Mo. Ann. Stat. § 595.209 (West Supp. 2008); N.H. Rev. Stat. Ann. § 21-M:8-k (LexisNexis 2008); Utah Code Ann. § 77-38-4 (2003). *See generally* National Center for Victims of Crime, *supra* note 10; National Conference of State Legislatures, *supra* note 10.

101. *See, e.g.*, Kan. Stat. Ann. § 74-7333 (2002).

102. *See* N.H. Rev. Stat. Ann. § 21-M:8-k (LexisNexis 2008); *see also* R.I. Gen. Laws § 12-28-4.1 (2002). *But see* Ariz. Rev. Stat. Ann. § 13-4423 (2001); Idaho Code Ann. § 19-5306 (2004).

103. *See* Ariz. Rev. Stat. Ann. § 13-4436 (Supp. 2007); S.D. Codified Laws § 23A-7-8.1 (2004); Utah Code Ann. § 77-38-10 (2003); *cf.* N.Y. Exec. Law § 647 (McKinney 2005).

104. 44 P.3d 756 (Utah 2002).

105. *See id.* at 757–60.

106. *See id.* at 760–66.

107. 253 Cal. Rptr. 484 (Cal. Ct. App. 1988).

108. *See id.* at 485–94.

109. *See id.* at 490–94; *see also* Wilson v. Commonwealth, 839 S.W.2d 17 (Ky. Ct. App. 1992).

110. *See* State v. Johnson, 907 P.2d 140 (Kan. 1995); Sharp v. State, 908 S.W.2d 752 (Mo. Ct. App. 1995); *cf.* Weston v. State, 2 S.W.3d 111 (Mo. Ct. App. 1999).

111. 794 P.2d 780 (Or. 1990).

112. *See id.* at 781–82.

113. *See id.* at 782–85. *Compare* Reed v. Becka, 511 S.E.2d 396 (S.C. Ct. App. 1999) (rejecting a victim veto of a plea agreement), *with* Commonwealth v. Latimore, 667 N.E.2d 818 (Mass. 1996) (upholding the prosecutor's consideration of the victim's views regarding a plea).

114. 527 F.3d 391 (5th Cir. 2008).

115. *See id.* 392–93.

116. *Id.* at 395 (citation omitted).

117. *See id.* at 394–96.

118. United States v. Blumhagen, No. 03-CR-56S, 2006 U.S. Dist. LEXIS 15380 (W.D.N.Y. Apr. 3, 2006).

119. United States v. Eberhard, 525 F.3d 175 (2d Cir. 2008); *see* United States v. Horsfall, 552 F.3d 1275 (11th Cir. 2008).

120. *In re* W.R. Huff Asset Management, 409 F.3d 555, 564 (2d Cir. 2005).

121. United States v. Rubin, 558 F. Supp. 2d 411, 424 (E.D.N.Y. 2008).

122. *See* Sarah N. Welling, *Victim Participation in Plea Bargains*, 65 Wash. U. L.Q. 301, 338 n.204 (1987).

123. *See* Hall, *supra* note 4, at 953–56.

124. *See* William F. McDonald, U.S. Dep't of Justice, Plea Bargaining: Critical Issues and Common Practices 68–69 (1985).

125. *See id.* at 61–62, 68–70.

126. *See* Susan W. Hillenbrand & Barbara E. Smith, American Bar Association, Executive Summary: Victim Rights Legislation: An Assessment of its Impact on Criminal Justice Practitioners and Victims 7, 20 (1989).

127. *See* DOERNER & LAB, *supra* note 64, at 271.

128. *See* Murphy, *supra* note 61, at 58; Sinclair, *supra* note 61, at 17.

129. *See* BEATTY ET AL., *supra* note 60, at 9–30, 42.

130. *See id.* at 35, 44, 87.

131. *See id.* at 36, 87, 132.

132. *See id.* at 45, 53–54.

133. Stickels et al., *supra* note 66, at 15–18.

134. *See* Anne M. Heinz & Wayne A. Kerstetter, *Pretrial Settlement Conference: Evaluation of a Reform in Plea Bargaining*, 13 L. & SOC'Y REV. 349, 353–54 (1979).

135. *See id.* at 356, 360–62, 364–65.

136. *See id.* at 356–65.

137. *See* EDWIN VILLMOARE & VIRGINIA V. NETO, U.S. DEP'T OF JUSTICE, VICTIM APPEARANCES AT SENTENCING HEARINGS UNDER THE CALIFORNIA VICTIMS' BILL OF RIGHTS 6 (1987).

138. *See* Karen Gorbach Rebrovich, Comment, *Factors Affecting the Plea-Bargaining Process in Erie County: Some Tentative Findings*, 26 BUFF. L. REV. 693, 697–705 (1977).

139. *See* Susan E. Gegan & Nicholas Ernesto Rodriguez, Note, *Victims' Roles in the Criminal Justice System: A Fallacy of Victim Empowerment?*, 8 ST. JOHN'S J. LEGAL COMMENT. 225, 232–33 (1992).

140. Welling, *supra* note 122, at 307–12, 345–56; *see also* Gittler, *supra* note 69, at 167; Karyn Ellen Polito, Note, *The Rights of Crime Victims in the Criminal Justice System: Is Justice Blind to the Victims of Crime?*, 16 NEW ENG. J. ON CRIM. & CIV. CONFINEMENT 241, 252–54 (1990); David A. Starkweather, Note, *The Retributive Theory of "Just Deserts" and Victim Participation in Plea Bargaining*, 67 IND. L.J. 853, 876–77 (1992)

141. *See* Goldstein, *supra* note 23, at 556–61.

142. *See* Donald G. Gifford, *Meaningful Reform of Plea Bargaining: The Control of Prosecutorial Discretion*, 1983 U. ILL. L. REV. 37, 90–95 (1983).

143. *See* FLETCHER, *supra* note 70, at 190–93, 247–48; Karen L. Kennard, Comment, *The Victim's Veto: A Way to Increase Victim Impact on Criminal Case Dispositions*, 77 CAL. L. REV. 417, 437–53 (1989).

144. *See* Kennard, *supra* note 143, at 437–53.

Notes for Chapter 6

1. *See generally* DOUGLAS E. BELOOF ET AL., VICTIMS IN CRIMINAL PROCEDURE 625–67 (2d ed. 2006); National Center for Victims of Crime, VictimLaw, http://www.victimlaw.info/ victimlaw/ (last visited Jan. 1, 2009); National Conference of State Legislatures, Victims' Rights Laws in the States, http://www.ncsl.org (last visited Jan. 1, 2009).

2. *See* OFFICE OF JUSTICE PROGRAMS, U.S. DEP'T OF JUSTICE, FOUR YEARS LATER: A REPORT ON THE PRESIDENT'S TASK FORCE ON VICTIMS OF CRIME 4 (1986).

3. *See* Peggy M. Tobolowsky, *"Constitutionalizing" Crime Victim Rights*, 33 CRIM. L. BULL. 395, 398–99 (1997).

4. *See* PRESIDENT'S TASK FORCE ON VICTIMS OF CRIME, FINAL REPORT 33 (1982).

5. *See id.* at 65–66.

6. *Id.* at 76.

7. *Id.* at 114; *see* LeRoy L. Lamborn, *Victim Participation in the Criminal Justice Process: The Proposals for a Constitutional Amendment*, 34 WAYNE L. REV. 125, 187–200 (1987).

8. PRESIDENT'S TASK FORCE ON VICTIMS OF CRIME, *supra* note 4, at 76–78.

9. *Id.* at 76–77.

10. *See* OFFICE FOR VICTIMS OF CRIME, U.S. DEP'T OF JUSTICE, NEW DIRECTIONS FROM THE FIELD: VICTIMS' RIGHTS AND SERVICES FOR THE 21ST CENTURY 17–18, 107–08 (1998).

11. *See* S.J. Res. 1, 108th Cong. (2003); H.R.J. Res. 48, 108th Cong. (2003); H.R.J. Res. 10, 108th Cong. (2003).

12. 18 U.S.C.A. § 3771 (West Supp. 2009).

13. Fed. R. Crim. P. 1, 32, 60; *see* U.S. Courts, Proposed Amendments to the Federal Rules of Criminal Procedure (effective Dec. 1, 2008), http://www.uscourts.gov/rules/ supct0408.html (last visited Jan. 2, 2009) (including the amendments to the federal rules and related reports).

14. *See* ALASKA CONST. art. I, § 24; ARIZ. CONST. art. 2, § 2.1; CAL. CONST. art. 1, § 28; CONN. CONST. art. I, § 8; IDAHO CONST. art. I, § 22; ILL. CONST. art. 1, § 8.1; IND. CONST. art. 1, § 13; LA. CONST. art. 1, § 25; MICH. CONST. art. 1, § 24; N.M. CONST. art. II, § 24; N.C. CONST. art. I, § 37; OR. CONST. art. I, § 42; S.C. CONST. art. I, § 24; TENN. CONST. art. I, § 35; TEX. CONST. art. 1, § 30; VA. CONST. art. I, § 8-A; WIS. CONST. art. 1, § 9m.

15. *See* ALA. CONST. art. I, § 6.01; COLO. CONST. art. 2, § 16a; FLA. CONST. art. 1, § 16; LA. CONST. art. 1, § 25; MD. CONST. art. 47; MISS. CONST. art. 3, § 26A; TENN. CONST. art. I, § 35; UTAH CONST. art. I, § 28.

16. *See* ALASKA CONST. art. I, § 24; ARIZ. CONST. art. 2, § 2.1; CAL. CONST. art. 1, § 28; CONN. CONST. art. I, § 8; IDAHO CONST. art. I, § 22; ILL. CONST. art. 1, § 8.1; KAN. CONST. art. 15, § 15; MICH. CONST. art. 1, § 24; MO. CONST. art. 1, § 32; NEB. CONST. art. I, § 28; NEV. CONST. art. 1, § 8; N.M. CONST. art. II, § 24; N.C. CONST. art. I, § 37; OKLA. CONST. art. 2, § 34; OR. CONST. art. I, § 42; R.I. CONST. art. 1, § 23; S.C. CONST. art. I, § 24; VA. CONST. art. I, § 8-A; WASH. CONST. art. 1, § 35; WIS. CONST. art. 1, § 9m.

17. *See supra* chapter 5, notes 85–86 and accompanying text.

18. *See, e.g.,* ARIZ. REV. STAT. ANN. § 13-4419 (2001); KAN. STAT. ANN. § 74-7333 (2002); LA. REV. STAT. ANN. § 46:1844 (Supp. 2008); N.M. STAT. ANN. § 31-26-4 (LexisNexis 2000); N.Y. EXEC. LAW § 642 (McKinney Supp. 2008).

19. *See, e.g.,* ALA. CODE §§ 15-23-73, -74 (LexisNexis 1995); 725 ILL. COMP. STAT. ANN. 120/6 (West Supp. 2008); MINN. STAT. ANN. § 611A.038 (West 2003); S.D. CODIFIED LAWS § 23A-28C-1 (2004); WYO. STAT. ANN. § 7-21-102 (2007).

20. *See, e.g.,* KY. REV. STAT. ANN. § 421.520 (LexisNexis 2005).

21. *See* Maureen McLeod, *An Examination of the Victim's Role at Sentencing: Results of a Survey of Probation Administrators*, 71 JUDICATURE 162, 163 (1987).

22. *See, e.g.,* 18 PA. STAT. ANN. § 11.201 (West Supp. 2008).

23. *See, e.g.,* CAL. PENAL CODE § 1191.1 (West 2004); MICH. COMP. LAWS ANN. § 780.763 (West 2007); WASH. REV. CODE ANN. § 9.94A.500 (West 2003).

24. *See, e.g.,* OHIO REV. CODE ANN. § 2930.14 (LexisNexis 2006).

25. *See* Donald J. Hall, *Victims' Voices in Criminal Court: The Need for Restraint*, 28 AM. CRIM. L. REV. 233, 242–43 (1991).

26. *See, e.g.,* 725 ILL. COMP. STAT. ANN. 120/6 (West Supp. 2008); ME. REV. STAT. ANN. tit. 17-A, § 1174 (2006); WYO. STAT. ANN. § 7-21-103 (2007).

27. *See* KY. REV. STAT. ANN. §§ 421.500, .520 (LexisNexis 2005).

28. *See* MO. ANN. STAT. §§ 557.026, .041 (West 1999).

29. *See* ARIZ. REV. STAT. ANN. §§ 13-4401, -4424, -4426 (2001 & Supp. 2007).

30. *See* Minn. Stat. Ann. §§ 611A.01, .037, .038 (West 2003 & Supp. 2008).

31. *See, e.g.,* Ga. Code Ann. §§ 17-10-1.1, -1.2 (West 2003); Wyo. Stat. Ann. § 7-21-101 (2007).

32. *See, e.g.,* Ga. Code Ann. § 17-10-1.2 (West 2003); Md. Code Ann., Crim. Proc. § 11-403 (2001); N.D. Cent. Code § 12.1-34-02 (Supp. 2007); *cf.* N.Y. Crim. Proc. Law § 380.50 (McKinney Supp. 2008). *But see, e.g.,* Ariz. Rev. Stat. Ann. § 13-4426.01 (Supp. 2007); N.H. Rev. Stat. Ann § 21-M:8-k (LexisNexis 2008); Okla. Stat. Ann. § 22-984.1 (West Supp. 2009).

33. *See* Ala. Code § 15-23-76 (LexisNexis 1995); Ga. Code Ann. §§ 17-10-1.1, –1.2 (West 2003); N.Y. Crim. Proc. Law § 380.50 (McKinney Supp. 2008); Utah Code Ann. § 77-38-10 (2003); Vt. Stat. Ann. tit. 13, § 5321 (Supp. 2007).

34. *See* Ariz. Rev. Stat. Ann. § 13-4436 (Supp. 2007); Md. Code Ann., Crim. Proc. § 11-403 (2001); *cf.* Alaska Stat. § 12.55.120 (2006) (authorizing a victim to file a petition for appellate review of a sentence below the crime's sentencing range).

35. *See, e.g.,* Payne v. Tennessee, 501 U.S. 808, 819–22, 825 (1991); People v. Mockel, 276 Cal. Rptr. 559, 562–63 (Cal. Ct. App. 1990).

36. Williams v. New York, 337 U.S. 241, 246 (1949).

37. 482 U.S. 496 (1987).

38. *Id.* at 502–03. *See generally* Paul Boudreaux, *Booth v. Maryland and the Individual Vengeance Rationale for Criminal Punishment,* 80 J. Crim. L. & Criminology 177 (1989); Dina R. Hellerstein, *The Victim Impact Statement: Reform or Reprisal,* 27 Am. Crim. L. Rev. 391 (1989); Phillip A. Talbert, Comment, *The Relevance of Victim Impact Statements to the Criminal Sentencing Decision,* 36 U.C.L.A. L. Rev. 199 (1988).

39. *See Booth,* 482 U.S. at 497–501, 509–15.

40. *See id.* at 504–09.

41. 490 U.S. 805 (1989).

42. *See id.* at 808–12.

43. *See id.* at 812; *Booth,* 482 U.S. at 507–08 n.10, 509 & n.12.

44. 501 U.S. 808 (1991).

45. *See id.* at 814–16, 819–30.

46. *See id.* at 830 & n.2; *id.* at 833 (O'Connor, J., joined by White and Kennedy, JJ., concurring); *see also, e.g.,* State v. Lovelace, 90 P.3d 298, 305 (Idaho 2004); State v. Bolton, 896 P.2d 830, 855 (Ariz. 1995); State v. Fautenberry, 650 N.E.2d 878, 882 (Ohio 1995). *But see* Salazar v. State, 973 P.2d 315, 325 (Okla. Crim. App. 1998); Conover v. State, 933 P.2d 904, 918–21 (Okla. Crim. App. 1997); Ledbetter v. State, 933 P.2d 880, 891 (Okla. Crim. App. 1997); Douglas E. Beloof, *Constitutional Implications of Crime Victims as Participants,* 88 Cornell L. Rev. 282 (2003) (advocating the constitutionality of victim sentencing recommendations in capital cases).

47. *See Payne,* 501 U.S. at 825–27; *see also id.* at 831 (O'Connor, J., joined by White and Kennedy, JJ., concurring). *But see* Kelly v. California, 129 S. Ct. 564 (2008) (Stevens, J., statement regarding certiorari denial; Souter, J., dissenting from certiorari denial) (criticizing lack of guidance from the Court regarding post-*Payne* expanded use of victim impact information in capital proceedings). *See generally* Jose Felipe Anderson, *Will the Punishment Fit the Victims? The Case for Pre-trial Disclosure, and the Uncharted Future of Victim Impact Information in Capital Jury Sentencing,* 28 Rutgers L.J. 367 (1997); Susan Bandes, *Empathy, Narrative, and Victim Impact Statements,* 63 U. Chi. L. Rev. 361 (1996); John H. Blume, *Ten Years of* Payne: *Victim Impact Evidence in Capital Cases,* 88 Cornell L. Rev. 257 (2003); Wayne A. Logan, *Through the Past Darkly: A Survey of the Uses and Abuses of*

Victim Impact Evidence in Capital Trials, 41 ARIZ. L. REV. 143 (1999); Wayne A. Logan, *Impact Evidence in Federal Capital Trials*, 19 FED. SENT'G REP. 5 (2006); Niru Shanker, *Getting a Grip on* Payne *and Restricting the Influence of Victim Impact Statements in Capital Sentencing: The Timothy McVeigh Case and Various State Approaches Compared*, 26 HASTINGS CONST. L.Q. 711 (1999); Ashley Paige Dugger, Note, *Victim Impact Evidence in Capital Sentencing: A History of Incompatibility*, 23 AM. J. CRIM. L. 375 (1996); Brian J. Johnson, Note, *The Response to* Payne v. Tennessee: *Giving the Victim's Family a Voice in the Capital Sentencing Process*, 30 IND. L. REV. 795 (1997); Amy K. Phillips, Note, *Thou Shalt Not Kill Any Nice People: The Problem of Victim Impact Statements in Capital Sentencing*, 35 AM. CRIM. L. REV. 93 (1997); Gregory B. Schneider, Note, *Victim Impact Statement: A Victim's Steam Valve*, 14 CRIM. JUST. J. 407 (1992); Beth E. Sullivan, Note, *Harnessing* Payne: *Controlling the Admission of Victim Impact Statements to Safeguard Capital Sentencing Hearings from Passion and Prejudice*, 25 FORDHAM URB. L.J. 601 (1998).

48. *See, e.g.,* Jones v. United States, 527 U.S. 373, 395–96, 402 (1999) (applying 18 U.S.C.A. § 3593 (West 2000 & Supp. 2009)); United States v. Nelson, 347 F.3d 701, 712–14 (8th Cir. 2003); State v. Muhammad, 678 A.2d 164, 176–77 (N.J. 1996) (applying N.J. STAT. ANN. § 2C:11-3 (West Supp. 2009)); Commonwealth v. Means, 773 A.2d 143 (Pa. 2001) (upholding 42 PA. CONS. STAT. ANN. § 9711 (West 2007) and identifying states that permit victim impact evidence in capital sentencing proceedings); State v. Gentry, 888 P.2d 1105, 1141 & n.93 (Wash. 1995). *But see* Olsen v. State, 67 P.3d 536, 594–600 (Wyo. 2003) (declining to permit victim impact evidence in capital proceedings in the absence of authorizing legislation and noting jurisdictions that enacted such legislation following *Payne*). *See generally* Blume, *supra* note 47; Logan, *Federal Capital Trials*, *supra* note 47; Shanker, *supra* note 47; Johnson, *supra* note 47; Phillips, *supra* note 47, at 100–01 n.56.

49. *See* Hicks v. State, 940 S.W.2d 855 (Ark. 1997); *see also id.* at 857 (Brown, J., joined by Imber, J., concurring); *cf.* State v. Garza, 163 P.3d 1006 (Ariz. 2007); Evans v. State, 637 A.2d 117, 129–32 (Md. 1994); State v. Koskovich, 776 A.2d 144 (N.J. 2001). *But see* Salazar v. State, 90 S.W.3d 330 (Tex. Crim. App. 2002); Salazar v. State, 118 S.W.3d 880 (Tex. Ct. App. 2003).

50. *See* State v. Worthington, 8 S.W.3d 83, 89–90 (Mo. 1999) (en banc); *cf.* People v. Panah, 107 P.3d 790 (Cal. 2005); State v. Wakefield, 921 A.2d 954 (N.J. 2007); Commonwealth v. Williams, 854 A.2d 440 (Pa. 2004).

51. *See* Conover v. State, 933 P.2d 904, 920–21, 923 (Okla. Crim. App. 1997); Ledbetter v. State, 933 P.2d 880, 891, 902 (Okla. Crim. App. 1997).

52. *See* Holmes v. State, 671 N.E.2d 841, 848–49 (Ind. 1996).

53. *See id.; see* State v. Roll, 942 S.W.2d 370, 378 (Mo. 1997) (en banc); *cf.* State v. Card, 825 P.2d 1081, 1089 (Idaho 1991).

54. *See* State v. Lovelace, 90 P.3d 298 (Idaho 2004). *But see* Beloof, *supra* note 46. Victim families' recommendations of sentences of life rather than death have also been deemed inadmissible sentencing recommendations. *See, e.g.,* Lynn v. Reinstein, 68 P.3d 412 (Ariz. 2003); Ortiz v. State, 869 A.2d 285 (Del. 2005); Ware v. State, 759 A.2d 764 (Md. Ct. App. 2000); *see also* Charles F. Baird & Elizabeth E. McGinn, *Re-Victimizing the Victim: How Prosecutorial and Judicial Discretion Are Being Exercised to Silence Victims Who Oppose Capital Punishment*, 15 STAN. L. & POL'Y REV. 447 (2004).

55. *See* State v. Muhammad, 678 A.2d 164, 169–76, 180 (N.J. 1996); *Conover*, 933 P.2d at 918–21; *Ledbetter*, 933 P.2d at 890–96; Cargle v. State, 909 P.2d 806, 828–29 (Okla. Crim. App. 1995). An error in the jury instruction regarding victim impact evidence, that directed

jurors to balance the backgrounds of the defendant and victim, contributed to the reversal of the defendant's death sentence in *State v. Koskovich*, 776 A.2d 144, 177–84 (N.J. 2001).

56. *See* 18 U.S.C.A. §3593 (West 2000 & Supp. 2009).

57. *See, e.g.,* United States v. Gooch, Crim. No. 04-128-23 (RMC), 2006 U.S. Dist. LEXIS 91892 (D.D.C. Dec. 20, 2006) (limiting victim impact evidence to victims of the capital crimes and noting that victim impact evidence regarding the non-capital crimes could be offered in a separate sentencing proceeding pursuant to the Crime Victims' Rights Act); *cf.* United States v. Sampson, 335 F. Supp. 2d 166 (D. Mass. 2004) (excluding a twenty-seven minute memorial video regarding the victim). *See generally* Blume, *supra* note 47, at 277–78; Logan, *Federal Capital Trials, supra* note 47.

58. *See, e.g.,* United States v. Mayhew, 380 F. Supp. 2d 936, 955–57 (S.D. Ohio 2005); United States v. Johnson, 362 F. Supp. 2d 1043, 1106–11 (N.D. Iowa 2005); United States v. Cooper, 91 F. Supp. 2d 90, 110–11 (D.D.C. 2000); United States v. Glover, 43 F. Supp. 2d 1217, 1234–36 (D. Kan. 1999). One trial court required the Government to disclose evidence that would "impeach or negatively reflect" on victim impact evidence pursuant to the Government's obligation to disclose exculpatory evidence to the defendant. United States v. Duncan, No. 05-80025 (E.D. Mich. Dec. 28, 2007). *See generally* Blume, *supra* note 47, at 277–78; Logan, *Federal Capital Trials, supra* note 47.

59. *See* United States v. McVeigh, 153 F.3d 1166, 1216–22 (10th Cir. 1998); Shanker, *supra* note 47, at 726–32.

60. *See* Jones v. United States, 527 U.S. 373, 402, 404–05 (1999).

61. *See* United States v. Bernard, 299 F.3d 467, 480–81 (5th Cir. 2002).

62. *See generally* Blume, *supra* note 47; Logan, *Federal Capital Trials, supra* note 47.

63. *See generally* Jay M. Zitter, Annotation, *Validity, Construction, and Application of State Constitutional or Statutory Victims' Bill of Rights,* 91 A.L.R. 5th 343, 419–25 (2001); National Center for Victims of Crime, *supra* note 1.

64. *See* People v. Lee, 795 N.E.2d 751, 765 (Ill. Ct. App. 2003).

65. *See* State v. Leon, 132 P.3d 462, 464–67 (Idaho Ct. App. 2006).

66. *See* People v. Oyola, 626 N.Y.S.2d 849, 850 (N.Y. App. Div. 1995); *cf.* People v. Pickens, 653 N.E.2d 778, 783 (Ill. App. Ct. 1995); State v. Yanez, 469 N.W.2d 452, 454–55 (Minn. Ct. App. 1991).

67. *See, e.g.,* People v. Mockel, 276 Cal. Rptr. 559, 561–62 (Cal. Ct. App. 1990); Sherroan v. Commonwealth, 142 S.W.3d 7, 24 (Ky. 2004); Sharp v. State, 908 S.W.2d 752, 756 (Mo. Ct. App. 1995); State v. Aker, 113 P.3d 384, 387–88 (N.M. Ct. App. 2005).

68. *See, e.g.,* People v. Jones, 14 Cal. Rptr. 2d 9, 13–15 (Cal. Ct. App. 1992); State v. Matteson, 851 P.2d 336, 338–40 (Idaho 1993); Brown v. State, 875 S.W.2d 38, 39–40 (Tex. App. 1994).

69. *See, e.g.,* State v. Sailer, 587 N.W.2d 756 (Iowa 1998); Swindle v. State, 881 So. 2d 174 (Miss. 2004); Mehring v. State, 860 P.2d 1101, 1116–17 (Wyo. 1993). *But see, e.g.,* State v. Matheson, 684 N.W.2d 243 (Iowa 2004); State v. Behrnes, 706 So. 2d 179 (La. Ct. App. 1997).

70. *See, e.g.,* Jones v. State, 675 N.E.2d 1084, 1089 (Ind. 1996); *Sherroan,* 142 S.W.3d at 23–24; State v. Acoff, 610 N.E.2d 619, 621 (Ohio Ct. App. 1992); Thomas v. Commonwealth, 559 S.E.2d 652 (Va. 2002); State v. Lindahl, 56 P.3d 589 (Wash. Ct. App. 2002). *But see, e.g.,* Terry v. Commonwealth, 153 S.W.3d 794, 804–05 (Ky. 2005).

71. *Aker,* 113 P.3d at 384.

72. *See* Buschauer v. State, 804 P.2d 1046, 1047–49 (Nev. 1990); *see also* Conover v. State, 933 P.2d 904, 922–23 (Okla. Crim. App. 1997).

73. *See* State v. Whitten, 667 A.2d 849, 851–52 (Me. 1995).

74. *See, e.g.,* State *ex rel.* Thomas v. Foreman, 118 P.3d 1117 (Ariz. Ct. App. 2005); People v. Zikorus, 197 Cal. Rptr. 509, 514–15 (Cal. Ct. App. 1983); State v. Guerrero, 940 P.2d 419 (Idaho Ct. App. 1997).

75. *See, e.g., Mockel,* 276 Cal. Rptr. at 562; State v. Phillips, 381 S.E.2d 325, 326–27 (N.C. 1989); *see also* State v. Moss, 13 S.W.3d 374, 384–85 (Tenn. Crim. App. 1999).

76. *See, e.g.,* People v. Wright, 590 N.Y.S.2d 365, 366 (N.Y. App. Div. 1992); People v. Lader, 494 N.Y.S.2d 33, 35–36 (N.Y. App. Div. 1985).

77. *See* McLeod, *supra* note 21, at 168.

78. *See generally* Zitter, *supra* note 63; National Center for Victims of Crime, *supra* note 1.

79. 523 N.W.2d 640 (Mich. Ct. App. 1994).

80. *See id.* at 641–44. *But see* ARIZ. REV. STAT. ANN. § 13-4436 (Supp. 2007) (authorizing re-opening a sentence, in specified circumstances, due to a violation of the victim's right to be heard).

81. 642 N.E.2d 12 (Ohio Ct. App. 1994).

82. *See id.* at 13–15.

83. 906 S.W.2d 349 (Ky. 1995).

84. *See id.* at 350–51.

85. 807 P.2d 1063 (Cal. 1991) (in bank).

86. *See id.* at 1066–68 & n.6; *see* Dix v. County of Shasta, 963 F.2d 1296, 1298–1301 (9th Cir. 1992) (finding no enforceable due process interest); *cf.* CAL. CONST. art. 1, § 28 (providing right to enforce victim rights, including right to be heard, in appellate court in recently amended provision).

87. 899 P.2d 939 (Ariz. 1995) (en banc)

88. *Id.* at 942; *see also id.* at 940–41.

89. *See id.* at 942–43.

90. 133 P.3d 692 (Alaska Ct. App. 2006).

91. *Id.* at 706; *cf.* ALASKA STAT. § 12.55.120 (2006) (permitting victim to seek appellate review of sentences below the sentencing range); Johnston v. Dobeski, 739 N.E.2d 121 (Ind. 2000); Hagen v. Commonwealth, 772 N.E.2d 32 (Mass. 2002) (finding no victim standing to intervene in certain sentencing-related matters). The appellate court did not address the availability of mandamus or other appellate review for a violation of a victim's right to be heard because there was no such rights violation in this case. *See Cooper,* 133 P.3d at 711.

92. *See, e.g.,* United States v. Ausburn, 502 F.3d 313, 323–24 (3d Cir. 2007) (sentence vacated on other grounds); United States v. Santana, 908 F.2d 506 (9th Cir. 1990); United States v. Smith, 893 F. Supp. 187 (E.D.N.Y. 1995).

93. *See* 18 U.S.C.A. § 3771 (West Supp. 2009) (superseding prior Fed. R. Crim. P. 32); *cf.* Jayne W. Barnard, *Allocution for Victims of Economic Crimes,* 77 NOTRE DAME L. REV. 39 (2001).

94. *See generally* Amy Baronevans, *Traps for the Unwary under the Crime Victims' Rights Act: Lessons from the Kenna Cases,* 19 FED. SENT'G REP. 49 (2006); Richard A. Bierschbach, *Allocution and the Purposes of Victim Participation under the CVRA,* 19 FED. SENT'G REP. 44 (2006); Russell P. Butler, *What Practitioners and Judges Need to Know Regarding Crime Victims' Participatory Rights in Federal Sentencing Proceedings,* 19 FED. SENT'G REP. 21 (2006); Mary Margaret Giannini, *Equal Rights for Equal Rites?: Victim Allocution, Defendant Allocution, and the Crime Victims' Rights Act,* 26 YALE L. & POL'Y REV. 431 (2008); Michael M. O'Hear, *Punishment, Democracy, and Victims,* 19 FED. SENT'G REP. 1 (2006).

95. *See* United States v. Degenhardt, 405 F. Supp. 2d 1341 (D. Utah 2005); *cf.* United States v. Sharp, 463 F. Supp. 2d 556, 565 n.17 (E.D. Va. 2006) (indicating, in dicta, that the Act is "silent" regarding whether the right to be heard can be satisfied by written submissions or requires an opportunity for an oral presentation); United States v. Marcello, 370 F. Supp. 2d 745 (N.D. Ill. 2005) (finding that the right to be heard regarding the pretrial release proceeding could be satisfied by the provision of written submissions by the victim under the facts of this case); United States v. Turner, 367 F. Supp. 2d 319, 333 (E.D.N.Y. 2005) (indicating, in dicta, that the Act's right to be heard includes the right to appear and directly address the court, but also noting the Act's authorization of alternatives in cases involving many victims).

96. 435 F.3d 1011 (9th Cir. 2006).

97. *See id.* at 1012–13.

98. *See id.* at 1013–17; *see also id.* at 1014 n.1; *cf. id.* at 1018–19 (Friedman, J., concurring) (cautioning about the "broad sweep" of the majority opinion beyond the facts of the instant case).

99. *See id.* at 1017–18. The appellate court noted the trial court's task to fashion a remedy that would vindicate the victim's right to speak at the second defendant's sentencing, but not "upset" the defendant's constitutionally protected rights. The appellate court also chose the remand option rather than the requested vacation of the sentence because the defendant was not a party to the mandamus proceeding and the vacation of his sentence in the mandamus proceeding without his participation or right to respond could violate the defendant's due process rights. *See id.* The trial court subsequently granted the victim's motion to re-open the sentencing proceeding, heard from the victim, received additional information about the defendant, and ultimately re-imposed the same sentence. *See* Baronevans, *supra* note 94.

100. *See* Kenna v. United States District Court, 453 F.3d 1136 (9th Cir. 2006) (per curiam); Matthew B. Riley, Note, *Victim Participation in the Criminal Justice System:* In re Kenna *and Victim Access to Presentence Reports*, 2007 Utah L. Rev. 235 (2007); *cf.* United States v. Ingrassia, Cr. 04-0455 (ADS) (JO), 2005 U.S. Dist. LEXIS 27817, at *48–*51 (E.D.N.Y. Sept. 5, 2005) (noting, in dicta, that the Act does not require disclosure of the presentence report, at least in the absence of a victim request).

101. 262 Fed. Appx. 510 (4th Cir. 2008) (per curiam) (unpublished opinion).

102. *See id.* at 510–13; *cf.* United States v. Citgo Petroleum, Cr. No. C-06-563, 2007 U.S. Dist. LEXIS 57686 (S.D. Tex. Aug. 8, 2007) (denying motion filed by the Government to unseal its submission for the presentence report for the victims and other purposes).

103. *See* United States v. Rubin, 558 F. Supp. 2d 411, 425 (E.D.N.Y. 2008) (denying motion filed by victims for information from the Government as moot and noting that the Act does not authorize disclosure of all information in the Government's files, but finding that the Government was already working with the victims to provide the requested information); United States v. Sacane, Crim. No. 3:05cr325, 2007 U.S. Dist. LEXIS 22178 (D. Conn. Mar. 28, 2007) (denying a victim request for financial information from the defendant for use in restitution hearing); *cf. In re* Antrobus, 519 F.3d 1123, 1126–27 (10th Cir. 2008) (denying victim request for Government investigative information to establish status as victims); United States v. Moussaoui, 483 F.3d 220 (4th Cir. 2007) (holding that the Act did not authorize the trial court to order disclosure of non-public investigative materials to victims for use in their civil suits).

104. *See Brock*, 262 Fed. Appx. at 510–13.

105. *Id.* at 512–13.

106. No. 08-4010, 2008 U.S. App. LEXIS 24319 (10th Cir. Dec. 2, 2008).

107. *See id.* at *2–*6.

108. *Id.* at *6.

109. *See id.* at *7, *18–*22.

110. *Id.* at *18; *see id.* at *6–*18, *24.

111. *See supra* note 92 and accompanying text. *See generally* Barnevans, *supra* note 94; Butler, *supra* note 94.

112. *See generally* Bandes, *supra* note 47; Paul G. Cassell, *Barbarians at the Gates? A Reply to the Critics of the Victims' Rights Amendment,* 1999 Utah L. Rev. 479, 486–97 (1999); Robert C. Davis & Barbara E. Smith, *The Effects of Victim Impact Statements on Sentencing Decisions: A Test in an Urban Setting,* 11 Just. Q. 453, 454–55 (1994); Edna Erez, *Who's Afraid of the Big Bad Victim? Victim Impact Statements as Victim Empowerment and Enhancement of Justice,* 1999 Crim. L. Rev. 545 (1999); Edna Erez, *Victim Participation in Sentencing: And the Debate Goes On...,* 3 Int'l Rev. Victimology 17, 18–21 (1994); Paul Gewirtz, *Victims and Voyeurs at the Criminal Trial,* 90 Nw. U. L. Rev. 863 (1996); Lynne N. Henderson, *The Wrongs of Victim's Rights,* 37 Stan. L. Rev. 937, 986–1006 (1985); Deborah P. Kelly & Edna Erez, *Victim Participation in the Criminal Justice System, in* Victims of Crime 231, 236–37 (Robert C. Davis et al. eds., 2d ed. 1997); Logan, *supra* note 47; Howard C. Rubel, *Victim Participation in Sentencing Proceedings,* 28 Crim. L.Q. 226, 237–42 (1985).

113. *See, e.g.,* Jolene C. Hernon & Brian Forst, U.S. Dep't of Justice, The Criminal Justice Response to Victim Harm 50–52, 60 (1984); Susan W. Hillenbrand & Barbara E. Smith, American Bar Association, Executive Summary: Victim Rights Legislation: An Assessment of its Impact on Criminal Justice Practitioners and Victims 16 (1989); Deborah P. Kelly, *Victims,* 34 Wayne L. Rev. 69, 72 (1987); Deborah P. Kelly, *Delivering Legal Services to Victims: An Evaluation and Prescription,* 9 Just. Sys. J. 62, 73–78, 84 (1984).

114. *See* McLeod, *supra* note 21, at 164–65.

115. *See* Hall, *supra* note 25, at 242 (describing Hillenbrand & Smith study, *supra* note 113).

116. Anthony Walsh, *Placebo Justice: Victim Recommendations and Offender Sentences in Sexual Assault Cases,* 77 J. Crim. L. & Criminology 1126, 1129–30 (1986).

117. *See* Edna Erez & Pamela Tontodonato, *The Effect of Victim Participation in Sentencing on Sentence Outcome,* 28 Criminology 451, 455 (1990).

118. *See* Edwin Villmoare & Virginia V. Neto, U.S. Dep't of Justice, Victim Appearances at Sentencing Hearings under the California Victims' Bill of Rights 42 (1987).

119. *See* David Beatty et al., National Victim Center, Statutory and Constitutional Protection of Victims' Rights: Implementation and Impact on Crime Victims 9–30, 35, 42 (1996); *see also* Dean G. Kilpatrick et al., U.S. Dep't of Justice, The Rights of Crime Victims—Does Legal Protection Make a Difference? (1998).

120. *See* Beatty et al., *supra* note 119, at 90–91.

121. *See* U.S Government Accountability Office, Crime Victims' Rights Act: Increasing Awareness, Modifying the Complaint Process, and Enhancing Compliance Monitoring Will Improve Implementation of the Act 86 (2008).

122. *See* Ilhong Yun et al., Crime Victims' Institute, Victim Impact Statements: What Victims Have to Say 9 (2005).

123. *See id.* at 9, 11–14.

124. *See* McLeod, *supra* note 21, at 165. *See generally* Erez, *Victim Participation, supra* note 112, at 26–28; Kelly & Erez, *supra* note 112, at 240–41.

125. *See, e.g.,* Anne M. Heinz & Wayne A. Kerstetter, *Pretrial Settlement Conference: Evaluation of a Reform in Plea Bargaining,* 13 L. & Soc'y Rev. 349, 357 (1979); Susan E.

Gegan & Nicholas Ernesto Rodriguez, Note, *Victims' Roles in the Criminal Justice System: A Fallacy of Empowerment?*, 8 St. John's J. Legal Comment. 225, 244–47 (1992).

126. *See* Jim Sinclair, *Partners for Justice: Crime Victims and State Policymakers in the Northeast Join Together for System Change*, 3 The Crime Victims Report 17, 27 (1999).

127. *See* Villmoare & Neto, *supra* note 118, at 42.

128. *See* U.S. Government Accountability Office, *supra* note 121, at 82.

129. *See* Edna Erez & Pamela Tontodonato, *Victim Participation in Sentencing and Satisfaction with Justice*, 9 Just. Q. 393, 400 (1992).

130. *See* Robert C. Davis & Barbara E. Smith, *Victim Impact Statements and Victim Satisfaction: An Unfulfilled Promise?*, 22 J. Crim. Just. 1, 8–9 (1994).

131. *See* Villmoare & Neto, *supra* note 118, at 42–43.

132. *See* U.S Government Accountability Office, *supra* note 121, at 86.

133. *See* McLeod, *supra* note 21, at 163–64, 167.

134. *See* Paul S. Hudson, *The Crime Victim and the Criminal Justice System: Time for a Change*, 11 Pepp. L. Rev. 23, 52 (1984).

135. *See* Hillenbrand & Smith, *supra* note 113, at 5, 11.

136. *See* Villmoare & Neto, *supra* note 118, at 59; *cf.* Heinz & Kerstetter, *supra* note 125, at 360.

137. *See generally* Erez, *Victim Participation, supra* note 112, at 22; Kelly & Erez, *supra* note 112, at 237.

138. *See* Walsh, *supra* note 116, at 1132–33, 1139.

139. *See* Erez & Tontodonato, *supra* note 117, at 455–56.

140. *See* Villmoare & Neto, *supra* note 118, at 43–44.

141. *See* Robert C. Davis et al., *Expanding the Victim's Role in the Criminal Court Dispositional Process: The Results of an Experiment*, 75 J. Crim. L. & Criminology 491, 493 n.8 (1984).

142. *See* Joel Henderson & G. Thomas Gitchoff, *Using Experts and Victims in the Sentencing Process*, 17 Crim. L. Bull. 226, 229–30 (1981); *cf.* Heinz & Kerstetter, *supra* note 125, at 359.

143. *See generally* Erez, *Victim Participation, supra* note 112, at 21; Hall, *supra* note 25, at 244–45.

144. *See* Hillenbrand & Smith, *supra* note 113, at 10; Hudson, *supra* note 134, at 52; *see also* Davis & Smith, *supra* note 112, at 466; Madeline Henley et al., *The Reactions of Prosecutors and Judges to Victim Impact Statements*, 3 Int'l Rev. Victimology 83, 90 (1994). *But see* Hernon & Forst, *supra* note 113, at 19–21.

145. *See* Hillenbrand & Smith, *supra* note 113, at 5, 10.

146. *See* Villmoare & Neto, *supra* note 118, at 37, 55–56, 59.

147. *See* Hillenbrand & Smith, *supra* note 113, at 10, 20.

148. *See id.* at 9; Hudson, *supra* note 134, at 52.

149. *See* Davis & Smith, *supra* note 112, at 466.

150. *See* Henley et al., *supra* note 144, at 87–89.

151. *See* Hall, *supra* note 25, at 246 (describing Hillenbrand & Smith study, *supra* note 113).

152. *See* Villmoare & Neto, *supra* note 118, at 56.

153. *See* Beatty et al., *supra* note 119, at 93.

154. *See* Mary Lay Schuster & Amy Propen, 2006 WATCH Victim Impact Statement Study (2006), *available at* http://www.mincava.umn/edu/documents/victimimpact/watchreport.pdf.

155. *See generally* Erez, *Victim Participation, supra* note 112, at 22–24; Kelly & Erez, *supra* note 112, at 238–39.

156. *See* Hernon & Forst, *supra* note 113, at 13, 33–38, 43.

157. *See* Walsh, *supra* note 116, at 1129–34.

158. *See* Davis et al., *supra* note 141, at 495–96, 498–501, 503–05.

159. *See* Davis & Smith, *supra* note 112, at 456–65.

160. *See* Erez & Tontodonato, *supra* note 117, at 454–67.

161. *See, e.g.,* Davis et al., *supra* note 141, at 503–05; Davis & Smith, *supra* note 112, at 457, 466–68; Erez, *Who's Afraid, supra* note 112, at 548; Hall, *supra* note 25, at 247; Henley et al., *supra* note 144, at 91–92.

162. *See* Walsh, *supra* note 116, at 1139, 1141.

163. *See* Davis & Smith, *supra* note 112, at 467–68.

164. Erez, *Victim Participation, supra* note 112, at 24.

165. *See, e.g.,* Beatty et al., *supra* note 119, at 37; Villmoare & Neto, *supra* note 118, at 44, 56; Davis et al., *supra* note 141, at 498 & n.25; Erez & Tontodonato, *supra* note 129, at 401; Hall, *supra* note 25, at 247.

166. *See* U.S Government Accountability Office, *supra* note 121, at 83–84.

167. *See* Hillenbrand & Smith, *supra* note 113, at 20.

168. *See* Beatty et al., *supra* note 119, at 44, 46, 53–54, 58–63.

169. *See generally* Erez, *Victim Participation, supra* note 112, at 24–26; Kelly & Erez, *supra* note 112, at 239–40.

170. *See* Davis & Smith, *supra* note 130, at 7–12.

171. *See* Davis et al., *supra* note 141, at 498 & n.25.

172. *See* Villmoare & Neto, *supra* note 118, at 44, 60.

173. *See* Erez & Tontodonato, *supra* note 129, at 400–13; *see also* Hernon & Forst, *supra* note 113 at 45, 47, 62–63.

174. *See* Pamela Tontodonato & Edna Erez, *Crime, Punishment, and Victim Distress*, 3 Int'l Rev. Victimology 33, 50–51 (1994).

175. *See* Davis & Smith, *supra* note 130, at 8–10; Erez & Tontodonato, *supra* note 129, at 401.

176. *See* Office of Justice Programs, *supra* note 2, at 4.

177. *See* President's Task Force on Victims of Crime, *supra* note 4, at 29–31.

178. *See id.* at 29.

179. *See id.* at 83–84.

180. *See* Office for Victims of Crime, *supra* note 10, at 17–18, 137–39, 142.

181. *See* 18 U.S.C.A. §§3583, 3624 (West 2000); U.S. Sentencing Guidelines §§5D1.1-.3 (West 2007 & Supp. 2009); Tobolowsky, *supra* note 3, at 399–400.

182. *See* S.J. Res. 1, 108th Cong. (2003); H.R.J. Res. 48, 108th Cong. (2003); H.R.J. Res. 10, 108th Cong. (2003).

183. 18 U.S.C.A. § 3771 (West Supp. 2009).

184. *See* Ala. Const. art. I, §6.01; Colo. Const. art. 2, § 16a; Fla. Const. art. 1, § 16; La. Const. art. 1, § 25; Md. Const. art. 47; Miss. Const. art. 3, § 26A; Tenn. Const. art. I, § 35; Utah Const. art. I, § 28.

185. *See* Alaska Const. art. I., § 24; Ariz. Const. art. 2, § 2.1; Cal. Const. art. 1, § 28; Idaho Const. art. I, § 22; Mo. Const. art. 1, § 32; Neb. Const. art. I, § 28; Nev. Const. art. 1, § 8; N.M. Const. art. II, § 24; N.C. Const. art. I, § 37; Okla. Const. art. 2, § 34; Wash. Const. art.1, § 35.

186. *Cf.* Maine State Parole Board, http://www.maine.gov/sos/cec/rules/ (providing that, at its hearing that is not generally open to the public, written statements from "interested" persons (including victims) may be considered by the parole board). *See generally* Beloof et al., *supra* note 1, at 667–68; National Center for Victims of Crime, *supra* note 1; National Conference of States Legislatures, *supra* note 1; Frances P. Bernat et al., *Victim Impact Laws and the Parole Process in the United States: Balancing Victim and Inmate Rights and Interests*, 3 Int'l Rev. Victimology 121 (1994); Maureen McLeod, *Getting Free: Victim Participation in Parole Board Decisions*, 4 Crim. Just. 12 (1989).

187. *See* Iowa Code Ann. §915.18 (West 2003); Md. Code Ann., Cor. Serv. §7-801 (LexisNexis 2008); *see also* N.D. Cent. Code §12.1-34-02 (Supp. 2007).

188. *See, e.g.*, Ark. Code Ann. §16-93-206 (Supp. 2007); Cal. Penal Code §3043 (West Supp. 2008); Okla. Stat. Ann. tit. 57, §332.2 (West 2004).

189. *See, e.g.*, Mo. Ann. Stat. §595.206 (West 2003).

190. *See, e.g.*, Mass. Ann. Laws ch. 127, §133A (LexisNexis 2003); R.I. Gen. Laws §12-28-6 (2002); Va. Code Ann. §53.1-155 (2005).

191. *See, e.g.*, Tex. Code Crim. Proc. Ann. art. 56.03 (Vernon 2006).

192. *See, e.g.*, Cal. Penal Code §§3043, 3043.2, 3043.25 (West Supp. 2008); *see also* Gegan & Rodriguez, *supra* note 125, at 241.

193. *See, e.g.*, Ky. Rev. Stat. Ann. §439.340 (LexisNexis Supp. 2007).

194. *See* Bernat et al., *supra* note 186, at 129; McLeod, *supra* note 186, at 14–15, 43.

195. *See* Cal. Penal Code §3043 (West Supp. 2008).

196. *See* 61 Pa. Stat. Ann. §331.22a (West Supp. 2009).

197. *See* Ky. Rev. Stat. Ann. §439.340 (LexisNexis Supp. 2007).

198. *See* 61 Pa. Stat. Ann. §331.22a (West Supp. 2009).

199. *See* Colo. Rev. Stat. Ann. §17-2-214 (West 2006).

200. *See* Ky. Rev. Stat. Ann. §439.340 (LexisNexis Supp. 2007); R.I. Gen. Laws §12-28-7 (2002).

201. *See* Ariz. Rev. Stat. Ann. §13-4436 (Supp. 2007).

202. *See* Okla. Stat. Ann. tit. 57, §332.2 (West 2004).

203. *See* Tenn. Code Ann. §40-28-505 (2006).

204. *See* 61 Pa. Stat. Ann. §331.22a (West Supp. 2009).

205. *See* Barnett v. State, 979 P.2d 1046 (Haw. 1999).

206. *See* Cicchinelli v. Pennsylvania Board of Probation and Parole, 760 A.2d 914 (Pa. Commw. Ct. 2000).

207. 875 P.2d 824 (Ariz. Ct. App. 1993).

208. 984 S.W.2d 918 (Tenn. Ct. App. 1998).

209. *See id.* at 919–25.

210. 703 A.2d 754 (R.I. 1997).

211. *See id.* at 755–56.

212. 947 F.2d 1338 (7th Cir. 1991).

213. *See id.* at 1340–41; *see also* Alston v. Robinson, 791 F. Supp. 569, 592 (D. Md. 1992).

214. 110 F.3d 299 (5th Cir. 1997).

215. *See id.* at 304–09; *cf.* Palmer v. Granholm, No. 1:06-cv-301, 2006 U.S. Dist. LEXIS 45333 (W.D. Mich. July 5, 2006) (rejecting the prisoner's due process and equal protection claims based on the denial of his parole in a case in which the victim opposed parole).

216. *See, e.g.*, Gegan & Rodriguez, *supra* note 125, at 242–43.

217. *See, e.g.*, Bernat et al., *supra* note 186, 134–38; McLeod, *supra* note 186, at 13; Donald R. Ranish & David Shichor, *The Victim's Role in the Penal Process: Recent Developments in California*, Fed. Probation, March 1985, at 50, 54–55; Mark W. May, Comment, *Victims' Rights and the Parole Hearing*, 15 J. Contemp. L. 71, 77–79 (1989).

218. *See, e.g.*, Bernat et al., *supra* note 186, at 128–32, 137; McLeod, *supra* note 186, at 14–15, 41–43; Marlene A. Young, *A Constitutional Amendment for Victims of Crime: The Victims' Perspective*, 34 Wayne L. Rev. 51, 62 n.25 (1987); Gegan & Rodriguez, *supra* note 125, at 242, 245.

219. *See* William H. Parsonage et al., *Victim Impact Testimony and Pennsylvania's Parole Decision Making Process: A Pilot Study*, 6 Crim. Just. Pol'y Rev. 187, 193 (1994).

220. *See* Villmoare & Neto, *supra* note 118, at 68–69; Ranish & Shichor, *supra* note 217, at 54.

221. *See* Beatty et al., *supra* note 119, at 35, 42.

222. *See id.* at 98.

223. *See* Kathryn Morgan & Brent L. Smith, *Victims, Punishment, and Parole: The Effect of Victim Participation on Parole Hearings*, 4 Criminology & Pub. Pol'y 333, 357 (2005).

224. *See* Bernat et al., *supra* note 186, at 125.

225. *See* McLeod, *supra* note 186, at 14, 43; *cf.* Villmoare & Neto, *supra* note 118, at 69.

226. *See* Beatty et al., *supra* note 119, at 98.

227. *See* Bernat et al., *supra* note 186, 124–25; Parsonage et al., *supra* note 219, at 192–200.

228. *See* Parsonage et al., *supra* note 219, at 194.

229. *See id.* at 195–202.

230. *See* Morgan & Smith, *supra* note 223; Brent Smith et al., *The Effect of Victim Participation on Parole Decisions: Results from a Southeastern State*, 8 Crim. Just. Pol'y Rev. 57 (1997); *cf.* Laura J. Moriarty, *Victim Participation at Parole Hearings: Balancing Victim, Offender, and Public Interest*, 4 Criminology & Pub. Pol'y 385 (2005).

231. *See* Joel M. Caplan, Parole Release Decisions in New Jersey: Effects of Positive and Negative Victim and Non-Victim Input (2008) (unpublished Ph.D. dissertation, University of Pennsylvania) (on file with author).

232. *See* Villmoare & Neto, *supra* note 118, at 69–70.

Notes for Chapter 7

1. *See generally* Douglas E. Beloof et al., Victims in Criminal Procedure 693–797 (2d ed. 2006); National Center for Victims of Crime, VictimLaw, http://www.victimlaw.info/victimlaw/ (last visited Jan. 1, 2009); National Conference of State Legislatures, Victims' Rights Laws in the States, http://www.ncsl.org (last visited Jan. 1, 2009).

2. *See generally* President's Task Force on Victims of Crime, Final Report (1982).

3. *See* Office for Victims of Crime, U.S. Dep't of Justice, New Directions from the Field: Victims' Rights and Services for the 21st Century 29–31, 33–34 (1998).

4. *See generally* National Conference of State Legislatures, *supra* note 1.

5. *See* 18 U.S.C.A. § 3771 (West Supp. 2009).

6. *See* S.J. Res. 1, 108th Cong. (2003); H.R.J. Res. 48, 108th Cong. (2003); H.R.J. Res. 10, 108th Cong. (2003).

7. *See* 18 U.S.C.A. § 3771 (West Supp. 2009).

8. *See id.*

9. *See id.*; 42 U.S.C.A. § 10607 (West 2005) (precluding a cause of action based on the failure to provide the prescribed victim notification and services).

10. *See* 18 U.S.C.A. § 3771 (West Supp. 2009).

11. *See* Crime Victims' Rights Act of 2004, Pub. L. No. 108–405, Title I, §§ 103–104, 118 Stat. 2260, 2264–65 (2004); 42 U.S.C.A. § 10603d (West 2005) (permitting additional grants pursuant to the crime victim assistance grant program).

12. *See* OFFICE FOR VICTIMS OF CRIME, U.S. DEP'T OF JUSTICE, ATTORNEY GENERAL GUIDELINES FOR VICTIM AND WITNESS ASSISTANCE (2005); Executive Office for United States Attorneys, Office of the Victims' Rights Ombudsman, http://www.usdoj.gov.usao/eousa/vr/index.html (last visited Jan. 3, 2009).

13. *See* Fed. R. Crim. P. 60; *see* U.S. Courts, Proposed Amendments to the Federal Rules of Criminal Procedure (effective Dec. 1, 2008), http://www.uscourts.gov/rules/ supct0408.html (last visited Jan. 2, 2009) (including the amendments to the federal rules and related reports).

14. *See, e.g.*, ALA. CONST. art. I, § 6.01; CAL. CONST. art. 1, § 28; MISS. CONST. art. 3, § 26A; N.C. CONST. art. I, § 37; S.C. CONST. art. I, § 24.

15. *See, e.g.*, CONN. CONST. art. I, § 8; ILL. CONST. art. 1, § 8.1; NEB. CONST. art. I, § 28; OKLA. CONST. art. 2, § 34; TEX. CONST. art. 1, § 30.

16. *See* IDAHO CONST. art. I, § 22; KAN. CONST. art. 15, § 15; LA. CONST. art. 1, § 25; MD. CONST. art. 47; MO. CONST. art. 1, § 32; NEV. CONST. art. 1, § 8; OHIO CONST. art. I, § 10a; OR. CONST. art. I, § 42; UTAH CONST. art. I, § 28; VA. CONST. art. I, § 8-A.

17. KAN. CONST. art. 15, § 15.

18. *See* MD. CONST. art. 47; NEV. CONST. art. 1, § 8; OR. CONST. art. I, § 42.

19. *See* CONN. CONST. art. I, § 8; ILL. CONST. art. 1, § 8.1; LA. CONST. art. 1, § 25; VA. CONST. art. I, § 8-A.

20. *See* WASH. CONST. art. 1, § 35; *see also* LA. CONST. art. 1, § 25.

21. *See* N.M. CONST. art. II, § 24; N.C. CONST. art. I, § 37; TEX. CONST. art. 1, § 30; *cf.* ARIZ. CONST. art. 2, § 2.1; LA. CONST. art. 1, § 25; S.C. CONST. art. I, § 24; WASH. CONST. art. 1, § 35.

22. *See* NEV. CONST. art. 1, § 8.

23. *See* S.C. CONST. art. I, § 24.

24. *See* CAL. CONST. art. 1, § 28.

25. *See* OR. CONST. art. I, § 42.

26. *See* TEX. CONST. art. 1, § 30.

27. *See, e.g.*, HAW. REV. STAT. ANN. § 801D-5 (LexisNexis 2007); ME. REV. STAT. ANN. tit. 17-A, § 1175 (Supp. 2007); 18 PA. STAT. ANN. § 11.5101 (West 2000); TENN. CODE ANN. § 40-38-108 (2006).

28. *See, e.g.*, GA. CODE ANN. § 17-17-15 (West 2003); R.I. GEN. LAWS § 12-28-7 (2002).

29. *See, e.g.*, CONN. GEN. STAT. § 54-223 (2007); 725 ILL. COMP. STAT. ANN. 120/9 (West Supp. 2008); LA. REV. STAT. ANN. § 46:1844 (Supp. 2008); TEX. CODE CRIM. PROC. ANN. art. 56.02 (Vernon Supp. 2008).

30. *See, e.g.*, ALA. CODE § 15-23-66 (LexisNexis 1995); GA. CODE ANN. § 17-17-15 (West 2003); MISS. CODE ANN. § 99-36-5 (West 2006); TEX. CODE CRIM. PROC. ANN. art. 56.02 (Vernon Supp. 2008); VT. STAT. ANN. tit. 13, § 5319 (1998).

31. *See, e.g.*, ALA. CODE § 15-23-83 (LexisNexis1995); DEL. CODE ANN. tit. 11, § 9402 (2007); OHIO REV. CODE ANN. § 2930.19 (LexisNexis 2006); TEX. CODE CRIM. PROC. ANN. art. 56.02 (Vernon Supp. 2008).

32. *See* Haw. Rev. Stat. Ann. § 801D-5 (LexisNexis 2007).

33. *See, e.g.*, Minn. Stat. Ann. § 611A.74 (West 2003); *see also* Joanna Edwards et al., Institute of Public Research, Evaluability Assessment: State Compliance Projects (2006); Office for Victims of Crime, U.S. Dep't of Justice, Victims' Rights Compliance Efforts: Experience in Three States (1998); U.S. Government Accountability Office, Crime Victims' Rights Act: Increasing Awareness, Modifying the Complaint Process, and Enhancing Compliance Monitoring Will Improve Implementation of the Act 44 n.53 (2008); Robert C. Davis & Carrie Mulford, *Victim Rights and New Remedies: Finally Getting Victims their Due*, 24 J. Contemp. Crim. Just. 198, 204–05 (2008); Glen Kercher & Matt Johnson, *Enforcement of the Rights of Crime Victims*, 3 Legislative Brief (2005); *States Establish Programs to Assure Agency Compliance with Victims' Rights Legislation*, 3 The Crime Victims Report 6 (1999).

34. *See* Colo. Rev. Stat. Ann. § 24-4.1-303 (West 2008); *cf.* Fla. Stat. Ann. § 960.001 (West Supp. 2008) (authorizing governor's application for injunctive relief regarding an agency that has failed to comply with victim rights provisions).

35. *See* Alaska Stat. §§ 24.65.010–.250 (2006); Stephen E. Branchflower, *The Alaska Office of Victims' Rights: A Model for America*, 21 Alaska L. Rev. 259 (2004). *But see* Cooper v. District Court, 133 P.3d 692 (Alaska Ct. App. 2006) (holding that neither the victim nor the Office of Victims' Rights had standing to seek appellate review of an alleged sentencing error); Richard Allen, Note, *Is the Office Closed? The Role of the Office of Victims' Rights after* Cooper v. District Court, 24 Alaska L. Rev. 263 (2007).

36. *See* Wis. Stat. Ann. §§ 950.08–.11 (West 2005).

37. *See* S.D. Codified Laws § 23A-28C-3 (2004); *cf.* Fla. Stat. Ann. § 960.001 (West Supp. 2008); Ind. Code Ann. § 35-40-2-1 (LexisNexis Supp. 2008) (granting the victim standing to assert prescribed rights, but also statutorily limiting certain remedies).

38. *See* N.C. Gen. Stat. § 15A-840 (2007); *cf.* La. Rev. Stat. Ann. § 46:1844 (Supp. 2008) (reflecting that mandamus actions are not precluded).

39. *See* Md. Code Ann., Crim. Proc. § 11-103 (LexisNexis Supp. 2007); *cf.* Alaska Stat. § 12.55.120 (2006) (authorizing a victim to file a petition for appellate review of a sentence below the crime's sentencing range).

40. *See* Ariz. Rev. Stat. Ann. § 13-4436 (Supp. 2007); Okla. Stat. Ann. tit. 57, § 332.2 (West 2004); 61 Pa. Stat. Ann. § 331.22a (West Supp. 2009); Tenn. Code Ann. § 40-28-505 (2006).

41. *See* Utah Code Ann. §§ 77-38-11, -12 (2003).

42. *See* Ariz. Rev. Stat. Ann. §§ 13-4436, -4437 (Supp. 2007).

43. *See, e.g.*, People v. Pfeiffer, 523 N.W.2d 640 (Mich. Ct. App. 1994).

44. *See, e.g.*, People v. Superior Court *ex rel.* Thompson, 202 Cal. Rptr. 585, 586 (Cal. Ct. App. 1984); State v. Holt, 874 P.2d 1183, 1186 (Kan. 1994); Bruegger v. Faribault County Sheriff's Department, 497 N.W.2d 260 (Minn. 1993). *But cf.* Melissa J. v. Superior Court *ex rel.* Williams, 237 Cal. Rptr. 5, 6–7 (Cal. Ct. App. 1987).

45. *See, e.g.*, Hoile v. State, 948 A.2d 30 (Md. 2008).

46. *See, e.g.*, State v. Bible, 858 P.2d 1152 (Ariz. 1993).

47. *See* State *ex rel.* Hance v. Arizona Board of Pardons and Paroles, 875 P.2d 824 (Ariz. Ct. App. 1993); Daniels v. Traughber, 984 S.W.2d 918 (Tenn. Ct. App. 1998).

48. *See* Alabama Board of Pardons and Paroles v. Brooks, 802 So. 2d 242 (Ala. Civ. App. 2001); Yang v. State, 703 A.2d 754 (R.I. 1997).

49. *See* Myers v. Daley, 521 N.E.2d 98 (Ill. App. Ct. 1987).

50. *See* Melissa J. v. Superior Court *ex rel.* Williams, 237 Cal. Rptr. 5 (Cal. Ct. App. 1987); Ford v. State, 829 So. 2d 946 (Fla. Dist. Ct. App. 2002).

51. *See* State v. Timmendequas, 737 A.2d 55 (N.J. 1999).

52. *See* State v. Holt, 874 P.2d 1183 (Kan. 1994).

53. *See* Dix v. Superior Court *ex rel.* People, 807 P.2d 1063 (Cal. 1991) (in bank).

54. *See* Cal. Const. art. 1, §28.

55. *See* State v. McDonnell, 794 P.2d 780 (Or. 1990).

56. *See* Reed v. Becka, 511 S.E.2d 396 (S.C. Ct. App. 1999).

57. *See* Schilling v. State of Wisconsin Crime Victims Rights Board, 692 N.W.2d 623, 624 (Wis. 2005).

58. 620 N.W.2d 763 (Neb. 2001).

59. *See id.* at 766–69.

60. *See* Neb. Rev. Stat. §81-1851 (Pamp. 2006); *see also* Neb. Rev. Stat. §§81-1843–50 (1999 & Pamp. 2006).

61. 540 S.E.2d 81 (S.C. 2000).

62. *See id.* at 82–86.

63. *See id.* at 85–87.

64. *See* Hoile v. State, 948 A.2d 30 (Md. 2008); People v. Pfeiffer, 523 N.W.2d 640 (Mich. Ct. App. 1994).

65. *See* State *ex rel.* Goldesberry v. Taylor, 233 S.W.3d 796 (Mo. Ct. App. 2007).

66. *See* State v. Casey, 44 P.3d 756 (Utah 2002).

67. *See id.* at 766 n.14; *cf.* State v. Means, 926 A.2d 328 (N.J. 2007) (finding that a prosecutor's failure to notify victims prior to entering a plea agreement was an insufficient basis by itself for the trial court to set aside a plea agreement).

68. *See* State v. Layman, 214 S.W.3d 442 (Tenn. 2007).

69. Linda R.S. v. Richard D., 410 U.S. 614, 619 (1973).

70. *See* Gansz v. People, 888 P.2d 256 (Colo. 1995) (en banc); *cf., e.g.,* Sandoval v. Farish, 675 P.2d 300 (Colo. 1984) (en banc); State *ex rel.* Rome v. Fountain, 678 P.2d 146 (Kan. 1984); Commonwealth v. Benz, 565 A.2d 764 (Pa. 1989); State v. Unnamed Defendant, 441 N.W.2d 696 (Wis. 1989) (describing cases under state general statutes permitting citizen challenges of governmental failure to prosecute cases).

71. *See* Johnston v. Dobeski, 739 N.E.2d 121 (Ind. 2000), *aff'g,* Johnston v. State, 702 N.E.2d 1085 (Ind. Ct. App. 1998).

72. *See* Hagen v. Commonwealth, 772 N.E.2d 32 (Mass. 2002).

73. *See* Cooper v. District Court, 133 P.3d 692 (Alaska Ct. App. 2006); State v. Lamberton, 899 P.2d 939 (Ariz. 1995) (en banc); Schroering v. McKinney, 906 S.W.2d 349 (Ky. 1995). *See generally* Susan Bandes, *Victim Standing,* 1999 Utah L. Rev. 331 (1999).

74. *Lamberton,* 899 P.2d at 942.

75. *See, e.g.,* Knutson v. County of Maricopa *ex rel.* Romley, 857 P.2d 1299 (Ariz. Ct. App. 1993); Bruegger v. Faribault County Sheriff's Department, 497 N.W.2d 260 (Minn. 1993).

76. Bandoni v. State, 715 A.2d 580 (R.I. 1998).

77. *See* Lewis v. Office of the Prosecuting Attorney, No. 05 CO 69, 2006 Ohio App. LEXIS 4601 (Ohio Ct. App. Sept. 5, 2006).

78. *See, e.g.,* Cianos v. State, 659 A.2d 291, 294 (Md. 1995).

79. *See* Mo. Ann. Stat. §595.209 (West Supp. 2008); *cf.* Ariz. Const. art. 2, §2.1; S.C. Const. art. I, §24.

80. 858 P.2d 1152 (Ariz. 1993).

81. *Id.* at 1205 (citations omitted).

82. *See id.* at 1206.

83. 836 P.2d 445 (Ariz. Ct. App. 1992).

84. *See id.* at 447–49.

85. *See id.* at 449.

86. *See id.* at 448, 450–54; *cf.* State v. Riggs, 942 P.2d 1159 (Ariz. 1997).

87. *See* David E. Aaronson, *New Rights and Remedies: The Federal Crime Victims' Rights Act of 2004*, 28 PACE L. REV. 623 (2008); Russell P. Butler, *What Practitioners and Judges Need to Know Regarding Crime Victims' Participatory Rights in Federal Sentencing Proceedings*, 19 FED. SENT'G REP. 21 (2006). *See generally* U.S. GOVERNMENT ACCOUNTABILITY OFFICE, *supra* note 33, at 119–31 (describing the federal cases decided pursuant to the Act reviewed through June 2008).

In light of the general absence of remedial provisions in the victim-related federal laws prior to the 2004 Act, federal reviewing courts had found that pre-Act laws did not grant victims standing to seek review of orders relating to matters addressed by the applicable rights provisions. *See* United States v. McVeigh, 106 F.3d 325, 334–36 (10th Cir. 1997); *see also* United States v. Mindel, 80 F.3d 394 (9th Cir. 1996); United States v. Kelley, 997 F.2d 806 (10th Cir. 1993); United States v. Johnson, 983 F.2d 216 (11th Cir. 1993); United States v. Grundhoefer, 916 F.2d 788 (2d Cir. 1990).

88. *See In re* Dean, 527 F.3d 391 (5th Cir. 2008) (per curiam); *In re* W.R. Huff Asset Management, 409 F.3d 555 (2d Cir. 2005); United States v. BP Products North America, Cr. No. H-07-434, 2008 U.S. Dist. LEXIS 12893 (S.D. Tex. Feb. 21, 2008); United States v. Rubin, 558 F. Supp. 2d 411 (E.D.N.Y. 2008) United States v. Stokes, No. 3:06-00204, 2007 WL 1849846 (M.D. Tenn. June 22, 2007); United States v. Saltsman, No. 07-CR-641, 2007 U.S. Dist. LEXIS 87044 (E.D.N.Y. Nov. 27, 2007); United States v. Turner, 367 F. Supp. 2d 319 (E.D.N.Y. 2005); United States v. Ingrassia, CR 04-0455, 2005 U.S. Dist. LEXIS 27817 (E.D.N.Y. Sept. 7, 2005).

89. *See In re* Mikhel, 453 F.3d 1137 (9th Cir. 2006) (per curiam); United States v. L.M., 425 F. Supp. 2d 948 (N.D. Iowa 2006); United States v. Turner, 367 F. Supp. 2d 319 (E.D.N.Y. 2005); United States v. Johnson, 362 F. Supp. 2d 1043 (N.D. Iowa 2005).

90. *See* United States v. Heaton, 458 F. Supp. 2d 1271 (D. Utah 2006).

91. *See In re* Dean, 527 F.3d 391 (5th Cir. 2008); United States v. Eberhard, 525 F.3d 175 (2d Cir. 2008); *In re* W.R. Huff Asset Management, 409 F.3d 555, 564 (2d Cir. 2005); United States v. Horsfall, 552 F.3d 1275 (11th Cir. 2008); United States v. Rubin, 558 F. Supp. 2d 411, 424 (E.D.N.Y. 2008); United States v. Blumhagen, No. 03-CR-56S, 2006 U.S. Dist. LEXIS 15380 (W.D.N.Y. Apr. 3, 2006).

92. *See* Kenna v. United States District Court, 435 F.3d 1011, 1013–17 (9th Cir. 2006); *see also* United States v. Degenhardt, 405 F. Supp. 2d 1341 (D. Utah 2005); *cf.* United States v. Sharp, 463 F. Supp. 2d 556 (E.D. Va. 2006); United States v. Marcello, 370 F. Supp. 2d 745 (N.D. Ill. 2005); United States v. Turner, 367 F. Supp. 2d 319, 333 (E.D.N.Y. 2005).

93. *See In re* Brock, 262 Fed. Appx. 510 (4th Cir. 2008) (per curiam) (unpublished opinion); Kenna v. United States District Court, 453 F.3d 1136 (9th Cir. 2006) (per curiam); *cf.* United States v. Ingrassia, Cr. 04-0455 (ADS) (JO), 2005 U.S. Dist. LEXIS 27817 (E.D.N.Y. Sept. 5, 2005).

94. *See* United States v. Hunter, 2008 U.S. App. LEXIS 24319 (10th Cir. 2008); *Brock*, 262 Fed. Appx. at 510.

95. *See generally* U.S. GOVERNMENT ACCOUNTABILITY OFFICE, *supra* note 33, at 119–31 (describing the federal cases decided pursuant to the Act reviewed through June 2008).

96. 409 F.3d 555 (2d Cir. 2005).

97. *See id.* at 562–63.

98. 435 F.3d 1011 (9th Cir. 2006).

99. *Id.* at 1017; *cf. In re* Walsh, 229 Fed. Appx. 58, 60 (3d Cir. 2007) (per curiam) (unpublished opinion) (referring to the "less demanding" mandamus standard under the Act and referencing *Kenna*).

100. 519 F. 3d 1123 (10th Cir. 2008).

101. *Id.* at 1130 (quoting Dalton v. United States, 733 F.2d 710, 716 (10th Cir. 1984)).

102. 527 F.3d 391, 393–94 (5th Cir. 2008).

103. *See In re* Brock, 262 Fed. Appx. 510 (4th Cir. 2008) (per curiam) (unpublished opinion); *In re* Jacobsen, No. 05-7086, 2005 U.S. App. LEXIS 13990 (D.C. Cir. July 8, 2005) (unpublished opinion).

104. *See* Crime Victims' Rights Act of 2004, Pub. L. No. 108-405, Title I, §§ 103–104, 118 Stat. 2260, 2264–65 (2004).

105. *See generally* U.S. GOVERNMENT ACCOUNTABILITY OFFICE, *supra* note 33.

106. *See id.* at 18–19; Executive Office for United States Attorneys, *supra* note 12.

107. *See* U.S. GOVERNMENT ACCOUNTABILITY OFFICE, *supra* note 33, at 36–39, 117–18.

108. *See id.* at 39–47, 90–93.

109. *See id.* at 55–60, 90–93.

110. *See id.* at 19, 47–48, 119–31.

111. *See id.* at 21–22, 52–54.

112. *See id.* at 48–50, 90–91.

113. *See supra* note 33.

114. *See* Kercher & Johnson, *supra* note 33, at 3. *See generally* EDWARDS ET AL., *supra* note 33.

115. *See* WISCONSIN CRIME VICTIMS RIGHTS BOARD, REPORT (2004). *But see* Schilling v. State of Wisconsin Crime Victims Rights Board, 692 N.W.2d 623, 624 (Wis. 2005); *supra* text accompanying note 57 (finding that the Board's private reprimand was not supported by the state constitutional rights provision).

116. *See* OFFICE FOR VICTIMS OF CRIME, *supra* note 33.

117. *See* D. VICTOR KESTER, OFFICE OF VICTIMS' RIGHTS ANNUAL REPORT (2008).

118. *See* KEVONNE SMALL ET AL., URBAN INSTITUTE, EVALUABILITY ASSESSMENT OF THE STATE AND FEDERAL CLINICS AND SYSTEM DEMONSTRATION PROJECT: FINAL REPORT (2006); Davis & Mulford, *supra* note 33, at 205–06; National Crime Victim Law Institute, http://www.ncvli.org (last visited Jan. 1, 2009).

119. *See* Crime Victims' Rights Act of 2004, Pub. L. No. 108-405, Title I, §§ 103–104, 118 Stat. 2260, 2264–65 (2004).

120. *See, e.g.,* John W. Gillis & Douglas E. Beloof, *The Next Step for a Maturing Victim Rights Movement: Enforcing Crime Victim Rights in the Courts*, 33 McGEORGE L. REV. 689 (2002).

121. *See* Douglas E. Beloof, *The Third Wave of Crime Victims' Rights: Standing, Remedy, and Review*, 2005 BYU L. REV. 255 (2005).

Notes for Chapter 8

1. *See* Ted. R. Miller et al., U.S. Dep't of Justice, Victim Costs and Consequences: A New Look 11 (1996).

2. *See id.* at 22–24; *see also* Susan Kiss Sarnoff, Paying for Crime: the Policies and Possibilities of Crime Victim Reimbursement 1–15 (1996); Mark A. Cohen & Ted R. Miller, *The Cost of Mental Health Care for Victims of Crime*, 13 J. Interpersonal Vio. 93 (1998); *Medical Costs of Crime*, 3 The Crime Victims Report 73 (1999).

3. *See* Miller et al., *supra* note 1, at 9.

4. *See id.* at 17; *see also* William G. Doerner & Steven P. Lab, Victimology 58–61 (5th ed. 2008).

5. *See* Richard M. Titus et al., *Victimization of Persons by Fraud*, 41 Crime & Delinq. 54, 58–59 (1995).

6. *See* Miller et al., *supra* note 1, at 19, 21.

7. *See, e.g.*, Marlene A. Young, *Victim Rights and Services: A Modern Saga*, *in* Victims of Crime 194 (Robert C. Davis et al. eds., 2d ed. 1997).

8. *See generally* Juan Cardenas, *The Crime Victim in the Prosecutorial Process*, 9 Harv. J. L. & Pub. Pol'y 357, 366–72 (1986); William F. McDonald, *Towards a Bicentennial Revolution in Criminal Justice: The Return of the Victim*, 13 Am. Crim. L. Rev. 649, 651–68 (1976).

9. *See* Stephen Schafer, Compensation and Restitution to Victims of Crime 9–11 (2d ed. 1970).

10. *See, e.g.*, Alan T. Harland, *Monetary Remedies for the Victims of Crime: Assessing the Role of the Criminal Courts*, 30 UCLA L. Rev. 52, 57 (1982).

11. *See* Alan T. Harland, *One Hundred Years of Restitution: An International Review and Prospectus for Research*, 8(1–2) Victimology 190, 192 (1983); Joe Hudson et al., *When Criminals Repay Their Victims: A Survey of Restitution Programs*, 60 Judicature 312, 313 (1977); Arthur J. Lurigio & Robert C. Davis, *Does a Threatening Letter Increase Compliance with Restitution Orders?: A Field Experiment*, 36 Crime & Delinq. 537, 538 (1990).

12. *See* Office of Justice Programs, U.S. Dep't of Justice, Four Years Later: A Report on the President's Task Force on Victims of Crime 4 (1986); *cf.* Steve Chesney et al., *A New Look at Restitution: Recent Legislation, Programs and Research*, 61 Judicature 348 (1978); Hudson et al., *supra* note 11, at 312.

13. *See* 18 U.S.C.A. §§ 3579–3580 (West 1985) (current version at 18 U.S.C.A. §§ 3663–3664 (West 2000 & Supp. 2009)); S. Rep. No. 97-532, at 9–10, 30–33 (1982); Peggy M. Tobolowsky, *Restitution in the Federal Criminal Justice System*, 77 Judicature 90 (1993).

14. *See* 18 U.S.C.A. § 3580(b) (West 1985) (current version at 18 U.S.C.A. § 3664 (West 2000 & Supp. 2009)); Fed. R. Crim. P. 32; S. Rep. No. 97-532, at 11–14 (1982).

15. *See* 18 U.S.C.A. §§ 3579–3580 (West 1985) (current version at 18 U.S.C.A. §§ 3663–3664 (West 2000 & Supp. 2009)); Tobolowsky, *supra* note 13, at 91–93.

16. *See* S. Rep. No. 97-532, at 30–31 (1982).

17. President's Task Force on Victims of Crime, Final Report 18 (1982).

18. *See id.* at 66, 78–79.

19. *Id.* at 79–80 (footnote omitted).

20. *See* Office for Victims of Crime, U.S. Dep't of Justice, Ordering Restitution to the Crime Victim (2002); Peggy M. Tobolowsky, *Crime Victim Restitution: Its Past, Present, and Future*, 36 Crim. L. Bull. 85 (2000). *See generally* National Center for Victims

of Crime, VictimLaw, http://www.victimlaw.info/victimlaw/ (last visited Jan. 1, 2009); National Conference of State Legislatures, Victims' Rights Laws in the States, http://www.ncsl.org (last visited Jan. 1, 2009).

21. *See* Office for Victims of Crime, U.S. Dep't of Justice, New Directions from the Field: Victims' Rights and Services for the 21st Century 19–20, 112–13, 136–37, 355–71 (1998).

22. *See* S.J. Res. 1, 108th Cong. (2003); H.R.J. Res. 48, 108th Cong. (2003); H.R.J. Res. 10, 108th Cong. (2003).

23. *See* Tobolowsky, *supra* note 13, at 92–93. *See generally* Tobolowsky, *supra* note 20.

24. *See* 18 U.S.C.A. §§ 3563(a), 3663A (West 2000 & Supp. 2009); *cf.* 18 U.S.C.A. § 16 (West 2000). *See generally* S. Rep. No. 104-179 (1995).

25. *See* 18 U.S.C.A. § 3663A (West 2000& Supp. 2009).

26. *See* 18 U.S.C.A. § 3663 (West 2000 & Supp. 2009); *see also* 18 U.S.C.A. § 3563(b) (West 2000 & Supp. 2009).

27. 18 U.S.C.A. § 3664 (West 2000 & Supp. 2009).

28. *See id.*

29. *See id.*

30. *See* 18 U.S.C.A. §§ 3612–3615, 3664 (West 2000 & Supp. 2009).

31. *See* 18 U.S.C.A. § 3771 (West Supp. 2009); see also Fed. R. Crim. P. 32.

32. *See* Alaska Const. art. I, §§ 12, 24; Ariz. Const. art. 2, § 2.1; Cal. Const. art. 1, § 28; Conn. Const. art. I, § 8; Idaho Const. art. I, § 22; Ill. Const. art. 1, § 8.1; La. Const. art. 1, § 25; Mich. Const. art. 1, § 24; Mo. Const. art. 1, § 32; N.M. Const. art. II, § 24; N.C. Const. art. I, § 37; Okla. Const. art. 2, § 34; Or. Const. art. I, § 42; R.I. Const. art. 1, § 23; S.C. Const. art. I, § 24; Tenn. Const. art. I, § 35; Tex. Const. art. 1, § 30; Va. Const. art. I, § 8-A; Wis. Const. art. 1, § 9m; *cf.* Mont. Const. art. II, § 28.

33. *See generally* Daniel McGillis, U.S. Dep't of Justice, Crime Victim Restitution: An Analysis of Approaches (1986); National Center for Victims of Crime, *supra* note 20; National Conference of State Legislatures, *supra* note 20.

34. *See, e.g.,* Colo. Rev. Stat. Ann. § 24-4.1-302.5 (West 2008); N.H. Rev. Stat. Ann. § 21-M:8-k (LexisNexis 2008); N.M. Stat. Ann. § 31-26-4 (Lexis Nexis 2000); S.D. Codified Laws § 23A-28C-1 (2004).

35. *See generally* National Center for Victims of Crime, *supra* note 20; National Conference of State Legislatures, *supra* note 20; Sarnoff, *supra* note 2, at 19; Barbara E. Smith & Susan W. Hillenbrand, *Making Victims Whole Again: Restitution, Victim-Offender Reconciliation Programs, and Compensation, in* Victims of Crime, *supra* note 7, at 245.

36. *See* National Center for Victims of Crime, *supra* note 20; National Conference of State Legislatures, *supra* note 20.

37. *See* Ariz. Rev. Stat. Ann. §§ 13-105, -603, -804 (2001 & Supp. 2008); *see also* Okla. Stat. Ann. tit. 22, § 991f (West 2003).

38. *See, e.g.,* Ala. Code §§ 15-18-65 to -68 (LexisNexis 1995); Fla. Stat. Ann § 775.089 (West 2005); Idaho Code Ann. § 19-5304 (Supp. 2008); Iowa Code Ann. §§ 910.1–.3 (West 2003 & Supp. 2008); Wash. Rev. Code Ann. § 9.94A.753 (West Supp. 2008); W. Va. Code Ann. § 61-11A-4 (LexisNexis Supp. 2008); Wyo. Stat. Ann. § 7-9-102 (2007).

39. *See, e.g.,* Ind. Code Ann. § 35-50-5-3 (LexisNexis Pamp. 2007); Ohio Rev. Code Ann. §§ 2929.18 (LexisNexis Supp. 2009); Neb. Rev. Stat. § 29-2280 (1995); Tenn. Code Ann. § 40-35-304 (2006).

40. *See* ALA. CODE § 15-18-66 (LexisNexis 1995); *see also* FLA. STAT. ANN. § 775.089 (West 2005).

41. *See, e.g.,* IND. CODE ANN. § 35-50-5-3 (LexisNexis Pamp. 2007); MINN. STAT. ANN. § 611A.01 (West Supp. 2008).

42. *See, e.g.,* IDAHO CODE ANN. § 19-5304 (Supp. 2008).

43. *See, e.g.,* IDAHO CODE ANN. § 19-5304 (Supp. 2008); IOWA CODE ANN. § 910.1 (West Supp. 2008); 18 PA. CONS. STAT. ANN. § 1106 (West Supp. 2008).

44. *See generally* National Center for Victims of Crime, *supra* note 20; National Conference of State Legislatures, *supra* note 20.

45. *See, e.g.,* 18 PA. CONS. STAT. ANN. § 1106 (West Supp. 2008).

46. WYO. STAT. ANN. § 7-9-101 (2007); *see also* ALA. CODE § 15-18-66 (LexisNexis 1995).

47. FLA. STAT. ANN. § 775.089 (West 2005).

48. *See* ARK. CODE ANN. § 5-4-205 (2006); *see also* COLO. REV. STAT. ANN. § 24-4.1-302.5 (West 2008).

49. *See* OKLA. STAT. ANN. tit. 22, § 991f (West 2003).

50. *See* IND. CODE ANN. § 35-50-5-3 (LexisNexis Pamp. 2007); TEX. CODE CRIM. PROC. ANN. art. 42.037 (Vernon Supp. 2008).

51. *See* IDAHO CODE § 19-5304 (Supp. 2008); *see also* WASH. REV. CODE ANN. § 9.94A.753 (West Supp. 2008).

52. IOWA CODE ANN. § 910.1 (West Supp. 2008); *see also* WYO. STAT. ANN. § 7-9-101 (2007).

53. *See generally* McGILLIS, *supra* note 33; Harland, *supra* note 10.

54. *See* Smith & Hillenbrand, *supra* note 35, at 249.

55. *See, e.g.,* ALA. CODE § 15-18-68 (LexisNexis 1995); W. VA. CODE ANN. § 61-11A-5 (LexisNexis 2005).

56. *See, e.g.,* FLA. STAT. ANN. § 775.089 (West 2005); MINN. STAT. ANN. § 611A.045 (West 2003); TEX. CODE CRIM. PROC. ANN. art. 42.037 (Vernon Supp. 2008).

57. *See, e.g.,* TEX. CODE CRIM. PROC. ANN. art. 42.037 (Vernon Supp. 2008). *See generally* OFFICE FOR VICTIMS OF CRIME, U.S. DEP'T OF JUSTICE, RESTITUTION: MAKING IT WORK (2002).

58. *See, e.g.,* ARIZ. REV. STAT. ANN. § 13-804 (2001); S.D. CODIFIED LAWS § 23A-27-25.1 (2004).

59. *See, e.g.,* ALA. CODE §§ 15-18-71 to -72 (LexisNexis 1995).

60. *See, e.g.,* ARIZ. REV. STAT. ANN. §§ 13-4436, -4437 (Supp. 2007).

61. *See* MD. CODE ANN., CRIM. PROC. § 11-103 (LexisNexis Supp. 2007).

62. WYO. STAT. ANN. § 7-9-111 (2007).

63. *See* Diane M. Allen, Annotation, *Restitutional Sentencing Under Victim and Witness Protection Act § 5 (18 USCS §§ 3579, 3580),* 79 A.L.R. Fed. 724 (1986); *see also* Fern L. Kletter, Annotation, *Mandatory Victims Restitution Act Constitutional Issues,* 20 A.L.R. Fed. 2d 239 (2007); *cf.* Irene J. Chase, Comment, *Making the Criminal Pay in Cash: The Ex Post Facto Implications of the Mandatory Victims Restitution Act of 1996,* 68 U. CHI. L. REV. 463 (2001).

64. *See, e.g.,* United States v. Palma, 760 F.2d 475, 479–80 (3d Cir. 1985); United States v. Brown, 744 F.2d 905, 908–11 (2d Cir. 1984); United States v. Satterfield, 743 F.2d 827, 836–39 (11th Cir. 1984); *cf.* United States v. Dubose, 146 F.3d 1141 (9th Cir.1998); Kelly v. Robinson, 479 U.S. 36, 52–53 (1986). *See generally* Allen, *supra* note 63, at 740–42. *But see generally* Margaret Raymond, Note, *The Unconstitutionality of the Victim and Witness Protection Act under the Seventh Amendment,* 84 COLUM. L. REV. 1590 (1984); Bonnie Arnett Von Roeder, Note, *The Right to a Jury Trial to Determine Restitution Under the Victim and Witness Protection Act of 1982,* 63 TEX. L. REV. 671 (1984).

65. 530 U.S. 466 (2000).

66. *See, e.g.,* United States v. Dupes, 513 F.3d 338 (2d Cir. 2008); United States v. Milkiewicz, 470 F.3d 390 (1st Cir. 2006); United States v. Beydoun, 469 F.3d 102 (5th Cir. 2006); United States v. Leahy, 438 F.3d 328 (3d Cir. 2006); United States v. Carruth, 418 F.3d 900 (8th Cir. 2005); *cf.* United States v. Bonner, 522 F.3d 804 (7th Cir. 2008).

67. *See, e.g., Palma,* 760 F.2d at 477; *Satterfield,* 743 F.2d at 839–841; *see also* United States v. Sunrhodes, 831 F.2d 1537, 1541–1542 (10th Cir. 1987); *cf. Dubose,* 146 F.3d at 1141.

68. *See, e.g., Palma,* 760 F.2d at 478; *Satterfield,* 743 F.2d at 841–42 (citing Williams v. Illinois, 399 U.S. 235 (1970)); *cf.* Tobolowsky, *supra* note 20, at 92–93 n.35.

69. *See, e.g.,* United States v. Sablan, 92 F.3d 865, 871 (9th Cir. 1996); *Palma,* 760 F.2d at 478–79; United States v. Keith, 754 F.2d 1388, 1393 (9th Cir.1985); *Brown,* 744 F.2d at 911; *Satterfield,* 743 F.2d at 842–43; *cf. Dubose,* 146 F.3d at 1141; Tobolowsky, *supra* note 20, at 92–93 n.35. *But see, e.g.,* United States v. Bailey, 975 F.2d 1028 (4th Cir. 1992). *See generally* Recent Decisions, *The Constitutionality of the Victim and Witness Protection Act of 1982,* 35 ALA. L. REV. 529, 543–49 (1984).

70. 461 U.S. 660 (1983).

71. *See id.* at 661–74.

72. *See* 18 U.S.C.A. §3579 (West 1985) (as amended 18 U.S.C.A. §3613A (West 2000 & Supp. 2009)).

73. *See* 18 U.S.C.A. §3614 (West 2000 & Supp. 2009).

74. *See* 18 U.S.C.A. §3579 (West 1985) (current version at 18 U.S.C.A. §3663 (West 2000 & Supp. 2009)).

75. *Compare, e.g.,* United States v. Duncan, 870 F.2d 1532, 1537 (10th Cir. 1989) *with, e.g.,* United States v. Barnette, 800 F.2d 1558, 1571 (11th Cir. 1986). *See* Lawrence P. Fletcher, Note, *Restitution in the Criminal Process: Procedures for Fixing the Offender's Liability,* 93 YALE L.J. 505, 507–16 (1984); Laura Munster Sever, Note, *The Victim and Witness Protection Act of 1982: Who Are the Victims of Which Offenses?* 20 VAL. U. L. REV. 109, 126–32 (1985); John F. Wagner Jr., Annotation, *Who Is "Victim," So As to be Entitled to Restitution under Victim and Witness Protection Act (18 USCS §§3663, 3664),* 108 A.L.R. FED. 828, 835–837 (1992).

76. Hughey v. United States, 495 U.S. 411, 413 (1990).

77. *See* 18 U.S.C.A. §§3663, 3663A (West 2000 & Supp. 2009); *cf., e.g.,* United States v. Adams, 363 F.3d 363 (5th Cir. 2004) (limiting restitution to offenses contained in plea agreement).

78. *See* United States v. Haggard, 41 F.3d 1320 (9th Cir. 1994); United States v. Allison, 599 F. Supp. 958 (N.D. Ala. 1985). *But see* United States v. Davenport, 445 F.3d 366 (4th Cir. 2006); United States v. Reed, 80 F.3d 1419 (9th Cir. 1996). *See generally* Beth Bates Holliday, Annotation, *Who Is a "Victim" Entitled to Restitution under the Mandatory Victims Restitution Act of 1996 (18 U.S.C.A. §3663A),* 26 A.L.R. Fed. 2d 283 (2008); Wagner, *supra* note 75; Allen, *supra* note 63.

79. *See* United States v. Washington, 434 F.3d 1265 (11th Cir. 2006); United States v. Vaknin, 112 F.3d 579 (1st Cir. 1997); United States v. Hensley, 91 F.3d 274 (1st Cir. 1996); *cf., e.g.,* United States v. Jackson, 982 F.2d 1279 (9th Cir. 1992); United States v. Farkas, 935 F.2d 962 (8th Cir. 1991). *But cf., e.g.,* United States v. Robertson, 493 F.3d 1322 (11th Cir. 2007); United States v. Dailey, 189 Fed. Appx. 212 (4th Cir. 2006); Gall v. United States, 21 F.3d 107 (6th Cir. 1994).

80. *See, e.g.,* United States v. Twitty, 107 F.3d 1482 (11th Cir. 1997); United States v. Blocker, 104 F.3d 720 (5th Cir. 1997).

81. *See, e.g.*, United States v. Pizzichiello, 272 F.3d 1232 (9th Cir. 2001); United States v. Patty, 992 F.2d 1045 (10th Cir. 1993); United States v. Rochester, 898 F.2d 971 (5th Cir. 1990).

82. *Compare* United States v. Amato, 540 F.3d 153 (2d Cir. 2008), United States v. DeRosier, 501 F.3d 888 (8th Cir. 2007), United States v. Scott, 405 F.3d 615 (7th Cir. 2005), *and* United States v. Bogart, 490 F. Supp. 2d 885 (S.D. Ohio 2007), *with* United States v. Schinnell, 80 F.3d 1064 (5th Cir. 1996), Government of the Virgin Islands v. Davis, 43 F.3d 41 (3rd Cir. 1994), United States v. Mullins, 971 F.2d 1138 (4th Cir. 1992), *and* United States v. Saad, 554 F. Supp. 2d 589 (E.D. Mich. 2008).

83. United States v. Grundhoefer, 916 F.2d 788, 791 (2d Cir. 1990); *see* United States v. Mindel, 80 F.3d 394 (9th Cir. 1996); United States v. Kelley, 997 F.2d 806 (10th Cir. 1993); United States v. Johnson, 983 F.2d 216 (11th Cir. 1993).

84. *See Mindel*, 80 F.3d at 398.

85. *Id.* at 397–98

86. *See* United States v. Perry, 360 F.3d 519 (6th Cir. 2004).

87. *See In re* Oak Brook Bank, No. 06-2331 (7th Cir. May 12, 2006).

88. *See In re* W.R. Huff Asset Management, 409 F.3d 555 (2d Cir. 2005); *see also* United States v. Purdue Frederick, 495 F. Supp. 2d 569 (W.D. Va. 2007).

89. *See In re* Butler, No. 06-20848 (5th Cir. Nov. 1, 2006); United States v. Lay, 456 F. Supp. 2d 869 (S.D. Tex. 2006).

90. *See, e.g.*, People v. Moser, 57 Cal. Rptr. 2d 647 (Cal. Ct. App. 1996); State v. Blakley, 534 N.W.2d 645, 648 (Iowa 1995).

91. *See, e.g.*, State v. Ihde, 532 N.W.2d 827, 829 (Iowa Ct. App. 1995); Monson v. Carver, 928 P.2d 1017, 1026–28 (Utah 1996).

92. *See, e.g.*, Rice v. State, 491 So. 2d 1049, 1052–53 (Ala. Crim. App. 1986); Cannon v. State, 272 S.E.2d 709, 710 (Ga. 1980).

93. *See, e.g.*, Hill v. Bradford, 565 So. 2d 208, 210 (Ala. 1990); Henry v. State, 468 So. 2d 896, 901–02 (Ala. Crim. App. 1984); State v. Steffy, 839 P.2d 1135 (Ariz. Ct. App. 1992); *cf.* State v. Alspach, 554 N.W.2d 882 (Iowa 1996); Walters v. Grossheim, 554 N.W.2d 530 (Iowa 1996).

94. *See, e.g.*, State v. Klawonn, 609 N.W.2d 515 (Iowa 2000); Wiggins v. State, 513 So. 2d 73, 79 (Ala. Crim. App. 1987).

95. *See, e.g.*, Hodges v. State, 158 P.3d 864 (Alaska Ct. App. 2007); State v. Stafford, 93 P.3d 572 (Colo. Ct. App. 2004); State v. Bybee, 768 P.2d 804 (Idaho Ct. App. 1989); State v. Tupa, 691 N.W.2d 579 (N.D. 2005); *cf.* People v. Frye, 27 Cal. Rptr. 2d 52 (Cal. Ct. App. 1994); State v. Edson, 985 P.2d 1253 (Or. 1999). *But cf.* State v. Martin, 79 P.3d 686 (Haw. Ct. App. 2003); Laker v. State, 869 N.E.2d 1216 (Ind. Ct. App. 2007).

96. *See, e.g.*, Seaton v. State, 811 P.2d 276 (Wyo. 1991).

97. *See, e.g.*, Jordan v. State, 939 S.W.2d 255 (Ark. 1997); *see also* Ariz. Rev. Stat. Ann. § 13-810 (Supp. 2008); *cf.* Fla. Stat. Ann. § 775.089 (West 2005); Tex. Code Crim. Proc. Ann. art. 42.037 (Vernon Supp. 2008); W. Va. Code § 61-11A-4 (LexisNexis 2005). *But see* State v. Nordahl, 680 N.W.2d 247 (N.D. 2004).

98. *See* Harland, *supra* note 10, at 78–89. *See generally* George Blum, Annotation, *Measure and Elements of Restitution to which Victim is Entitled under State Criminal Statute*, 15 A.L.R. 5th 391 (1993); Kimberly J. Winbush, Annotation, *Persons or Entities Entitled to Restitution as "Victim" under State Criminal Restitution Statute*, 92 A.L.R. 5th 35 (2001).

99. *See, e.g.*, State v. Clinton, 890 P.2d 74 (Ariz. Ct. App. 1995); Bell v. State, 652 So. 2d 1192 (Fla. Dist. Ct. App. 1995).

100. *See, e.g.*, Ellis v. State, 641 So. 2d 333 (Ala. Crim. App. 1994). *But see, e.g.*, State v. Gribble, 636 N.W.2d 488 (Wis. Ct. App. 2001).

101. *See, e.g.*, State v. Adams, 941 P.2d 908 (Ariz. Ct. App. 1997); People v. Littlejohn, 403 N.W.2d 215 (Mich. Ct. App. 1987); State v. Campbell, 620 N.E.2d 150 (Ohio Ct. App. 1993).

102. *See, e.g.*, People v. Cruz, 615 N.E.2d 1017 (N.Y. 1993); Commonwealth v. Pozza, 750 A.2d 889 (Pa. Super. Ct. 2000); LaFleur v. State, 848 S.W.2d 266 (Tex. App. 1993); State v. Baker, 626 N.W.2d 862 (Wis. Ct. App. 2001). *But see, e.g.*, People v. Martinez, 115 P.3d 62 (Cal. 2005); State v. Haase, 716 N.W.2d 526 (Wis. Ct. App. 2006).

103. *See, e.g.*, Nix v. State, 925 S.W.2d 802 (Ark. Ct. App. 1996) (en banc); State v. Lewis, 917 S.W.2d 251 (Tenn. Crim. App. 1995).

104. *Compare, e.g.*, Roberts v. People, 130 P.3d 1005 (Colo. 2007), Hearn v. Commonwealth, 80 S.W.3d 432 (Ky. 2002), Commonwealth v. McIntyre, 767 N.E.2d 578 (Mass. 2002), State v. Palubicki, 727 N.W.2d 662 (Minn. 2007), State v. Johnson, 704 N.W.2d 625 (Wis. Ct. App. 2005), *with, e.g.*, State v. Foy, 859 P.2d 789 (Ariz. Ct. App. 1993), Myers v. State, 629 So. 2d 279 (Fla. Dist. Ct. App. 1993), State v. Newman, 623 A.2d 1355 (N.J. 1993), State v. Hefa, 871 P.2d 1093 (Wash. Ct. App. 1994).

105. *See, e.g.*, Franks v. State, 644 So. 2d 1277 (Ala. Crim. App. 1993); Commonwealth v. Cannon, 563 A.2d 918 (Pa. Super. Ct. 1989). *But see, e.g.*, C.W. v. State, 655 So. 2d 87 (Fla. 1995). *See generally* Bradford C. Mank, *The Scope of Criminal Restitution: Awarding Unliquidated Damages in Sentencing Hearings*, 17 Cap. U. L. Rev. 55 (1987).

106. *See, e.g.*, Cooper v. District Court, 133 P.3d 692 (Alaska Ct. App. 2006); State v. Lamberton, 899 P.2d 939 (Ariz. 1995) (en banc); Schroering v. McKinney, 906 S.W.2d 349 (Ky. 1995).

107. Melissa J. v. Superior Court *ex rel.* Williams, 237 Cal. Rptr. 5, 6–7 (Cal. Ct. App. 1987).

108. Ford v. State, 829 So. 2d 946 (Fla. Ct. App. 2002).

109. *See* State v. Korsen, 111 P.3d 130 (Idaho 2005); *cf.* Surland v. State, 895 A.2d 1034 (Md. 2006); State v. Devin, 142 P.3d 599 (Wash. 2006). *See generally* Timothy A. Razel, Note, *Dying to Get Away With It: How the Abatement Doctrine Thwarts Justice And What Should be Done Instead*, 75 Fordham L. Rev. 2193 (2007); Joseph Sauder, Comment, *How a Criminal Defendant's Death Pending Direct Appeal Affects the Victim's Right to Restitution under the Abatement Ab Initio Doctrine*, 71 Temp. L. Rev. 347 (1998).

110. *But cf.* Md. Code Ann., Crim. Proc. § 11-103 (LexisNexis Supp. 2007) (authorizing a violent crime victim to appeal from an interlocutory or final order that denies or fails to consider a victim's right to restitution).

111. *See, e.g.*, Office for Victims of Crime, *supra* note 21, 355–71; Paul S. Hudson, *The Crime Victim and the Criminal Justice System: Time for a Change*, 11 Pepp. L. Rev. 23, 45–47 (1984); Young, *supra* note 7.

112. *See, e.g.*, Schafer, *supra* note 9, at 117–22; Richard C. Boldt, *Restitution, Criminal Law, and the Ideology of Individuality*, 77 J. Crim. L. & Criminology 969, 974–75 (1986); Richard E. Laster, *Criminal Restitution: A Survey of Its Past History and An Analysis of Its Present Usefulness*, 5 U. Rich. L. Rev. 71, 80–83, 97–98 (1970); *cf.* Leslie Sebba, Third Parties: Victims and the Criminal Justice System 168–91 (1996).

113. *See, e.g.*, Elizabeth Q. DeValve et al., Crime Victims' Institute, Understanding the Experiences and Needs of Crime Victims (2005); Schafer, *supra* note 9, at 123–29; Boldt, *supra* note 112, at 975–77; Joe Hudson & Burt Galaway, *Restitution Program Models with Adult Offenders, in* Criminal Justice, Restitution, and Reconcilia-

TION 165, 174 (Burt Galaway & Joe Hudson eds., 1990); Sara Manaugh, *The Vengeful Logic of Modern Criminal Restitution*, 1 LAW, CULTURE & HUMAN. 359 (2005); Note, *Victim Restitution in the Criminal Process: A Procedural Analysis*, 97 HARV. L. REV. 931, 937–41 (1984).

114. *See* MCGILLIS, *supra* note 33, at 43–60; Hudson & Galaway, *supra* note 113, at 171–72.

115. *See, e.g.*, Harland, *supra* note 11, at 195–96; Hudson & Gallaway, *supra* note 113, at 172, 175; *cf.* R. Barry Ruback & Mark H. Bergstrom, *Economic Sanctions in Criminal Justice: Purposes, Effects, and Implications*, 33 CRIM. J. & BEHAV. 242 (2006). *See generally* DOERNER & LAB, *supra* note 4, at 84–91.

116. *See* MILLER ET AL., *supra* note 1, at 17.

117. *See generally* SARNOFF, *supra* note 2.

118. *See* Harland, *supra* note 10, at 64; Laster, *supra* note 112, at 83–84.

119. MICHAEL R. RAND, U.S. DEP'T OF JUSTICE, CRIMINAL VICTIMIZATION, 2008, at 6 (2009).

120. FEDERAL BUREAU OF INVESTIGATION, U.S. DEP'T OF JUSTICE, CRIME IN THE UNITED STATES, 2008 (2009), *available at* http://www.fbi.gov/ucr/cius2008/offenses/clearances/index.html.

121. *Id.*, *available at* http://www.fbi.gov/ucr/cius2008/arrests/index.html.

122. *See* SAMUEL WALKER, SENSE AND NONSENSE ABOUT CRIME AND DRUGS: A POLICY GUIDE 49 (6th ed. 2006).

123. *See, e.g.*, Harland, *supra* note 10, at 64–65, 68; Laster, *supra* note 112, at 84–86.

124. *See* Chesney at al., *supra* note 12, at 355–56; Alan T. Harland & Cathryn J. Rosen, *Impediments to the Recovery of Restitution by Crime Victims*, 5 VIOLENCE AND VICTIMS 127, 128–29 (1990); Smith & Hillenbrand, *supra* note 35, at 249; Tobolowsky, *supra* note 20, at 103 n.71.

125. *See* MATTHEW R. DUROSE & PATRICK A. LANGAN, U.S. DEP'T OF JUSTICE, FELONY SENTENCES IN STATE COURTS, 2002, at 1, 10 (2004); Tobolowsky, *supra* note 20, at 103 n.73.

126. *See* DUROSE & LANGAN, *supra* note 125, at 10; PATRICK A. LANGAN & JODI M. BROWN, U.S. DEP'T OF JUSTICE, FELONY SENTENCES IN STATE COURTS, 1994, at 10 (1997); PATRICK A. LANGAN & JOHN M. DAWSON, U.S. DEP'T OF JUSTICE, FELONY SENTENCES IN STATE COURTS, 1988, at 7 (1990).

127. *See* DUROSE & LANGAN, *supra* note 125, at 10.

128. *See, e.g.*, U.S. SENTENCING COMM'N, 2008 SOURCEBOOK OF FEDERAL SENTENCING STATISTICS tbl. 15 (2009); U.S. SENTENCING COMM'N, ANNUAL REPORT 1988, at 35 (1989).

129. *See* U.S. SENTENCING COMM'N, ANNUAL REPORT 1988, *supra* note 128, at 35.

130. *See* U.S. SENTENCING COMM'N, 2008 SOURCEBOOK OF FEDERAL SENTENCING STATISTICS, *supra* note 128, at tbl. 15; U.S. SENTENCING COMM'N, ANNUAL REPORT 1995, at 65 tbl. 20 (1996).

131. *See* U.S. SENTENCING COMM'N, 2008 SOURCEBOOK OF FEDERAL SENTENCING STATISTICS, *supra* note 128, at tbl. 15.

132. *Cf.* 18 U.S.C.A. § 3663A (West 2000 & Supp. 2008).

133. *See* DAVID BEATTY ET AL., NATIONAL VICTIM CENTER, STATUTORY AND CONSTITUTIONAL PROTECTION OF VICTIMS' RIGHTS: IMPLEMENTATION AND IMPACT ON CRIME VICTIMS 9–30, 39 (1996); *see also* DEAN G. KILPATRICK ET AL., U.S. DEP'T OF JUSTICE, THE RIGHTS OF CRIME VICTIMS—DOES LEGAL PROTECTION MAKE A DIFFERENCE? (1998); *cf.* Maureen C. Outlaw & R. Barry Ruback, *Predictors and Outcomes of Victim Restitution Orders*, 16 JUST. Q. 847, 856 (1999).

134. *See* BEATTY ET AL., *supra* note 133, at 94.

135. *See, e.g.*, Outlaw & Ruback, *supra* note 133, at 857.

136. *See* BEATTY ET AL., *supra* note 133, at 95–96, 137–39.

137. *See* Harland & Rosen, *supra* note 124.

138. *See* R. Barry Ruback et al., *Assessing the Impact of Statutory Change: A Statewide Multilevel Analysis of Restitution Orders in Pennsylvania*, 51 CRIME & DELINQ. 318 (2005); R. Barry Ruback & Jennifer N. Shaffer, *The Role of Victim-Related Factors in Victim Restitution: A Multi-Method Analysis of Restitution in Pennsylvania*, 29 LAW & HUMAN BEHAV. 657 (2005); *cf.* Olga Tsoudis, *The Likelihood of Victim Restitution in Mock Cases: Are the "Rules of the Game" Different from Prison and Probation?*, 28 SOC. BEHAV. & PERSONALITY 481 (2000). *See generally* Ruback & Bergstrom, *supra* note 115, at 251–53.

139. *See generally* National Center for Victims of Crime, *supra* note 20; National Conference of State Legislatures, *supra* note 20.

140. *See* S. REP. NO. 104–179, at 18 (1995).

141. *See* Burt Galaway, *Is Restitution Practical?*, FED. PROBATION, Sept. 1977, at 3, 3–5; Harland & Rosen, *supra* note 125.

142. *See* OFFICE FOR VICTIMS OF CRIME, *supra* note 21, at 357.

143. *See* MCGILLIS, *supra* note 33, at 44–45.

144. *See* Robert C. Davis et al., *Increasing Offender Compliance with Restitution Orders*, 74 JUDICATURE 245, 246 (1991).

145. *See* MCGILLIS, *supra* note 33, at 45–48.

146. *See* Davis et al., *supra* note 144, at 246.

147. *See* BEATTY ET AL., *supra* note 133, at 95–96, 137–39; *cf.* G. Frederick Allen & Harvey Treger, *Fines and Restitution Orders: Probationers' Perceptions*, FED. PROBATION, June 1994, at 34, 37; Lurigio & Davis, *supra* note 11, at 539; Outlaw & Ruback, *supra* note 133, at 856.

148. *See* U.S. GOVERNMENT ACCOUNTABILITY OFFICE, CRIMINAL DEBT: ACTIONS STILL NEEDED TO ADDRESS DEFICIENCIES IN JUSTICE'S COLLECTION PROCESSES 2–3 (2004); U.S. GOVERNMENT ACCOUNTABILITY OFFICE, CRIMINAL DEBT: OVERSIGHT AND ACTIONS NEEDED TO ADDRESS DEFICIENCIES IN COLLECTION PROCESSES (2001).

149. *See, e.g.*, OFFICE FOR VICTIMS OF CRIME, *supra* note 21, at 357–58; U.S. GOVERNMENT ACCOUNTABILITY OFFICE (2004 study), *supra* note 148; Allen & Treger, *supra* note 147, at 38–40; Davis et al., *supra* note 144, at 246; Harland & Rosen, *supra* note 124, at 135.

150. *See* OFFICE FOR VICTIMS OF CRIME, *supra* note 21, at 358–63; Linda F. Frank, *The Collection of Restitution: An Often Overlooked Service to Crime Victims*, 8 ST. JOHN'S J. LEGAL COMMENT. 107 (1992); Francis W. Maiolino et al., *Computer-Supported Restitution Programming in County Probation and Parole, in* CRIMINAL JUSTICE, RESTITUTION, AND RECONCILIATION, *supra* note 113, at 155.

151. *See* Davis et al., *supra* note 144, at 247.

152. *See* Allen & Treger, *supra* note 147, at 36–39; *cf.* OFFICE FOR VICTIMS OF CRIME, *supra* note 21, at 358; Joe Hudson et al., *When Criminals Repay Their Victims: A Survey of Restitution Programs*, 60 JUDICATURE 312, 318 (1977); Maiolino et al., *supra* note 150, at 158.

153. *See* Allen & Treger, *supra* note 147, at 37–38.

154. *See* Lurigio & Davis, *supra* note 11, at 541–44.

155. *See* Robert C. Davis & Tanya M. Bannister, *Improving Collection of Court-Ordered Restitution*, 79 JUDICATURE 30, 31–32 (1995).

156. *See* Lurigio & Davis, *supra* note 11, at 543 (describing earlier study by Lurigio).

157. *See id.* at 544.

158. *See* Davis et al., *supra* note 144, at 246–47.

159. *See* Outlaw & Ruback, *supra* note 133, at 857–59.

160. *See* Jeff Latimer et al., *The Effectiveness of Restorative Justice Practices: A Meta-Analysis*, 85 Prison J. 127, 137 (2005).

161. *See* Davis et al., *supra* note 144, at 248; Lurigio & Davis, *supra* note 11, at 544–46.

162. *See* Edna Erez & Pamela Tontodonato, *Victim Participation in Sentencing and Satisfaction with Justice*, 9 Just. Q. 393, 404–13 (1992). Pamela Tontodonato & Edna Erez, *Crime, Punishment, and Victim Distress*, 3 Int'l Rev. Victimology 33, 37–38, 50–51 (1994).

163. *See* McGillis, *supra* note 33, at 48–49 (describing study by Joe Hudson et al.); *cf.* Robert C. Davis et al., *Expanding the Victim's Role in the Criminal Court Dispositional Process: The Results of an Experiment*, 75 J. Crim. L. & Criminology 491, 493 n.8 (1984).

164. *See* McGillis, *supra* note 33, at 47–48; *cf.* Dean G. Kilpatrick & Randy K. Otto, *Constitutionally Guaranteed Participation in Criminal Justice Proceedings for Victims: Potential Effects on Psychological Functioning*, 34 Wayne L. Rev. 7 (1987); Peggy M. Tobolowsky, *Victim Participation in the Criminal Justice Process: Fifteen Years after the President's Task Force on Victims of Crime*, 25 New Eng. J. On Crim. & Civ. Confinement 21, 84–90 (1999).

165. *See* McGillis, *supra* note 33, at 48 (describing Hudson et al. study).

166. *See* Robert C. Davis et al., *Restitution: The Victim's Viewpoint*, 15 Just. Sys. J. 746, 750–53 (1992).

167. *See id.* at 753–56.

168. *See id.* at 753–55.

169. *See* Davis & Bannister, *supra* note 155, at 32–33.

170. *See, e.g.*, Erez & Tontodonato, *supra* note 162, at 410–13; Smith & Hillenbrand, *supra* note 35, at 249–50.

171. *See* McGillis, *supra* note 33, at 57–59.

172. *See id.* at 52–53, 58–59.

173. *See id.*; Thomas C. Castellano, *Assessing Restitution's Impact on Recidivism: A Review of the Evaluative Research*, *in* Critical Issues in Victimology: International Perspectives 233, 236 (Emilio C. Viano ed. 1992) (describing Hudson & Chesney study).

174. *See* Allen & Treger, *supra* note 147, at 34, 35–36, 38.

175. *See* Castellano, *supra* note 173, at 235–40.

176. *See id.* at 236–40; *see also* McGillis, *supra* note 33, at 54, 58; Steve Chesney et al., *A New Look at Restitution: Recent Legislation, Programs and Research*, 61 Judicature 348, 356–57 (1978); Anne L. Schneider, *Restitution and Recidivism Rates of Juvenile Offenders: Results from Four Experimental Sites*, 24 Criminology 533, 536 (1986).

177. *See* Chesney et al., *supra* note 176, at 356–57.

178. *See* McGillis, *supra* note 33, at 58; Gallaway, *supra* note 141, at 6.

179. *See* Castellano, *supra* note 173, at 236–40.

180. *See id.* at 240.

181. *See id.* at 240–45; *see also* Laurie Ervin & Anne Schneider, *Explaining the Effects of Restitution on Offenders: Results from a National Experiment in Juvenile Courts*, *in* Criminal Justice, Restitution, and Reconciliation, *supra* note 113, at 183; Schneider, *supra* note 176, at 533; Tobolowsky, *supra* note 20, at 113 n.108; *cf.* M.S. Rowley, *Recidivism of Juvenile Offenders in a Diversion Restitution Program (Compared to a Matched Group of Offenders Processed Through Court)*, *in* Criminal Justice, Restitution, and Reconciliation, *supra* note 113, at 217.

182. *See* Outlaw & Ruback, *supra* note 133, at 857, 860.

183. *See id.* at 860–64.

184. *See id.* at 867–68.

185. *See* McGILLIS, *supra* note 33, at 52–58.

186. *See* McGILLIS, *supra* note 33, at 52–55; Galaway, *supra* note 141, at 6–7; Hudson et al., *supra* note 11, at 318; Carol Shapiro, *Is Restitution Legislation the Chameleon of the Victims' Movement?*, *in* CRIMINAL JUSTICE, RESTITUTION, AND RECONCILIATION, *supra* note 113, at 73, 76.

187. *See* McGILLIS, *supra* note 33, at 53–55; *see also* Frank, *supra* note 150, at 128–31.

188. *See* S. REP. No. 104–179, at 26 (1995).

189. *See* U.S. GOVERNMENT ACCOUNTABILITY OFFICE (2004 study), *supra* note 148; U.S. GOVERNMENT ACCOUNTABILITY OFFICE (2001 study), *supra* note 148.

190. *See* McGILLIS, *supra* note 33, at 54–55.

191. *See* 18 U.S.C.A. §§ 3663, 3663A (West 2000 & Supp. 2009).

192. *See* Galaway, *supra* note 141, at 6.

193. *See* Frank, *supra* note 150, at 123; Richard Lawrence, *Restitution as a Cost-Effective Alternative to Incarceration*, *in* CRIMINAL JUSTICE, RESTITUTION, AND RECONCILIATION, *supra* note 113, at 207.

194. *Cf.* SCHAFER, *supra* note 9, at 126–27; McDonald, *supra* note 8, at 672.

195. *See* McGILLIS, *supra* note 33, at 55.

196. *See id.* at 35–40, 55–56; Tobolowsky, *supra* note 20, at 114–16.

197. *See* Harland & Rosen, *supra* note 124, at 138; *see also* SCHAFER, *supra* note 9, at 125.

198. *See, e.g.,* McGILLIS, *supra* note 33, 61–62; Allen & Treger, *supra* note 147, at 38–39; Davis et al., *supra* note 144, at 247–48.

199. *See, e.g.,* OFFICE FOR VICTIMS OF CRIME, *supra* note 21, at 364–69.

200. *See id.*; *see also* Frank, *supra* note 150, at 121; Maiolino et al., *supra* note 150, at 134.

201. *See, e.g.,* Shapiro, *supra* note 186; Tobolowsky, *supra* note 20, at 116–26.

202. Portions of this chapter have been reprinted from Peggy M. Tobolowsky, *Crime Victim Restitution: Its Past, Present, and Future*, 36 CRIM. L. BULL. 85 (2000) with the permission of the West Group.

Notes for Chapter 9

1. *See* WILLIAM G. DOERNER & STEVEN P. LAB, VICTIMOLOGY 97 (5th ed. 2008); LESLIE SEBBA, THIRD PARTIES: VICTIMS AND THE CRIMINAL JUSTICE SYSTEM 227 (1996); Gerald F. Ramker & Martin S. Meagher, *Crime Victim Compensation: A Survey of State Programs*, FED. PROBATION, March 1982, at 68.

2. *See* DOERNER & LAB, *supra* note 1, at 97; SEBBA, *supra* note 1, at 227.

3. *See* DOERNER & LAB, *supra* note 1, at 97; William E. Hoelzel, *A Survey of 27 Victim Compensation Programs*, 63 JUDICATURE 485 (1980); Ramker & Meagher, *supra* note 1, at 68.

4. *See* Robert J. McCormack, *Compensating Victims of Violent Crime*, 8 JUST. Q. 329, 331 (1991); Marlene A. Young, *Victim Rights and Services: A Modern Saga*, *in* VICTIMS OF CRIME 194, 195 (Robert C. Davis et al. eds., 2d ed. 1997).

5. *See* Hoelzel, *supra* note 3; Ramker & Meagher, *supra* note 1.

6. *See* Alan T. Harland, *Victim Compensation: Programs and Issues*, *in* PERSPECTIVES ON CRIME VICTIMS 412 (Burt Galaway & Joe Hudson eds., 1981); Hoelzel, *supra* note 3; LeRoy L. Lamborn, *Victim Compensation Programs: An Overview*, *in* PERSPECTIVES ON CRIME, *supra*, at 418; Ramker & Meagher, *supra* note 1.

7. *See* PRESIDENT'S TASK FORCE ON VICTIMS OF CRIME, FINAL REPORT 39 (1982).

8. *See id.* at 38–43.

9. *See id.* at 43–46.

10. *See id.* at 46.

11. *See id.* at 34.

12. *See* OFFICE FOR VICTIMS OF CRIME, U.S. DEP'T OF JUSTICE, NEW DIRECTIONS FROM THE FIELD: VICTIMS' RIGHTS AND SERVICES FOR THE 21ST CENTURY 325–36 (1998).

13. *See id.* at 337–53.

14. *See* 18 U.S.C.A. § 3771 (West Supp. 2009); S.J. Res. 1, 108th Cong. (2003); H.R.J. Res. 48, 108th Cong. (2003); H.R.J. Res. 10, 108th Cong. (2003).

15. *See* Hoelzel, *supra* note 3, at 493, 495; Ramker & Meagher, *supra* note 1, at 69–71.

16. *See* 42 U.S.C.A. § 10601 (as amended, West 2005 & Supp. 2009); *see also* 18 U.S.C.A. § 3013 (as amended, West 2000); *cf.* 18 U.S.C.A. § 3681 (as amended, West 2000).

17. *See* 42 U.S.C.A. § 10602 (as amended, West 2005 & Supp. 2009).

18. *See* 18 U.S.C.A. § 3013 (West 2000); 42 U.S.C.A. § 10601 (West 2005 & Supp. 2009). *See generally* STEVE DERENE, NATIONAL ASSOCIATION OF VOCA ASSISTANCE ADMINISTRATORS, CRIME VICTIMS FUND REPORT: PAST, PRESENT, AND FUTURE (2005).

19. *See* 42 U.S.C.A. § 10602 (West 2005 & Supp. 2009).

20. *See* OFFICE FOR VICTIMS OF CRIME, U.S. DEP'T OF JUSTICE, VICTIMS OF CRIME ACT OF 1984, AS AMENDED: A REPORT TO THE PRESIDENT AND THE CONGRESS 8 (1999). Two special federal compensation programs have been established for victims of the 2001 terrorist attack in New York and for victims of international terrorism. *See* DAN EDDY, STATE CRIME VICTIM COMPENSATION PROGRAMS: NATURE AND SCOPE 3 (2003).

21. *See* 42 U.S.C.A. § 10607 (West 2005).

22. R.I. CONST. art. 1, § 23.

23. *See* WIS. CONST. art. 1, § 9m.

24. *See, e.g.,* WIS. STAT. ANN. § 950.04 (West Supp.2007).

25. *See, e.g.,* COLO. REV. STAT. ANN. § 24-4.1-302.5 (West 2008); KAN. STAT. ANN. § 74-7333 (2002); WYO. STAT. ANN. § 1-40-203 (2007).

26. *See, e.g.,* LA. REV. STAT. ANN. § 46:1817 (1999); N.Y. EXEC. LAW § 625-a (McKinney Supp. 2009); UTAH CODE ANN. § 63-25a-428 (2004).

27. *See generally* EDDY, *supra* note 20; LISA NEWMARK ET AL., THE NATIONAL EVALUATION OF STATE VICTIMS OF CRIME ACT ASSISTANCE AND COMPENSATION PROGRAMS: TRENDS AND STRATEGIES FOR THE FUTURE (2003); LISA NEWMARK & MEGAN SCHAFFER, CRIME VICTIMS COMPENSATION IN MARYLAND: ACCOMPLISHMENTS AND STRATEGIES FOR THE FUTURE (2003); DALE G. PARENT ET AL., U.S. DEP'T OF JUSTICE, COMPENSATING CRIME VICTIMS: A SUMMARY OF POLICIES AND PRACTICES (1992); SUSAN KISS SARNOFF, PAYING FOR CRIME: THE POLICIES AND POSSIBILITIES OF CRIME VICTIM REIMBURSEMENT 57–81 (1996); Susan Kiss Sarnoff, A National Survey of State Crime Victim Compensation Programs: Policies and Administrative Methods (1993) (unpublished Ph.D. dissertation, Adelphi University) (on file with author); National Association of Crime Victim Compensation Boards, Program Directory, http://www.nacvcb.org/progdir.html (last visited June 1, 2009); National Center for Victims of Crime, VictimLaw, http://www.victimlaw.info/victimlaw/ (last visited Jan. 1, 2009); National Conference of State Legislatures, Victims' Rights Laws in the States, http://www.ncsl.org (last visited Jan. 1, 2009).

28. *See, e.g.,* Ky. Rev. Stat. Ann § 346.185 (LexisNexis 2005); *see also* Office for Victims of Crime, U.S. Dep't of Justice, Report to the Nation 2007, at 32–33 (2007). *See generally* National Association of Crime Victim Compensation Boards, *supra* note 27.

29. *See, e.g.,* Ark. Code Ann. § 16-90-703 (2006); Wis. Stat. Ann. § 949.06 (West Supp. 2008).

30. *See, e.g.,* Ala. Code § 15-23-12 (LexisNexis Supp. 2008); N.C. Gen. Stat. § 15B-11 (2007); Wash. Rev. Code Ann. § 7.68.060 (West 2007). *See generally* National Association of Crime Victim Compensation Boards, *supra* note 27.

31. *See, e.g.,* Ark. Code Ann. § 16-90-712 (2006); Haw. Rev. Stat. Ann. § 351-62 (LexisNexis 2004); R.I. Gen. Laws § 12-25-22 (2002). *See generally* National Association of Crime Victim Compensation Boards, *supra* note 27.

32. *See, e.g.,* Colo. Rev. Stat. Ann. § 24-4.1-108 (West 2008); Iowa Code Ann. § 915.87 (West 2003).

33. *See, e.g.,* La. Rev. Stat. Ann. § 46:1809 (1999).

34. *See, e.g.,* Ind. Code Ann. § 5-2-6.1-21, –35 (LexisNexis 2006). *See generally* National Association of Crime Victim Compensation Boards, *supra* note 27.

35. *See, e.g.,* Neb. Rev. Stat. § 81-1822 (2008).

36. *See, e.g.,* Ala. Code §§ 15-23-3, -9, -12, -14 (LexisNexis 1995 & Supp. 2008); Iowa Code Ann. §§ 915.87, .92 (West 2003).

37. *See, e.g.,* N.C. Gen. Stat. § 15B-11 (2007); Vt. Stat. Ann. tit. 13, § 5356 (Supp. 2008). *See generally* National Association of Crime Victim Compensation Boards, *supra* note 27.

38. *See* Cal. Gov't Code § 13957 (West Supp. 2009); Tex. Code Crim. Proc. Ann. art. 56.42 (Vernon 2006).

39. *See* N.Y. Exec. Law § 631 (McKinney Supp. 2009); Wash. Rev. Code Ann. § 7.68.085 (West 2007).

40. *See, e.g.,* Tex. Code Crim. Proc. Ann. art. 56.42 (Vernon 2006).

41. *See, e.g.,* N.Y. Exec. Law § 631 (McKinney Supp. 2009). *See generally* National Association of Crime Victim Compensation Boards, *supra* note 27.

42. *See, e.g.,* Fla. Stat. Ann. § 960.195 (West 2006); N.Y. Exec. Law § 631 (McKinney Supp. 2009).

43. *See* Haw. Rev. Stat. Ann. § 351-33 (LexisNexis 2004); Tenn. Code Ann. § 29-13-106 (Supp. 2008).

44. *See, e.g.,* N.Y. Exec. Law §§ 627–628 (McKinney Supp. 2009); *see also* Eddy, *supra* note 20, at 2–3, 9. *See generally* National Association of Crime Victim Compensation Boards, *supra* note 27.

45. *See generally* Andrea G. Nadel, Annotation, *Statutes Providing for Governmental Compensation for Victims of Crime,* 20 A.L.R. 4th 63 (1983).

46. *See* McComas v. Criminal Injuries Compensation Bd., 594 A.2d 583 (Md. Ct. Spec. App. 1991); Ortell v. Crime Victim's Compensation Bd., 552 A.2d 766 (Pa. Commw. Ct. 1989).

47. *See* Meditrust Financial Services Corp. v. Crime Victims Bd., 640 N.Y.S.2d 676 (N.Y. App. Div. 1996); Smith v. Crime Victim's Compensation Bd., 498 A.2d 489 (Pa. Commw. Ct. 1985).

48. *See* McCullough v. State, 490 A.2d 967 (R.I. 1985).

49. *See In re* John W., 48 Cal. Rptr. 2d 899, 909 (Cal. Ct. App. 1996); Marshall v. Commonwealth, 602 N.E.2d 204 (Mass. 1992); *In re* Raymond, 698 N.E.2d 92 (Ohio Ct. Cl. 1994).

50. *See In re* Hugley, 629 N.E.2d 1136 (Ohio Ct. Cl. 1993); *McCullough*, 490 A.2d at 967; *cf.* Pack v. State, 819 P.2d 280 (Okla. Crim. App. 1991). *But see In re* Douglas, 684 N.E.2d 753 (Ohio Ct. Cl. 1996).

51. *See In re* Williams, 698 N.E.2d 114 (Ohio Ct. Cl. 1995).

52. *See In re* Kramer, 684 N.E.2d 751 (Ohio Ct. Cl. 1995); *In re* Marcus-Bey, 643 N.E.2d 626 (Ohio Ct. Cl. 1994).

53. *See In re* Dale, 643 N.E.2d 614 (Ohio Ct. Cl. 1993); *In re* Chaney, 643 N.E.2d 612 (Ohio Ct. Cl. 1993).

54. *See In re* Simmons, 579 N.E.2d 311 (Ohio Ct. Cl. 1989); *In re* Ferrell, 553 N.E.2d 1096 (Ohio Ct. Cl.1988).

55. *See* Ellis v. North Carolina Crime Victims Compensation Comm'n, 432 S.E.2d 160 (N.C. Ct. App. 1993); *In re* Smith, 698 N.E.2d 131 (Ohio Ct. Cl. 1997). *But see In re* Rodgers, 577 N.E.2d 162 (Ohio Ct. Cl. 1988). *See generally Simmons*, 579 N.E.2d at 312.

56. *See In re* Dillon, 620 N.E.2d 302 (Ohio Ct. Cl. 1993); *cf. In re* Holbrook, 619 N.E.2d 1250 (Ohio Ct. Cl. 1993). *But cf. In re* Weber, 579 N.E.2d 307 (Ohio Ct. Cl. 1989).

57. *See In re* Guffey, 593 N.E.2d 496 (Ohio Ct. Cl. 1990).

58. *See* Starkman v. Frischetti, 675 N.Y.S.2d 703 (N.Y. App. Div. 1998); *In re* Wilson, 579 N.E.2d 314 (Ohio Ct. Cl. 1989).

59. *See* Hullum v. Commonwealth, 487 N.E.2d 477 (Mass. 1986).

60. *See In re* Reede, 619 N.E.2d 1212 (Ohio Ct. Cl. 1992).

61. *See In re* Edmundson, 625 P.2d 372 (Haw. 1981).

62. *See In re* Bradley, 706 N.E.2d 1278 (Ohio Ct. Cl. 1998).

63. *See* Graham v. State Bd. Of Control, 39 Cal. Rptr. 2d 146 (Cal. Ct. App. 1995); *In re* Dillon, 620 N.E.2d 302 (Ohio Ct. Cl. 1993).

64. *See* Carter v. State, 897 So. 2d 149 (La. Ct. App. 2004); Archer v. Crime Victims Compensation Bd., 305 N.W.2d 259 (Mich. Ct. App. 1981). *But see* Callicutt v. Crime Victims Bd., 665 N.Y.S.2d 125 (N.Y. App. Div. 1997).

65. *See Carter*, 897 So. 2d at 149; Calloway-Gaines v. Crime Victim Services Comm'n, 616 N.W.2d 674 (Mich. 2000); Smith v. Crime Victims Compensation Bd., 344 N.W.2d 23, 25 (Mich. Ct. App. 1983); *In re* Kramer, 684 N.E.2d 751 (Ohio Ct. Cl. 1995); Ciaverelli v. Crime Victim's Compensation Bd., 621 A.2d 1232, 1234 (Pa. Commw. 1993).

66. *See* United States v. Munoz-Flores, 495 U.S. 385 (1990).

67. See, e.g., United States v. Cooper, 870 F.2d 586 (11th Cir. 1989); United States v. Smith, 818 F.2d 687 (9th Cir. 1987); United States v. Pagan, 785 F.2d 378 (2d Cir. 1986).

68. *See* State v. Champe, 373 So. 2d 874 (Fla. 1978); People v. Matthews, 508 N.W.2d 173 (Mich. Ct. App. 1993).

69. *See* People v. Ramirez, 46 Cal. Rptr. 2d 530, 534 (Cal. Ct. App. 1995); Bird v. State, 939 P.2d 735, 739 (Wyo. 1997); *cf.* State v. Pindale, 592 A.2d 300, 313 (N.J. Super. Ct. App. Div. 1991). *But see* Meerscheidt v. State, 931 P.2d 220, 228 (Wyo. 1997).

70. *See* DOERNER & LAB, *supra* note 1, at 99–100; SARNOFF, *supra* note 27, at 3–5; SEBBA, *supra* note 1, at 240–48; Robert Elias, *Community Control, Criminal Justice and Victim Services, in* FROM CRIME POLICY TO VICTIM POLICY: REORIENTING THE JUSTICE SYSTEM, at 290, 302–08 (Ezzat A. Fattah ed., 1986); Harland, *supra* note 6, at 415–16; Ramker & Meagher, *supra* note 1, at 74–75.

71. *See* SARNOFF, *supra* note 27, at 5–6; *cf.* SEBBA, *supra* note 1, at 240–48.

72. *See* SARNOFF, *supra* note 27, at 71, 73; Robert Elias, *The Symbolic Politics of Victim Compensation*, 8(1–2) VICTIMOLOGY 213, 219–22 (1983); David R. Miers, *Compensation and Conceptions of Victims of Crime*, 8(1–2) VICTIMOLOGY 204 (1983).

73. *See* PARENT ET AL., *supra* note 27, at 5, 12–13, A-16; *cf.* SARNOFF, *supra* note 27, at 106–08, 113–14, 138–47, 157–84; McCormack, *supra* note 4, at 331, 334–37.

74. *See* OFFICE FOR VICTIMS OF CRIME, *supra* note 20, at 8–9, 57–60; Office for Victims of Crime, U.S. Dep't of Justice, Nationwide Analysis, 1998 Victims of Crime Act Performance Report, http://www.ojp.usdoj.gov/fund/vocanpr_vc98_1.html (last visited June 1, 2009).

75. *See* Office for Victims of Crime, U.S. Dep't of Justice, Nationwide Analysis, 2008 Victims of Crime Act Performance Report, http://www.ojp.usdoj.gov/fund/vocanpr_vc08.html (last visited June 1, 2009).

76. *See* SEBBA, *supra* note 1, at 231; William G. Doerner & Steven P. Lab, *The Impact of Crime Compensation Upon Victim Attitudes Toward the Criminal Justice System*, 5 VICTIMOLOGY 61, 65 (1980); Robert Elias, *Alienating the Victim: Compensation and Victim Attitudes*, 40 J. SOC. ISSUES 103, 106, 110 (1984); *cf.* Hoelzel, *supra* note 3, at 495.

77. *See generally* McCormack, *supra* note 4.

78. *See* PARENT ET AL., *supra* note 27, at 5–6, 16–17, A-1 to -3; *cf.* SARNOFF, *supra* note 27, at 122–23.

79. *See* CRIME VICTIMS' INSTITUTE, OFFICE OF THE ATTORNEY GENERAL, STATE OF TEXAS, THE IMPACT OF CRIME ON VICTIMS: A BASELINE STUDY ON PROGRAM SERVICE DELIVERY, 1997–98, FINAL REPORT 74–95, 102, 168 (1999).

80. *See* NEWMARK ET AL., *supra* note 27, at 33, 274–76; *see also* Fran S. Danis, DOMESTIC VIOLENCE AND CRIME VICTIM COMPENSATION: A RESEARCH AGENDA, 9 VIOLENCE AGAINST WOMEN 374 (2003).

81. *See* NEWMARK ET AL., *supra* note 27, at 93–100; *cf.* Hayden P. Smith, *Violent Crime and Victim Compensation: Implications for Social Justice*, 21 VIOLENCE AND VICTIMS 307 (2006).

82. *See* NEWMARK ET AL., *supra* note 27, at 97, 99.

83. *See supra* notes 29–43 and accompanying text.

84. *See* NEWMARK ET AL., *supra* note 27, at 28, 259–61.

85. *See* OFFICE FOR VICTIMS OF CRIME, *supra* note 12, at 337.

86. *See* NEWMARK ET AL., *supra* note 27, at 30, 265, 270.

87. *See supra* notes 73–75 and accompanying text; *see also* OFFICE FOR VICTIMS OF CRIME, *supra* note 28, at 29.

88. *See* SARNOFF, *supra* note 27, at 74; SEBBA, *supra* note 1, at 230; Elias, *supra* note 72, at 218; McCormack, *supra* note 4, at 336; Ramker & Meagher, *supra* note 1, at 76.

89. *See* PARENT ET AL., *supra* note 27, at 13–15, A-15.

90. *See, e.g.,* FLA. STAT. ANN. § 960.001 (West Supp. 2008); MICH. COMP. LAWS ANN. § 780.753 (West 2007); MINN. STAT. ANN. § 611A.02 (West Supp. 2008); *see also* Ramker & Meagher, *supra* note 1, at 74; *cf.* OFFICE FOR VICTIMS OF CRIME, *supra* note 12, at 333–34; PARENT ET AL., *supra* note 27, at 14–16.

91. *See* CRIME VICTIMS' INSTITUTE, *supra* note 79, at 26–36, 54, 56, 100–01.

92. *See* Robert W. Taylor et al., An Analysis of the Texas Crime Victims' Compensation Fund: Predictors of Access, Utilization and Efficiency 46–48, 58, 70–75, 88, 103, 120, 130, 132, 138, 145–47, 188(1997) (unpublished manuscript, on file with author).

93. *See* NEWMARK ET AL., *supra* note 27, at 26, 252–54.

94. *See id.* at 110–11, 315–16.

95. *See* NEWMARK & SCHAFFER, *supra* note 27, at 43–49, App. G.

96. *See id.* at App. G.

97. *See* Jennifer Alvidrez, *Reduction of State Victim Compensation Disparities in Disadvantaged Crime Victims Through Active Outreach and Assistance: A Randomized Trial,* 98 Am. J. Pub. Health 882 (2008).

98. *See* Ramker & Meagher, *supra* note 1, at 74.

99. *See* Parent et al., *supra* note 27, at 9–10.

100. *See* Eddy, *supra* note 20, at 2.

101. *See* Crime Victims' Institute, *supra* note 79, at 53, 56; Parent et al., *supra* note 27, at 9; McCormack, *supra* note 4, at 336–38; *cf.* Sarnoff, *supra* note 27, at 75–76.

102. *See* 42 U.S.C.A. § 10603 (West 2005 & Supp. 2009).

103. *See* Eddy, *supra* note 20, at 2–3.

104. *See* Parent et al., *supra* note 27, at 9–10, 13, 35–37, A-15, A-16; *cf.* Sarnoff, *supra* note 27, at 149–50.

105. *See* 42 U.S.C.A. § 10602 (West 2005 & Supp. 2009).

106. *See* Parent et al., *supra* note 27, at 14, A-16.

107. *See* McCormack, *supra* note 4, at 338–39.

108. *See* Office for Victims of Crime, *supra* note 12, at 335–36.

109. *See* Office for Victims of Crime, *supra* note 20, at 57–61; Office for Victims of Crime, *supra* note 12, at 327–29, 334–36.

110. *See* Newmark et al., *supra* note 27, at 24–25, 250–51.

111. *See* Eddy, *supra* note 20, at 4–6. *See generally* Derene, *supra* note 18.

112. *See* Eddy, *supra* note 20, at 4–6. *See generally* Derene, *supra* note 18.

113. *See* Newmark et al., *supra* note 27, at 22, 24–25.

114. *See generally* National Association of Crime Victim Compensation Boards, *supra* note 27.

115. *See* Doerner & Lab, *supra* note 1, at 104–06; Doerner & Lab, *supra* note 76, at 62; Elias, *supra* note 76, at 107–08.

116. *See* Doerner & Lab, *supra* note 76.

117. *See id.*

118. *See* Elias, *supra* note 76, at 110–11.

119. *See id.* at 111–14; Elias, *supra* note 72, at 219.

120. *See* Newmark et al., *supra* note 27, at 92–93, 118–23, 126, 325–32.

121. *See* Newmark & Schaffer, *supra* note 27, at 29, 35–36, 40–42.

Notes for Chapter 10

1. *See generally* A.S. Diamond, Primitive Law (2d ed. 1950); Harold J. Berman, *The Background of the Western Legal Tradition in the Folklaw of the Peoples of Europe,* 45 U. Chi. L. Rev. 553 (1978).

2. *See generally* William F. McDonald, *Towards a Bicentennial Revolution in Criminal Justice: The Return of the Victim,* 13 Am. Crim. L. Rev. 649 (1976).

3. *See generally* Susan Kiss Sarnoff, Paying for Crime: The Policies and Possibilities of Crime Victim Reimbursement (1996).

4. *See generally* WILLIAM L. PROSSER, HANDBOOK OF THE LAW OF TORTS (4th ed. 1971); MARSHALL S. SHAPO, BASIC PRINCIPLES OF TORT LAW (1999); JAMES H. STARK & HOWARD W. GOLDSTEIN, THE RIGHTS OF CRIME VICTIMS 188–264 (1985).

5. *See* PROSSER, *supra* note 4; STARK & GOLDSTEIN, *supra* note 4.

6. *See* OFFICE FOR VICTIMS OF CRIME, U.S. DEP'T OF JUSTICE, NEW DIRECTIONS FROM THE FIELD: VICTIMS' RIGHTS AND SERVICES FOR THE 21ST CENTURY 249–61, 373–80 (1998); National Crime Victim Bar Association, http://www.victimbar.org (last visited June 1, 2009).

7. *See* 18 U.S.C.A. § 3771 (West Supp. 2009); S.J. Res. 1, 108th Cong. (2003); H.R.J. Res. 48, 108th Cong. (2003); H.R.J. Res. 10, 108th Cong. (2003).

8. *See* 28 U.S.C.A. § 1332 (West 2006 & Supp. 2009).

9. *See* 28 U.S.C.A. § 1331 (West 2006); *see also* 28 U.S.C.A. § 1343 (West 2006); Bivens v. Six Unknown Named Agents of Federal Bureau of Narcotics, 403 U.S. 388 (1971); *cf.* Cort v. Ash, 422 U.S. 66 (1975).

10. *See, e.g.,* 42 U.S.C.A. §§ 1983, 1985, 3613 (West 2003).

11. *See* 42 U.S.C.A. § 13981 (West 2005).

12. *See* United States v. Morrison, 529 U.S. 598 (2000).

13. *See* 28 U.S.C.A. § 1346 (West 2006); 28 U.S.C.A. §§ 2674, 2680 (West 2006 & Supp. 2009).

14. *See* 42 U.S.C.A. § 1983 (West 2003).

15. *See, e.g.,* Vance v. County of Santa Clara, 928 F. Supp. 993, 995–96 (N.D. Cal. 1996); *cf.* DARRELL L. ROSS, CIVIL LIABILITY IN CRIMINAL JUSTICE (4th ed. 2006).

16. *See generally* PROSSER, *supra* note 4, at 1–138; STARK & GOLDSTEIN, *supra* note 4, at 190–208, 217–22.

17. *See, e.g.,* ALA. CODE § 6-5-410 (LexisNexis 2005); MINN. STAT. ANN. § 573.02 (West Supp. 2008); WIS. STAT. ANN. §§ 895.03, .04 (West 2006). *See generally* PROSSER, *supra* note 4, at 898–914; STARK & GOLDSTEIN, *supra* note 4, at 208–09.

18. *See generally* PROSSER, *supra* note 4, at 139–491; STARK & GOLDSTEIN, *supra* note 4, at 217–46.

19. *See, e.g.,* CAL. PENAL CODE §§ 496, 637.2 (West 1999); CONN. GEN. STAT. § 52-564 (2009); IND. CODE ANN. § 34-24-3-1 (LexisNexis 2008); MINN. STAT. ANN. § 609.53 (West 2009); WYO. STAT. ANN. § 1-1-127 (2009).

20. *See, e.g.,* CAL. CIV. CODE §§ 1708.5, .7 (West 2009).

21. *See, e.g.,* CONN. GEN. STAT. § 52-577d (2009); ME. REV. STAT. ANN. tit. 14, § 752-C (2003); NEV. REV. STAT. ANN. § 11.215 (LexisNexis 2008).

22. *See, e.g.,* FLA. STAT. ANN. § 775.085 (West 2005); IDAHO CODE ANN. §§ 18-7902, -7903 (2004); MICH. COMP. LAWS ANN. § 750.147b (West 2004). *See generally* Anti-Defamation League, State Hate Crime Statutory Provisions, http://www.adl.org/99hatecrime/state_hate_crime_laws.pdf (last visited June 10, 2009).

23. *See* PRESIDENT'S TASK FORCE ON VICTIMS OF CRIME, FINAL REPORT 18 (1982); SARNOFF, *supra* note 3, at 50–51; STARK & GOLDSTEIN, *supra* note 4, at 265–80; Michelle G. Lewis Liebeskind, *Back to Basics for Victims: Striking Son of Sam Laws in Favor of an Amended Restitutionary Scheme*, 1994 ANN. SURV. AM. L. 29 (1994); Orly Nosrati, Note, *Son of Sam Laws: Killing Free Speech or Promoting Killer Profits?*, 20 WHITTIER L. REV. 949 (1999); *Anti-Profit Laws Assure that Victims Receive Restitution*, 3 CRIME VICTIMS RPT. 43 (1999).

24. *See* Simon & Schuster v. New York Crime Victims Bd., 502 U.S. 105 (1991).

25. *See, e.g.,* 18 U.S.C.A. §§ 3681–3682 (West 2000); FLA. STAT. ANN. § 944.512 (West Supp. 2009); MINN. STAT. ANN. § 611A.68 (West 2009); N.Y. EXEC. LAW § 632-a (McKinney

2005); Wis. Stat. Ann. § 949.165 (West Supp. 2008); *see also* Stark & Goldstein, *supra* note 4, at 265–80; Liebeskind, *supra* note 23.

26. *See* Brown v. Robinson, 747 S.W.2d 24 (Tex. App. 1988). *See generally* Jay M. Zitter, Annotation, *Excessiveness or Inadequacy of Compensatory Damages for False Imprisonment or Arrest*, 48 A.L.R. 4th 165 (1986).

27. *See* Reyes v. Greatway Ins. Co., 582 N.W.2d 480 (Wis. Ct. App. 1998), *aff'd*, 597 N.W.2d 687 (Wis. 1999).

28. *See* Pluid v. B.K., 948 P.2d 981 (Alaska 1997).

29. *See* Hattori v. Peairs, 662 So. 2d 509 (La. Ct. App. 1995).

30. *See* Beam v. Kingsley, 566 S.E.2d 437 (Ga. Ct. App. 2002); *cf.* Warhurst v. White, 838 S.W.2d 350 (Ark. 1992).

31. *See* Stewart v. Bader, 907 A.2d 931 (N.H. 2006); *cf.* Page v. Fulton, 30 S.W.3d 61 (Tex. App. 2000); Nelson v. Schubert, 994 P.2d 225 (Wash. Ct. App. 2000).

32. *See* Johnson v. Smith, 878 F. Supp. 1150 (N.D. Ill. 1995); *cf.* Annotation, *Modern Status of Intentional Infliction of Mental Distress as Independent Tort; "Outrage,"* 38 A.L.R. 4th 998 (1985). *See generally* George L. Blum, Annotation, *Validity, Construction, and Effect of "Hate Crimes" Statutes, "Ethnic Intimidation" Statutes, or the Like*, 22 A.L.R. 5th 261 (1994).

33. *See* Troutt v. Charcoal Steak House, Inc., 835 F. Supp. 899 (W.D. Va. 1993), *aff'd*, 37 F.3d 1495 (4th Cir. 1994); *cf.* Little v. Windmere Relocation, 301 F.3d 958 (9th Cir. 2001).

34. *See* Johnson v. Hugo's Skateway, 974 F.2d 1408 (4th Cir. 1992).

35. *See* Buggie v. Cutler, 636 N.Y.S.2d 357 (N.Y. App. Div. 1995); *see also Stewart*, 907 A.2d at 931.

36. *See* Stark & Goldstein, *supra* note 4, at 213–15.

37. *See id.* at 212–13; *cf.* Baxter v. Palmigiano, 425 U.S. 308 (1976); Nat'l Acceptance Co. of America v. Bathalter, 705 F.2d 924 (7th Cir. 1983); *Johnson*, 878 F. Supp. at 1151–52.

38. *See* Stark & Goldstein, *supra* note 4, at 217–18.

39. Brown v. Robinson, 747 S.W.2d 24, 26 (Tex. App. 1988).

40. *See* Reyes v. Greatway Ins. Co., 582 N.W.2d 480 (Wis. Ct. App. 1998), *aff'd*, 597 N.W.2d 687 (Wis. 1999); *cf.* Pacific Mut. Life Ins. Co. v. Haslip, 499 U.S. 1 (1991). *See generally* Jane Massey Draper, Annotation, *Excessiveness or Inadequacy of Punitive Damages Awarded in Personal Injury or Death Cases*, 12 A.L.R. 5th 195 (1993).

41. *See Reyes*, 486 N.W.2d at 487–88.

42. *See* Cater v. Cater, 846 S.W.2d 173 (Ark. 1993).

43. *See* Buggie v. Cutler, 636 N.Y.S.2d 357 (N.Y. App. Div. 1995).

44. *See generally* James L. Rigelhaupt, Jr., Annotation, *Construction and Application of Provision of Liability Insurance Policy Expressly Excluding Injuries Intended or Expected by Insured*, 31 A.L.R. 4th 957 (1984).

45. *See* Raby v. Moe, 450 N.W.2d 452, 457 (Wis. 1990); *cf.* Skiathos v. Essex Ins. Co., 396 F. Supp. 2d 624 (D. Md. 2005); Sennett v. U.S. Fidelity & Guaranty Co., 757 So. 2d 206 (Miss. 2000); Doe v. Interstate Fire & Casualty Co., 738 N.E.2d 1243 (Ohio 2000).

46. *See* Frank Carrington, *Victims' Rights Litigation: A Wave of the Future?*, 11 U. Rich. L. Rev. 447 (1977); Gregory A. Crouse, Comment, *Negligence Liability for the Criminal Acts of Another*, 15 J. Marshall L. Rev. 459 (1982); Frank Carrington, *Crime Victims' Rights: Courts Are More Willing to Grant Remedies*, Trial, Jan. 1988, at 78; Frank Carrington, *Victims' Rights: A New Tort? Five Years Later*, Trial, Dec. 1983, at 50; Frank Carrington, *Victims' Rights: A New Tort?*, Trial, June 1978, at 39. *See generally* Stark & Goldstein, *supra* note 4, at 222–49.

47. *See* Restatement of Torts viii–ix (1934).

48. *See* Restatement (Second) of Torts §§ 314–324A, 344 (1965).

49. *See id.* at §§ 314A–314B, 344.

50. *See id.* at §§ 315–319.

51. *See id.* at §§ 321–324A.

52. *See* Restatement of Torts, *supra* note 47, at ix.

53. *See* Stark & Goldstein, *supra* note 4, at 222–26.

54. *See, e.g.,* Kline v. Santa Barbara Consolidated Ry. Co., 90 P. 125 (1907).

55. *See* Stark & Goldstein, *supra* note 4, at 226–27.

56. *See* Washington Metro. Area Transit Auth. v. O'Neill, 633 A.2d 834 (D.C. 1993).

57. *See* Stark & Goldstein, *supra* note 4, at 227–28. *See generally* Annotation, *Liability of Hotel or Motel Operator for Injury to Guest Resulting from Assault by Third Party,* 28 A.L.R. 4th 80 (1984); Jay M. Zitter, Annotation, *Liability of Hotel or Motel for Guest's Loss of Money from Room by Theft or Robbery Committed by Person Other than Defendant's Servant,* 28 A.L.R. 4th 120 (1984).

58. *See* Garzilli v. Howard Johnson Motor Lodges, Inc., 419 F. Supp. 1210 (E.D.N.Y. 1976).

59. *See* Courtney v. Remler, 566 F. Supp. 1225 (D.S.C. 1983), *aff'd,* 745 F.2d 50 (4th Cir. 1984); *cf.* Burnett v. Stagner Hotel Courts, Inc., 821 F. Supp. 678 (N.D. Ga. 1993), *aff'd,* 42 F.3d 645 (11th Cir. 1994); Canterino v. Mirage Casino-Hotel, 42 P.3d 808 (Nev. 2002); Taboada v. Daly Seven, 626 S.E.2d 428 (Va. 2006).

60. *See* Restatement (Second) of Torts, *supra* note 48, at § 344; Stark & Goldstein, *supra* note 4, at 233–34; Robert C. Bishop, Annotation, *Liability of Storekeeper for Death of or Injury to Customer in Course of Robbery,* 72 A.L.R. 3d 1269 (1976); Joseph T. Bockrath, Annotation, *Liability of Bank for Injuries Sustained by Customer in Course of Bank Robbery,* 51 A.L.R. 3d 711 (1973); Marjorie A. Caner, Annotation, *Liability of Owner or Operator of Shopping Center, or Business Housed Therein, for Injury to Patron on Premises from Criminal Attack by Third Party,* 31 A.L.R. 5th 550 (1995); Deborah T. Landis, Annotation, *Liability of Owner or Operator of Shopping Center, or Business Housed Therein, for Injury to Patron on Premises from Criminal Attack by Third Party,* 93 A.L.R. 3d 999 (1979); James O. Pearson, Annotation, *Liability of Owner or Operator of Theatre or Other Amusement to Patron Assaulted by Another Patron,* 75 A.L.R. 3d 441 (1977).

61. *See* Brown v. J.C. Penney Co., Inc., 688 P.2d 811 (Or. 1984) (in banc).

62. *See* Jackson v. Swordfish Investments, 620 S.E.2d 54 (S.C. 2005); *cf.* Russell v. McDonald's Corp., 576 So. 2d 1213 (La. Ct. App. 1991).

63. *See* Stark & Goldstein, *supra* note 4, at 228–29; Joan Teshima, Annotation, *Tavernkeeper's Liability to Patron for Third Person's Assault,* 43 A.L.R. 4th 281 (1986); Ferdinand S. Tinio, Annotation, *Civil Damage Act: Liability of One Who Furnishes Liquor to Another for Consumption by Third Parties, for Injury Caused by Consumer,* 64 A.L.R. 3d 922 (1975); Annotation, *Liability of Innkeeper, Restauranteur, or Tavern Keeper for Injury Occurring on or About Premises to Guest or Patron by Person Other than Proprietor or his Servant,* 70 A.L.R. 2d 628 (1960).

64. *See* Mason v. Royal Dequindre, Inc., 566 N.W.2d 199 (Mich. 1997).

65. *See* Fast Eddie's v. Hall, 688 N.E.2d 1270 (Ind. Ct. App. 1997).

66. *See* Stark & Goldstein, *supra* note 4, at 230–33; Tracy A. Bateman & Susan Thomas, Annotation, *Landlord's Liability for Failure to Protect Tenant from Criminal Acts of Third Person,* 43 A.L.R. 5th 207 (1996); Gary D. Spivey, Annotation, *Landlord's Obligation to Protect Tenant Against Criminal Activities of Third Persons,* 43 A.L.R. 3d 331 (1972).

67. 439 F.2d 477 (D.C. Cir. 1970).

68. *See id.*; *cf.* Rodriguez v. Cambridge Housing Authority, 823 N.E.2d 1249 (Mass. 2005).

69. *See* Doe v. Prudential-Bache/A.G. Spanos Realty Partners, L.P., 492 S.E.2d 865 (Ga. 1997); *cf.* South *ex rel.* South v. McCarter, 119 P.3d 1 (Kan. 2005).

70. *See* STARK & GOLDSTEIN, *supra* note 4, at 235–36.

71. *See id.* at 237–38; Allan E. Korpela, Annotation, *Tort Liability of Public Schools and Institutions of Higher Learning for Injuries Caused by Acts of Fellow Students*, 36 A.L.R. 3d 330 (1971); Joel E. Smith, Annotation, *Liability of University, College, or Other School for Failure to Protect Student from Crime*, 1 A.L.R. 4th 1099 (1980).

72. *See* Lillie v. Thompson, 332 U.S. 459 (1947).

73. *See* Gross v. Family Services Agency, Inc., 716 So. 2d 337, 338 (Fla. Dist. Ct. App. 1998), *aff'd sub nom.* Nova Southeastern University, Inc. v. Gross, 758 So. 2d 86 (Fla. 2000).

74. *See* STARK & GOLDSTEIN, *supra* note 4, at 236, 238–40.

75. *See* Joseph T. Bockrath, Annotation, *Liability of Municipality or Other Governmental Unit for Failure to Provide Police Protection*, 46 A.L.R. 3d 1084 (1972); Colleen R. Courtade, Annotation, *What Constitutes Policy or Custom for Purposes of Determining Liability of Local Governmental Unit Under 42 USCS § 1983 — Modern Cases*, 81 A.L.R. Fed. 549 (1987); Jean F. Rydstrom, Annotation, *Claims Based on Law Enforcement and Regulatory Activities as Within 28 USCS § 2680(a) Excepting from Federal Tort Claims Act Claims Involving "Discretionary Function or Duty,"* 36 A.L.R. Fed. 240 (1978).

76. *See* John H. Derrick, Annotation, *Modern Status of Rule Excusing Governmental Unit for Tort Liability on Theory That Only General, Not Particular, Duty Was Owed Under Circumstances*, 38 A.L.R. 4th 1194 (1985); Caroll J. Miller, Annotation, *Governmental Tort Liability for Failure to Provide Police Protection to Specifically Threatened Crime Victim*, 46 A.L.R. 4th 948 (1986); Robert A. Shapiro, Annotation, *Personal Liability of Policeman, Sheriff, or Similar Peace Officer or his Bond, for Injury Suffered as a Result of Failure to Enforce Law or Arrest Lawbreaker*, 41 A.L.R. 3d 700 (1972); Jay M. Zitter, Annotation, *Liability for Failure of Police Response to Emergency Call*, 39 A.L.R. 4th 691 (1985).

77. *See* DeShaney v. Winnebago Cty. Dep't Soc. Servs., 489 U.S. 189, 195, 197 (1989).

78. *See id.* at 201–03; *cf.* Ricketts v. City of Columbia, Missouri, 36 F.3d 775 (8th Cir. 1994). *But cf.* Thurman v. City of Torrington, 595 F. Supp. 1521 (D. Conn. 1984).

79. *See* Town of Castle Rock v. Gonzales, 545 U.S. 748 (2005).

80. *See* Massee v. Thompson, 90 P.3d 394 (Mont. 2004); *cf.* Moore v. Green, 848 N.E.2d 1015 (Ill. 2006).

81. *See* Taylor v. Phelan, 9 F.3d 882 (10th Cir. 1993); *cf.* Harvey v. County of Snohomish, 134 P.3d 216 (Wash. 2006).

82. *See* Wallace v. City of Los Angeles, 16 Cal. Rptr. 2d 113 (Cal. Ct. App. 1993); *cf.* Ozik v. Gramins, 799 N.E.2d 871 (Ill. Ct. App. 2003).

83. *See* STARK & GOLDSTEIN, *supra* note 4, at 239–40.

84. *See* RESTATEMENT (SECOND) OF TORTS, *supra* note 48, at §§ 315–319.

85. *See* STARK & GOLDSTEIN, *supra* note 4, at 245–46; Wade R. Habeeb, Annotation, *Parents' Liability for Injury or Damage Intentionally Inflicted by Minor Child*, 54 A.L.R. 3d 974 (1973); *cf.* Kimberly C. Simmons, Annotation, *Liability of Adult Assailant's Family to Third Party for Physical Assault*, 25 A.L.R. 5th 1 (1994).

86. *See* Barrett v. Pacheco, 815 P.2d 834 (Wash. Ct. App. 1991).

87. *See* Long v. Turk, 962 P.2d 1093 (Kan. 1998); *cf.* Gritzner v. Michael R., 611 N.W.2d 906 (Wis. 2000).

88. *See, e.g.,* Colo. Rev. Stat. Ann. §§ 13-21-107, -107.5 (West 2005); Mich. Comp. Laws Ann. § 600.2913 (West 2000); Wis. Stat. Ann. § 895.035 (West 2006). *See generally* Annotation, *Validity and Construction of Statutes Making Parents Liable for Torts Committed by Their Minor Children,* 8 A.L.R. 3d 612 (1966).

89. *See* N.E.M. *ex rel.* Kryshak v. Strigel, 559 N.W.2d 256 (Wis. 1997); *cf.* Lavin v. Jordan, 16 S.W.3d 362 (Tenn. 2000).

90. *See* Stark & Goldstein, *supra* note 4, at 234–35; Diane M. Allen, Annotation, *Liability of Supervisory Officials and Governmental Entities for Having Failed to Adequately Train, Supervise, or Control Individual Peace Officers Who Violate Plaintiff's Civil Rights Under 42 USCS. § 1983* (1984); Phoebe Carter, Annotation, *Employer's Liability for Assault, Theft, or Similar Intentional Wrong Committed by Employee at Home or Business of Customer,* 13 A.L.R. 5th 217 (1993); John H. Derrick, Annotation, *Landlord's Tort Liability to Tenant for Personal Injury or Property Damage Resulting from Criminal Conduct of Employee,* 38 A.L.R. 4th 240 (1985); Ferdinand S. Tinio, Annotation, *Employer's Knowledge of Employee's Past Criminal Record as Affecting Liability for Employee's Tortious Conduct,* 48 A.L.R. 3d 359 (1973).

91. *See* Big B, Inc. v. Cottingham, 634 So. 2d 999 (Ala. 1993); *cf.* Costner v. Adams, 121 S.W.3d 164 (Ark. Ct. App. 2003); Sparks Reg'l Med. Ctr. v. Smith, 976 S.W.2d 396 (Ark. Ct. App. 1998); Zsigo v. Hurley Medical Center, 716 N.W.2d 220 (Mich. 2007); Baker v. Saint Francis Hospital, 126 P.3d 602 (Okla. 2005); Doe v. Forrest, 853 A.2d 48 (Vt. 2004).

92. *See* Stark & Goldstein, *supra* note 4, at 243–45; Donald T. Kramer, Annotation, *Liability of One Releasing Institutionalized Mental Patient for Harm He Causes,* 38 A.L.R. 3d 699 (1971); John C. Williams, Annotation, *Liability of One Treating Mentally Afflicted Patient for Failure to Warn or Protect Third Persons Threatened by Patient,* 83 A.L.R. 3d 1201 (1978); *cf.* Janet Boeth Jones, Annotation, *Governmental Tort Liability for Injuries Caused by Negligently Released Individual,* 6 A.L.R. 4th 1155 (1981).

93. *See* Semler v. Psychiatric Institute, 538 F.2d 121 (4th Cir. 1976).

94. 551 P.2d 334 (Cal. 1976) (in bank).

95. *See id.; cf.* Long v. Broadlawns Medical Center, 656 N.W.2d 71 (Iowa 2002); Bradley v. Ray, 904 S.W.2d 302 (Mo. Ct. App. 1995); Doe v. Marion, 605 S.E.2d 556 (S.C. Ct. App. 2004); Peter F. Lake, *Revisiting Tarasoff,* 58 Alb. L. Rev. (1994).

96. *See* Stark & Goldstein, *supra* note 4, at 24–42; Jones, *supra* note 92; Janet Boeth Jones, Annotation, *Immunity of Public Officer from Liability for Injuries Caused by Negligently Released Individual,* 5 A.L.R. 4th 773 (1981); *cf.* Steven J. Gaynor, Annotation, *Liability of Private Operator of "Halfway House" or Group Home Housing Convicted Prisoners Before Final Release for Injury to Third Person Caused by Inmate,* 9 A.L.R. 5th 969 (1993); Janet Boeth Jones, Annotation, *Liability of Governmental Officer or Entity for Failure to Warn or Notify of Release of Potentially Dangerous Individual from Custody,* 12 A.L.R. 4th 722 (1982); Don F. Vaccaro, Annotation, *Liability of Public Officer or Body for Harm Done by Prisoner Permitted to Escape,* 44 A.L.R. 3d 899 (1972).

97. *See* Grimm v. Arizona Bd. of Pardons and Paroles, 564 P.2d 1227 (Ariz. 1977) (in banc); *cf.* President's Task Force on Victims of Crime, *supra* note 23, at 54–55.

98. *See* Martinez v. California, 444 U.S. 277 (1980).

99. *See* Stark & Goldstein, *supra* note 4, at 242–43; Francis M. Dougherty, Annotation, *Probation Officer's Liability for Negligent Supervision of Probationer,* 44 A.L.R. 4th 638 (1986).

100. *See* National Crime Victim Bar Association, http://www.victimbar.org (last visited June 1, 2009)

101. *See, e.g.,* Coughlin v. Hilton Hotels Corp., 879 F. Supp. 1047 (D. Nev. 1995), *aff'd sub nom.* Coughlin v. Tailhook Ass'n, 112 F.3d 1052 (9th Cir. 1997); Stewart v. Bader, 907 A.2d 931 (N.H. 2006); Hattori v. Peairs, 662 So. 2d 509 (La. Ct. App. 1995).

102. *See generally* WILLIAM G. DOERNER & STEVEN P. LAB, VICTIMOLOGY 92–96 (5th ed. 2008); OFFICE FOR VICTIMS OF CRIME, *supra* note 6, at 373–75; SARNOFF, *supra* note 3, at 44–55; STARK & GOLDSTEIN, *supra* note 4, at 191–98; Mary Kay Barbieri, Commentary, *Civil Suits for Sexual Assault Victims: The Down Side,* 4 J. INTERPERSONAL VIO. 110 (1989); Lucy Berliner, Commentary, *Another Option for Victims: Civil Damage Suits,* 4 J. INTERPERSONAL VIO. 107 (1989); Robert K. Dawson, Commentary, *Civil Suits for Sexual Assault Victims: The Up Side,* 4 J. INTERPERSONAL VIO. 114 (1989).

103. *See* STARK & GOLDSTEIN, *supra* note 4, at 193–94.

104. *See* Dawson, *supra* note 102, at 114–15; Beth G. Baldinger & D. Thomas Nelson, *Crime Victims and Psychological Injuries,* TRIAL, Feb. 1995, at 56, 57.

105. *See* Baldinger & Nelson, *supra* note 104.

106. *See* Morris Dees & Ellen Bowden, *Taking Hate Groups to Court,* TRIAL, Feb. 1995, at 20; Daren Fonda, *Under Fire,* TIME, Sept. 4, 2000, at 32; John K. Wiley, *Idahoans Hope Case Alters Area's Image: Verdict Returned Against Supremacists,* DALLAS MORNING NEWS, Sept. 9, 2000, at 4A.

107. *See* STARK & GOLDSTEIN, *supra* note 4, at 192–93.

108. *See* SARNOFF, *supra* note 3, at 52; STARK & GOLDSTEIN, *supra* note 4, at 265–80; Liebeskind, *supra* note 23, at 45.

109. *See* SARNOFF, *supra* note 3, at 51.

110. *See* Barbieri, *supra* note 102.

111. *Cf.* SARNOFF, *supra* note 3, at 48–50.

112. *See* Bradford C. Mank, *The Scope of Criminal Restitution: Awarding Unliquidated Damages in Sentencing Hearings,* 17 CAP. U. L. REV. 55 (1987).

113. *See* Juan Cardenas, *The Crime Victim in the Prosecutorial Process,* 9 HARV. J. L. & PUB. POL'Y 357 (1986); *cf.* Matti Joutsen, *Victim Participation in Proceedings and Sentencing in Europe,* 3 INT'L REV. VICTIMOLOGY 57 (1994); Mike Maguire & Joanna Shapland, *Provision for Victims in an International Context, in* VICTIMS OF CRIME 211 (Robert C. Davis et al. eds., 2d ed. 1997).

Notes for Chapter 11

1. *See* Frank Carrington & George Nicholson, *The Victims' Movement: An Idea Whose Time Has Come,* 11 PEPP. L. REV. 1 (1984).

2. *See* OFFICE OF JUSTICE PROGRAMS, U.S. DEP'T OF JUSTICE, FOUR YEARS LATER: A REPORT ON THE PRESIDENT'S TASK FORCE ON VICTIMS OF CRIME 4–5 (1986); Carrington & Nicholson, *supra* note 1.

3. *See* PRESIDENT'S TASK FORCE ON VICTIMS OF CRIME, FINAL REPORT (1982).

4. *See* ALA. CONST. art. I, §6.01; ALASKA CONST. art. I, §§12, 24; ARIZ. CONST. art. 2, §2.1; CAL. CONST. art. 1, §28; COLO. CONST. art. 2, §16a; CONN. CONST. art. I, §8; FLA. CONST. art. 1, §16; IDAHO CONST. art. I, §22; ILL. CONST. art. 1, §8.1; IND. CONST. art. 1, §13; KAN. CONST. art. 15, §15; LA. CONST. art. 1, §25; MD. CONST. art. 47; MICH. CONST. art. 1, §24; MISS. CONST. art. 3, §26A; MO. CONST. art. 1, §32; MONT. CONST. art.

II, § 28; Neb. Const. art. I, § 28; Nev. Const. art. 1, § 8; N.J. Const. art. 1, § 22; N.M. Const. art. II, § 24; N.C. Const. art. I, § 37; Ohio Const. art. I, § 10a; Okla. Const. art. 2, § 34; Or. Const. art. I, §§ 42, 43; R.I. Const. art. 1, § 23; S.C. Const. art. I, § 24; Tenn. Const. art. I, § 35; Tex. Const. art. 1, § 30; Utah Const. art. I, § 28; Va. Const. art. I, § 8-A; Wash. Const. art. 1, § 35; Wis. Const. art. 1, § 9 m. *See generally* App. 3.

5. *See* S.J. Res. 1, 108th Cong. (2003); H.R.J. Res. 48, 108th Cong. (2003); H.R.J. Res. 10, 108th Cong. (2003).

6. *See* David Beatty et al., National Victim Center, Statutory and Constitutional Protection of Victims' Rights: Implementation and Impact on Crime Victims 6 (1996); Office for Victims of Crime, U.S. Dep't of Justice, New Directions from the Field: Victims' Rights and Services for the 21st Century ix (1998).

7. *See generally* Office for Victims of Crime, *supra* note 6; National Center for Victims of Crime, VictimLaw, http://www.victimlaw.info/victimlaw/ (last visited Jan. 1, 2009); National Conference of State Legislatures, Victims' Rights Laws in the States, http://www.ncsl.org (last visited Jan. 1, 2009).

8. *See* Beatty et al., *supra* note 6, at 143–49; *see also* Dean G. Kilpatrick et al., U.S. Dep't of Justice, The Rights of Crime Victims—Does Legal Protection Make a Difference? (1998).

9. *See* Beatty et al., *supra* note 6, at 144–46.

10. *See id.* at 102–04, 112–20, 146–49.

11. *See id.* at 99, 149.

12. *See id.* at 143–49.

13. *See* Office for Victims of Crime, *supra* note 6.

14. *See id.* at vii–viii.

15. *See id.* at 9–37, 59–69, 82–92, 104–15, 132–43, 337–51, 364–69, 376–78; *cf.* Douglas Evan Beloof, *The Third Model of Criminal Process: The Victim Participation Model*, 1999 Utah L. Rev. 289 (1999).

16. *See* Douglas E. Beloof, *The Third Wave of Crime Victims' Rights: Standing, Remedy, and Review*, 2005 BYU L. Rev. 255, 256–331 (2005).

17. *See id.* at 257–60, 343–44.

18. *See id.* at 300–23, 344–45.

19. *See id.* at 323–30, 345–50.

20. *See id.* at 342–43, 353–54; *see also* 18 U.S.C.A. § 3771 (West Supp. 2009); 42 U.S.C.A. § 10603d–e (West 2005); Crime Victims' Rights Act of 2004, Pub. L. No. 108-405, Title I, § 103, 118 Stat. 2260, 2264–65 (2004); David E. Aaronson, *New Rights and Remedies: The Federal Crime Victims' Rights Act of 2004*, 28 Pace L. Rev. 623, 631–34, 662–68 (2008).

21. *See* Office for Victims of Crime, *supra* note 6, at 9–12; President's Task Force on Victims of Crime, *supra* note 3, at 114–15.

22. *See, e.g.,* S. Rep. No. 108-191, at 1–30 (2003); Office for Victims of Crime, *supra* note 6, at 9–12; Beloof, *supra* note 16; Paul G. Cassell, *Barbarians at the Gates? A Reply to the Critics of the Victims' Rights Amendment*, 1999 Utah L. Rev. 479 (1999); Dean G. Kilpatrick & Randy K. Otto, *Constitutionally Guaranteed Participation in Criminal Proceedings for Victims: Potential Effects on Psychological Functioning*, 34 Wayne L. Rev. 7(1987); Steven J. Twist, *The Crime Victims' Rights Amendment and Two Good and Perfect Things*, 1999 Utah L. Rev. 369 (1999); Marlene A. Young, *A Constitutional Amendment for Victims of Crime: A Victims' Perspective*, 34 Wayne L. Rev. 51 (1987); Jennie L. Cassie, Note, *Passing the Victims' Rights Amendment: A Nation's March Toward a More Perfect Union*, 24 New. Eng. J. On

CRIM. & CIV. CONFINEMENT 647 (1998); Sue Anna Moss Cellini, Note, *The Proposed Victims' Rights Amendment to the Constitution of the United States: Opening the Door of the Criminal Justice System to the Victim*, 14 ARIZ. J. COMP. & INT'L L. 839, 856–66 (1997); Dayva B. Gewurz & Maria A. Mercurio, Note, *The Victims' Bill of Rights: Are Victims All Dressed Up with No Place to Go?*, 8 ST. JOHN'S J. LEGAL COMMENT. 251 (1992); *cf.* John W. Gillis & Douglas E. Beloof, *The Next Step for a Maturing Victim Rights Movement: Enforcing Crime Victim Rights in the Courts*, 33 MCGEORGE L. REV. 689 (2002).

23. *See* S.J. Res. 1, 108th Cong. (2003); H.J. Res. 48, 108th Cong. (2003); H.J. Res. 10, 108th Cong. (2003); S. REP. NO. 108–191, at 4, 30–44 (2003); *cf.* LeRoy L. Lamborn, *Victim Participation in the Criminal Justice Process: The Proposals for a Constitutional Amendment*, 34 WAYNE L. REV. 125 (1987); Robert P. Mosteller & H. Jefferson Powell, Essay, *With Disdain for the Constitutional Craft: The Proposed Victims' Rights Amendment*, 78 N.C. L. REV. 393 (2000); Peggy M. Tobolowsky, *"Constitutionalizing" Crime Victim Rights*, 33 CRIM. L. BULL. 395 (1997).

24. *See, e.g.*, S. REP. NO. 108–191, at 56–110 (2003); James M. Dolliver, *Victims' Rights Constitutional Amendment: A Bad Idea Whose Time Should Not Come*, 34 WAYNE L. REV. 87 (1987); Lynne Henderson, *Revisiting Victim's Rights*, 1999 UTAH L. REV. 383 (1999); Rachel King, *Why a Victims' Rights Constitutional Amendment is a Bad Idea: Practical Experiences from Crime Victims*, 68 U. CIN. L. REV. 357, 400 (2000); Robert P. Mosteller, *The Unnecessary Victims' Rights Amendment*, 1999 UTAH L. REV. 443, 450–51 (1999).

25. Mosteller, *supra* note 23, at 449–50.

26. *See, e.g.*, DANIEL VAN NESS & KAREN HEETDERKS STRONG, RESTORING JUSTICE (1997); Ezzat A. Fattah, *Toward a Victim Policy Aimed at Healing, Not Suffering*, in VICTIMS OF CRIME 257 (Robert C. Davis et al. eds, 2d ed. 1997); Marlene A. Young, *Restorative Community Justice in the United States: A New Paradigm*, 6 INT'L REV. VICTIMOLOGY 265 (1999); *Restorative Justice: An Interview with Visiting Fellow Thomas Quinn*, NAT'L INST. JUST. J., March 1998, at 10.

27. *See* MARK S. UMBREIT ET AL., U.S. DEP'T OF JUSTICE, DIRECTORY OF VICTIM-OFFENDER MEDIATION PROGRAMS IN THE UNITED STATES (2000); MARK S. UMBREIT ET AL., U.S. DEP'T OF JUSTICE, NATIONAL SURVEY OF VICTIM-OFFENDER MEDIATION PROGRAMS (2000).

28. *See Restorative Justice, supra* note 25. *See generally* MARK S. UMBREIT ET AL., VICTIM MEETS OFFENDER: THE IMPACT OF RESTORATIVE JUSTICE AND MEDIATION (1994).

29. *See Restorative Justice, supra* note 25.

Table of Cases

Alabama Board of Pardons and Paroles v. Brooks, 39, 138, 288, 312

Alston v. Robinson, 309

Apprendi v. New Jersey, 160, 319

Archer v. Crime Victims Compensation Bd., 191, 328

Armatta v. Kitzhaber, 266

Baker v. Saint Francis Hospital, 335

Bandoni v. State, 37–38, 141, 288, 313

Barnett v. State, 123, 309

Barrett v. Pacheco, 221, 334

Baxter v. Palmigiano, 332

Beam v. Kingsley, 210, 332

Bearden v. Georgia, 161–62, 164, 319

Bell v. State, 320

Big B, Inc. v. Cottingham, 221–22, 335

Bird v. State, 328

Bivens v. Six Unknown Named Agents of Federal Bureau of Narcotics, 331

Booth v. Maryland, 96–98, 100, 301

Bradley v. Ray, 335

Brown v. J.C. Penney Co., Inc., 215, 333

Brown v. Robinson, 209, 211–12, 332

Brown v. State, 303

Bruegger v. Faribault County Sheriff's Department, 312, 313

Buggie v. Cutler, 211, 212, 332

Burnett v. Stagner Hotel Courts, Inc., 333

Buschauer v. State, 101, 303

C.W. v. State, 321

Cain v. State, 292

Callicutt v. Crime Victims Bd., 328

Calloway-Gaines v. Crime Victim Services Comm'n, 328

Cannon v. State, 320

Canterino v. Mirage Casino-Hotel, 333

Carey v. Musladin, 292

Cargle v. State, 99, 302

Carter v. State, 191, 328

Cater v. Cater, 212, 332

Cianos v. State, 37, 288, 313

Ciaverelli v. Crime Victim's Compensation Bd., 328

Cicchinelli v. Pennsylvania Board of Probation and Parole, 123, 309

Claiborne v. State, 58, 292

Commonwealth v. Benz, 72, 295, 313

Commonwealth v. Cannon, 321

Commonwealth v. Carbone, 292

Commonwealth v. Harris, 292

Commonwealth v. Lattimore, 298

Commonwealth v. McIntyre, 321
Commonwealth v. Means, 302
Commonwealth v. Pozza, 321
Commonwealth v. Pritchard, 72, 296
Commonwealth v. Williams, 302
Conover v. State, 98–99, 301, 302, 303
Cooper v. District Court, 103–04, 141, 304, 312, 313, 321
Cort v. Ash, 331
Costner v. Adams, 335
Coughlin v. Hilton Hotels Corp., 336
Coughlin v. Tailhook Ass'n, 336
Courtney v. Remler, 215, 333
Dalton v. United States, 315
Daniels v. Traughber, 123, 138, 309, 312
DeShaney v. Winnebago Cty. Dep't Soc. Servs., 218–19, 334
Dix v. County of Shasta, 42, 288, 304
Dix v. Superior Court ex rel. People, 35–36, 103, 138, 287, 304, 313
Doe v. Forrest, 335
Doe v. Interstate Fire & Casualty Co., 332
Doe v. Marion, 335
Doe v. Prudential-Bache/A.G. Spanos Realty Partners, L.P., 217, 334
East v. Johnson, 296
East v. Scott, 296
Ellis v. North Carolina Crime Victims Compensation Comm'n, 191, 328
Ellis v. State, 321
Evans v. State, 302

Ex parte Littlefield, 18, 139–40, 282, 313
Fast Eddie's v. Hall, 216, 333
Ford v. State, 39, 138, 165, 288, 313, 321
Franks v. State, 321
Fuselier v. State, 292
Gall v. United States, 319
Gansz v. People, 70–71, 141, 295, 313
Garzilli v. Howard Johnson Motor Lodges, Inc., 215, 333
Gavcus v. Maroney, 295
Globe Newspaper Co. v. Superior Court, 289
Government of the Virgin Islands v. Davis, 320
Graham v. State Bd. Of Control, 191, 328
Grimm v. Arizona Bd. of Pardons and Paroles, 222–23, 335
Grimsley v. State, 59, 292
Gritzner v. Michael R., 334
Gross v. Family Services Agency, Inc., 218, 334
Hagen v. Commonwealth, 141, 304, 313
Hall v. State, 59, 292
Harvey v. County of Snohomish, 334
Hattori v. Peairs, 210, 332, 336
Hearn v. Commonwealth, 321
Henry v. State, 320
Hicks v. State, 98, 302
Hill v. Bradford, 320
Hodges v. State, 320
Hoile v. State, 36–37, 140, 288, 312, 313
Holmes v. State, 99, 302
Hughey v. United States, 162, 319

Hullum v. Commonwealth, 191,
   328
In re Antrobus, 19, 144, 283, 305,
   315
In re Bradley, 328
In re Brock, 106–07, 144–45, 305,
   314, 315
In re Butler, 163, 320
In re Chaney, 191, 328
In re Dale, 191, 328
In re Dean, 41–42, 82–83, 144,
   288, 298, 314, 315
In re Dillon, 191, 328
In re Douglas, 328
In re Edmundson, 191, 328
In re Ferrell, 191, 328
In re Guffey, 191, 328
In re Holbrook, 328
In re Hugley, 190, 328
In re Jacobsen, 144–45, 315
In re Jane Doe, 283
In re John W., 190, 327
In re Kramer, 191, 328
In re Marcus-Bey, 191, 328
In re Mikhel, 61, 292–93, 314
In re Oak Brook Bank, 320
In re Raymond, 190, 327
In re Reede, 191, 328
In re Rodgers, 328
In re Simmons, 191, 328
In re Smith, 191, 328
In re Stewart, 19, 283
In re Walsh, 315
In re Weber, 328
In re Williams, 190, 328
In re Wilson, 328
In re W.R. Huff Asset Management,
   40–41, 83, 144, 163, 288, 298,
   314, 315, 320

Inmates of Attica Correctional Fa-
   cility v. Rockefeller, 295
Jackson v. Henderson, 288
Jackson v. Swordfish Investments,
   215, 333
Jimenez v. State, 58, 292
Johnson v. Hugo's Skateway,
   210–11, 332
Johnson v. Rodriguez, 124, 309
Johnson v. Smith, 210, 332
Johnston v. Dobeski, 141, 304, 313
Jones v. State, 303
Jones v. United States, 100, 302,
   303
Jordan v. State, 320
Kelly v. California, 301
Kelly v. Robinson, 318
Kenna v. United States District
   Court, 104–05, 144, 304, 305,
   314, 315
Kenna v. United States District
   Court (II), 105–06, 144, 305,
   314
Kline v. 1500 Massachusetts Avenue
   Apartment Corporation, 217
Kline v. Santa Barbara Consolidated
   Ry. Co., 34, 217, 333
Knapp v. Martone, 17, 282
Knutson v. County of Maricopa *ex
   rel.* Romley, 313
LaFleur v. State, 321
Laker v. State, 320
Lamb v. Kontgias, 288
Lamm v. Nebraska Board of Par-
   dons, 139, 313
Lavin v. Jordan, 335
Ledbetter v. State, 99, 301, 302
Leeke v. Timmerman, 295
Lewis v. Office of the Prosecuting
   Attorney, 141, 313

Lillie v. Thompson, 217–18, 334
Linda R.S. v. Richard D., 69, 295, 313
Little v. Windmere Relocation, 332
Lodowski v. State, 37, 288
Long v. Broadlawns Medical Center, 335
Long v. Turk, 221, 334
Lopez-Sanchez v. State, 37, 288
Lynn v. Reinstein, 282, 302
Marshall v. Commonwealth, 190, 327
Martinez v. California, 223, 335
Mask v. State, 59, 292
Mason v. Royal Dequindre, Inc., 216, 333
Massee v. Thompson, 219, 334
McComas v. Criminal Injuries Compensation Bd., 327
McCullough v. State, 190, 327, 328
McGowan v. State, 59, 292
Meditrust Financial Services Corp. v. Crime Victims Bd., 327
Meerscheidt v. State, 328
Mehring v. State, 303
Melissa J. v. Superior Court ex rel. Williams, 38–39, 138, 165, 288, 312, 313, 321
Miller v. State, 59, 292
Monson v. Carver, 320
Moody v. Larsen, 71, 295
Moore v. Green, 334
Mosley v. Klincar, 124, 309
Myers v. Daley, 38, 138, 288, 312
Myers v. State, 321
N.E.M. ex rel. Kryshak v. Strigel, 221, 335
Nat'l Acceptance Co. of America v. Bathalter, 326, 332, 338
Nelson v. Schubert, 332

Nix v. State, 321
Nova Southeastern University, Inc. v. Gross, 334
Olsen v. State, 302
Ortell v. Crime Victim's Compensation Bd., 327
Ortiz v. State, 302
Overstreet v. State, 292
Ozik v. Gramins, 334
Pacific Mut. Life Ins. Co. v. Haslip, 332
Pack v. State, 328
Page v. Fulton, 332
Palmer v. Granholm, 309
Patterson v. Mahoney, 282
Payne v. Tennessee, 97–100, 301, 302
People v. Cruz, 321
People v. Frye, 320
People v. Johns, 292
People v. Jones, 303
People v. Lader, 304
People v. Lee, 100, 303
People v. Littlejohn, 321
People v. Martinez, 321
People v. Matthews, 328
People v. Mockel, 301, 303, 304
People v. Moser, 320
People v. Oyola, 100, 303
People v. Panah, 302
People v. Patten, 292
People v. Pfeiffer, 36, 102, 140, 287, 291, 304, 312, 313, 342
People v. Pickens, 303
People v. Ramirez, 328
People v. Stringham, 81, 298
People v. Superior Court ex rel. v. Thompson, 287, 288, 312
People v. Williams, 295
People v. Wright, 304

People v. Zikorus, 304
Person v. Miller, 296
Pluid v. B.K., 210, 332
Press-Enterprise Co. v. Superior
  Court, 289
Raby v. Moe, 212–13, 332
Reed v. Becka, 139, 298, 313
Reyes v. Greatway Ins. Co, 209–10,
  212, 332
Rice v. State, 320
Ricketts v. City of Columbia, Mis-
  souri, 334
Roberts v. People, 321
Robinson v. State, 292
Rodriguez v. Cambridge Housing
  Authority, 334
Russell v. McDonald's Corp., 333
Salazar v. State, 301, 302
Salt Lake City v. Johnson, 295
Sandoval v. Farish, 71, 295, 313
Saum v. Widnall, 283, 292
Schilling v. State of Wisconsin
  Crime Victims Rights Board,
  139, 313, 315
Schroering v. McKinney, 103, 141,
  304, 313, 321
Searcy v. Paletz, 283
Seaton v. State, 320
Semler v. Psychiatric Institute, 335
Sennett v. U.S. Fidelity & Guaranty
  Co., 332
Sharp v. State, 81–82, 298, 303
Sherroan v. Commonwealth, 303
Simon & Schuster v. New York
  Crime Victims Bd., 209, 331
Sireci v. State, 292
Skiathos v. Essex Ins. Co., 332
Smith v. Crime Victim's Compensa-
  tion Bd., 327, 328
Solomon v. State, 58, 292

South Carolina v. Gathers, 96–98,
  301
South ex rel. South v. McCarter, 334
Sparks Reg'l Med. Ctr. v. Smith,
  335
Stapleford v. Houghton, 18, 282
Starkman v. Frischetti, 328
State ex rel. Goldesberry v. Taylor,
  57, 140, 291, 313
State ex rel. Hance v. Arizona Board
  of Pardons and Paroles, 25–26,
  34, 123, 138, 309, 312
State ex rel. Rome v. Fountain, 72,
  313
State ex rel. Romley v. Superior
  Court, 17–18, 142, 282, 296, 314
State ex rel. Thomas v. Foreman,
  304
State ex rel. Thomas v. Klein, 21,
  284
State ex rel. Unnamed Petitioner v.
  Circuit Court for Walworth
  County, 295
State v. Acoff, 303
State v. Aker, 101, 303
State v. Adams, 321
State v. Alspach, 320
State v. Baker, 321
State v. Behrnes, 303
State v. Beltran-Felix, 57–58,
  291–92
State v. Bible, 142–43, 312, 313
State v. Blakley, 320
State v. Bolton, 301
State v. Bruce, 102, 304
State v. Bybee, 320
State v. Campbell, 321
State v. Card, 302
State v. Casey, 80–81, 140, 298, 313
State v. Champe, 328

State v. Clinton, 320
State v. Cosey, 292
State v. David G.K., 282
State v. Devin, 321
State v. Edson, 320
State v. Fautenberry, 301
State v. Foy, 321
State v. Fulminante, 57, 291
State v. Garza, 302
State v. Gentry, 302
State v. Gribble, 321
State v. Guerrero, 304
State v. Haase, 321
State v. Heath, 292
State v. Hefa, 321
State v. Holt, 35, 287, 312, 313
State v. Ihde, 320
State v. Imperiale, 344
State v. Johnson (Kan.), 81–82, 298
State v. Johnson, 321
State v. Kinder, 296
State v. Klawonn, 320
State v. Korsen, 321
State v. Koskovich, 302, 303
State v. Lamberton, 103, 141, 304, 313, 321
State v. Layman, 70, 140, 295, 313
State v. Leon, 100, 303
State v. Lewis, 321
State v. Lindahl, 303
State v. Lovelace, 99, 301, 302
State v. Martin, 320
State v. Matteson, 303
State v. McDonnell, 82, 138–39, 298, 313
State v. Means, 39, 288, 313
State v. Moss, 304
State v. Muhammad, 99, 302
State v. Newman, 321
State v. Nordahl, 320

State v. Phillips, 304
State v. Pindale, 328
State v. Palubicki, 321
State v. Rangel, 292
State v. Riggs, 314
State v. Roll, 302
State v. Roscoe, 17, 282
State v. Sailer, 303
State v. Schoening, 291
State v. Sims, 287
State v. Stafford, 320
State v. Stauffer, 18, 282
State v. Steffy, 320
State v. Superior Court, 18, 282
State v. Timmendequas, 56–57, 291, 313
State v. Tupa, 320
State v. Unnamed Defendant, 72, 295, 313
State v. Wakefield, 302
State v. Whitten, 101, 304
State v. Williams, 292
State v. Worthington, 98, 302
State v. Yanez, 303
Stephens v. State, 57, 291
Stewart v. Bader, 210, 332, 336
Surland v. State, 321
Swindle v. State, 303
Taboada v. Daly Seven, 333
Tarasoff v. Regents of the University of California, 222, 335
Taylor v. Newton Division of District Court Department, 295
Taylor v. Phelan, 219, 334
Terry v. Commonwealth, 303
Thomas v. Commonwealth, 303
Thurman v. City of Torrington, 334
Town of Castle Rock v. Gonzales, 219, 334

Troutt v. Charcoal Steak House,
  Inc., 210, 332
United States v. Adams, 319
United States v. Allison, 319
United States v. Amato, 320
United States v. Ausburn, 304
United States v. Bailey, 319
United States v. Bernard, 100, 303
United States v. Barnette, 319
United States v. Beydoun, 319
United States v. Blocker, 319
United States v. Blumhagen, 83,
  298, 314
United States v. Bogart, 320
United States v. Bonner, 319
United States v. BP Products North
  America, 283, 288, 314
United States v. Brown, 318, 319
United States v. Carruth, 319
United States v. Cooper, 303, 328
United States v. Dailey, 319
United States v. Davenport, 319
United States v. Degenhardt, 104,
  305, 314
United States v. DeRosier, 320
United States v. Dubose, 318, 319
United States v. Duncan (10th Cir.),
  319
United States v. Duncan, 303
United States v. Dupes, 319
United States v. Eberhard, 83, 298,
  314
United States v. Edwards, 293
United States v. Farkas, 319
United States v. Glover, 303
United States v. Gooch, 303
United States v. Grundhoefer, 314,
  320
United States v. Heaton, 73, 143,
  296, 314

United States v. Haggard, 319
United States v. Hensley, 319
United States v. Horsfall, 298, 314
United States v. Hunter, 107, 144,
  305–06, 314
United States v. Ingrassia, 41, 283,
  287, 288, 305, 314
United States v. Jackson, 319
United States v. Johnson (11th
  Cir.), 314, 320
United States v. Johnson, 60, 292,
  303, 314
United States v. Keith, 319
United States v. Kelley, 314, 320
United States v. Lay, 320
United States v. Leahy, 319
United States v. L.M., 60–61, 292,
  314
United States v. Marcello, 305, 314
United States v. Mayhew, 303
United States v. McVeigh, 59–60,
  99, 292, 302, 303, 314
United States v. Merkosky, 283
United States v. Milkiewicz, 319
United States v. Mindel, 314, 320
United States v. Morrison, 331
United States v. Moussaoui, 305
United States v. Mullins, 320
United States v. Munoz-Flores, 192,
  328
United States v. Nelson, 302
United States v. Pagan, 328
United States v. Palma, 318, 319
United States v. Patty, 320
United States v. Perry, 163, 320
United States v. Pizzichiello, 320
United States v. Purdue Frederick,
  320
United States v. Reed, 319
United States v. Robertson, 319

United States v. Rochester, 320
United States v. Rubin, 83–84, 285,
    288, 298, 305, 314
United States v. Saad, 320
United States v. Sablan, 319
United States v. Sacane, 305
United States v. Saltsman, 288, 314
United States v. Sampson, 62, 293,
    303
United States v. Santana, 304
United States v. Satterfield, 318,
    319
United States v. Schinnell, 320
United States v. Scott, 320
United States v. Sharp, 18–19, 283,
    305, 314
United States v. Smith, 304, 328
United States v. Stokes, 288, 314
United States v. Sunrhodes, 319
United States v. Turner, 18, 41,
    61–62, 283, 288, 293, 305, 314
United States v. Twitty, 319
United States v. Vaknin, 319
United States v. Visinaiz, 62, 293
United States v. Washington, 319

Vance v. County of Santa Clara,
    331
Wallace v. City of Los Angeles,
    219–20, 334
Wallace v. State, 18, 282
Walters v. Grossheim, 320
Ware v. State, 302
Warhurst v. White, 332
Washington Metro. Area Transit
    Auth. v. O'Neill, 214, 333
Watts v. State, 292
Wayte v. United States, 295
Weston v. State, 298
Wheeler v. State, 292
Wiggins v. State, 320
Williams v. Illinois, 319
Williams v. New York, 95, 301
Wilson v. Commonwealth, 298
Woods v. Linahan, 296
Yang v. State, 123–24, 138, 309,
    312
Young v. United States ex rel. Vuit-
    ton et Fils S.A., 73, 296
Zsigo v. Hurley Medical Center, 335

Index

American Law Institute, 153, 213

Charge, 24, 32, 65–76, 79–80,
114–16, 135
Charging decision, 29, 65–76, 88,
143
Civil suit, 73, 153, 167, 193,
205–26
Common law, 37–38, 49–50, 68,
71, 73, 74, 141, 206–11, 213,
215, 218, 221
Commutation, 32, 139
Constitutional Amendment, 12,
15–16, 20, 23, 25, 29, 31, 52,
53, 67, 77, 92, 93, 120, 132, 139,
155, 157, 186, 207, 227, 230–33,
242–76
Crime Victims' Rights Act of 2004,
xiii, 12, 16, 20, 23–24, 26,
29–30, 53, 67, 77–78, 93, 120,
131, 132–33, 145, 149, 157, 231

Due Process, 42, 50, 57, 73, 88, 98,
101, 123, 125, 142–43, 160, 161,
164, 192, 218–19, 233, 248, 251,
263, 266, 271, 272, 274

Eighth Amendment, 96–98, 160,
161
Equal protection, 124, 161, 164, 192

Fifth Amendment, 160, 161
First Amendment, 49, 60, 209
Fourteenth Amendment, 50, 98
Fry, Margery, 7, 183

Hentig, Hans von, 6

Johnson, Lyndon, 7

Mendelsohn, Beniamin, 6

Negligence, 37–38, 141, 206, 208,
214–16, 218–22, 225, 237
New Directions From the Field, 13,
20, 23, 29, 33, 51–52, 67, 77,
92–93, 119–20, 131, 154–55,
185–86, 196, 206, 229–30, 232

Pardon, 32, 55, 139, 245, 246, 262,
265
Parole, 9–11, 15–16, 25–32,
34–35, 39, 43–44, 49–55, 63,
65, 91, 119–29, 136, 138, 155,
157, 159, 177, 222–23, 227,
236–38, 240, 245–76
Plea, 10, 18, 20, 29–32, 34–35, 37,
39, 41–42, 44, 57, 63, 65, 71,
76–89, 94, 107, 114, 133, 134,
137, 139–40, 142–43, 155, 158,
162, 165, 210–11, 231, 238,
245–76

President's Task Force, xiii, 10,
    15–16, 20, 23, 28–29, 44,
    50–51, 52, 55, 64, 65–67,
    75–77, 80, 84–85, 89, 91–92,
    104, 108, 114–15, 119, 122, 129,
    131, 149, 153–154, 157, 160,
    165, 181, 184–86, 206, 213, 223,
    225, 227–30, 232, 234, 235–43
Private prosecution, 6, 76
Property crime, 3, 12, 44, 66,
    155–56, 158, 163, 167–68, 175,
    190, 217, 221

Reagan, Ronald, xiii, 10, 227
Restitution, 5, 6, 7, 10–13, 35,
    37–39, 94–95, 106, 112, 114–16,
    118, 132, 136, 138, 151–81,
    183–84, 189, 190, 193, 205, 223,
    225, 227–28, 232–33, 236–39,
    245–76
Restorative justice, 173, 233
Right to be heard, 27, 41, 65–129,
    133–34, 137–38, 140, 143, 231,
    245–76
Right to be present, 10, 31, 49–64,
    79, 140, 243, 245–76
Right to notice, 23–47, 141,
    245–76
Rule on witnesses, 49–50

Sentence, 11–13, 15, 25, 30–32,
    35–37, 45, 53, 57, 63, 79, 82–83,
    88, 91–119, 122, 126, 128,
    133–34, 137–38, 140–42, 144,
    153–57, 159–61, 163, 167–70,
    173–77, 179, 212, 224, 227–28,
    233, 236, 245–76
Seventh Amendment, 160

Sixth Amendment, 10, 42, 49–50,
    160, 242–43

Tort, 37–38, 141, 190, 206–13,
    219–21
Trial, 10, 12, 15–19, 30, 31, 32–36,
    38–42, 44, 49–53, 56–64,
    70–71, 73, 78, 81–83, 86, 88, 93,
    96–99, 101–07, 109, 125,
    132–33, 134–35, 137–46, 161,
    163, 165, 191, 211–12, 215, 217,
    220, 222–23, 225, 231–32, 236,
    239, 243, 245–76

Uniform Crime Reports, 3, 7, 167

Victim assistance, 8, 9, 12, 24,
    44–45, 99, 156, 186, 197, 199,
    240
Victim compensation, 7–12,
    152–53, 158, 167, 169, 183–204,
    205, 223, 227–28, 237, 240, 242
Victim impact, 11, 27, 36, 42, 59,
    80, 91–104, 106–18, 121,
    123–26, 153, 169, 227, 233, 236
Victim satisfaction, 45, 63, 75, 86,
    108, 111, 117–19, 129, 145–46,
    174–75, 201–03, 233
Victim service, 8–10, 13, 23, 27,
    30, 33, 151, 185, 197–99,
    227–29, 239, 242
Victims' movement, 8–10, 65, 153,
    205, 227
Violent crime, 3, 11, 15, 20, 27–29,
    38, 52, 66, 77, 91–92, 104, 110,
    121, 123, 136, 155, 167, 184,
    188, 190, 193–95, 197, 201–03,
    232, 238–42, 245